Sportswomen at the Olympics

A Global Content Analysis of Newspaper Coverage

Edited by

Toni Bruce
University of Waikato, New Zealand

Jorid Hovden
The Norwegian University of Science and Technology, Norway

Pirkko Markula
University of Alberta, Canada

SENSE PUBLISHERS
ROTTERDAM/BOSTON/TAIPEI

A C.I.P. record for this book is available from the Library of Congress.

ISBN: 978-94-6091-105-7 (paperback)
ISBN: 978-94-6091-106-4 (hardback)
ISBN: 978-94-6091-107-1 (e-book)

Published by: Sense Publishers,
P.O. Box 21858,
3001 AW Rotterdam
The Netherlands
http://www.sensepublishers.com

Printed on acid-free paper

CONTENTS

CONTENTS

Europe: Eastern Europe

North America

Asia: West Asia

Asia: East Asia

Africa

Oceania

ACKNOWLEDGMENTS

In part, this book is a tribute to the value of academic sabbaticals which allow researchers to exchange ideas with international colleagues. The idea for an international collaboration came when Jorid Hovden (then at Finnmark University College, Norway) spent time with Toni Bruce while visiting the University of Waikato (New Zealand) and was enhanced when Toni later visited Norway and Europe on sabbatical as part of developing the project. Through our discussions, we not only realised we had a shared interest in issues of gender but became aware that, despite being at opposite ends of the globe, there were strong similarities in the ways that Norwegians and New Zealanders thought about the world. From this position of mutual interest, we embarked upon a comparison of Olympic media coverage during the 2004 Olympic Games. After deciding to see if any of our international colleagues would like to join us, our potential countries of collaboration grew from two to 24, the majority of which were not English-speaking nations. At this point, Pirkko Markula agreed to join the editorial team. As in most collaborations of such size, not all interested researchers were able to see the project through: some had to withdraw as a result of illness, others because of more pressing responsibilities, and some because their institutions failed to see the value of joining the largest international comparison of its type. By the time we went to press, we had gained one country, Turkey, and lost others, including Iran, Tanzania, North Korea, Ireland, Israel, Greece and Australia, which would have broadened the scope of comparison even further.

An international collaboration such as this could not be successful without the commitment and passion of many different people, not least the researchers and authors of the chapters which comprise this book. We would like to thank all of them for their enthusiasm, patience and willingness to contribute to broadening our understanding of how a global event like the Olympics plays out in the sports media in a range of national contexts. We also acknowledge the hard work done by the individuals and teams in 14 countries who analysed data in their own (non-English) language newspapers and then translated their work into English for a broad audience. Susan Chapman, a PhD student in the Department of Sport and Leisure Studies at the University of Waikato, helped a number of researchers with their analysis of data using Excel. Her commitment and expertise in this area is much appreciated. Jane Burnett brought a meticulous approach to formatting the chapters and Stephanie Chia helped ensure consistency across them. The French language expertise provided by Nick Grey and Fabrice Desmarais was important in making sure nothing was 'lost in translation'.

Finally, we would like to thank our institutions, particularly the University of Waikato, Finnmark University College and The Norwegian University of Science and Technology, for their support of this project, which included the provision of grants for research and editorial support as well as sabbatical and conference leave.

PREFACE

The Olympic Games today represent the world's largest sport and media event. During the Olympics, sport is momentarily placed at the centre of the world's attention as large audiences avidly follow broadcast and news media coverage (Puijk, 2000). The Games that are the focus of this book, the 2004 summer Olympics in Athens, were characterised as 'the biggest show ever'. More than 35,000 hours of live events were beamed to 220 countries and territories and it is estimated that almost 4 billion people had access to coverage of the Games (International Olympic Committee [IOC], 2004; IOC, 2008).

With such an expansive scope, the Olympic Games offer a powerful public platform to showcase the achievements of women athletes. And it is evident that there are many achievements available for showcasing. In Athens, women competed in a record number of sports (27) and events (135) and were eligible for more than 400 medals (IOC, 2004; "Women in", 2004). The proportion of women competing in the Games offers a clear indication of how far women have come in their fight for access to sports fields, pools, courts and arenas. Although females made up less than 15% of all Olympic participants until the 1970s, by the 2004 Games in Athens, the overall proportion of female competitors exceeded 40% for the first time. Today, the International Olympic Committee (IOC) actively promotes women's increased participation in the Olympic movement through a range of strategic developments.

Just as the numbers show a major increase in female involvement in elite sport so, too, have attitudes changed significantly. We have clearly come a long way from the first modern Olympic Games in 1896, when founder Baron de Coubertin felt "women should not soil the Olympic Games with their sweat" (Pfister, Habermann & Ottesen, 2004, p. 5), and just as far from the 1970s when a United States judge in a court case about equal sports access for girls was reputed to have said, "Athletic competition builds character in our boys. We do not need that kind of character in our girls, the women of tomorrow" (Dyer, 1982, p. 109). However, although the societal attitudes embedded in these comments have been firmly rejected as females have successfully taken to the field of play, the struggle for sporting equality is far from over, especially in the area of media coverage.

Despite exponential growth in female sports participation, research over more than three decades consistently shows the invisibility of sportswomen in the global sports media. Although this invisibility appears to be moderated during global media events such as the Olympics in which both males and females compete, media coverage clearly has not kept up with the rapid growth in female participation. Researchers remain concerned about the generally low levels of coverage which, they argue, constitute an ongoing marginalisation and trivialisation of female athleticism. Although studies across many nations show this broad trend, the research has been critiqued for inconsistencies in methods and times of analysis, and types of media analysed. Thus, comparisons between countries, and even within countries, have been difficult to make, due to the variability in how the research has been conducted.

This book brings together, in one place, the largest quantitative collection of content analyses of media coverage focused on a single event and using the same methodology. It presents the results of the *Global Women in Sports Media Project* which was designed to broaden the scope of quantitative sport media analyses beyond research that centred on the English-speaking world by including research from across Europe, Africa and Asia. With contributions from all major world regions except Latin America, and analysing newspapers published in 14 languages, this book will allow for substantial international and cross-cultural comparison of the current status of female athletes in the global sports media. It includes chapters from countries such as Turkey, South Korea, China, the Czech Republic, Hungary and South Africa which have only infrequently been included in international comparisons of this type. It draws upon the work of both established and emerging scholars to assess the progress – or lack of it – made by the global media in providing equitable coverage that recognises the involvement and success of female athletes.

ORGANISATION OF THE BOOK

To prevent repetition, Chapter 1 contextualises the existing international research on media coverage of sportswomen and identifies the key themes that inform the broader project. Chapter 2 aims to enable comparisons over time by providing enough detail that others can replicate the study. As a result, it includes a practical guide to the method of content analysis for the use of the many novice undergraduate and postgraduate students embarking in this type of research, while also addressing the methodological and theoretical underpinnings of this type of research.

The findings are divided into five major sections, each of which represents a United Nations-defined world region. We begin with Europe. The first part introduces the findings from Northern Europe, including the United Kingdom and the Scandinavian countries of Denmark, Norway and Sweden. The focus then shifts to Western and Southern Europe with chapters from Belgium, France, Germany and Spain. Eastern Europe is represented by the Czech Republic and Hungary. The second section focuses on North America and includes Canada and the US. In the third section, we highlight chapters from Asia, beginning with Turkey from West Asia and concluding with China, Japan and South Korea from East Asia. Finally, the regions of Africa and Oceania are represented by chapters from South Africa and New Zealand. The authors of each country chapter locate their findings in the broader context of gender relations and the status of sportswomen in that country. They also provide in-depth reviews of research conducted in their own countries to complement the overview provided in Chapter 1. As a result, the reviews of research from each country bring together a wealth of material, much of which may not have been accessible or previously published in English. We conclude the book by summarising the major trends across the different nations and look at the implications for future research regarding women in the Olympic media.

REFERENCES

Dyer, K. (1982). *Challenging the men*. St Lucia: University of Queensland Press.
International Olympic Committee. (2008). *Athens 2004*. Retrieved April 29, 2007, from http://www. olympic.org/uk/games/past/index_uk.asp?OLGT=1&OLGY=2004
International Olympic Committee. (2004). *AΘHNA*. Lausanne: IOC.
Pfister, G., Habermann, U., & Ottesen, L. (2004). *Women at the top – on women, sport and management*. Copenhagen: Institute of Exercise and Sport Sciences.
Puijk, R. (2000). A global media event? Coverage of the 1994 Lillehammer Olympic Games. *International Review for the Sociology of Sport, 35*, 309–330.
Women in the Olympic Games. (2004, February). *Olympic Review*, p. 1. Retrieved from http:// multimedia.olympic.org/pdf/en_report_792.pdf

PIRKKO MARKULA, TONI BRUCE AND JORID HOVDEN

1. KEY THEMES IN THE RESEARCH ON MEDIA COVERAGE OF WOMEN'S SPORT

INTRODUCTION

In order to set the scene for the rest of the book, in this chapter we review the major trends in more than 50 published quantitative studies on media coverage of sporting women. A large portion of the substantive body of research published in English focuses on the United States and, to a lesser extent, Australia, the United Kingdom, New Zealand, Canada and a range of European countries. The trends identified in this review are further developed throughout the book as each country chapter reviews research in its own national context, much of which may not be published in English.

We first briefly discuss the media-sport relationship, before examining the relative invisibility of women athletes in routine sport media coverage; a trend which contributes to the 'symbolic annihilation' of women in sport. We then examine how women athletes are represented in the Olympics, with particular focus on newspaper representations. Throughout, we indicate how the major trends identified in the literature inform the research project that frames this book.

SPORT MEDIA AND THE OLYMPIC GAMES

In the first decade of the 21st century there can be little doubt that life is significantly mediated. Indeed, researchers argue that "no place in the world can escape entirely the power of contemporary media, although different places (and populations) experience that power in different ways and to different degrees" (Grossberg, Wartella, Whitney & Wise, 2006, pp. xvii–xviii). The power of contemporary media is particularly evident in major international sport festivals such as the Olympic Games, in which the symbiotic relationship between the most powerful multinational media corporations and Olympic sport has turned them into global spectacles (Coakley, 2001). The Games represent powerful global and secular rituals that engage more people in shared experience than any other institutions or cultural activities (Burstyn, 1999). At the same time, they are presented as bodily dramas, where the athletes reflect and act as national symbols of dominant cultural values and ideologies (e.g., MacAloon, 1987; Messner 1988; Rudie, 1994). Thus, media coverage of the Games is both global and local: showing patterns that extend across countries while also being represented differently to different national audiences (Bernstein, 2000).

T. Bruce, J. Hovden and P. Markula (eds.),
Sportswomen at the Olympics: A Global Content Analysis of Newspaper Coverage, 1–18.

As the media preserve, transmit and create important cultural information, they powerfully shape how and what we know about sport in general and women's sport in particular (Pedersen, Whisenant & Schneider, 2003). Phillips argues that "regardless of what is actually happening, it is the media's interpretation of that event that shapes our attitudes, values and perceptions about the world and about our culture" (1997, p. 20). In this sense, the media has significant symbolic power that influences public perceptions of women's sport.

Yet, the symbiotic relationship of sport and media benefits some groups and excludes others (Pedersen et al., 2003). Indeed, as discussed in the next section, routine media coverage of women's sport symbolically reinforces dominant ideological beliefs in the superiority of men and makes the dominant gender order in sport appear as 'natural' and fair (e.g., Birrell, 2000).

SYMBOLIC ANNIHILATION – INEQUALITY IN ROUTINE COVERAGE

In this section, we focus on the substantial research into what has been called routine, normal, general or everyday coverage. This type of coverage makes up the bulk of sports media content and excludes major events such as the Olympic Games.

While the results differ depending on cultural context, one of the long-standing criticisms of sport media is its routine exclusion of women (Theberge & Birrell, 1994). Although female coverage ranges from zero to almost 23% in the research reviewed here, most studies find that women receive less than 10% of routine newspaper or TV sport coverage.[1] Further, when compared to the average across all newspapers in a single study, closer analysis of the raw data consistently demonstrates a much wider range of results for individual newspapers. This trend is found in studies in Australia, New Zealand and the US where, for example, an average of 12% might be made up of a range from 4% to 22% (Sage & Furst, 1994; see also Eastman & Billings, 2000; Fountaine & McGregor, 1999; Phillips, 1997; Stoddart, 1994).

The Australian finding that sportswomen "have struggled to get consistent, long-term and supportive attention" (Phillips, 1997, p. 19) rings true for many Western nations (see Table 1). In addition, rather than a steady upward trend as women's participation in sport has increased, the studies reveal consistently low levels of coverage, with women's sport receiving less than 5% of all sports coverage as recently as the mid-1990s (e.g., Matheson & Flatten, 1996; McGregor & Fountaine, 1997; Szabo, 2001). "Women are invisible" was the summary of a recent study involving 37 newspapers in 10 countries which found an average of only 6% of coverage going to women (Jorgensen, 2005, p. 3). Even when mixed coverage was included, females appeared in only 12% of all sports coverage.

Media throughout the English-speaking world follows the same pattern of male-dominated sports reporting. For example, Canadian newspapers allocated just over 6% of sports coverage to women (Crossman, Hyslop & Guthrie, 1994). In US newspapers, women's sport coverage has ranged from less than 1% to 14% (Bryant, 1980; Duncan, Messner & Williams, 1991; Eastman & Billings, 2000; Sage & Furst, 1994; Szabo, 2001). The United Kingdom findings range from zero to 12% (Bernstein, 2002; Donohoe, 2003, 2004; Matheson & Flatten, 1996; Valgeirsson & Snyder, 1986).

Table 1. Female sports coverage[1] in selected countries

Country	Range of routine newspaper coverage %	Range of Olympic newspaper coverage %
Australia	0 – 23	9–40
Belgium		32
Canada	6	11 – > 40[2]
Denmark		37
France		34
Germany	4 – 7	15–29
Iceland	9	
Israel	< 1 – 5	
Italy	<1	2–28
Netherlands	6	33
New Zealand	4 – 14	16 – 24
Norway	5 – 10	
South Africa	9[3]	42
United Kingdom	< 1 – 12	22 – 32[4]
USA	< 1 – 14	14 – 17

[1] Coverage relates to female-only coverage and does not include mixed coverage.
[2] This range highlights coverage since the mid 1960s (Lee, 1992; Urquhart & Crossman, 1999).
[3] This percentage excludes Olympic and Paralympic results from Serra's (2005) data.
[4] These studies looked only at Olympic athletics or track and field coverage (Alexander, 1994; King, 2007).

In Australia and New Zealand, the results are similar but slightly higher. Across numerous studies, women's coverage has varied within a very small range, generally between 5% and 15%. In New Zealand, coverage of women's sport has averaged 10% since research began and, rather than a trend of gradual improvement, some of the higher levels of routine newspaper coverage were found in the 1980s (Bruce, 2008; Ferkins, 1992; Fountaine & McGregor, 1999; McGregor & Fountaine, 1997). Although Australian coverage did not exceed 2% in the 1980s (Menzies, 1989), a longitudinal study found that women received a steady increase in regional newspaper coverage from just over 1% in 1890 to just over 17% in 1990 (Brown, 1995). Regional or non-commercial newspapers and television stations have tended to give more coverage to women's sport than major metropolitan newspapers or commercial broadcasters (Alston, 1996; Brown, 1995; Bruce, Mikosza, Hayles & Whittington, 1999; Mikosza, 1997; Phillips, 1997; Stoddart, 1994).

A recent six-month South African study found an average of almost 14% coverage for females, but this percentage also included coverage of the 2004 Olympic Games (Serra, 2005). Excluding the Olympic and Paralympic results, the routine percentage was approximately 9%.

While there is less information about sport media coverage in non-English-speaking countries, the findings again reflect the trend of extremely low coverage for female athletes. In published studies since the 1970s, routine coverage has not passed 10% in Denmark, Germany, Iceland, the Netherlands, Norway or Sweden (Fasting & Tangen, 1983; Jorgensen, 2002; Klein, 1988; Knoppers & Elling, 2004; Valgeirsson & Snyder, 1986). Jorgensen's (2002) cross-cultural analysis of Scandinavian countries concluded that "if not for female handballers and Norwegian female skiers, women would be almost absent from the sports pages" (p. 4). In Italy, one study found that "outside the Olympic Games women's sports took less than 1 percent of newspaper coverage" (Aversa & Cence, 1992, cited in Capranica & Aversa, 2002, p. 338). Similarly, research in Israel reports very low levels (below 1% in some cases) of women's sport coverage (Bernstein & Galily, 2008).

The electronic media appears to marginalise women's sport to an even greater extent than the print media. For example, while newspaper coverage may reach 14%, television news and highlight shows seldom give women's sport more than 5% and are sometimes well below this level (Duncan, Messner & Willms, 2005; Eastman & Billings, 2000; Tuggle, 1997). In Denmark, the Netherlands, Sweden and the UK, researchers found that women's sport never exceeded 10% on national television stations (Bernstein, 2002; Knoppers & Elling, 2004; Koivula, 1999; Szabo, 2001); a finding that is also true for New Zealand coverage since 1985 (Bruce, 2008). In one case, a three-month study of a popular UK channel found that female athletes received no coverage at all (Szabo, 2001). The majority of Australian studies reported that female coverage on major television stations languished between 1% and 2%.

While studies of newspaper photographs tend to show similar low levels of coverage for female athletes, some researchers discovered that women athletes received a higher percentage of images than of text (e.g., Duncan et al., 1991; Eastman & Billings, 2000; Matheson & Flatten, 1984; Shifflett & Revelle, 1994; Wann et al., 1998). The percentage of female photographs was sometimes close to double the percentage given to text. For example, a UK study found that female athletes received 12% of text and 22% of images in one newspaper, and 10% of text and 20% of images in another (Matheson & Flatten, 1984). Studies in the US found that women's sport coverage comprised almost 4% of text and 7% of images in California newspapers (Duncan et al., 1991) and 14% of text and 19% of images in *USA Today* (Eastman & Billings, 2000). Eastman and Billings concluded, however, that women's relatively larger photographic coverage showed "a lingering tendency to use women athletes for their glamour or sex appeal without serious treatment of their activities" (2000, p. 204). Therefore, photographs, while more numerous than textual coverage, may be used to trivialise sportswomen.

Because women's sport in the mainstream media is almost invisible, the audience necessarily gets a false impression that women's sport does not exist (e.g., Alexander, 1994; Bernstein, 2002). Gerbner (1978) characterised women's under-representation in the media as 'symbolic annihilation' because, as he argued, such exclusion convincingly demonstrates that women do not matter in our culture (Theberge & Birrell, 1994). Therefore, based on the extensive evidence of women's marginalisation in routine sport media coverage, we hypothesised that in the non-Olympic coverage during the Athens Olympic Games, female athletes would receive unequal and lesser newspaper coverage compared to male athletes.

INCREASED VISIBILITY: WOMEN'S COVERAGE DURING MAJOR EVENTS

While the majority of routine sport reporting focuses on men's sport, women's sport is more visible during major international events. For example, Alexander (1994) showed evidence of more parity between men's and women's sport in UK coverage of the World Athletic Championships. During the Commonwealth Games, women's coverage increases to around 30% in both Australia (Pringle & Gordon, 1995) and the UK (Donohoe, 2003) and has exceeded that of males in New Zealand (Wensing, 2003). One might assume, as Bernstein (2002) points out, that during an international sport event, any successful athlete "will get extensive media attention in his or her home country regardless of their sex" (p. 418). Therefore, in the next section we consider media coverage of the Olympic Games, which has received extensive attention.

THE OLYMPIC GAMES: BETTER BUT BY NO MEANS EQUAL

Across a wide range of countries, there is a general trend of increased media coverage of women's sport during the Olympic Games both in newspapers (see Table 1) and on television.[2] Capranica et al. (2005) even identify the Olympic Games as "a path-breaking event" for newspaper coverage of women's sport (p. 214). Although the amount of reported increase varies, based on the newspapers selected for analysis, cultural context, and the exact measures used by the researchers, it appears that some time in the 1980s we begin to see a shift to higher levels of coverage. With a few exceptions, women's Olympic coverage was generally below 20% into the 1980s in many countries but has increased to around 30% since then. Longitudinal comparisons demonstrate a gradual increase over the past three decades. For example, an extensive longitudinal study of Canadian winter Olympic coverage in the *Globe and Mail* newspaper found that women received more space in the later years (from 1964 to 1992) than during the earlier period (1924 to1960) (Urquhart & Crossman, 1999). Similar findings emerged from German research, where a comparison of reports of female Olympians between 1952 and 1980 found that the percentage of women's Olympic coverage rose from almost 15% to just over 29% (Pfister, 1987).

Up until the early 1990s, the North American increase above routine coverage was relatively small, with women receiving between 13% and 17% of Olympics coverage and men receiving between 54% and 57% in Canadian newspapers (Lee, 1992; Urquhart & Crossman, 1999). However, from the 1990s onwards, US research has reported women receiving a much higher proportion of coverage. A content analysis that included the 1996 and 2000 summer Games coverage in *USA*

Today found that women received 25% of articles; a percentage that rose to 43% when mixed coverage was included (Pemberton, Shields, Gilbert, Shen & Said, 2004). Similarly, a review of coverage in five major US newspapers during the 1996 Atlanta Games reported that women received 38% of the coverage (Kinnick, 1998). Equivalent findings emerged from another analysis of the Atlanta Games, in which women athletes featured in 36% of articles with photographs and 31% of articles without a photograph in newspapers from the US, Canada and Great Britain (Vincent, Imwold, Masemann & Johnson, 2002).

Recent research in Europe and Oceania also suggests that women receive about one third of Olympic coverage. The results of European research conducted 20 years apart are remarkably consistent. A study of the 1980 Olympics (in Germany) and the 2000 Olympics (in Belgium, Denmark, France and Italy) both found that females averaged 29% of coverage (Pfister, 1987; Capranica et al., 2005). However, the recent study reported a range of results, with Denmark achieving the highest percentage of coverage at 37% (Capranica et al., 2005). In Australia, the media has dedicated slightly in excess of 30% of coverage to female athletes since the mid-1990s. Coverage of women's sport in seven major newspapers during the 1996 Olympics averaged 33%, rising to 41% when the female proportion of mixed coverage was included (Mikosza, 1996). Coverage in individual newspapers ranged from just over 29% to almost 40% in 1996; and from 32% to 40% in 2000 (Mikosza, 1996; Payne, 2004). Australian coverage has clearly increased from below 20% in the 1980s (Hindson, 1989). The only New Zealand research found low levels of coverage of between 22% and 24% in the 1988 and 1992 Olympics (see Bruce, 2008). These levels appear similar to Israeli 1992 coverage in which men received three times more coverage than female athletes (Bernstein & Galily, 2008). According this research, women's coverage in Australian and European newspapers has tended to be slightly higher than the North American Olympic coverage, although Vincent et al. (2002) recently found few significant differences between European and North American newspapers.

The trend of increased coverage is also seen in analyses of photographs and, just as with routine coverage, some studies found the female athletes received more photographic coverage than text. Australian research reported that the percentage of female photographs was more than double the percentage of articles during the 1984 and 1988 Olympics (Hindson, 1989) and was higher in two out of three newspapers in 1992 (Embrey, Hall & Gunter, 1993). In Canadian winter Olympic coverage between 1924 and 1992, newspapers devoted only 14% of text but 25% of photographs to females (Urquhart & Crossman, 1999). In the UK, females received 15% of all coverage but 25% of the photographic coverage of Olympics athletics events during the late 1980s in British newspapers (Lee, 1992). In other studies, the overall percentage for female photographic coverage has ranged from 33% in a study of four European countries (Capranica et al., 2005) to 48% in five US newspapers (Hardin, Chance, Dodd & Hardin, 2002). In both cases, there were a range of results: from 39% to 55% in US newspapers (Hardin et al., 2002), and from 24% to 49% in different European countries (Capranica et al., 2005). Another cross-cultural study reported high levels of photographic coverage, averaging 43% when results from Canada, the UK and US were combined (Vincent et al., 2002). Based on these findings, women athletes receive a lower percentage of photographs than men yet this coverage, like the overall coverage, increases during the Olympic Games.

It may be, as Pemberton et al. (2004) concluded, that at the international elite level, "we may be closing in on the day when an athlete is an athlete, and sport media coverage truly reflective of those who compete" (p. 95). Consequently, we hypothesised that during the Olympic Games in Athens 2004, female athletes would receive relatively equal newspaper coverage compared to male athletes.

COVERAGE RELATIVE TO PARTICIPATION IN THE GAMES

During the Olympics, while women's overall coverage remains lower than men's, women have tended to be represented relative to their proportions on national Olympic teams. Longitudinal studies in Europe and North America, for example, have found that women's sport receives equivalent and sometimes proportionally more coverage than men's sport in relation to the proportion of female participation (Capranica et al., 2005; Pemberton et al., 2004; Pfister, 1987; Urquhart & Crossman, 1999). For example, in *USA Today* coverage of recent Olympiads, women athletes represented 34% (Atlanta) and 38% (Sydney) of participants but received 41% (Atlanta) and almost 46% (Sydney) of all articles when mixed coverage was included (Pemberton et al., 2004). Capranica et al. (2005) concluded that in several European countries "female athletes receive an equitable amount of coverage during the Olympic Games, especially when their national participation rate is considered" (p. 220). This is also true for photographs, where coverage is relative to or even higher than the female proportion on Olympic teams (Capranica et al., 2005; Pemberton et al., 2004). Nevertheless, several studies have found exceptions to this pattern. For example, during the 1992 summer Games, Australian women were 37% of the team and won 38% of the medals but their overall coverage ranged between 24% and 30% (Embrey et al., 1993). An analysis of British newspaper coverage of the 1992 Olympics athletics events identified a ratio of 3:1 in favour of men; a finding that could not be explained by the higher proportion of male athletes on the British team or the men's greater success (Alexander, 1994). In Canada, despite an overall trend towards proportional coverage, and a higher proportion of photographs from 1964–1992, Urquhart and Crossman (1999) identified five Olympiads "when women received extremely poor coverage in relation to the number of female competitors" (p. 198). They noted, however, that Canadian women won few medals in those five Olympiads and, as we discuss in our next theme, argued that medal success may influence coverage of females. Overall, these studies provide an optimistic picture of gender equality in Olympic sport reporting. Mirroring the more recent optimism, we hypothesised that female and male athletes would receive coverage relative to their proportions on the Olympic team during the Athens Games.

THE INTERSECTION OF NATIONALISM AND MEDAL SUCCESS

There is some evidence that factors other than gender might create increased media visibility for females in international competitions. In this section, we discuss two key intersecting factors – medal success and nationalism.

Successful athletes, regardless of their gender, become the focus of media attention, especially during major international sporting events. Indeed, the media focus on those who win gold medals (Darnell & Sparks, 2005; Pemberton et al., 2004; Wensing, 2003). MacAloon (1987) argues that "female achievements…are of equal status with those of men in the context of a national medal struggle which is 'gender-blind'" (p. 118). Thus, it should not be surprising that several studies have demonstrated that women who win or are expected to win medals receive more attention in the media. For example, throughout the twentieth century, Canadian newspaper coverage of female Winter Olympians ebbed and flowed with their medal success, leading the researchers to conclude that "media coverage may have been performance biased" (Urquhart & Crossman, 1999, p. 198). During the 2000 Games, the five women who were among the top 10 most-mentioned athletes on US prime time television coverage were all gold medallists, as were four of the men (Billings & Eastman, 2002). The growth in women's events in the Games means that increased opportunities for Olympic success should result in increased media coverage. As a result, we hypothesised that female and male athletes would receive coverage relative to the proportion of Olympic medals they won.

Nationalism is another key factor that may result in increased coverage for female athletes. While women have not historically been seen as carriers of national identity, all athletes and teams who represent the nation "have a potential for constructing symbols of national identity" (see von der Lippe, 2003, p. 379). Indeed, Wensing and Bruce (2003) reflect a growing belief among sport media researchers when they argue that "coverage during international sports events … may be less likely to be marked by gendered … discourses or narratives than reporting on everyday sports, at least for sportswomen whose success is closely tied to a nation's sense of self " (p. 393). In many countries, the media focus on athletes who represent the nation, whether in routine stories, Olympic reports or coverage of other international events. For example, in three Scandinavian countries, more than 60% of routine coverage focused on 'domestic' athletes and "40 per cent of international articles spotlight a national athlete who is partaking" (Jorgensen, 2002, p. 4). In New Zealand, 70% of articles and 73% of images in Commonwealth Games reports focused on New Zealanders (Wensing, 2003). During the 1992 Olympic Games, two separate studies also found a large 'national' emphasis. In the UK, the 10 most photographed athletes in athletics events were all British (Alexander, 1994) and 88% of front page Olympic stories featured British athletes (Bernstein, 2000). In Israel, 100% of front page Olympic stories were about Israeli athletes (Bernstein, 2000). The author concluded that:

> There is a clear trend that shows that Olympic stories deemed most newsworthy and considered by newspaper editors to be of interest to the general public and not only to the devoted sports fans (who read the sports pages) were the stories related to the nation's own performance. (Bernstein, 2000, p. 361)

It is possible that nationalism may be even more important for female coverage than for males. In contrast to men's coverage during the 1991 World Athletics Championships, British coverage of women was "to a great extent limited to coverage of British women alone" (Alexander, 1994, p. 652). This finding led Alexander to conclude that "the situation seems to be that male athletics is interpreted on a world-wide scale, but women's athletics is only seen of importance if there is a British contestant" (1994, p. 652).

However, despite the overarching nationalism that generally marks media coverage some sports have stronger links to national identity than others. As MacAloon (1987) argues, "whole nations may be distinguished by their appreciation for or domination of certain sports and by their weakness, disinterest, or even shock at others" (p. 115). This claim is supported by research which found that sports routinely covered by the media outside of the Olympics received more coverage during the Olympics, even if the home nation was not competing (Bernstein, 2000). It was also evident in two cross-national studies which found that different countries highlighted different female Olympic sports; such as judo and tennis (Belgium), handball, badminton and sailing (Denmark), fencing and basketball (Italy), and field hockey (UK) (Capranica et al., 2005; Vincent, Imwold, Johnson & Massey, 2003). Similarly, European research discovered that attention to women's handball during the 1998 European championships varied by country. In contrast to only about 5% in German newspapers, women's handball received about 30% in Norway (von der Lippe, 2002), where the sport has a long tradition of media interest (Jorgensen, 2002).

These findings resulted in the hypothesis that female athletes who won medals in sports that were historically linked to national identity would receive more coverage than female medal winners in other sports.

SPOTLIGHT ON FEMININITY

While several of the themes discussed above appear to demonstrate a shift towards more equitable coverage, some researchers caution that a focus on the 'raw' numbers might provide an overly optimistic picture of the equality of women's Olympic representation in newspapers. Therefore, in addition to investigating the amount of coverage sportswomen receive, it is valuable to analyse the content more closely. One way of providing further insight into the content is to examine the types of women's sports that receive media coverage. To connect the type of sport to larger issues of gender inequality, many researchers classify women's sports into sex appropriate and sex inappropriate sports, following Matteo (1986), or into acceptable/feminine or non-acceptable/masculine sports, following Metheny (1965). Acceptable/feminine sports include individual sports that focus on aesthetics instead of the power, strength and/or contact required by many team sports. For example, ice-skating, diving, swimming, badminton or volleyball (which, while a team sport, does not require contact with the opponents) were considered female appropriate sports in Metheny's original classification.[3] Media scholars argue further that if women athletes are only depicted in feminine or female-appropriate sports it limits women's equal access to sport. For example, Jones, Murrell and Jackson (1999) conclude that "as a result of beliefs concerning the sex appropriateness of particular sports, women who participate in male-appropriate sports must challenge traditional sex role stereotypes by combating the belief that their participation is less valuable than men's involvement" (p. 184). Furthermore, limiting women's media representation to feminine or acceptable sports trivialises women's achievements, because their physical prowess in other sports is not fully appreciated. Therefore, a stereotypical focus on feminine sports in the media portrayal of women athletes generates and supports "sexist ideologies and beliefs about gender" (Jones et al., 1999, p. 184). We should point out, however, that beliefs about the gender-appropriateness of particular sports are not universally shared, and need to be defined on a nation-by-nation basis. For example, handball is seen as women's sport in Norway, as a gender-neutral sport in Denmark and as a male sport in Germany (von der Lippe, 2002).

North American newspapers have tended to focus on sports that are traditionally stereotyped as feminine in both Olympic and routine coverage (e.g., Duncan et al., 2005). In Canadian and US Olympic coverage, Lee (1992) found that female athletes were highly represented in individual sports, particularly in swimming and gymnastics, which she argued "emphasize aesthetic characteristics – appearance, beauty, form, and grace – and are seen as culturally acceptable sports for women" (p. 206). In the US, Pemberton et al. (2004) argued that Olympic "coverage for women remained largely focused on sports/events traditionally stereotyped as 'appropriate' for women and girls" (p. 94). This trend was moderated only in relation to gold medals: "Unless a 'gold medal' was at stake, the coverage of less 'feminine' sports/events was at best thin" (Pemberton et al., 2004, p. 94). Therefore, while women did receive coverage proportional to their participation, the coverage tended to focus on sports or events traditionally seen as appropriate for females.

Vincent et al. (2003) found that more than half the articles and photographs in Canadian, UK and US Olympic coverage were of gymnastics and swimming, and more than three-quarters of the most prominent photographs focused on these historically gender-appropriate sports, as well as diving and tennis. Another study found that photographic coverage in USA Today suggested "a lingering tendency to use women athletes for their glamour or sex appeal without serious treatment of their activities" (Eastman & Billings, 2000, p. 204). Certainly, research throughout the 1980s on both Olympic and routine coverage found evidence of imagery that highlighted gender difference. For example German media in the 1980s represented the female body "as barely covered nakedness in skin-tight sports clothes, graceful positions, fully stretched bodies, legs wide apart…sportswomen have been degraded to mere sex objects" (Klein, 1986, p. 145; see also Duncan, 1990). Although more recent research on routine US news broadcasts found "less frequent trivialization and humorous sexualisation" of women (Duncan et al., 2005, p. 5), an analysis of beach volleyball during the 2004 Games concluded that sexuality and sexual difference were "highly evident" in US broadcast images (Bissell & Duke, 2007, p. 35).

To further explore trivialisation of women athletes in newspaper coverage during the 2004 Olympic Games, we hypothesized that female athletes competing in sports more strongly linked to femininity or dressed in ways that highlight gender difference would receive more coverage than those competing in sports more strongly linked to masculinity or dressed in ways that did not highlight gender difference.

WOMEN AND MEN IN ACTION: SIMILARITIES IN PHOTOGRAPHIC COVERAGE

A key issue in the research has been the way in which females are represented in images. Research suggests that when female Olympic athletes are photographed, they tend to be shown in similar kinds of photographs to men[4] (e.g., Alexander, 1994; Lee, 1992; Hardin et al., 2002; Pemberton et al., 2004; Vincent et al., 2002). For both genders, the most common photographs show athletes in action or in competitive settings; a finding which is also true for some studies of non-Olympic coverage (e.g., Klein, 1988; Pedersen, 2002). Studies of Canadian, South African, UK and US newspapers report that men and women are most often shown in action or sport settings, and that the percentages differ very little by gender (e.g., Lee, 1992). A number of studies of the 2000 Games demonstrate that the trends in distribution by photo type (such as action, in a sport setting, not competing or posed) are remarkably similar by gender, although there may be minor percentage differences. More than 40% of images of men and women athletes showed them in action in *USA Today* coverage of the Sydney and Atlanta Games (Pemberton et al., 2004). Hardin et al. (2002) found that 78% of women and 81% of male athletes were represented in active rather than passive images in US newspapers. Comparing UK, US and Canadian coverage, Vincent et al. (2002) reported that both women and men were most commonly represented in competitive situations (female, 51%; male, 52%). Women were slightly more often depicted not competing but males were found more often in 'posed' photographs. Furthermore, an approximately equal number of photographs showed female athletes competing in so-called gender appropriate (22%) and gender inappropriate (21%) sports. The researchers concluded, positively, that national newspapers in all three countries gave generally equitable coverage to both genders (Vincent et al., 2002). From the 2004 Olympics, South African research reported that both males (65%) and females (60%) were most often represented in action (Serra, 2005).

As a result of this research, we hypothesised that female and male athletes would be portrayed similarly in photographs.

CONCLUSION

The extensive literature on the amount of women's coverage in the sport media demonstrates clearly that outside of major sporting events female athletes receive very little coverage. However, during the Olympic Games there is a significant increase and, in many cases, even though women receive less overall coverage than men, the Olympic coverage tends to be proportionate to the number of women athletes in national teams. This development, some researchers conclude, is a positive result of several factors.

First, women's increased media visibility demonstrates that some of the gender equality policies initiated by the IOC have taken effect. For example, Capranica et al. (2005) argue that these initiatives have increased both women's participation and women's events in the Games and, thus, enabled growing acceptance of women's sport in general.

Second, the increased visibility of women's sport in the Olympic movement has created a better market for women's mediated sport. Women's sport is now more popular and also attracts greater audiences, especially during the Olympic Games (e.g., Capranica et al., 2005; MacAloon, 1987; Vincent et al., 2002). Vincent et al. (2002) also argue that the media might currently perceive physically active women as a lucrative niche market and, therefore, the increased media coverage "may be reflecting the increased commercial potential of women's sport and physical activity and the marketing requirements of their advertisers" (p. 333). Third, as discussed earlier, some researchers point out that nationalism and success are factors that create media visibility during international level competitions. Therefore, women who are expected to win medals or who are successful will receive more attention in the media of the country they represent. In this sense, national identity overrides the athlete's gender identity (e.g., Bernstein, 2002; Wensing & Bruce, 2003).

While these are positive developments, most researchers are only cautiously optimistic about gender equality in Olympic media representation. Several studies found that while the amount of coverage for women's sport might have increased, the media still tended to focus only on few women's events. This was particularly evident in the US media, where women's gymnastics was the major focus. Currently, gymnastics is classified as a feminine/appropriate sport as it promotes such traditionally feminine qualities as smallness and flexibility. Some researchers also pointed out that female individual sports received more coverage than team sports because the former are considered feminine sports and are, thus, more acceptable in terms of female participation. Consequently, the media may promote an acceptance of sportswomen as long as they participate in appropriately feminine sports that do not require obvious strength, power or physical contact. Capranica et al. (2005), however, maintain that factors other than gender appropriateness dictate the content for Olympic sport coverage in the European media:

> the lack of any "gender-appropriate sports" effect on coverage and the differences among countries in the amount of articles and photos dedicated to sports reflecting high national medal expectancies, achievements, and sport participation, confirm that gender may not be the most relevant issue for media coverage in a global multisport event. In this regard, the Olympic Games contribute to the general promotion of women in sports, giving visibility to female athletes who compete in traditionally male-appropriate sports. (p. 221)

Several studies also pointed out that while the IOC or the media at the executive level may engage in positive action to promote gender equality, this sentiment does not necessarily reach the grassroots level of sport reporting. Male reporters greatly outnumber female reporters in most countries and they tend know, write and talk about men's sport (Bruce, 2008; Capranica et al., 2005; Eastman & Billings, 1999; Garrison & Salwen, 1989; Knoppers & Elling, 2004; Lowes, 1999; Strong, 2007; Theberge & Cronk, 1986). They also believe that audiences are primarily interested in men's sports; a claim that is challenged during Olympic broadcasts which not only attract large numbers of female viewers but have also indicated "no audience preference for men's sport" (Capranica & Aversa, 2002, p. 347). This finding led the authors to argue that the supposedly 'market-driven' media argument that audiences want to read about men's sport is merely an "ideological justification for what is in fact a *socially constructed* 'audience preference' for men's sport" (Capranica & Aversa, 2002, p. 347, emphasis added). Their claim is further supported by the finding that noticeable gender imbalances remain even in print media where no commercial imperative drives journalists' choices (Shifflett & Revelle, 1994; Wann, Schrader, Allison & McGeorge, 1998). The overwhelming male domination of sports journalism has led some researchers to argue that until there is more occupational equality we will not witness a significant change in the content of sport reporting.

Finally, we should not forget that Olympic Games media coverage does not represent the routine level of women's sport coverage. Outside of the Olympics, women's representation in the sport media remains dismally low. Researchers continue to be concerned about the level of routine media coverage which, they argue, constitutes an ongoing marginalisation and trivialisation of female athleticism. Tuggle and Owen (1999) suggest that viewers express less interest in women's sport because they have very little exposure to it between Olympics. Despite exponential growth in female sports participation, research over more than a quarter of a century consistently shows the invisibility of sportswomen in the global sports media and demonstrates that media coverage has not kept pace with changes in the gender makeup of sport.

The existing research demonstrates that although women are winning on the podium, they are still mostly missing in action in terms of media coverage, especially outside of major events. If women's sports are ignored, the patriarchal, male sport model is further legitimised as the hegemonic structure for sport. With the sports media acting as the primary source through which most people gain their ideas about what is important and valuable, the absence of sportswomen in the sports media appears to reinforce historical but still widespread cultural assumptions that sport is a male domain. However, because Olympic media coverage moderates women's usual invisibility, it clearly has the potential to challenge these cultural assumptions. As Vincent et al. argue:

> The unique format of international sporting events such as the Olympic Games is ideal to provide the print and electronic media with an opportunity to balance social responsibility with economic rationales and provide an equitable amount and type of coverage of female athletes competing in all sports. (2003, p. 18)

NOTES

[1] Throughout the review, we have rounded all percentages to whole numbers. See original research for the exact figures.

[2] Because our project analyses newspaper coverage during the Olympic Games, we focus our review on this type of media coverage. There is also considerable research on televised coverage of women's Olympic sport (e.g., Billings & Eastman, 2002; Capranica & Aversa, 2002; Eastman & Billings, 1999; Higgs & Weiller, 1994; Higgs, Weiller & Martin, 2003; Knoppers & Elling, 2004; Toohey, 1997; Tuggle & Owen, 1999). This research suggests that airtime for women's sport has steadily risen and females receive almost as much coverage as men in a number of countries, (e.g., Billings & Eastman, 2002; Eastman & Billings, 2000; Knoppers & Elling, 2004). Research on Australian online media also found that women received almost half the coverage (Jones, 2004). The research also indicates that females receive more television coverage than newspaper coverage (e.g., Knoppers & Elling, 2004; Toohey, 1997); a finding which contrasts with the research on routine coverage. In addition, while televised coverage in the US tends to focus on 'feminine' sports such as gymnastics, swimming and diving (e.g., Eastman & Billings, 2000; Higgs, Weiller & Martin, 2003; Tuggle & Owen, 1999), this trend is not necessarily found in Europe (Capranica & Aversa, 2002) or Australia (Toohey, 1997).

[3] The methodological tool of dividing sport events into 'appropriate' and 'inappropriate' for women is based on Metheny's (1965) study of perceptions of gender appropriateness of different sports among US college women in the 1960s. Sports that the college women found *inappropriate* included wrestling, judo, boxing, weight-lifting, hammer throw, pole vault, the longer foot races, high hurdles, and all forms of team games except volleyball. In 1964, women were excluded from these events in the Olympic Games. Currently, only wrestling is not offered as a women's Olympic event. Sports that they felt *appropriate for women of lower socio-economic status* included shot put, discus, javelin, shorter foot races, low hurdles, long jump, gymnastic events, and free exercise. Metheny reasoned that in the United States, 'Negro' women were disproportionately represented in the track and field events (shot put, discus, javelin and sprint events) and this might influence college women's perceptions of their suitability for certain, but not all, women. Moreover, Metheny pointed out that women of Germanic and Slavic ancestry in the United States tended to engage in gymnastics at club level in their ethnic communities rather than colleges which probably made the college women classify gymnastics as an unsuitable for themselves. Sports that were identified as *wholly appropriate* for college women in the US included swimming, diving, skiing, figure skating, golf, archery, bowling, fencing, squash, badminton, tennis and volleyball. Metheny noted that some of these sports required considerable amounts of time and money. More recent research by Reimer and Visio (2003) suggests that some team sports, such as soccer and basketball, are now seen as appropriate for both genders: Indeed, they argue that "perceptions of best sports for girls seem to be expanding to include more masculine sports" (p. 203).

[4] The idea of classifying photographs based on their content derives from Rintala and Birrell's (1984) study. Lee (1992), Pringle and Gordon (1995) and Vincent et al. (2002), among others, have used this study to devise their content analysis for the photographic coverage.

REFERENCES

Alexander, S. (1994). Newspaper coverage of athletics as a function of gender. *Women's Studies International Forum, 17*, 655–662.

Alston, M. (1996). *Goals for women: Improving media representation of women's sport*. Centre for Rural Social Research, Wagga. Wagga: Charles Sturt University.

Bernstein, A. (2000). "Things you can see from there you can't see from here": Globalization, media, and the Olympics. *Journal of Sport & Social Issues, 24*(4), 351–369.

Bernstein, A. (2002). Is it time for a victory lap? Changes in the media coverage of women in sport. *International Review for the Sociology of Sport, 37*, 415–428.

Bernstein, A., & Galily, Y. (2008). Games and sets: Women, media and sport in Israel. *Nashim: A Journal of Jewish Women's Studies & Gender Issues, 15*, 175–196.

Billings, A. C., & Eastman, S. T. (2002). Selective representation of gender, ethnicity, and nationality in American television coverage of the 2000 Summer Olympics. *International Review for the Sociology of Sport, 37*, 351–370.

Bissell, K. L., & Duke, A. M. (2007). Bump, set, spike: An analysis of commentary and camera angles of women's beach volleyball during the 2004 Summer Olympics. *Journal of Promotion Management, 13*(1/2), 35–53.

Brown, P. (1995). Gender, the press and history: Coverage of women's sport in the Newcastle Herald, 1890–1990. *Media Information Australia, 75*, 24–34.

Bruce, T. (2008). Women, sport and the media. In C. Obel, T Bruce, & S. Thompson (Eds.), *Outstanding: Research about women and sport in New Zealand* (pp. 51–71). Hamilton, NZ: Wilf Malcolm Institute for Educational Research.

Bruce, T., Falcous, M., & Thorpe, H. (2007). The mass media and sport. In C. Collins & S. Jackson (Eds.), *Sport in Aotearoa/New Zealand society* (2nd ed., pp. 147–169). Auckland: Thomson.

Bruce, T., Mikosza, J., Hayles, C., & Whittington, J. (1999). *Marching in place: Media coverage of women's sport in Australia, 1999.* Unpublished manuscript, University of Canberra, Canberra, Australia.

Bryant, J. (1980). A two-year selective investigation of the female in sport as reported in the paper media. *Arena Review, 4*(2), 32–40.

Burstyn, V. (1999). *The rites of men: Manhood, politics and the culture of sport.* Toronto, ON: University of Toronto Press.

Capranica, L., & Aversa, F. (2002). Italian television sport coverage during the 2000 Sydney Olympic Games. *International Review for the Sociology of Sport, 37*, 337–349.

Capranica, L., Minganti, C., Billat, V., Hanghoj, S., Piacentini, M. F., Cumps, E., et al. (2005). Newspaper coverage of women's sports during the 2000 Sydney Olympic Games: Belgium, Denmark, France, and Italy. *Research Quarterly for Exercise and Sport, 76*, 212–223.

Coakley, J. (2001). *Sport in society: Issues & controversies.* Boston: McGraw-Hill.

Crossman, J., Hyslop, P., & Guthrie, B. (1994). A content analysis of the sports section of Canada's national newspaper with respect to gender and professional/amateur status. *International Review for the Sociology of Sport, 29*, 123–134.

Darnell, S. C., & Sparks, R. (2005). Inside the promotional vortex: Canadian media construction of Sydney Olympic triathlete Simon Whitfield. *International Review for the Sociology of Sport, 40, 357–376.*

Davis, L. (1997). *The swimsuit issue and sport. Hegemonic masculinity in sports illustrated.* Albany, NY: The State University of New York Press.

Donohoe, H. (2003). *Britain's best kept secrets.* London: Women's Sports Foundation UK.

Donohoe, H. (2004). Media blackout. *Sports Management, 8*(1), 26–28.

Duncan, M. C., Messner, M., & Willms, N. (2005). *Gender in televised sports: News and highlights shows, 1989–2004.* Los Angeles: Amateur Athletic Foundation of Los Angeles.

Duncan, M. C., Messner, M., & Williams, L. (1991). *Coverage of women's sports in four daily newspapers.* Los Angeles: Amateur Athletic Foundation.

Dyer, K. (1982). *Challenging the men.* St. Lucia: University of Queensland Press.

Eastman, S. T., & Billings, A. C. (1999). Gender parity in the Olympics: Hyping women athletes, favoring men athletes. *Journal of Sport & Social Issues, 23*, 140–170.

Eastman, S. T., & Billings, A. C. (2000). Sportscasting and sports reporting: The power of gender bias. *Journal of Sport & Social Issues, 24*, 192–213.

Embrey, L., Hall, A., & Gunter, A. (1993). *Print media coverage of the 1992 winter and summer Olympics in two Australian states.* Paper presented at the International Association of Physical Education and Sports for Girls and Women [IAPESGW] Congress, Melbourne, Australia.

Fasting, K., & Tangen, J. (1983). Gender and sport in Norwegian mass media. *International Review for the Sociology of Sport, 18*(1), 61–70.

Ferkins, L. (1992). New Zealand women in sport: An untapped media resource. *New Zealand Journal of Health, Physical Education and Recreation, 25*(4), 15–18.

Fountaine, S., & McGregor, J. (1999). The loneliness of the long distance gender researcher: Are journalists right about the coverage of women's sport? *Australian Journalism Review, 21*(3), 113–126.

Garrison, B., & Salwen, M. (1989). Newspaper sports journalists: A profile of the profession. *Journal of Sport and Social Issues, 13*(2), 57–68.

Gerbner, G. (1978). The dynamics of cultural resistance. In G. Tuchman, A. K. Daniels, & J. Benet (Eds.), *Hearth and home: Images of women in mass media.* New York: Oxford University Press.

Grossberg, L., Wartella, E., Whitney, D. C., & Wise, J. M. (2006). *Media making: Mass media in a popular culture* (2nd ed.). Thousand Oaks, CA: Sage.

Hardin, M., Chance, J., Dodd, J. E., & Hardin, B. (2002). Olympic photo coverage fair to female athletes. *Newspaper Research Journal, 23*(2/3), 64–78.

Higgs, T. C., & Weiller, K. H. (1994). Gender bias and the 1992 summer Olympic Games: An analysis of television coverage. *Journal of Sport & Social Issues, 18*, 234–246.

Higgs, T. C., Weiller, K. H., & Martin, S. B. (2003). Gender bias in the 1996 Olympic Games: A comparative analysis. *Journal of Sport & Social Issues, 27*, 52–64.

Hindson, L. J. (1989). *A newspaper content analysis of the Australian's treatment of female and male athletes in the 1984 and 1988 Summer Olympic Games.* Unpublished master's thesis, the University of Iowa.

Jones, R., Murrell, A., & Jackson, J. (1999). Pretty vs powerful in the sports pages: Print media coverage of U.S. Olympic gold medal winning teams. *Journal of Sport & Social Issues, 23*, 183–192.

Jorgensen, S. S. (2005, October 31). The world's best advertising agency: The sports press. *Mandagmorgen [Mondaymorning], 37*, pp. 1–7.

Jorgensen, S. S. (2002, November). Industry or independence? Survey of the Scandinavian sports press. *Mondaymorning*, Special issue, pp. 1–8.

King, C. (2007). Media portrayals of male and female athletes: A text and picture analysis of British national newspaper coverage of the Olympic games since 1948. *International Review for the Sociology of Sport, 42*(2), 187–199.

Kinnick, K. N. (1998, Fall). Gender bias in newspaper profiles of 1996 Olympic athletes: A content analysis of five major dailies. *Women's Studies in Communication, 21*(2), 212–237.

Klein, M.-L. (1988). Women in the discourse of sport reports. *International Review for the Sociology of Sport, 23*(2), 139–152.

Knoppers, A., & Elling, A. (2004). 'We do not engage in promotional journalism': Discursive strategies used by sport journalists to describe the selection process. *International Review for the Sociology of Sport, 39*(1), 57–73.

Koivula, N. (1999). Gender stereotyping in televised media sport coverage. *Sex Roles, 41*(7/8), 589–603.

Lee, J. (1992). Media portrayals of male and female Olympic athletes: Analyses of newspaper accounts of the 1984 and 1988 summer games. *International Review for the Sociology of Sport, 27*, 197–219.

Matteo, S. (1986). The effect of sex and gender-schematic processing on sport participation. *Sex Roles, 15*, 417–432.

MacAloon, J. J. (1987, Fall). Missing stories: American politics and Olympic discourse. *Gannett Center Journal, 1*(2), 111–142.

Mathesen, H., & Flatten, K. (1996). Newspaper representation of women athletes in 1984 and 1994. *Women in Sport and Physical Activity Journal, 5*(2), 65–83.

McGregor, J., & Fountaine, S. (1997). Gender equity in retreat: The declining representation of women's sport in the New Zealand print media. *Metro, 112*, 38–44.

Menzies, H. (1989). Women's sport – treatment by the media. In K. Dyer (Ed.), *Sportswomen towards 2000: A celebration* (pp. 220–231). Adelaide: University of Adelaide.

Messner, M. (1988). Sports and male domination: The female athlete as contested terrain. *Sociology of Sport Journal, 3*, 197–211.

Metheny, E. (1965). *Connotations of movement in sport and dance.* Dubuque: William C. Brown.

Mikosza, J. (1996). *Report on newspaper reportage and images: Atlanta Olympic Games.* Canberra: Womensport Australia.

Mikosza, J. (1997). *Inching forward.* Canberra: Womensport Australia.

Payne, R. (2004). Rethinking the status of female Olympians in the Australian press. *Media Information Australia, 110*, 120–131.

Pedersen, P. M. (2002). Examining equity in newspaper photographs: A content analysis of the print media photographic coverage of interscholastic athletics. *International Review for the Sociology of Sport, 37*, 303–318.

Pedersen, P. M., Whisenant, W. A., & Schneider, R. G. (2003). Using a content analysis to examine the gendering of sports newspaper personnel and their coverage. *Journal of Sport Management, 17*, 376–393.

Pemberton, C., Shields, S., Gilbert, L., Shen, X., & Said, H. (2004). A look at print media coverage across four Olympiads. *Women in Sport and Physical Activity Journal, 13*, 87–99.

Pfister, G. (1987). Women in the Olympic (1952–1980): An analysis of German newspapers (Beauty awards vs gold medals). In R. Jackson & T. McPhail (Eds), *Olympic movement and mass media conference* (pp. 27–33). Calgary: Hurford.

Phillips, M. (1997). *An illusory image: A report on the media coverage and portrayal of women's sport in Australia 1996*. Canberra: Australian Sports Commission.

Pringle, R., & Gordon, S. (1995, Winter). A content analysis of western Australian print media coverage of the 1990 Commonwealth Games with particular reference to gender differences. *The ACHPER Healthy Lifestyles Journal*, 4–8.

Riemer, B. A., & Visio, M. E. (2003). Gender typing of sports: An investigation of Metheny's classification. *Research Quarterly for Exercise and Sport, 74*, 193–204.

Rintala, J., & Birrell, S. (1984). Fair treatment for the active female: A content analysis of *Young Athlete* magazine. *Sociology of Sport Journal, 1*(3), 213–250.

Rudie, I. (1994). Sport: A way of speaking about society? In Sekretariatet for kvinneforskning (Ed.), *Kvinner - En utfordring for idretten?* Oslo: Norges Forskningsråd.

Serra, P. (2005). *The construction and deconstruction of gender through sport reporting in selected South African newspapers*. Unpublished master's thesis, University of Johannesburg, Johannesburg, South Africa.

Shifflett, B., & Revelle, R. (1996). Gender equity in sports media coverage: A review of the NCAA News. In R. E. Lapchick (Ed.), *Sport in society: Equal opportunity or business as usual?* London: Sage.

Stoddart, B. (1994). *Invisible games: A report on the media coverage of women's sport, 1992*. Canberra: Sport and Recreation Ministers' Council.

Strong, C. (2007). Female journalists shun sports reporting: Lack of opportunity or lack of attractiveness? *Communication Journal of New Zealand, 8*(2), 7–18.

Szabo, A. (2001). Men versus women in the sports media: Fair play? In H. Ruskin & M. Lammer (Eds.), *Fair play: Violence in sport and society* (pp. 158–175). *The Cossell Center for Physical Education, Leisure and Health Promotion*. Jerusalem: The Hebrew University of Jerusalem.

Theberge, N., & Birrell, S. (1994). The sociological study of women and sport. In D. M. Costa & S. R. Guthrie (Eds.), *Women and sport: Interdisciplinary perspectives* (pp. 323–359). Champaign, IL: Human Kinetics.

Theberge, N., & Cronk, A. (1986). Work routines in newspaper sports departments and the coverage of women's sports. *Sociology of Sport Journal, 3*, 195–203.

Toohey, K. (1997). Australian television, gender and the Olympic games. *International Review for the Sociology of Sport, 32*, 19–29.

Tuggle, C. A. (1997). Differences in television sports coverage of men's and women's athletics: ESPN SportsCenter and CNN Sports Tonight. *Journal of Broadcasting and Electronic Media, 41*, 14–24.

Tuggle, C. A., & Owen, A. (1999). A descriptive analysis of NBC's coverage of the Centennial Olympics: The "Games of the Woman"? *Journal of Sport & Social Issues, 23*, 171–182.

Urquhart, J., & Crossman, J. (1999). The Globe and mail coverage of the winter Olympic games. *Journal of Sport & Social Issues, 23*, 193–202.

Valgeirsson, G., & Snyder, E. E. (1986). A cross-cultural comparison of newspaper sports sections. *International Review for the Sociology of Sport, 21*(2/3), 131–140.

Vincent, J., Imwold, C., Johnson, J. T., & Massey, C. D. (2003). Newspaper coverage of female athletes competing in selected sports in the centennial Olympic games: The more things change the more they stay the same. *Women in Sport & Physical Activity Journal, 12*, 1–21.

Vincent, J., Imwold, C., Masemann, V., & Johnson, J. T. (2002). A comparison of selected 'serious' and 'popular' British, Canadian, and United States newspaper coverage of female and male athletes competing in the Centennial Olympic Games. *International Review for the Sociology of Sport, 37,* 319–335.

von der Lippe, G. (2002). Media image: Sport, gender and national identities in five European countries. *International Review for the Sociology of Sport, 37*(3/4), 371–396.

Wann, D. L., Schrader, M. P., Allison, J. A., & McGeorge, K. K. (1998). The inequitable newspaper coverage of men's and women's athletics at small, medium, and large universities. *Journal of Sport and Social Issues, 22,* 79–87.

Weiller, K. H., Higgs, C. T., & Martin, S. B. (2004). Gender bias in the 1996 Olympic Games: Audience perception and effects. *Women in Sport and Physical Activity Journal, 13,* 8–17.

Wensing, E. H. (2003). *Print media constructions of New Zealand national identity at the 2002 Commonwealth Games.* Unpublished master's thesis, University of Waikato, New Zealand.

Wensing, E. H., & Bruce, T. (2003). Bending the rules: Media representations of gender during an international sporting event. *International Review for the Sociology of Sport, 38,* 387–396.

TONI BRUCE, JORID HOVDEN AND PIRKKO MARKULA

2. CONTENT ANALYSIS, LIBERAL FEMINISM AND THE IMPORTANCE OF MAPPING THE MEDIA TERRAIN

Content analysis is a popular and widely used method for the study of gender differences in media coverage; a tradition to which this book contributes. Briefly, its goal is "the accurate representation of a body of messages" (Wimmer & Dominick, 2003, p. 141). Content analysis aims to understand what the media produces by systematically quantifying media content, using pre-determined categories, and analysing the results statistically (Deacon, Pickering, Golding & Murdoch, 1999; Riffe, Lacy & Fico, 1998; Wimmer & Dominick, 2003).

In sport, gender has attracted by far the most attention, although researchers have used content analysis to consider other areas of sociological interest such as coverage of race (Billings & Eastman, 2002; Bruce, 2004; Eastman & Billings, 2001; Rada, 1996; Rada & Wulfemeyer, 2005; Rainville & McCormick, 1977) or disability (Schantz & Gilbert, 2001; Schell & Duncan, 1999). For well over quarter of a century, researchers have steadily counted and measured their way through newspaper, magazine and television coverage, en route to demonstrating how the sports media has ignored, trivialised, devalued and often sexualised female athletes. More recently, content analysis has been used to assess how these patterns are replicated or disrupted in the online environment (Cipywnyk, 2006; Jones, 2004, 2006).

There are those who suggest there is no further need for content analyses of gender difference and that we should now turn our attention to more important questions or different methods. Such critics suggest that there is little need to conduct or publish these kinds of studies when they so often tell us the same thing, particularly in Western countries with a history of content analysis research (e.g., Australia, Canada, New Zealand, the United Kingdom and the United States).

In contrast, we suggest that the very fact that these studies demonstrate such limited change, during a period of unprecedented growth and development in women's sport in many countries, is exactly what makes this kind of work important. It is precisely the documented lack of change that challenges us to continue the fight for the public recognition and respect that sportswomen around the world deserve for their dedication, skill and performance. We agree with Turner (1997) that content analyses of the sports media "are themselves a damning indictment of the institutionalised sexism of sports reporting" (p. 298). Ongoing systematic documentation allows us to explore the historical reproduction of gender and

T. Bruce, J. Hovden and P. Markula (eds.),
Sportswomen at the Olympics: A Global Content Analysis of Newspaper Coverage, 19–30.
© *2010 Sense Publishers. All rights reserved.*

contributes to theorising about why some forms of representation and stereotypes persist and others do not. In addition, policy makers "notoriously prefer 'hard data'" (van Zoonen, 1994, p. 73) and, thus, quantitative analyses of content can be used effectively in legislating and arguing for change. As van Zoonen (1994) argues, the method of content analysis produces results that are grounded in traditional scientific expectations of objectivity and, as a result, are generally accepted as reliable and true.

In this chapter, we describe and assess the quantitative methods used in the *Global Women in Sports Media Project*. We begin by considering the theoretical framework that underpins much of the quantitative research on media coverage of sportswomen. Next, we discuss the value of content analysis as a method. Finally, we outline the ways in which it has been used by the researchers in this book and consider some of the issues that arose in attempting to follow one methodology across a range of countries.

CONTENT ANALYSIS OF GENDER: THEORETICAL UNDERPINNINGS

Many of the previous content analyses of sports media have been conducted from an explicit or implicit liberal feminist position that focuses on ensuring that female athletes achieve equality with male athletes in terms of amount and type of coverage. This position reflects the broader liberal feminist focus on "the removal of barriers to the achievement of equality with men" (Curthoys, 2005, p. 129; hooks, 1984; Jaggar & Rothenberg Struhl, 1978; Jones & Jones, 1999; van Zoonen, 1994). Thus, while seldom acknowledged by researchers, we argue that the fundamental assumptions of liberal feminism are a driving force behind the conduct of this kind of analysis. This approach draws heavily on a transmission model of communication which assumes "a rather straightforward relation between media and society, accusing the mass media of conveying a distorted picture of women's lives and experiences and demanding a more accurate reflection instead" (van Zoonen, 1994, p. 68; Grossberg, Wartella, Whitney & Wise, 2006).

Following liberal feminist thinking, researchers argue that women athletes deserve what male athletes have in terms of media acknowledgement and visibility. Thus, unlike radical feminists for example, researchers who conduct content analyses of sport have seldom argued for a significant revolution in how the sports media and sport are organised. Rather, their work has come from a liberal position seeking equality *within* the existing structures of sport and sports media. This theoretical approach implicitly believes that once discrimination has been highlighted then it is logical for steps to be taken to end that discrimination. It focuses on legal and government intervention, believing that affirmative action programmes and equal opportunity policies are the way to bring about gender relations that are more equal (Jones & Jones, 1999). Current sports media coverage appears to reflect what Jones and Jones (1999) call a *cultural lag* in which the significant social changes in women's lives "are only partially reflected and represented by the media" (p. 66). The liberal feminist position holds that media representations of women should eventually "catch up with their actual social position" and provide "a more accurate view" of women's lives and experiences (Jones & Jones, 1999, p. 66).

Liberal feminism has, however, endured extensive critique. The limits of liberal feminism have been highlighted by critics who argue that it primarily reflects the beliefs and experiences of white, middle class women (see hooks, 1984; van Zoonen, 1994). Some have argued that feminism must go beyond focusing on gaining "social equality with men" (hooks, 1984, p. 31), and recognisee that because "patriarchal domination shares an ideological foundation with racism and other forms of group oppression...there is no hope that it can be eradicated while these systems remain intact" (hooks, 1984, p. 22). At the same time, however, liberal feminism's focus on reform has been successful in instigating legal and political changes in many countries (see Curthoys, 2005; hooks, 1984; Jagger & Rothenberg Stuhl, 1978, Skjeie & Teigen, 2003), and hooks acknowledges that "such reforms have helped many women make significant strides towards social equality with men in a number of areas" (1984, p. 157). As discussed in the individual country chapters, nations such as Norway and the United States have enacted laws which have led to large increases in female participation in sport and sport administration. Yet these increases have rarely been represented in increased media interest in or coverage of women's sport. Nor has bringing inequality to the attention of the sports media resulted in substantive change (Fountaine & McGregor, 1999), except perhaps in the case of major events such as the Olympic Games, when nationalism rather than gender appears to become a stronger determinant of coverage. Almost 30 years of content analysis on sports media coverage of women in a variety of predominantly Western countries appears to have done little to challenge the persistent ideology that sees female sport as inferior and second-rate. While increasing numbers of women successfully compete in sport, the male-dominated sports media shows virtually no change in the amount of coverage of everyday or within-nation women's sport.

Despite our awareness of the critiques of liberal feminism, we have chosen to engage in content analysis in this project because we firmly believe that Winston (1990) is correct when he argues that "the objective, systematic and quantitative description of communication ... is a thing to be sought after. If we cannot have such a description of [the media's] content, then how, in any real sense, can we know what it is?" (p. 62). For sport researchers analysing the ways in which female athletes are represented, accurate summaries or 'maps' of what the media actually produces are central to any argument for change. As Winston agues, "without the 'map', no case can be sustained as to any kind of cultural skewedness except on the basis of one-off examples of misrepresentation ... and if no case can be made, then there is none to answer" (1990, p. 62). Further, for researchers wanting to consider questions about what media practices produce the content or what effects the content might have on those who consume it, knowledge of the content must come first. Indeed, some suggest that without knowledge of media content such questions "are meaningless" (Riffe et al., 1998, p. 32). Therefore, while acknowledging that much content analysis research is underpinned by a liberal feminist position, we chose this method because it provided the most appropriate way to gather and compare results across a large international sample. It also was the most appropriate way to begin, in some countries, the ground-breaking work of determining 'what the content is'.

THE VALUE OF CONTENT ANALYSIS

Like all methods of media analysis, content analysis is a tool that researchers can use to gain a more rigorous and reflective understanding of particular media texts (Grossberg et al., 2006). It aims to understand the nature of what the media produces by systematically quantifying media content, using pre-determined categories, and analysing the results statistically (Deacon et al., 1999; Riffe et al., 1999; Wimmer & Dominick, 2003).

One of the key advantages of content analysis is its ability to consider the big picture; "delineating trends, patterns and absences over large aggregates of texts" (Deacon et al., 1999, p. 117). This means that researchers can summarize large amounts of information and present their results succinctly. As a result, it is particularly appropriate for research such as ours which explores questions about patterns of media representation across a wide range of countries. In addition, Deacon et al. argue that:

> The great advantage of content analysis is that it is methodical. It stipulates that all material within a chosen sample must be submitted to the same set of categories, which have been explicitly identified. To this extent it ensures a reasonable degree of reliability in the establishment of a pattern of media representation. (1999, p. 133)

Equally importantly, they point out that:

> It also provides a guard against temptations inherent in less rigorous approaches, of selecting items that seem to fit the case you may want to prove, or allowing your impression of a developing pattern of representation to be guided by your pre-existing prejudices and assumptions. (Deacon et al., 1999, p. 133)

Even critics of content analysis (e.g., McKee, 2001; Turner, 1997; van Zoonen, 1994; Winston, 1990) recognise its value in producing descriptions or 'maps' of media content. Certainly, content analysis of gender in the sports media has a long and well-established history; and the 'maps' of content identified across time, countries and continents have been widely used by organisations, Governments, teachers and researchers as part of a broader discussion of sexism in sport.

THE PROCESS OF CONDUCTING CONTENT ANALYSIS

The methods followed in the *Global Women in Sports Media Project* were developed so that researchers in each country could collect, input and analyse the same data in a similar fashion. Of course, it is never as simple as this and, as you will see throughout the book, researchers from each country made their own decisions about what data was of most relevance. Their choices reflect a number of factors including the relationship of this study to previous research in their countries, the questions or hypotheses that were most relevant to their own interests, stylistic differences in newspapers, expectations for research quality in their institutions and, in some cases, the availability of graduate students or research assistants to do the "often laborious and tedious" (Wimmer & Dominick, 2003, p. 145) work of measurement. Our aim was to produce a body of work that was systematic, objective and rigorous, while also being accessible to a wide range of readers including undergraduate students, policy makers, sports organisations and interested members of the public. To enable such readers to make sense of the results and compare them across different nations, we recommended that each country limit the analysis to descriptive statistics.

Although we attempted to maintain the same methodology across all studies, some countries undertook their data collection across slightly different time frames, decided to focus only on coverage of the Olympics (excluding any stories unrelated to the Olympics from their collection and analysis), or measured either space or the number of articles and photographs. As a result, although this chapter outlines the key elements of the project methodology, each country chapter outlines methodological issues specific to the data gathering undertaken in that country.

A typical content analysis project follows the following steps: developing hypotheses, 'defining the universe', sampling, developing the instrument and statistical analysis (Deacon et al., 1999; Riffe et al., 1998; Wimmer & Dominick, 2003; Winston, 1990). In the following section we discuss how we structured our project based on these steps.

Developing the Guiding Hypotheses

The first step in content analysis is formulating research questions or hypotheses. These can come from existing theory, prior research, industry definitions or practical/grounded problems. In our case, the seven guiding hypotheses derived primarily from the substantial body of existing international research (see Chapter 1), and we attempted to assess whether the 2004 Olympic coverage supported or challenged the results of previous studies. We noted that not all hypotheses would be relevant to each country and that hypotheses 5 and 7 would need to be defined on a country-by-country basis.

Hypothesis 1: In coverage of the Olympics, female athletes will receive relatively equal newspaper coverage compared to male athletes.

Hypothesis 2: In non-Olympic coverage, female athletes will receive unequal and lesser newspaper coverage compared to male athletes.

Hypothesis 3: Female and male athletes will receive coverage relative to their proportions on the Olympic team.

Hypothesis 4: Female and male athletes will receive coverage relative to the proportion of Olympic medals they win.

Hypothesis 5: Female athletes competing in sports more strongly linked to femininity or dressed in ways that highlight gender difference will receive more coverage than those competing in sports more strongly linked to masculinity or dressed in ways that do not highlight gender difference.

Hypothesis 6: Female and male athletes will be portrayed similarly in photographs.

Hypothesis 7: Female athletes who win medals in sports that are historically linked to national identity will receive more coverage than female medal winners in other sports.

As will be apparent in the various chapters, although all countries gathered data relevant to the guiding hypotheses, the authors of each chapter decided which results were the most relevant to their own contexts.

Defining the Universe

Another key decision is specifying the boundaries of the body of content to be analysed, a process that Wimmer and Dominick call "defining the universe" (2003, p. 145). To ensure comparisons could be made across the countries, the sample was limited to newspaper coverage (rather than including television news, live broadcasts, radio or internet coverage, for example) and, in most countries, to the largest circulation or most prominent newspaper. This definition of 'the universe' recognised that media environments differ significantly across countries and relied upon the researchers' local knowledge to identify the most appropriate newspaper outlet. Where possible, authors selected a newspaper with national circulation, such as in the Czech Republic, Japan, South Korea, Spain and USA. Others, such as Canada, Hungary, New Zealand, Norway and Sweden, selected the largest circulation daily newspaper, even if it did not have 'national' distribution. Some countries, such as Belgium, China and South Africa, focused on popular or large circulation regional newspapers, especially in cases where there were distinct regions within the nation. In still others, such as Denmark, the UK and Germany, the cultural importance of both tabloid and broadsheet newspapers led the researchers to analyse one example of each type. In France, the researchers compared a general newspaper and sports-only newspaper, and the Turkish researchers examined three mass circulation newspapers which appeal to different audiences. Although each country was initially asked to analyse only coverage in the sports section and on the front page of the newspaper, once the study began it became apparent that there were substantial variations in how newspapers in different countries presented the Olympics. For example, some placed all or most Olympics coverage into special Olympic supplements while others provided specific Olympic pages in the general news section. As a result, researchers in each country gathered the most appropriate sample in their case and described this in their methods section.

Sampling

Because our questions related to media coverage during the Olympic Games, the *sample* time frame selected in this study was relatively straightforward. We chose a purposive sample, defined by the time frame of the 2004 Olympics. We offered two options for the period of analysis: the longer period included a week either side of the Games to permit collection of preview and review stories and the shorter period began with the opening ceremony and concluded with the closing ceremony; thus focusing only the days during which competition was taking place.

The *unit of analysis* was the 'story' or 'article', which included any material written under a headline and included any attached photographs, graphics or illustrations and their accompanying captions. One area of difference related to the analysis of results data. Some studies counted each result report as a separate story and analysed by gender; others categorized it as mixed even if only one set of results included female sport; others excluded the results from analysis (deciding that results would accurately reflect Olympic performances by gender and, thus, would not reflect media choices grounded in gender difference).

Instrumentation

The instrument for gathering data was an Excel spreadsheet containing 15 different elements, which were chosen to allow researchers a wide range of possible avenues for analysis, and to gather data related to the guiding hypotheses. In regard to the newspaper articles, the elements included the name of the newspaper, the day and date, the sport, whether the article was an Olympics story or not, gender of the article, identification of key individuals or teams discussed in the article, position or location of the article (e.g., front page, main sports page, inside sports page, etc.), the article focus or topic (e.g., sports event, athlete or team, facilities, sport organisation), the type of story (e.g., profile or feature story, event report, results, editorial) and the size of the article. In relation to images (which often have a different focus from the written text), the elements included image size, gender, type of image (e.g., sport action, sport-related, with medals, headshot or mugshot, logo, graphic), who was featured, and whether the image was in black and white or colour.

Validity and Reliability

The heart of any content analysis is the categories developed to classify the media content. In most sports media content analyses, the focus is on *face validity* which means that categories actually measure what they propose to measure. All categories should be mutually exclusive, exhaustive and reliable. In our study, this meant that each story could fit into only one category and that different coders would agree on the categories in most instances. In this project, the key categories were those related to gender. In line with previous research, we identified four 'gender' categories: male, female, mixed and neutral. The male category included articles that focused only on male athletes or, in longer feature stories (also called personality profiles or human interest stories) on male coaches or sports personnel. The female category included all articles focused only on female athletes (or on female coaches or sports personnel in feature stories). The mixed category included any stories that featured both males and females. In major events like the Olympic Games there are often high numbers of mixed stories, particularly in daily summaries of results or when multiple individuals or teams win medals on the same day. What this form of data gathering did not make possible was an analysis of the relative weight of male or female content within such stories, although some previous research has investigated this aspect. The neutral category (also called 'other' in some research) included all stories that did not focus on individuals or teams associated with the Games, such as stories about security plans for the Games, descriptions of various stadia, explanations of drug testing processes and features on the city of Athens. While the four 'gender' categories appear, in principle, to be relatively straightforward, valid coding is one of the most difficult elements of this kind of content analysis. In all cases, we emphasized that coders should be consistent with their choices and explain in their methods if and where they deviated from the project recommendations. For example, some countries such as Germany adapted the template to allow comparisons with existing German research, which meant dividing mixed stories and counting them twice (once as male, and once as female).

Reliability is another key issue for content analyses. This concept means that repeated measurement of the same material would result in similar decisions or conclusions. In studies such as this, where different people code material using the same template, it is recommended that training sessions and pilot studies be conducted to achieve *intercoder reliability*. However, given the difficulty of such an approach because of the geographical spread of researchers, wide range of native languages, different structures of national newspapers and levels of researcher experience, we concluded that this approach was not feasible. Instead, we provided a description and English-language newspaper example of how to measure and categorize stories, and set up a web-based discussion forum through which researchers could pose questions to the project leaders. The project leaders also visited a number of research teams and met with coders to discuss specific issues related to allocating stories to appropriate categories. The different layout of newspapers and the range of native languages (Chinese, Czech, Danish, English, Dutch, French, German, Hungarian, Japanese, Korean, Norwegian, Swedish, Spanish and Turkish) resulted in much discussion of the terms used in the template. For example, while the terms "feature story" and "headshot" or "mugshot" are commonly used by sports journalists in English-speaking countries, they were unfamiliar to a number of researchers. Much of the discussion on the web forum and via email revolved around explaining what kinds of material would appear in each category of story or photograph. Thus, issues of reliability and how to 'translate' categories became an important and ongoing aspect of the research project discussion.

Statistical Analysis

A common form of analysis used in quantitative studies involves descriptive statistics, such as percentages, means, medians and modes, which allow readers to easily grasp the importance of the findings, even without an extensive background in statistical analysis (Riffe et al., 1998). Given our explicit intention of making the results accessible to a wide range of readers, we asked researchers to limit their analysis and discussion to descriptive statistics. We note that of the more advanced statistical tests, the chi-square test is the most commonly used because content analysis data tends to nominal in form, although previous studies have also used t-tests, anovas and Newman Kreuls tests (e.g., Billings & Eastman, 2002; Pedersen, 2002; Vincent, Imwold, Masemann & Johnson, 2002).

LOOKING TO THE FUTURE: A STATISTICAL COMPARISON OF MEASURING SPACE OR COUNTING NUMBERS

Much of the quantitative research on media coverage of women's sport has measured space in squared centimetres or inches. This method of assessing the quantity of coverage involves a considerable investment of time and, in some ways, limits the number of researchers who can be involved in large, collaborative studies of this kind. The emphasis on measuring space is also apparent in the bulk of research at the Masters and PhD level where we suspect that 'merely' counting the number of articles might be considered too 'easy'. However, to our knowledge, previous researchers have not attempted to measure the association between measuring space or measuring numbers. As a result, we decided to use the results of this project to consider whether it was necessary to measure space as well as counting the number of articles and photographs in Olympic analyses (see BOX, Tom Cavanagh). As Tom Cavanagh's analysis demonstrates, admittedly based on a small sample of 10 countries, although there are small percentage differences between the results for space and for number of Olympic articles, the two measurement methods are significantly correlated. We want to suggest that this finding opens up exciting possibilities for future international collaborations which, by counting the number of articles and photographs, could be done in an efficient fashion and allow comparisons across a wide range of media types, time frames and countries, at least in terms of assessing Olympic coverage. It also opens up opportunities for fulfilling Winston's (1990) recommendation for more robust content analyses which must be based "on a sufficiently large body of output...so that the true regularities of ideological production can be described without the distortion of particular news incidents...skewing the results" (p. 61; see also Fountaine & McGregor, 1999). If counting numbers of Olympic articles provides results that are significantly associated with those measuring space, then the possibilities for time-strapped academic researchers and graduate students to expand their research time frames are much greater.

CONCLUSIONS

Whilst acknowledging that content analysis has theoretical and analytical limitations, it is a powerful method that provides the kind of hard data that governments and sports organisations value. It is also the most appropriate in studies such as this where researchers wish to compare results across a large international sample such as ours, which comprised 18 countries and newspapers published in 14 different languages. Large content analyses of this type are rare yet, precisely because they follow the same methodology and present results statistically, they permit us to explore global trends and differences that might be more difficult to investigate using other methods. The results of the analyses included in this volume suggest that it is important to continue to track and record the mass media's failure to adequately acknowledge women's sport and, at the same time, to explore the conditions, such as during the Olympic Games, under which female athletes may more closely approach equality with males.

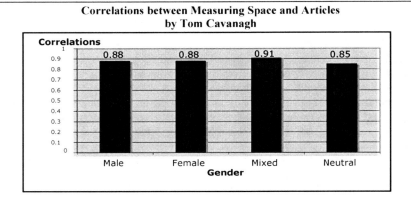

Means and Standard Deviations Comparing Measurement of Percentage of Space with Percentage of Articles

| | *Space* | | | | *Articles* | |
	n	*M*	*SD*	*n*	*M*	*SD*
Male	10	37.90	6.54	10	39.33	6.47
Female	10	25.46	7.70	10	26.45	6.04
Mixed	10	20.56	10.16	10	17.05	8.91
Neutral	10	16.06	8.17	10	17.18	9.51

Note: n = The number of participants (countries) in the sample; M = The mean is simply the average of all the items in a sample; SD = The standard deviation is a measure of how spread out your data are. * Alpha set at $p \leq .05$.

Results: To investigate if there was a statistically significant association between measuring space and counting numbers of Olympic articles, a Pearson product moment correlation was computed for each variable, with these results: male – $r(8) = .88$, $p = .001$; female – $r(8) = .88$, $p = .001$; mixed – $r(8) = .91$, $p = .000$; and neutral – $r(8) = .85$, $p = .002$. The results are interpreted as meaning the correlations are strong to very strong. Correlation analysis is a statistical test conducted to determine the degree of relationship between two sets of data. In this type of analysis results below .60 are not acceptable, between .60 and .69 are minimally acceptable, between .70 and .79 are adequate, between .80 and .89 are good, and between .90 and .99 are very good. Thus, results over .80 are interpreted in this case as meaning that a researcher can substitute counting the number of Olympic articles for measuring space. The 10 countries contained in this analysis are a representative sample of the total 18 countries taking part in the study and, therefore, these results can be generalized to the whole project.

Content analyses provide important 'hard data' to convince policy and programme decision-makers about the need for change and to promote public awareness and debate. Yet, as we discuss in the final chapter of the book, even policies and programmes designed to raise awareness and encourage change appear to have had only limited impact on how the sports news media generally represent female athletes. Unfortunately, demonstrating discrimination does not directly translate into stopping discrimination.

REFERENCES

Billings, A. C., & Eastman, S. T. (2002). Selective representation of gender, ethnicity, and nationality in American television coverage of the 2000 Summer Olympics. *International Review for the Sociology of Sport, 27*, 351–370.

Bruce, T. (2004). Marking the boundaries of the 'normal' in televised sports: The play-by-play of race. *Media, Culture & Society, 26*(6), 861–879.

Cipywnyk, P. Z. (2006). *Comparing Torino 2006 winter Olympics coverage on the websites of public broadcasters in Canada (CBC) and Japan (NHK)*. The Olympic Communication Research Consortium, Royal Roads University, Victoria, B.C., Canada. Retrieved August 17, 2007, from http://www.royalroads.net/olympics/studies/comparingTorino2006coverage.php

Curthoys, A. (2005). Feminism. In T. Bennett, L. Grossberg, & M. Morris (Eds.), *New keywords: A revised vocabulary of culture and society* (pp. 128–130). Malden, MA: Blackwell.

Deacon, D., Pickering, M., Golding, P., & Murdoch, G. (1999). *Researching communications: A practical guide to methods in media and cultural analysis*. London: Arnold.

Eastman, S. T., & Billings, A. C. (2001). Biased voices of sports: Racial and gender stereotyping in college basketball announcing. *The Howard Journal of Communications, 12*, 183–201.

Fountaine, S., & McGregor, J. (1999). The loneliness of the long distance gender researcher: Are journalists right about the coverage of women's sport? *Australian Journalism Review, 21*, 113–126.

Grossberg, L., Wartella, E., Whitney, D. C., & Wise, J. M. (2006). *Media making: Mass media in a popular culture* (2nd ed.). Thousand Oaks, CA: Sage.

hooks, b. (1984). *Feminist theory: From margin to center*. Boston: South End Press.

Jaggar, A. M., & Rothenberg Struhl, P. (1978). *Feminist frameworks: Alternative theoretical accounts of the relations between women and men*. New York: McGraw-Hill.

Jones, D. (2006). The representation of female athletes in online images of successive Olympic Games. *Pacific Journalism Review, 12*, 108–129.

Jones, D. (2004). Half the story? Olympic women on ABC News Online. *Media International Australia, 110*, 132–146.

Jones, M., & Jones, E. (1999). *Mass media*. London: Macmillan.

McKee, A. (2001). A beginner's guide to textual analysis. *Metro, 127/128*, 138–149.

Pedersen, P. M. (2002). Examining equity in newspaper photographs: A content analysis of the print media photographic coverage of interscholastic athletes. *International Review for the Sociology of Sport, 37*, 303–318.

Rada, J. (1996). Color blind-sided: Racial bias in network television's coverage of professional football games. *The Howard Journal of Communications, 7*, 231–240.

Rada, J. A., & Wulfemeyer, K. T. (2005). Color coded: Racial descriptors in television coverage of intercollegiate sports. *Journal of Broadcasting and Electronic Media, 49*, 65–85.

Rainville, R., & McCormick, E. (1977). Extent of covert racial prejudice in pro football announcers' speech. *Journalism Quarterly, 54*, 20–26.

Riffe, D., Lacy, S., & Fico, F. G. (1998). *Analyzing media messages: Using quantitative content analysis in research*. Mahwah, NJ: Lawrence Erlbaum Associates.

Schantz, O., & Gilbert, K. (2001). An ideal misconstrued: Newspaper coverage of the Atlanta Paralympic games in France and Germany. *Sociology of Sport Journal, 18*, 69–94.

Schell, L. A., & Duncan, M. C. (1999). A content analysis of CBS' coverage of the 1996 Paralympic games. *Adapted Physical Activity Quarterly, 16*, 27–47.

Skjeie, H., & Teigen, M. (2003). *Menn imellom* [Among men]. Oslo: Gyldendal Akademisk.

Turner, G. (1997). Media texts and messages. In S. Cunningham & G. Turner (Eds.), *The media in Australia: Industries, texts, audiences* (2nd ed., pp. 293–347). St Leonards, NSW: Allen & Unwin.

Van Zoonen, L. (1994). *Feminist media studies*. London: Sage Publications.

Vincent, J., Imwold, C., Masemann, V., & Johnson, J. T. (2002). A comparison of selected 'serious' and 'popular' British, Canadian, and United States newspaper coverage of female and male athletes competing in the Centennial Olympic Games: Did female athletes receive equitable coverage in the 'Games of the Women'? *International Review for the Sociology of Sport, 37*(3/4), 319–335.

Wimmer, R. D., & Dominick, J. R. (2003). *Mass media research: An introduction* (7th ed.). Belmont, CA: Wadsworth/ThomsonLearning.

Winston, B. (1990). On counting the wrong things. In M. Alvarado & J. O. Thompson (Eds.), *The media reader* (pp. 50–64). London: BFI.

EUROPE: NORTHERN EUROPE

GERTRUD PFISTER

3. DENMARK

Nationalism, Gender and Media Sports: A Content Analysis
of Danish Newspapers

INTRODUCTION

It is a widespread belief, and also the claim of the 'Olympic family', that the Olympic Games contribute to peace and international understanding, as well as to the emancipation of women. Since the rise of modern sport, national superiority was based primarily on the performances of male athletes. Today, physical activity is a women's as well as a men's domain, at least in the Western world, and the IOC has declared the promotion of women's sports to be one of its main aims. Progress has been made particularly with regard to the numbers of competing women with the result that, since the turn of the 21st century, around 40% of Olympic participants are female. Both the movement's aims, international understanding and women's emancipation, can be achieved only with the help of the mass media.

In this chapter, three main questions are addressed: 1) What do the media present and what do audiences learn about 'others' (i.e., the athletes of other nations and the 'second sex') at the Olympic Games?; 2) How do nationality and gender interact or, in other words, is nationality more important than gender or vice versa?; and 3) How can gender differences in media coverage be explained? In order to answer these questions, a quantitative and qualitative content analysis of the coverage of the 2004 Olympic Games was conducted in two Danish newspapers. In this chapter, the focus is on the quantitative results.

Denmark is a Western industrial nation with a high percentage of employed women, large numbers of sportingly active people and claims to be highly cosmopolitan. Like the other Scandinavian countries, Denmark is a social-democratic welfare state based on values like equality and solidarity which, according to Leira (1992), aims to guarantee equal opportunities and reduce economic, gender and ethnic differences. The Danish state uses taxes to provide the necessary funds for welfare and takes on control and responsibility for social security, free health care and education, and day care of children, the elderly and the sick (Anttonnen, 1999; Esping-Andersen, 1990).

However, Bergman (2008, 4) emphasizes that gender equality policies in Nordic countries "are characterized by gender equality paradoxes and policy inconsistencies". There is a discrepancy between the objectives and the position of men and women (Borchorst, 2006). In Denmark, women are still highly under-represented in the top

T. Bruce, J. Hovden and P. Markula (eds.),
Sportswomen at the Olympics: A Global Content Analysis of Newspaper Coverage, 33–46.
© *2010 Sense Publishers. All rights reserved.*

echelons of both private enterprise and academia (Højgaard & Søndergaard, 2003; Lister, 2006; Tienari, Søderberg, Holgersen & Vaara, 2005). The percentage of women among the top leaders of private companies is around 4%, and only 22% of the 6,000 academic positions at Danish universities and under 10% of the professorships are occupied by women (Henningsen, 2004). There is a more balanced gender representation in public administration and also in political institutions (Dybkjær, 2004).

Despite the Nordic welfare system and the emphasis on egalitarianism, Denmark has a gender-segregated labour market, not only vertically but also horizontally. "A high percentage of women in the Nordic countries work in female-dominated caring and household-related occupations, where wages are typically relatively low" (Tienari et al., 2005, p. 223; see also Lister, 2006). Although Denmark has an equally high employment rate for men and women, women are more often part-time workers than men, and women's salaries are, on average, 20% lower than men's. However, 95% of Danes agree that women have the same right to jobs as men even if jobs are scarce (EU average was 86%), and more than 80% believe women should have a paid job (Eurobarometer, 2005).

The gender equality policies of the Danish state are characterized by Borchorst (2003) as reactive because they stress the equal *opportunities* of women and men and not the actual situation. As in the liberal feminist movement, gender equality is looked upon as a matter of free choice and an issue concerning women *and* men (Tienari et al., 2005). Although a number of laws are concerned with gender discrimination,[1] none includes sanctions in case gender equality is not reached. Quotas have never been regarded as desirable and, with few exceptions,[2] have not been implemented (see also Skjeie & Borchorst, 2003). Gender equality, equality policies and especially feminism are currently not an issue of debate: Gender equality is perceived as achieved, gender hierarchies are looked upon as the outcome of individual decisions, and proactive measures are not considered necessary (Borchorst & Dahlerup, 2003).

MAPPING THE FIELD: MEN AND WOMEN IN DANISH SPORTS ORGANISATIONS

Physical activities are widespread in Denmark: 58% of men and 57% of women report that they are physically active at least once per week; 30% are active three or more times (Bille, Fridberg, Storgaard & Wulff, 2005). The most popular activities are hiking, jogging, fitness training, swimming and badminton. A closer look reveals considerable gender differences, especially with regard to sports. Whereas gymnastics/aerobics/dance, yoga and horseback riding attract more women than men, soccer, cycling as sport, and badminton are dominated by men (Bille et al., 2005; see also Overbye & Roessler, 2006). The main sport providers in Denmark are clubs which are supported by the Danish state, organised according to the principles of democracy and autonomy and based on volunteer work: 67% of children and 35% of the adult Danish population are members of a sport club. In the clubs, adult women are a clear minority: 43% of men and 27% of women are members.

Danish sport has two major umbrella organisations with somewhat different aims and ideologies. The Danish Sports Federation [DIF] (1,650,000 members) is responsible for 'sport for all' *and* elite sports. The Danish Gymnastics and Sports Associations [DGI] (1,240,000 members) cater exclusively to 'sport for all' and emphasize "the importance of fellowship, challenge and health in order to promote the educative qualities of the association activities" (DGI, 2008, 16). DGI has traditionally had a strong focus on gymnastics which explains the relatively high percentage of women among the members and leaders of this organisation (see Table 1). In 2003, of the 7,048 senior officials above club level, working in an honorary capacity in the Danish sports system, 31% were women. A comparison of the percentages of senior officials with the percentages of female members reveals significant differences. Furthermore, it can be said that the higher the positions, the lower the percentage of women working in these positions becomes.

Table 1. Percentages of female leaders[3] and members

Organisation	Executive body umbrella organisation	Chairpersons	Senior officials	Members
DIF	10%	12%	22%	39%
DGI	33%	36%	42%	47%

Source: Habermann, Ottesen and Pfister (2003)

GENDERED SPORTS COVERAGE AND SPORT CONSUMPTION – OBSERVATIONS ON THE STATE OF RESEARCH

Sport today is a global spectacle and sport consumption plays a huge role in Danish society. Only 18% of the Danish population is 'not' or 'very little' interested in media sport: more than 47% watch sport always or often (Hedal, 2004). However, sport consumption is a highly gendered activity. In 2005, 40% of men but only 21% of women were 'very much' or 'much' interested in media sport (Hedal, 2006b).

The sports media, like sport in general, was invented by men for men (Stevens, 1987). In Denmark, as elsewhere, 'national' sports attract increasing attention with more than 50% of the coverage (a figure which is constantly rising) while numerous other sports are condemned to oblivion (Hedal, 2006a). A content analysis of five Danish newspapers ranging from serious press to tabloids showed that men's soccer got 47% of the coverage, followed by cycling (15%) and team handball (men and women, 5%), while all other sports scored less than 5% (Jørgensen, 2005). A survey of the TV coverage of sports showed that 28% of the airtime devoted to sport was given to men's football, 14% to handball (men and women) and 13% to men's cycling. Of the audiences, 38% watched football, 26% watched handball and 38% watched cycling (Hedal, 2006b).

In contrast to the sports coverage in many other countries, among the top three Danish mediated sports is one 'gender neutral' discipline, namely team handball, a sport with a long tradition in Denmark. In recent decades, women were even more successful than men, which guaranteed them a place in the media and in the hearts of the male and female fans. An analysis of seven Danish TV channels showed that, in 2004, women's handball got double the attention of TV viewers compared to the men's game (Hedal, 2006a).

As in numerous other countries, in Denmark female athletes do not get adequate newspaper coverage. According to an analysis of five Danish newspapers, conducted in 2005, women's coverage was under 10% (Jørgensen, 2005). These results demonstrate clearly that the symbolic annihilation of women in and through media sports has not changed – at least in its everyday coverage (see also Knoppers & Elling, 2004).

During international events such as the Olympic Games women attract much more attention than they normally do. An analysis of 3,281 Danish newspaper articles and TV transmissions during the 2004 Olympic Games revealed that 44% of the coverage was given to men, 31% to women and 13% to both genders (Lund 2004). Danish research supports United States studies which found that, besides gender, a decisive influence on coverage is exerted by ethnicity and nationality, not least because audiences seem interested only in 'their' athletes and stars (Billings & Eastman, 2002). If no Danish teams are involved, 38% watch men's international football matches but only 10% are interested in women's handball without Danish participation (Hedal 2004).[4] In Hedal's (2004) study, 82% found it important that they could watch or read about Danish athletes. Lund's research on the 2004 Games supports the strong focus on national athletes and events, revealing that 75% of the interviewed or quoted athletes were Danes (Lund, 2004).

METHODS

Two Danish newspapers were chosen for this research: firstly, *Politiken*, founded in 1884, a politically independent and critical broadsheet with a social-liberal orientation, and Denmark's leading newspaper with around 200,000 readers; and, secondly, *BT*, founded in 1916, a tabloid which claims to be *the* Danish sports newspaper with 417,000 readers and which exhibits all the typical characteristics of the popular press. The analysis is based on sports articles and pictures published from August 11 to 30, 2004. The sample included the sports section and the front page of the two newspapers, and the articles and pictures were counted separately. The results sections were not included because they merely consisted of names and numbers without any additional information or evaluation. Except where otherwise noted, 'coverage' refers to the data based on the number of articles. In addition to the quantitative research, some qualitative analysis was conducted which will be discussed in the conclusion.

RESULTS OF THE QUANTITATIVE ANALYSIS OF TWO DANISH NEWSPAPERS

Politiken published a total of 1,178 articles and 657 pictures. Besides the Olympic coverage there were also reports and pictures relating to the most important sporting events taking place parallel to the Olympic Games. The non-Olympic sports coverage of the newspaper contained 245 articles (see Table 2). These articles gave the impression that women's sport did not exist at all: 84% of the articles (206) being reports about men and men's events and only 2% (5 articles) being about women and women's events. Of the non-Olympic articles, 60% covered Denmark's No. 1 sport, men's football. Six articles covered male and female athletes, and 28 did not refer to athletes at all. The second newspaper, *BT*, published 904 articles in the same period. In the 439 reports on non-Olympic sports, women and women's sports formed a minority of 2% of the articles (see Table 2). These results support the results of the above mentioned study about the marginalisation of women in the 'everyday' sports coverage.

Table 2. 2004 Non-Olympic sports articles in two Danish newspapers

	Men (n)	%	Women (n)	%	Mixed (n)	%	Neutral (n)	%	Total
Politiken	206	84	5	2	6	2	28	11	245
BT	392	89	10	2	2	0.5	35	8	439
Total	598	87	15	2	8	1	63	9	684

Although women's non-Olympic sport was almost invisible in both newspapers, *Politiken* and *BT* gave different levels of emphasis to the Olympic Games. *BT*'s coverage was almost even with 49% given to non-Olympic coverage and 51% to the Olympics (see Table 3). In contrast, *Politiken* emphasized the Olympics, giving almost 80% of its coverage to the Olympic Games.

Table 3. Division between Olympic and Non-Olympic articles by gender

Gender	Olympic Politiken %	Olympic BT %	Non-Olympic Politiken %	Non-Olympic BT %
Male	72.0	38.0	28.0	62.0
Female	98.0	93.0	2.0	7.0
Mixed	93.0	96.0	7.0	4.0
Neutral	76.0	57.0	24.0	43.0
Total	79.0	51.0	21.0	49.0

In the Olympic coverage in both newspapers, too, women were greatly under-represented, receiving only 26% of articles overall, compared to men who received 55% (see Table 4). In *Politiken*, 57% of the articles were about men, 25% about women, 8% about both sexes, and 10% did not fit into the gender-differentiated category because the article did not report about athletes. In *BT*'s coverage of the Olympics, female athletes are under-represented to almost the same degree as in *Politiken*, with 51% of the articles dealing with men and only 28% with women. These results show that female Olympians get more attention than women on the sports pages outside the Games. However, they are marginalised compared with the men.

Table 4. 2004 Olympic Games coverage in two Danish newspapers

	Men (n)	%	Women (n)	%	Mixed (n)	%	Neutral (n)	%	Total
Articles									
Politiken	530	57	232	25	81	8	90	10	933 100%
BT	239	51	131	28	48	10	47	10	465 100%
Total	769	55	363	26	129	9	137	10	1,398 100%
Pictures									
Politiken	278	56	164	33	35	7	20	4	497 100%
BT	154	56	93	34	22	8	6	2	275 100%
Total pictures	432	56	257	33	57	7	26	3	772 100%
Total coverage	1,201	55	620	29	186	8	163	8	2,170 100%

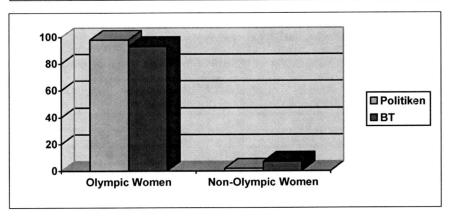

Figure 1. Division between Olympic and non-Olympic coverage by percentage of articles about women.

Of interest is the gender difference in how much of the coverage was focused on the Olympics (see Table 3). For men, between 72% (Politiken) and 38% (BT) of the articles were reports about the Olympics. The difference in percentages between the two newspapers can be explained by the high importance of men's soccer which covered around 80% of the non-Olympic coverage of BT which has an emphasis on sports and feels an obligation to also provide sport fans with the news outside the Olympics. For women, the Olympics percentages are much higher, rising to 98% (*Politiken*) and 93% (*BT*). Thus, almost all the articles on women were Olympic stories (see Figure 1). With regard to the photos, the results show that women are slightly better represented in the photos than in the text, which could support the idea that images of the 'beautiful sex' are popular among journalists (and readers).

SEARCHING FOR EXPLANATIONS

In the light of other international studies, such as Vincent et al. (2002), the under-representation of female athletes in the Danish press is surprising, especially if we take into consideration the 41% participation rate of women in the 2004 Olympic Games. What may be the reasons for this lack of attention? In order to answer this question, it might be of help to examine the selection criteria used by the mass media. The selection of events, athletes and stories by journalists is based on certain 'realities' (Lowes, 1999). However, it can be assumed that the journalists follow certain rules and, besides gender, the following factors may be important: the performance and success of athletes, the type of sport, suspense and sensation, the gender and 'personal taste' of journalists, newspaper policy and, most importantly, the nationality of athletes (Strauß, Kolb & Lames, 2002). Therefore, the number and the success of male and female athletes from Denmark, as well as the coverage of Danish athletes, are factors which might help to explain the gendered coverage in the two newspapers.

Highly conspicuous in the Danish Olympic delegation is the fact that, while men were greatly over-represented among leaders/coaches (93%) and officials (71%), the percentage of women athletes (48%) was only slightly lower than that of men (see Table 5).

Table 5. The Danish delegation

	Leaders/Coaches[5]		Officials		Athletes		Total	
	Women	Men	Women	Men	Women	Men	Women	Men
Number	3	39	4	10	44	48	51	97
Percentage	7%	93%	29%	71%	48%	52%	34%	66%

Table 6. Danish athletes covered by Politiken and BT as a percentage of total Olympic coverage

	Danish athletes	Non-Danish athletes	Mixed nationalities or neutral coverage
Politiken (n = 933 articles)	50%	44%	6%
BT (n = 465 articles)	43%	41%	17%

Both newspapers focused on the Danish athletes (see Table 6). In its 933 articles on the Olympic Games, *Politiken* reported about Danish athletes in 50% of the articles and about non-Danish athletes in 44%. Only 8% of the articles about foreign athletes carried pictures, as compared with 55% of articles related to Danish athletes. *BT* focused on Danish athletes in 43% of its reporting, giving them, however, more than half the space. Of the articles about Danish athletes, 70% carried pictures. Both papers thus focused on less than 1% of the more than 11,000 athletes competing at the Games.

An analysis of the correlation between gender and nationality in *Politiken* articles shows clearly that Danish women athletes were not represented in relation to their proportion of the Danish delegation (48%). Danish men were focused upon in 60% of the articles, women in only 20% and men and women or mixed teams in 11% of the articles. In the articles about non-Danish athletes 58% referred to men, 34% to women and 6% to both sexes. In *BT* the coverage of the Danish female athletes was more extensive than the coverage of women from other countries: 55% of the Danish articles focused on male athletes and 36% on female athletes, while 63% of the non-Danish articles dealt with foreign male athletes and only 30% with foreign female athletes.

Table 7. Gender and coverage of Danish and Non-Danish athletes in Politiken and BT by percentage

	Danish athletes		Non-Danish athletes	
	Politiken (n=462)	BT (n=198)	Politiken (n=408)	BT (n=189)
Male	60%	55%	59%	63%
Female	20%	36%	34%	30%
Mixed	11%	9%	6%	7%

Female athletes seem to have less national appeal than males, at least in *Politiken*, where 39% of women's coverage but 52% of the reports about men referred to Danish athletes. In *BT*, 44% of the articles about women and 46% of the reports about men had Danish athletes in the focus (data not included in Table 7).

A closer look reveals that these results, including the differences between *BT* and *Politiken*, stem at least partly from the successful Danish women's handball team, which gained a gold medal. In *BT*, women's handball was given at least 4 pages every day, with the space increasing as the final decision drew closer: In fact, 47 articles (36% of the entire women's coverage) were devoted to women's team handball – at the cost of the coverage of women from other countries.

DANISH SPORTS AND PERFORMANCE

Denmark entered athletes only for a limited selection of events. However, the number of participants (91) was remarkable, given the fact that Denmark has just five million inhabitants. The sports in which Danish athletes competed mirror, at least partly, popular Danish sports like cycling, badminton, table tennis, sailing and team handball.[6] With regard to the chances of women receiving media attention, though, it must be borne in mind that Denmark did not send a team to the most popular sport, men's football. In both newspapers there is a clear emphasis on those sports/events in which Danes competed, and the patterns of Danish participation may explain some of the gender differences. The women concentrated on nine sports, especially on handball with 15 participants, whereas the men participated in 16 sports, although often with very few athletes and mostly not very successfully. But because all the Danish athletes got some media attention, the higher number of events with male Danish participants (16 versus 9) could have caused a higher number of articles with a focus on male athletes. Often the 15 players of the handball team were covered in one article.

Since success is one of the most important criteria for receiving public attention, can the gendered coverage be explained by the better results of the male athletes? The Danish delegation won eight Olympic medals: two gold (one in men's lightweight rowing and one in women's team handball) and six bronze medals.[7] These can be divided into four medals for men/men's teams, three for women/women's teams and one in a mixed event. Thus, the achievements of the Danish male and female athletes are almost even, particularly if one takes into consideration that the women's gold medal was in one of the most popular sports, handball, which is of especial significance. In *Politiken*, women's team handball ranked first in the coverage of women's sports and second in the coverage of sport overall, representing 13% of articles on women's sports and 4% of the total number of articles on Olympic sport. In *BT*, women's handball was the event given the greatest coverage, with 35% of articles on women's sports and 10% of all articles on sport being devoted to it. However, this was not enough to balance the unequal coverage of male and female athletes overall.

To sum up, the gendered Olympic coverage can partly be explained by the composition of the Danish delegation, especially the slightly lower number of women taking part and the smaller number of sports in which women competed. Also playing a role was perhaps the slightly greater number of medals won by the men. However, this does not explain the extent of the difference in media coverage. Nor does it explain the media dominance of male athletes from other countries.

GENDER, NATIONALITY AND JOURNALISTS' 'TASTE'

Media sports construct and present multiple Olympic Games. In the Danish press Denmark was the focus: the coverage in *BT* starting with a calendar of the competitions in which Danish athletes competed, along with the pictures of the whole delegation and an overview of Danish medal chances (on 13 August), and ending with the results of the Danish delegation. Besides the coverage of their 'own' Danish athletes, the journalists chose from the numerous Olympic events those athletes and sports which, for one reason or another, they found interesting. Interest depends, among other things, on gender. All the journalists of both newspapers were men, and they saw the Games from their gendered and 'nationalised' perspective.

When one takes a closer look at the types of sports covered in the Olympic coverage, the following lists emerge (see Table 8). All in all, *Politiken* covered 47 sports but only in three disciplines (handball, gymnastics and water polo) was there a significantly larger coverage of women's sports. In seven events the coverage was almost equal, and in 37 sports more articles were devoted to men.

Table 8. Olympic sports receiving the most coverage in Politiken and BT

Politiken		*BT*	
Sport, gender	%	Sport, gender	%
Athletics, men	5	Handball, women	10
Handball, women	4	Athletics, men	6
Gymnastics, women	3	Handball, men	4
Football, men	3	Cycling, men	4
Cycling, men	3	Sailing, men	3
Table tennis, men	3	Running, women	3
Athletics, men	2	Sailing men,	3
Swimming, women	2	Swimming, men	3
Swimming, men	2	Rowing, men	3
Sailing, women	2	Swimming, women	3
Rowing, men	2	Table tennis, men	3
Boxing, men	2	Boxing, men	2
Water polo, women	2	Sailing, women	2

Note: Other sports were under 2% of Olympic coverage.

BT covered 33 sports and there were more articles on male athletes in all events with the exception of team handball (47:18) and gymnastics (5:3). At the same time, it must be borne in mind that both newspapers covered only a very small percentage of the 202 Olympic events. As mentioned above, the coverage of Olympic events with no Danish participation depended on the choice and thus the 'taste' of the journalists, who had a large number of sports, athletes and issues from which to choose. In their choices, journalists try to meet the – imagined – taste of their readers (Strauß, Kolb & Lames, 2002). Here, it must be assumed that interest in a particular sport grows with the length and intensity of consumption and thus is relatively constant among adults (Schellhaaß, 2003). Reports on a particular sport arouse interest, and the reader's interest has, in turn, an effect on the reporting in a reciprocal process. Sports journalists orient their articles towards men – and thus towards the majority of readers – and both develop similar preferences (Helland, 2003; Knoppers & Elling, 2004). Accordingly, sports like men's handball and football, which are popular in Denmark, were the focus of those reports which covered sporting events in which there was no Danish participation. There were some exceptions. Women's gymnastics and women's water polo (10 articles) were given special attention in *Politiken*: gymnastics because of the glamour and tragedy of the child-woman phenomenon, as was seen in an article which discussed the problems of the training, starting at an early age, the pressure to stay slim and the need to present an attractive feminine image. Water polo was interesting because it provided an example of women intruding into former men's domains. The range of sports covered in *Politiken* was much broader (47 versus 33 sports) than in *BT*, where interest in sports with no Danish participation was relatively small. As is typical of tabloid newspapers, *BT* focused on a small number of sports and, even more than *Politiken*, on famous Danish athletes such as Wilson Kipketer, the black Danish runner and, above all, the 'golden girls' of the handball team which won a gold medal in one of the most popular Danish sports.

THE CONSTRUCTION OF GENDER AND NATIONALITY

The results of the qualitative analysis show that the majority of articles in both papers took male and female athletes seriously. It was not so much the human interest stories but rather the sport, the event and the performance that received most attention. However, there were traces of androcentric perspectives in both papers. For example, *Politiken* raised the question of the reconcilability of motherhood and top-level competitive sports (15 August) and published more or less erotic pictures of female beach volleyball players (13 August). In addition, a number of advertisements which complemented the coverage of events could be categorised as 'sexism on the sidelines'. Further, in *BT*, a long article was devoted to the sexualisation of female athletes. Claiming to discuss and even criticise this trend, the newspaper printed many pictures of nude athletes, making it clear that the more nude skin, the more money for the women. However, there was one exception. The handball players were presented as national heroines in this article and it was emphasized that the 'handball girls' were covered in the media because of their performance and not because of their appearance. A closer look, though, reveals that the handball players' appearance was indeed discussed – albeit in a more sophisticated way. The very fact that the newspaper mentioned the unimportance of appearance in handball players shows a gender bias. At the same time, this study confirms the findings of other research that the Danes identify with their handball stars, regardless of their gender (Hedal, 2004). The emphasis on women's handball in the Olympic coverage has already been mentioned: In *Politiken* and *BT* handball ranked first in the coverage of women's sport, and in *BT* it ranked first among all articles on sport. As stated in the introduction, women's handball is, after football, the second most popular sport in Denmark. The case of the handball players demonstrates, furthermore, how the newspapers construct national identity. In the headlines we are informed that Denmark won the gold medal, that members of the royal family are fans, that 'we' are the best in the world, etcetera. Thus, identification is created with the successful team – and at the same time with Denmark.

CONCLUSION

The coverage of the Olympic Games was strongly focused on Danish participants and on events in which Danish athletes competed. This is a form of nationalism, in which 'others' are made invisible. Moreover, the reader is encouraged to identify with the athletes by a variety of means: by the selection of topics, the forms of address, metaphors, etcetera. In this manner, the Olympic Games were harnessed to a 'national project'.

Both newspapers focused on male athletes in their Olympic coverage. In spite of the 'equality doxa' and the relatively even gender balance in the Danish delegation, female Danish athletes were given considerably less attention than their male counterparts. In the case of the handball team, the nationalistic narrative was intertwined with gender issues and condensed into ambiguous images in which femininity and the appearance of the players were the topics of discussion. However, the nationalist discourse superimposed itself on and even overrode categories of gender so that, in the end, nationalism managed to overcome gender prejudices. Female athletes were nationalised and identified as medal winners first and as women second.

NOTES

[1] These include the Equal Pay Act (adopted in 1976), the Equal Treatment Act (1978), the Act of Equal Opportunities for Men and Women on the Appointment of Members of Public Committees, Commissions, etc. (1985), the Sex Discrimination Act (1988) and the Act on Equal Opportunities for Men and Women with respect to the Appointment of Members of Certain Executive Committees or Governing Bodies (1990).

[2] For a short time quotas were imposed for local and European elections.

[3] Leaders were defined as members of the governing bodies and committees on the national and regional levels. In Denmark, as in other European countries where sport is based on associations and federations, sports organisations are run by unpaid volunteers who have great power since they form the decision-making committees.

[4] Hedal's (2004) study is published in 2 sections (one with results and one with additional information and tables). This information comes from the second section.

[5] Leaders/coaches include physiotherapists and other support staff.

[6] Denmark competed in athletics (men [m], women [w]), badminton (m, w), table tennis (m), wrestling (1m), archery (1m), cycling (m, w), team handball (w), kayaking (m), horse riding (m, w), rowing (m, w), sailing (m, w), shooting (m, w), swimming (m, w), taekwondo (m), trampoline (1m), triathlon (1m).

[7] The bronze medals were in table tennis doubles (m), badminton doubles (mixed), 800m (m), shot put (m), sailing yngling (w), sailing Europe (w).

REFERENCES

Anderson, B. (1983). *Imagined communities: Reflections on the origin and spread of nationalism.* London: Verso.

Anttonen, A. (1999, February). *Civil society, genus and the welfare state.* Paper presented at the Civil Society between Market and State conference, Stockholm, Sweden.

Bille, T., Fridberg, T., Storgaard, S., & Wulff, E. (2005). *Danskernes kultur – og fritidsaktiviteter 2004 – med udviklingslinjer tilbage til 1964.* København: Forlaget akf.

Billings, A. C., & Eastman, S. T. (2002). Selective representation of gender, ethnicity, and nationality in American television coverage of the 2000 Summer Olympics. *International Review for the Sociology of Sport, 37*, 351–370.

Bergman, S. (2008, March 31). Women-friendly Nordic societies? euro/topics website. Retrieved April 21, 2008, from http://www.eurotopics.net/en/magazin/frauen-20083/artikel_bergman_frauen_norden/

Borchorst, A. (2001). Still friendly: Danish women and welfare state restructuring. *Social Politics, 8*, 203–205.

Borchorst, A. (2003). *Køn, magt og beslutninger*. Århus: AKA-print.

Borchorst, A. (2006). *Daddy leave and gender equality: The Danish case in a Scandinavian perspective*. Aalborg: Institute for History, International and Social Studies, Aalborg University.

Borchorst, A., & Dahlerup, D. (2003). *Ligestillingspolitik som diskurs og praksis*. København: Samfundslitteratur.

Capranica, L., & Aversa, F. (2002). Italian television sport coverage of women's sports during the 2000 Sydney Olympic Games. *International Review for the Sociology of Sport, 37*, 337–349.

Connell, R. W. (2001). *Gender*. Cambridge: Polity.

Crawford, G. (2004). *Consuming sport*. London/New York: Routledge.

DGI (2008). *Om DGI-Verdensholdet – Promotion*. Retrieved April 23, 2008, from http://www.dgi.dk/OmDGI/Verdensholdet/nyheder/Promotion_%5Ba11710%5D.aspx

Dybkjær, L. (2004, February). Et europæisk perspektiv på kvinder og forskning. *Kvinden og Samfundet, 120*(1), 26–28.

Eastman, S. T., & Billings, A. C. (1999). Gender parity in the Olympics: Hyping women athletes, favoring men athletes. *Journal of Sport and Social Issues, 23*, 140–170.

Eurobarometer. (2005). *Social values, science and technology*. Retrieved April 21, 2008, from http://ec.europa.eu/pu-blic_opinion/archives/ebs/ebs_225_report_en.pdf

Esping Andersen, G. (1990). *The three worlds of welfare capitalism*. Cambridge: Polity Press.

Hedal, M. (2004). *Motivation og tv-sport*. Copenhagen: Københavns Universitet.

Hedal, M. (2006a). *Sport på dansk tv – En analyse af samspillet mellem sport og dansk tv, 1993–2005*. København: Idrættens Analyseinstitut. Retrieved April 21, 2008, from http://www.idan.dk/upload/sportp%C3%A5dansktv.pdf

Hedal, M. (2006b, December 9). Tv polariserer idrætten. *Overblik. Nyt fra Idan, 9*, p. 1. Retrieved April 21, 2008, from http://www.idan.dk/upload/nyhedsbrev9december2006_001.pdf

Helland, K. (2003). *Sport, medier og journalistikk. Med fotballandslaget til EM*. Bergen: Fagbokforlaget.

Henningsen, I. (2004). Underrekrutering af kvinder på danske universiteter. *Kvinden og Samfundet, 120*(1), 20–22.

Højgaard, L., & Søndergaard, D. M. (Eds.). (2003). *Akademisk tilblivelse*. København: Akademisk Forlag.

Jørgensen, S. S. (2005). *The world's best advertisement agency: The sports press*. Retrieved April 21, 2008, from http://www.playthegame.org/upload/sport_press_survey_english.pdf

Knoppers, A., & Elling, A. (2004). "We do not engage in promotional journalism" – Discursive strategies used by sport journalists to describe the selection process. *International Review for the Sociology of Sport, 39*(1), 57–73.

Leira, A. (1992). *Welfare states and working mothers*. New York: Cambridge University Press.

Lister, R. (2006). Children (but not women) first: New labour, child welfare and gender. *Critical Social Policy, 26*, 315–335.

Lorber, J. (1994). *Paradoxes of gender*. New Haven, CT: Yale University Press.

Lowes, M. (1999). *Inside the sports pages: Work routines, professional ideologies, and the manufacture of sports news*. Toronto: University of Toronto Press.

Lund, A. B. (2004). *Journalistik og etik under OL 2004*. Retrieved April 21, 2008, from http://www.idan.dk/vidensbank/forskninganalyser/stamkort.aspx?publikationID=9b4338e4-8ecf-496c-8f25-96aa00000000&/

Habermann, U., Ottesen, L. S., & Pfister, G. (2003). *Kvinder på toppen – om kvinder, idræt og ledelse*. København: Institut for Idræt, Københavns Universitet. Retrieved April 21, 2008, from http://cms.ku.dk/upload/application/pdf/552e02e2/Kvinder_paa_toppen_1.pdf

Overbye, M., & Roessler, K. (2006). *Kvinder og mænd i idrættens rum*. Odense: Syddansk Universitet. Retrieved April 21, 2008, from http://www.idan.dk/Vidensbank/Forskninganalyser.aspx?currentstart=5&ResultPrPage=5&Kortvisning=-False&emneID=5709eafe-a138-4d7e-9ac1-d7446a154d31

Pfister, G. (2004). Gender, sport und massenmedien. In C. Kugelmann, G. Pfister, & C. Zipprich (Eds.), *Geschlechterforschung im Sport. Differenz und/oder Gleichheit* (pp. 59–88). Hamburg: Czwalina.

Schellhaaß, H. (2003). *Strategien zur vermarktung des sports im fernsehen.* Köln: Institut für Rundfunkökonomie an der Universität zu Köln.

Skjeie, H., & Borchorst, A. (2003). Changing the patterns of gender and power in society. *NIKK magasin, 3,* 4–9.

Stevens, J. (1987). The rise of the sports page. *Gannett Center Journal, 1*(2), 1–11.

Strauß, B., Kolb, M., & Lames, M. (Eds.). (2002). *Sport-goes-media.de.* Schorndorf: Hofmann.

Tienari, J., Søderberg, A.-M., Holgersen, C., & Vaara, E. (2005). Gender and national identity constructions in the cross-border merger context. *Gender, Work and Organization, 12*(3), 217–241.

Vincent, J., Imwold, C., Masemann, V., & Johnson, J. T. (2002). A comparison of selected "serious" and "popular" British, Canadian and United States newspaper coverage of female and male athletes competing in the centennial Olympic Games. *International Review for the Sociology of Sport, 37,* 319–335.

Gertrud Pfister
University of Copenhagen
Denmark

JORID HOVDEN AND AINA HINDENES

4. NORWAY

Gender in Olympic Newspaper Coverage – Towards Stability or Change?

INTRODUCTION

During recent decades the sports media coverage in most western countries has increased extensively, particularly the newspaper and television coverage. The companies that control these media are partially dependent on sports for their commercial success (Coakley, 2001). However, studies mapping the representation of men and women in the sports media show distinct gender-based disparities, and women seem to have remained short-changed since the 1980s (e.g., Bernstein, 2002; Hall, 1997; Hartmann-Tews & Rulofs, 2005; Pemberton, Shields, Gilbert, Shen & Said, 2004). In Norway and the Nordic countries, as little as 10–15% of the print sport coverage is devoted to female athletes (NIKK, 2006). Hence, it is obvious that the daily sport media coverage still represents an image of sport as a male domain. The findings also agree on the fact that the amount of coverage of female athletes remains far below women's involvement and participation in sports. The relative marginalisation of women in the daily sports media coverage seems, however, not to be valid to the same extent for studies focusing on the coverage of gender-mixed mega sports events such as the Olympic Games. Several studies (e.g., Pemberton et al., 2004) indicate that during such events, the coverage of women's sport increases, often dramatically, and represents more than 25% of the total numbers of articles.

In this chapter, we present some results from a study focussing on gender disparities in Olympic media coverage in Norway. The study is part of the *Global Women in Sports Media Project* in which the main objectives are to map different gendered aspects of the media coverage during the 2004 summer Olympic Games as a basis for conducting comparative analyses among multiple nations. This part focuses on the amount of print media coverage dedicated to female and male athletes during the 2004 Olympic Games in the biggest and most profiled newspaper on sports in Norway, *Verdens Gang*. Before we move to the analysis, we provide general background on the status of gender relations and gender equality policies in Norway as well as in Norwegian sport and sports media.

GENDER EQUALITY POLICIES IN NORWAY

Norway is seen worldwide as a champion in gender equality policies. In the recently published *Global Gender Gap Report 2006* (Hausmann, Tyson & Zahidi, 2006), Norway is ranked the second best out of 115 countries. Norway's world-leading

T. Bruce, J. Hovden and P. Markula (eds.),
Sportswomen at the Olympics: A Global Content Analysis of Newspaper Coverage, 47–60.

position in terms of gender equality is, among other factors, caused by a 40-year political focus on gender issues in public policies. The Norwegian feminist researcher Helga Hernes has called the gender political strategies chosen in the 1970s and 1980s 'state feminism' (Hernes, 1987). The Norwegian 'state feminism' was characterised by a strategic alliance between the state and the women's movement; a top-down feminism implemented through an intersection of gender equality policies and social policies.

In 1978 – as one of the first countries in the world – the Norwegian Parliament passed a Gender Equality Act, with the objective of promoting equality between the sexes within all sectors of society, with special emphasis on improving the situation for women in education, work and cultural and professional development. In 1988, a provision was suggested and included in the Gender Equality Act requiring a 40% representation of both sexes on all public boards, councils and committees (Skjeie & Teigen, 2003). This provision serves not only to increase the percentage of women in central government, municipalities and county councils, and committees in general, but also helps to redress any imbalances in representation on committees where men tend to congregate in 'heavyweight' areas, such as economics, agriculture, communications and technology. One outcome of this provision – or gender quota regulation – is that no Government has since been formed in Norway, whether social democratic, conservative or centre, with less than 40% female members. In Norwegian politics, gender quotas have proved to be the most effective means of achieving a more equal distribution of women and men in political bodies as well as in public boards and committees in all sectors of the Norwegian society (Skjeie & Teigen, 2003).

On the other hand, in Norway, as elsewhere, we still find big discrepancies between political statements, objectives and political realities. Research recently conducted on how power is distributed within powerful societal institutions shows that men possess on average 84% of the top positions (Skjeie & Teigen, 2003). In institutions like the media, church and sports we still find the situation where the few women in top positions occur as 'spectacular' exceptions (Hovden, 2006).

GENDER EQUALITY IN SPORT

Historical sport studies (e.g., Olstad & Tønneson, 1986) have characterised the development of organised sport in Norway in the 1970s as a 'sport revolution' due to the explosive increase in participation among women and children. Until this period, sport had mostly been a domain for young males, and women had access only to a limited variety of sports. Nowadays, the organised sports system in Norway, the Norwegian Olympic Committee and Confederation of Sports (NOCCS), includes about 1.9 million memberships out of a population of 4.6 million. Women represent about 40% of NOCCS memberships. In addition, surveys (e.g., Breivik, & Vaagebo, 1999) conclude that regarding participation in non-competitive recreation and fitness activities, Norwegian women are as physically active as men, but the participation patterns are still quite gender-specific in terms of types of activities and forms of organisation.

Despite women possessing nearly 40% of the memberships in the NOCCS, we find only about 10% women in the organisational top positions (Hovden, 2006). In the most competition-oriented sports clubs, there are few women leaders (Enjolras, Seippel & Waldahl, 2005). Similar gender/power relations are documented in coaching. Female elite coaches represent a very small minority, and most female coaches are found in children's and youth sports (Enjolras et al., 2005; Karlsen, 1995).

In 1987, a law regulating gender quotas was suggested and passed in the NOOCS requiring a minimum representation of at least one of each gender in all organisational decision-making bodies.[1] The passing of the gender quota law has resulted in an increased representation of female board and committee members at all organisational levels. Women possess, for example, 29% of the board member positions in national sports federations (NIF, 2003). On the other hand, the gender quota law has not brought more women into the president positions of federations and clubs; the most powerful and prestigious positions within the organised sport system (Hovden, 2000). A recent study of local sport clubs (Enjolras et al., 2005) also registers that 22% of the clubs have no women on their executive boards. In other words, many organisational bodies do not practice the gender quota law and no political sanctions are directed towards those bodies. This indicates that although women are as physically active as men and are successful athletes, the politics and management of sport remain a predominantly male domain, where men possess the power of definition and, hence, the most significant role in defining conditions for women's participation and possibilities.

GENDER AND MEDIA COVERAGE

The immense increase in the media coverage of top sports in Norway during the last decade does not seem to have led to a corresponding interest in sports media studies. The media researcher Knut Helland states that in Norway media sports is a neglected field of research and, thus, also mirrors the current status of quantitative sport media studies on gender and gender disparities (Helland, 2003). The few studies available indicate, however, that female athletes are markedly under-represented both in television and newspaper coverage and the trends identified over time are more characterised by stability than change (Pettersen, 1978; Fasting & Tangen, 1983; Hovden, 1996; Lippe, 1998; Olafsson, 2006).

The first published study showed that women's sports received about 5% of the total numbers of articles and 4% of the total article space (cm^2) in the everyday coverage in four of the biggest Norwegian newspapers in 1973 (Pettersen, 1978). Eight years later in 1981, Kari Fasting and Jan Ove Tangen conducted a similar comparative study. The results showed that the coverage of women's sport had now increased to about 10% both in terms of numbers and article space (Fasting & Tangen, 1983). Concerning qualitative aspects, Fasting and Tangen (1983) also noticed that male journalists presented sex-discriminating statements in which female athletes and women's sports were trivialised.

In 1996, a very limited study examined the everyday domination of newspaper coverage of male football (soccer) and the consequences for women's sport coverage (Hovden, 1996). Two of the biggest Norwegian newspapers in the middle of the football season were studied for one week (August 19–25). The results indicated that the coverage of men's sports made up a total of 80–95%, and most days over 90% of the coverage was dedicated to men's football. The few articles about women's sports were, on the whole, concentrated on a conflict between two of the best and most famous handball players.

A recent study has examined newspaper coverage in terms of gender in five different countries including Norway (Olafsson, 2006). The Norwegian data indicated that about 80% of the current coverage is concentrated on men's sports, 11% on women's sports and 9% on mixed sports where both sexes are included in the articles. In addition, the content analyses revealed that sports media is dominated by a few good women and a large crowd of men, where the visible women are represented by a few top female athletes. One of the conclusions of the textual analyses was that more coverage of female athletes would most probably also lead to more sexualisation, gender stereotyping and commodification of women's bodies (Olafsson, 2006).

From these studies, we suggest that female athletes and women's sports in Norway in the everyday print media coverage, over a time period of about 30 years, seems to be in 5-15% range. Norwegian studies examining gender aspects in the media coverage during mega events like Olympic Games have, however, not been conducted. From this point of departure, it will be interesting to see if the Olympic newspaper coverage in this study will follow the tendency found in other Western studies (e.g. Pemberton et al., 2004) that the coverage of female athletes and female sports increases dramatically through such events.

METHODS

The study includes the largest Norwegian daily newspaper, *Verdens Gang*, which is also the newspaper that profiles sport the most. *Verdens Gang* is categorised as a tabloid paper and has a circulation of 1.337 million in a population of 4.7 million people. All space of both non-Olympic and Olympic sport was measured in cm^2 and all articles and photographs were counted. The data collection lasted from August 11 to August 29, the period from the first to the last day of the Olympic Games in Athens.

We made use of the *Global Women in Sports Media* project template for measuring and recording and followed the specific instructions made regarding procedures and categorising to ensure consistent data collection, as well as to establish an adequate platform for further comparative analyses. The coverage was divided into four categories: (1) female coverage; (2) male coverage; (3) mixed coverage in which both male and female athletes were featured and (4) neutral coverage which had no reference to male or female athletes/sports but included topics like the opening ceremony, doping discussions or descriptions of facilities.

In the analyses we have used the category *article space* for the total of both text space and photo space. In tables and figures, all percentages have been rounded to one decimal point. The data program *Excel* was used for the coding of data as well as for generating the descriptive statistics. We used the *Global Women in Sports Media Project* guiding hypotheses, based on former research on gender in the sports media, as a tool for organising, analysing and discussing our findings.

FINDINGS AND DISCUSSION

Olympic and Non-Olympic Sport

The total amount of sport coverage (article space) during the time period of 11–29 August was 215,462.2cm^2. Out of this total, the text space was 140,317.7cm^2 or 65.1% of the total, and the photo space was 75,144.5cm^2 or 34.9% of the total. Female athletes received 16% of the total text coverage (see Table 1) and male athletes 53%. This gender distribution indicates that female athletes received more coverage than in previous studies (e.g., Hovden, 1996; NIKK 2006).

Table 1. Gender distribution in the total coverage

Gender category	cm^2	%
Male	114292.6	53
Female	33670.2	16
Mixed	6,115.9	3
Neutral	61383.3	18
Total	215,462.2	100

The results regarding total numbers of photos show a pattern quite similar to numbers of articles; 17% for the female category and 61.5% for the male category (see Table 2). There is, however, a slightly smaller difference between the genders linked to the numbers of photos; 20.2% versus 59.2% (see Table 2). This may indicate that articles focussing on female athletes include more photos than articles focussing on male athletes.

Table 2. Gender distribution in the total numbers of articles and photos

Gender	Articles (n)	Articles %	Photos (n)	Photos %
Male	274	61.5	474	59.5
Female	77	17.0	161	20.2
Mixed	8	2.0	23	3.0
Neutral	87	19.5	138	17.3
Total	446	100	796	100

In the following sections, we focus on the gender distribution between Olympic and non-Olympic coverage and see if the levels of coverage between the genders differ as much as former studies indicate. We also consider whether the total increase in female coverage is caused by a markedly higher coverage of Olympic sport compared to non-Olympic sport.

Non-Olympic Coverage

The study shows that 48% of the total coverage is non-Olympic coverage and 52% is Olympic coverage. The findings related to non-Olympic coverage show surprisingly low rates for women, and indicate an even stronger marginalisation of female athletes than in the former Norwegian studies (e.g., Fasting & Tangen, 1983; Hovden, 1996; Olafsson, 2006). Female athletes receive only about 1% of the non-Olympic coverage both regarding text space and photo space (see Table 3).

Table 3. Gender distribution of text and photo space in non-Olympic coverage

Gender category	Text cm²	%	Photo cm²	%
Male	65,832.7	64	26,296.3	94
Female	1,212.3	1	11.3	≤ 1
Mixed	640.5	≤ 1	116.0	≤ 1
Neutral	35,237.8	34	1,608.5	6
Total	102,923.3	100	28,032.1	100

When we look at numbers of texts and photos the results are even more surprising. The non-Olympic coverage shows that, during the Olympic period, only three articles and one photo were dedicated to female athletes not participating in the Olympics (see Table 4). This can, in fact, be characterised as a further marginalisation of female athletes and women's sport compared to former findings (Fasting & Tangen, 1983; Hovden, 1996; Olafsson, 2006; Pettersen, 1978).

Table 4. Gender distribution of texts and photos in non-Olympic coverage

Gender category	Text (n)	Text %	Photo (n)	Photo %
Male	169	75	264	83
Female	3	1.5	1	0.5
Mixed	1	0.5	1	0.5
Neutral	52	23	51	16
Total	225	100	317	100

Olympic Coverage

When looking at the gender-based disparities in the Olympic coverage that, as mentioned, make up 52% of the total coverage, we can see that female athletes receive quite another level of Olympic coverage compared to non-Olympic.

The results indicate that female athletes receive 29% of the text space and 39% of the photo space, while their male counterparts received 43% of text space and 46% of photo space (see Table 5). Hence, we find here a much more gender-balanced picture than in non-Olympic sport or in the everyday level identified in the previous studies (e.g., Fasting & Tangen, 1983; Hovden, 1996; Olafsson, 2006). On the other hand, the findings still indicate that women and men do not receive equal Olympic coverage.

Table 5. Gender distribution of text and photo space in Olympic coverage

Gender	Text cm²	Text %	Photo cm²	Photo %
Male	48,459.9	43	21,887.2	46
Female	32,458.0	29	17,993.3	39
Mixed	5,475.5	5	3,332.4	7
Neutral	26,145.6	23	3,899.9	8
Total	112,539.0	100	47,112.8	100

When looking at the numbers of articles (see Table 6) the results show quite similar gender differences.

Table 6. Gender distribution of numbers of texts and photos in Olympics coverage

Gender	Text (n)	Text %	Photo (n)	Photo %
Male	105	48	217	45
Female	74	33	162	33
Mixed	7	3	22	5
Neutral	35	16	83	17
Total	221	100	484	100

The distribution between text and photo space (see Table 7) indicates that female athletes in Olympic coverage are distinctly more exposed through photos than text. It is, however, worth remembering that although females in Olympic coverage are more visible than usual, males athletes still receive markedly more text space (43% vs. 29%) and slightly more photo space (46% vs. 39%) than their female counterparts (see Table 5).

Table 7. Distribution between text and photo space by gender

Gender category	Male (%)	Female (%)	Mixed (%)	Neutral (%)
Text space	55	45	49	85
Photo space	45	55	52	15
Total space by gender category	100	100	100	100

Gender, Newspaper Coverage and Olympic Performances

The Norwegian Olympic team in Athens 2004 included 52 athletes; 17 of them (32.7%) were female while 35 (67.3%) were male. Olympic media studies (e.g., Bernstein, 2002; Pemberton et al., 2004) find that newspaper coverage is closely linked to performances, with most coverage dedicated to medal winners. Norway received 6 medals during the Olympics; 5 gold medals and 1 bronze. Male athletes contributed with gold medals in javelin, kayak (K-1) and rowing, in addition to a bronze medal in kayak (K-2). One of the two medal winners in K-2 was also the gold medal winner in K-1 (and, thus, the K-1 and K-2 coverage is combined in Table 8). Female athletes won gold medals in mountain-biking and sailing. Comparing the medal-winning sports by gender, the gold medal in athletics (javelin) for men receives the highest text space (34% of the total), while the two female medal winners in sailing and mountain-biking receive more coverage than the male gold medal winners in rowing and kayaking (see Table 8).

Table 8. Distribution of text/photo space of medal winners by sports and gender

Sports	Medal/gender	Text cm²	Text %	Photo cm²	Photo %
Athletics (javelin)	Gold/male	16,274.9	34	7,954.9	32
Sailing	Gold/female	14,043.8	30	8,232.2	33
Mountain biking	Gold/female	6,923.2	15	3,388.3	14
Rowing	Gold/male	5,295.3	11	2,892.0	12
Kayak (K-1, K-2)	Gold & Bronze/male	4,728.0	10	2,294.2	9
Total		47,165.2	100	24,761.6	100

There are several factors that may partially explain this finding. Regarding the two most-covered sports, in addition to the significance of gender, winning a medal in a traditional Olympic sport like javelin is considered more prestigious than in women's sailing. Another explanatory factor may be that javelin is one of the most winning summer Olympics sports in Norway and before the Games Andreas Torkildsen was not a favourite to win the gold but one of the outsiders. His gold medal was thus celebrated both as a sensation and as one carried by tradition. Both the female gold medallists were big favourites to win the gold and fulfilled the expectations on them. The data in Table 8 show that the gold medallist in sailing for women, Siren Sundby, is close (only 4% less) to Torkildsen in text coverage and receives a higher percentage of photo space (33% vs. 32%). This is also not very surprising due to the fact that sailing is historically the most winning summer Olympic sport in Norway. It is also interesting to register that 64% of the medal-winner texts and 65% of photographic coverage goes to the two gold medal winners representing prestigious and traditional summer Olympic sports, and the other four medal winners share the remaining coverage. If we look at the total text and photo space for the medal-winning sports (Table 9), we find that female athletes receive relatively more of the total coverage compared to their numbers of medals. Male athletes won 67% of the medals and received 56% of the coverage. From this point of analysis, female medal winners receive slightly more coverage than their male counterparts.

Table 9. Proportion of media coverage by gender in relation to Olympic medals won

	Medals (n)	*Medals %*	*Coverage cm²*	*Medals %*
Female	2	33	20,966.9	44
Male	4	67	26,298.2	56
Total	6	100	47,165.1	100

Coverage and Gender Stereotyping

Sports media studies (e.g., Koivula, 1999; Rowe, 1999) maintain that female and male athletes are depicted differently in media. Male athletes are, for example, more often depicted in sport-action and women more often in non-sport settings. This trend seems to be only partly confirmed in this study (see Figure 1). The data show that female athletes are more frequently depicted both in non-sports settings and in sports action compared to their male counterparts.

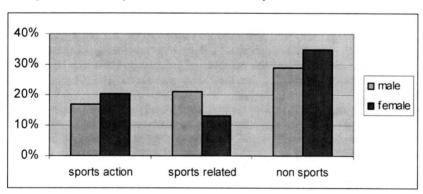

Figure 1. Types of image focus by gender.

It is also interesting to find that both male and female athletes are most frequently depicted in non-sports settings. One explanatory factor could be that this study is based on the coverage of a tabloid newspaper, in which aspects like personalisation and intimacy are emphasized (Lippe, 2005; Rowe, 1999).

One of the central hypotheses in the global study was to explore if female athletes competing in sports more linked to femininity or dressed in ways that highlighted gender difference received relatively more coverage than those competing in sports more strongly linked to masculinity or dressed in ways that did not highlight gender differences. From the Norwegian analysis, it is, however, very difficult to draw firm conclusions on the 'femininity hypothesis' because the female Olympic athletes involved, except the beach volleyball players, were not participating in sports that specifically highlight femininity or gender differences. The distribution of female coverage (see Table 10) shows that the females in the two gold winning sports received over 60% of the total coverage.

Table 10. The distribution of the female Olympic coverage by sports

Sports	Space %	Number of articles %
Sailing	42.3	47.0
Mountain-biking	20.7	19.2
Athletics	13.4	13.6
Beach volleyball	11.3	12.4
Cycling	7.2	5.8
Taekwondo	1.9	1.4
Tennis	1.5	0.5
Gymnastics	0.9	0.1
Kayak	0.7	0.0
Total	100	100

This picture seems to indicate that performances override any significance linked to emphasized femininity and heterosexual attributes. On the other hand, the data show that beach volleyball is ranked as the 4th most covered sport (with 11.3% of the total space and 12.4% of the numbers of articles) and this can be seen as an over-representation considering that the Norwegian players did not qualify for the quarterfinals.

If we look more closely at the results related to sailing and mountain-biking, we register that sailing receives more than twice as much coverage as mountain-biking. How can we explain this difference? Can this finding in some way be linked to the "femininity hypothesis"? It is difficult to say whether or not sports like sailing and mountain-biking are masculine or feminine when referring to stereotyped connotations of masculinity and femininity. When we compare these two sports, we can argue that mountain-biking, in some ways, is considered as a more masculine sport than sailing. Mountain-biking is a sport that demands capacities associated with hegemonic masculinity like strength, endurance, courage, toughness and risk-taking. The athletes have, for example, to be fearless, determined and offensive to maintain the speed downhill. Ongoing textual analyses (Hovden, 2007) of media narratives of the Norwegian mountain-biking gold medal winner Gunn-Rita Dahle seem to fit into this kind of image. She is profiled as a hard, strong, fearless and goal-oriented woman with lots of guts. Her appearance does not mirror emphasized femininity. In the Olympics she had, for example, her hair cut very short and in other championships she has even shaved her head.

The sailor, Siren Sundby, who receives almost half of the total female coverage, is in certain ways profiled differently. She has long blond hair and is profiled as a gentle, open and heterosexually attractive woman, but simultaneously also as an ambitious, hard-working and serious athlete. She is several times photographed together with her boyfriend, and in one article she is depicted knitting a birthday gift for her coach; a scarf decorated with the Norwegian flag (Hovden, 2007). The latter can be interpreted as a form of trivialisation, which often characterises the media exposure of female athletes (e.g., Duncan & Messner, 1998; Koivula, 1999). The narratives thus indicate that Siren Sundby is profiled as more feminine than Gunn-Rita Dahle and this could be one reason why Siren Sundby receives considerably more newspaper coverage. On the other hand, there are several other factors that may explain why sailing receives much higher media coverage. Firstly, an Olympic sailing competition takes place over several days, which obviously increases the media coverage. Secondly, Siren Sundby was almost disqualified during the qualification races and this situation generated a lot of media focus. In other words, several factors seem to explain the extensive media focus on the female sailing event. In addition, sailing in Norway is an upper class sport and a sport that traditionally is linked to national identity.

Olympic Coverage, Gender and National Identity

Sailing has been part of the Olympic program since 1900 and represents Norway's most winning summer Olympic sport with a total of over 50 Olympic medals. Further our King, King Harald V, has twice participated in the Olympic sailing competition and was also the first elected president of the Norwegian Sailing Federation (www.seiling.no). This position makes sailing a sport associated with traditions, prestige and national identity.

On the other hand, only one female (Linda Andersen in 1992) had won a gold medal in sailing before the Athens Olympics. Wensing and Bruce (2003) indicate that winning an Olympic gold medal in sports strongly linked to national identity seems to moderate the under-representation of female athletes in media and make it possible to celebrate female athletes as symbols of national identity and national pride. In this study, the coverage of Siren Sundby seems to confirm this connection.

SUMMARY AND CONCLUDING REMARKS

The results of the Norwegian study show that male athletes still receive distinctly more of the total media coverage during the 2004 Olympic period than their female counterparts, regarding both text and photo space. The male over-representation in coverage can, among other factors, be explained by an almost total male domination of the non-Olympic coverage. Female athletes received only about 1% of the non-Olympic coverage, regarding both space and numbers of texts and photos. This status, which in fact represents a lower rate than former studies, can be interpreted as an annihilation of women's participation, performances and contributions to sport.

The Olympic coverage shows a dramatic increase in female coverage compared to non-Olympic coverage. Although a notable increase, the overall gender distribution still indicates that women are not equally represented in Olympic coverage. However, when comparing the female coverage with the proportion of the Olympic medals won, we find that the two female gold medal winners receive slightly more coverage than their male counterparts. It is also worth noting that most of the female media coverage is concentrated around two female athletes; the two gold medal winners.

Former media studies show that female athletes are more often depicted in non-sports settings than in sports action. This study does not support these findings. Our analysis indicates more similarities than gender disparities regarding image focus.

It is difficult to state if and in which ways the analysis confirm the 'femininity hypothesis'. When supporting the content analysis with textual analysis (Hovden, 2007), we suggest that the female gold medal winner in sailing, Siren Sundby, who received the highest female coverage (about 30% of the total) was profiled as more feminine than the other gold medallist, mountain-biker Gunn Rita Dahle. However, the reasons why sailing receives so much print media coverage are found not only to be gender-related but to be part of a more complex picture. Sailing is, for example, historically the most winning summer Olympic sport in Norway and represents a sport linked to national identity. Hence, it seems like an Olympic gold medal in one of our national sports has contributed to moderating the under-representation of female athletes.

Overall, the Norwegian study documents that big events such as the Olympics give us a unique opportunity to celebrate and enjoy female success and excellence in sports. However, the analyses of both Olympic and non-Olympic coverage seem to indicate that female athletes become visible only on certain premises: the visibility is linked to a few female athletes who either win or are expected to win medals, while a variety of men's sports and achievements, particularly their everyday sporting exploits, are found worthy of far more attention. Hence, our findings trace both features of stability and change. There is still a way to go towards equal visibility and recognition of female and male athletes in Norwegian newspaper coverage. Gendered media representations, sports media included, play a powerful symbolic role in the construction of gender and modern gender identities in our societies (e.g., Bourdieu, 2000; Coakley, 2001). From this point of analysis, the lack of gender balance found in this study should represent an important gender political challenge for a nation like Norway, which markets itself as one of the leading nations regarding gender equality policies.

NOTES

[1] The provision included in the Gender Equality Act requiring 40% representation of both genders on all public boards came in 1988; one year after the gender quota was passed in the NOCCS This indicates that the organised sport system in Norway was very early in implementing gender equality policies in their decision-making bodies. This was, among other factors, caused by close relations between women in sports and women in the women's movement. On the other hand, the socialistic and social democratic political parties in Norway have practiced a radical gender quota in their nomination process since the beginning of the 1980s; nominating 50% of each gender on their lists.

REFERENCES

Bernstein, A. (2002). Is it time for a victory lap? *International Review for the Sociology of Sport, 37*, 3–4), 415–428.
Bourdieu, P. (2000). *Den maskuline dominans.* Oslo: Pax Forlag A/S.

Breivik, G., & Vaagebo, O. (1999). *Jakten på det gode liv. Utviklingen i fysisk aktivitet i den norske befolkning i perioden 1985 – 1997.* Oslo: Norges Idrettshøgskole.

Coakley, J. (2001). *Sport in society: Issues and controversies.* Colorado Springs, CO: McGraw-Hill International Editions.

Duncan, M. C., & Messner, M. (1998). The media image of sport and gender. In L. Wenner (Ed.), *Media Sport.* London: Routledge.

Enjolras, B., Seippel, O., & Waldahl, R. (2005). *Norsk idrett: Organisering, fellesskap og politikk.* Oslo: Akilles.

Fasting, K., & Tangen, J. O. (1983). Kvinneidrett i massemediene. In G. von der Lippe (Ed.), *Kvinner og idrett. Fra myte til realitet.* Oslo: Gyldendal Norsk Forlag.

Hall, M. A. (1987). *Feminism and sporting bodies: Essays on theory and practice.* Champaign, IL: Human Kinetics.

Hartmann-Tews, I., & Rulofs, B. (2005). "Goldmädel, Rennmiezen und Turnkuken" revisited – A comparison of newspaper coverage of sports and gender representation in Germany 1979–1999. In A. Hoffmann & E. Trangbæk (Eds.), *International perspectives on sorting women in past and present* (pp. 307–321). Copenhagen: Institute of Exercise and Sport Sciences.

Hausmann, R., Tyson, L., & Zahidi, S. (2006). *The global gender gap report 2006.* Geneva: World Economic Forum.

Helland, K. (2003). *Sport, medier og journalistikk. Med fotballlandslaget til EM.* Bergen: Fagbokforlaget.

Hernes, H. (1987). *Welfare state and women power. Essays in state feminism.* Oslo: Universitetsforlaget.

Hovden, J. (1996). Mediesportens janusansikt i et kjønnsperspektiv. In Sekretariatet for kvinneforskning (Eds), *Kjønn i media.* Arbeidsnotat nr 2/96 (pp. 40–54). Oslo: Norges Forskningsråd.

Hovden, J. (2000). *Makt, motstand og ambivalens. Betydningar av kjønn i idretten.* Dr.polit. avhandling (Unpublished doctoral dissertation). Universitetet i Tromsø (University of Tromso), Tromsø, Norway.

Hovden, J. (2006). The gender order as a policy issue in sport. A study of Norwegian sport organizations. *NORA (Nordic Journal of Women Studies), 14*(1), 41–53.

Hovden, J. (2007). *Siren og Gunn-Rita i olympiske mediediskursar. Nokre eksplorative funn.* Unpublished paper, Høgskolen i Finnmark, Alta.

Karlsen, S. (1995). *Idrettsskolen i fokus.* Hovedfagsoppgave (Unpublished master's thesis). Norges Idrettshøgskole (Norwegian School of Sport Sciences), Oslo, Norway.

Koivula, N. (1999). *Gender in sport.* Stockholm: University Press.

Lippe, G. von der. (1998). Toppidrett og kjønn i mediene. In S. Loland (Ed.), *Toppidrettens pris* (pp. 106–119). Oslo: Universitetsforlaget.

Lippe, G. von der. (2005). Klesdiskursen i sandvolleyball i OL-04. *Norsk Medietidsskrift, 12*(3), 234–255.

NIF. (2002). *Tilstandsrapport for norsk idrett.* Oslo: Norges Idrettsforbund og Olympiske Komite.

NIKK. (2006). *Kön och sport in nordiska massmedier och ungdomars praktiker. En forskningsoversikt och en bibliografi.* Oslo: Nordisk institutt for kvinne-og kjønnsforskning (Nordic Institute for Women and Gender Research).

Olafsson, K. (Ed.). (2006). *Sports, media and stereotypes. Women and men in sports and media.* Acureyri: Center for Gender Equality. Retrieved from http://www. mujerydeporte.org/documentos/docs/sms_summary_report.pdf

Olstad, F., & Tonnesson, S. (1986). *Norsk idrettshistorie. Folkehelse, trim, stjerner 1939–1986.* Oslo: Aschehoug.

Pemberton, C., Shields, S., Gilbert, L., Shen, X., & Said, H. (2004). A look at print media coverage across four Olympiads. *Women in Sport and Physical Activity Journal, 13*(2), 87–100.

Pettersen, P. (1978). *Idrett og presse.* Hovedfagsoppgave. (Unpublished master's thesis). Norges idrettshøgskole (Norwegian School of Sport Sciences), Oslo, Norway.

Rowe, D. (1999). *Sport, culture and the media.* Philadelphia: Open University Press.

Skjeie, H., & Teigen, M. (2003). *Menn imellom*. Oslo: Gyldendal Akademisk.

Wensing, E., & Bruce, T. (2003). Bending the rules: Media representations of gender during an international sporting event. *International Review for the Sociology of Sport, 38*(4), 387–396.

Jorid Hovden
Finnmark University College/
The Norwegian University of Science and Technology
Norway

Aina Hindenes
The Norwegian School of Sport Sciences
Norway

HELENA TOLVHED

5. SWEDEN

Swedish Media Coverage of Athens 2004

GENDER RELATIONS IN SWEDEN AND IN SWEDISH SPORT

In *The Global Gender Gap Report 2006* (Hausmann, Tyson & Zahidi, 2006),
Sweden (with a population of just over 9 million) was named the gender equality
world champion in an index combining four areas: economic participation and
opportunity, educational attainment, political empowerment, and health and survival.
Much has been done to achieve gender equality in Swedish society and politics,
particularly in the last 35 years. From the beginning of the 1960s, more and more
women entered the labour market, and a number of reforms and laws facilitating
women's paid employment were introduced during the 1970s. In 2006, 49% of all
members of the parliament (Riksdagen) were women. However, women still hold
less than 10% of industrial management positions and continue to be severely
under-represented in top corporate leadership positions. In higher education and
research, only 14% of professors are women. Women's incomes are about 83% of
men's and surveys show they still take most of the household responsibilities
("Swedish gender", 2006).

The Swedish Sports Confederation (Riksidrottsförbundet), established in 1903,
is the umbrella organisation of the Swedish sports movement with 2 million
members. The Confederation has a democratic structure and is led by the executive
committee, consisting of 11 members elected by the biannual General Assembly.
About 42% of the active members in the Swedish Sports Confederation are women,
and the Swedish Sports Confederation has taken an active approach to gender
equality. Women are, however, still under-represented as coaches, trainers and
board members. Those making decisions are not yet sufficiently representative of
sports participants. A recent survey by the Swedish public service broadcaster,
Sveriges Television, found that in Sweden's four largest team sports (soccer, ice
hockey, basketball and handball) only 7.9% of sports club management positions
were held by women (*Sportspegeln*, 2006). In 2005, Karin Mattsson was the first
woman to be elected president. She was elected after a rather heated debate in the
media, which ended only when her male opponent turned down his candidacy for
the post. However, in general, the Swedish Sports Confederation shows a decreasing
proportion of women the further up in the system one looks. While in the district
federations 42% of members of executives are women, they make up only 27% of
the executives of the 67 specialised sports federations on the national level, and

T. Bruce, J. Hovden and P. Markula (eds.),
Sportswomen at the Olympics: A Global Content Analysis of Newspaper Coverage, 61–71.
© 2010 Sense Publishers. All rights reserved.

only 15% of chairpersons in the latter. Only a minority of the specialised sports federations have reached the Swedish Sports Confederation's gender equity goals of at least 40% each of women and men in all of its decision-making bodies. In fact, there have not been any dramatic changes in the last 10 years, which suggests that not all specialised sports federations view gender equality as an important issue ("Kvinnor och", 2005).

PREVIOUS RESEARCH INTO GENDER DIFFERENCES AND SPORT IN SWEDEN

These gender differences in women's involvement in sport federations appear to emanate from the way in which sport and physical education developed in Sweden. Previous research suggests that men and women (and male and female) have been regarded as two distinct categories in Swedish sport, supported by biological and cultural assumptions that males and females are naturally different.

Lundqvist Wanneberg's (2004) examination of physical education in Sweden from 1919 to 1962, a period when influences from the Swedish Ling gymnastics were still strong, found a profound division into female and male forms of physical education, where girls and boys after puberty were to be raised into two different, gender-coded types of citizens. Boys were guided towards exercises that emphasized and worked on strength, determination and competition (with more influences from modern sport), and girls towards aesthetic exercises aimed at developing grace and agility. Girls' gymnastics often gave a lot of scope to rhythmic movements such as singing and dancing games. The division in physical education was based on ideas of girls' bodily sexual development, a process thought to require so much energy that they could not physically develop in the same way as boys. Also, women and girls were thought to lack competitive instincts and aggressiveness (Lundquist Wanneberg, 2004).

Olofsson's (1989) study of women's conditions within the Swedish sports movement in the 20th century led her to conclude that men's domination throughout the development of the early sport movement in the 19th century also came to characterize the following century. Olofsson (1989) observed that sport "...has been created by men for men and it has also been described by men" (p. 198, emphasis in original) and, consequently, the sports movement "...is much more of a men's movement than the popular movement it has been alleged to be by the leadership and by earlier research. Men have the power which means that they control women and their sports activities" (pp. 198–199).

Olofsson (1989) found that sport, because of its strong emphasis on biology and its traditions of naturalizing differences between men and women, historically has lagged behind the official work for equality between men and women. Her study showed that it was only after external political and social pressure in a society where the issue of gender equality was on the public agenda that the Swedish sports movement in the 1970s opened its doors to women (Olofsson, 1989).

Hjelm and Olofsson (2004) focused on the example of women's soccer in Sweden. As a team sport, traditionally closely connected with the concept of masculinity, soccer has been a particularly controversial sport for women. In the interwar period, male soccer experts vigorously attacked initiatives to start women's soccer teams and matches. The first women's soccer league in Sweden was formed in Umeå in the beginning of the 1950s, and was followed by other leagues during the latter half of the 1960s. Hjelm and Olofsson argue that the break-through in the 1960s was due to:

... the increasing number of women employed outside the home as well as the shift in social values, particularly those that had to do with attitudes towards what was 'feminine' and 'masculine', which inspired women to overcome traditional norms within sport also. (2004, p. 195)

The historical resistance from the Swedish Football Association meant that women's soccer was not represented in the decision-making bodies until the 1980s. Still today, there are conflicts over the distribution of clubs' common resources, and the boards of directors are frequently dominated by advocates of men's soccer.

Gender researcher Håkan Larsson (2001) argues that since the 1990s, neo-liberal discourses have come to influence the ways of reasoning about gender and gender equity in sport in Sweden. In these discourses, the sport subject is constructed as an individual and as a gender-specific subject. Larsson is critical of today's gender equity policies, which he finds counterproductive in the way that they produce two distinct and clearly differentiated gender subjects and construct the gendered and heterosexual 'sportsman' and 'sportswoman'.

PREVIOUS RESEARCH ON GENDER DIFFERENCES IN SWEDISH SPORTS MEDIA

There are also distinct differences when it comes to media coverage of men's and women's sport. According to surveys by the Swedish Sports Confederation, in 2005 television in Sweden (including public service and three commercial stations) devoted 1,273 hours (86.6%) to men's sport, but only 197 hours (13.4%) to women's sport ("Verksamhetsberättelse", 2005).

In 2005, the five specialised sports federations with the largest number of active women in Sweden were those for track and field (233,700 active women), soccer (197,285), gymnastics (174,920), equestrian (170,831) and golf (167,598) ("Kvinnor och", 2005). However, when it comes to media interest in these five sports, there seems to be a bias against those that are dominated by female participants. The federation with the largest proportion (over 85%) of female participants, the Equestrian Federation, is ranked 11 of the 15 sports most shown on TV in Sweden. The Gymnastics Federation, with over 80% female participants, did not even make the list ("Verksamhetsberättelse", 2005).

According to Hjelm and Olofsson (2004), women's soccer was generally portrayed in a positive light by the media in the 1960s. In the radical public debate on gender roles, journalists considered soccer to be an example of women encroaching on areas previously dominated by men and struggling against traditional attitudes. Remarks that had been common a few decades earlier, claiming that soccer was unwomanly, physically dangerous or that women simply could not play, did not win any great acceptance (Hjelm & Olofsson, 2004). However, in more recent decades the media has tended to marginalise women's soccer, while the number of female soccer players has grown consistently. The 2001 European Championship, where Sweden won a silver medal, is often considered to be something of a breakthrough in the media, although coverage is still far from comparable to that for the men's national team.

My own qualitative discourse analysis of popular magazine coverage from nine summer Olympics from 1948 to 1980 showed that women athletes were not considered as being serious athletes in the same way that males were (Tolvhed, 2005). They were frequently sexualised, with coverage focusing on their good looks and attractiveness rather than athletic performance, and the media even portraying the Olympics as first and foremost a beauty contest for female participants. Articles on women athletes tended to focus on life outside of sports activities, with emphasis on family, romance or general plans for the future. Women's sport was hence trivialised, and female athletes were frequently quoted saying that sport was just a hobby to them. While male athletes were represented as *sports*men, with an emphasis on their superior physical abilities and remarkable willpower, female Olympians were predominately represented as *women*. Representations of female athletes displayed a passive female body and upheld the boundaries between the sexes.

Furthermore, in a Cold War context, fears of sport's masculinising effect on the female body and mind were negotiated by displacing images of mannish women onto women athletes from the Eastern block. Female athletes from communist countries were predominantly represented as large, 'unsexed' and unattractive, and direct comparisons with more 'feminine' Swedish (or Western) Olympians were not uncommon. The reader was hereby assured that 'our' women, even the ones involved in top level sport, were 'proper' women and did not challenge the gender order. I argue that a specific kind of respectable Swedish femininity – western, white, heterosexual and middle-class – was constructed and reproduced (Tolvhed, 2005).

No content analyses of sports coverage in newspapers have been done in Sweden. However, Natalie Koivula (1999a, 1999b) examined a sample of sports news broadcasts on the Swedish public service broadcaster and on one national commercial station during one year (September 1, 1995, through August 31, 1996; a total of 1,470 minutes). In addition, a follow-up examination was done in 1998 (528 minutes). The results showed significant gender differences regarding both quantity and type of coverage. Less than 10% of sports news air-time was devoted to female athletes. Even considering the fact that there are fewer competing women athletes, the coverage was far from equitable with participation. Women competing in team sports were found to be particularly invisible, and amounted to a small proportion of the total coverage of women's sports. Koivula (1999a, 1999b) concluded that the largest part of the coverage was devoted to men in sports traditionally considered as masculine, and also that a large part of coverage of female athletes focused upon female-appropriate sports. She also found the use of gendered language, where men's sports were presented as a universal norm while women in sports were regarded as an anomaly. Sports in which women participated were more often gender marked, as in 'women's soccer', than those in which men participated. Women were referred to by only first name more than three times more often than men, and also frequently referred to as 'girls'. This means that while men were given status of adults, women were reduced to children (Koivula, 1999a, 1999b).

It is clear that more research into gender aspects of Swedish media coverage remains to be done. However, the qualitative and quantitative research studies that have been accomplished so far suggest that female athletes have been marginalised in comparison to males, and that their sport performances have been trivialised and regarded as less important.

METHODS

The newspaper used for this study was *Dagens Nyheter*, Sweden's largest morning paper (363,400 copies on weekdays in 2004), and the time period for data gathering was August 7 to September 5, 2004. Information was taken from the front page, the sports section and from special Olympic supplements. For practical reasons, the results section in each individual issue of *Dagens Nyheter* was counted as one article and categorised as 'mixed' (the consequences of this will be discussed below). Photographic space is counted as a subsection of 'total space', which means that 'total space' includes text as well as images. Stories were categorised as 'mixed' if females as well as males were mentioned, while the 'neutral' category included stories that were about non-gender specific issues such as security for the Games, ticketing, descriptions of facilities and transport options.

RESULTS OF THE CONTENT ANALYSIS FOR SWEDEN

At the Olympic Games in Athens 2004, 52 women (46%) and 61 men (54%) competed for Sweden. Swedish athletes won a total of seven medals. The four gold medals were won by female heptathlete Carolina Klüft, male high jumper Stefan Holm, male triple jumper Christian Olsson and the male canoe/kayak team of Henrik Nilsson and Markus Oscarsson. A silver medal was won by male wrestler Ara Abrahamian, and the two bronze medals by the mixed equestrian jump team (this medal was later changed to a silver medal) and the female sailing team of Therese Torgersson and Vendela Zachrisson.

Almost two-thirds of the total sports coverage during this period was from the Olympics (187,108 cm^2, 63.7%), while only just over one-third (106,453 cm^2, 36.3%) was non-Olympic coverage (see Tables 1, 2 & 4). For men, the percentage of coverage ranged from a low of 31.77% of space for Olympic coverage to a high of 65.68% for non-Olympic coverage. Women, on the other hand, received 32.63% of Olympic but a mere 7.91% of non-Olympic space in cm^2.

Table 1. All coverage in Dagens Nyheter during the 2004 Olympic Games

Measurement	Male	Female	Mixed	Neutral	Total
Space in cm^2	129,357	69,473	68,319	26,412	293,561
Percentage (%)	44.06	23.67	23.27	9.00	100%
Images in cm^2	50,704	36,085	11,767	10,853	109,409
Percentage (%)	46.34	32.98	10.76	9.92	37.27
Number of stories	472	186	124	88	870
Percentage (%)	54.25	21.38	14.25	10.11	100%
Number of images	186	108	42	23	359
Percentage (%)	51.81	30.08	11.70	6.41	41.26

When looking only at Olympic coverage, female athletes actually received more of this than males; 32.63% of coverage in cm^2 for females compared to 31.77% for males. However, men gained slightly more in number of articles; 36.12% of stories were about male athletes and 31.46% about females (see Table 2). The Olympic coverage that was categorised as mixed – since it included stories about both males and females – covered 22.08% of space in cm^2, whereas 13.52% referred to the neutral category.

Table 2. Olympics-only coverage in Dagens Nyheter during the 2004 Olympic Games

Measurement	Male	Female	Mixed	Neutral	Total
Total space in cm^2	59,442	61,050	41,319	25,297	187,108
Percentage (%)	31.77	32.63	22.08	13.52	100%
Images in cm^2	27,092	31,938	10,673	10,522	80,225
Percentage (%)	33.77	39.81	13.30	13.12	42.88
Number of stories	186	162	86	81	515
Percentage (%)	36.12	31.46	16.7	15.73	100%
Number of images	91	93	38	21	243
Percentage (%)	37.45	38.27	15.64	8.64	47.18

The relatively equal amount of Olympic coverage for male and females is in line with previous international research, which has shown that in major sport events, such as the Olympic Games, female athletes tend to become more visible (e.g., Bernstein, 2002). Also, Sweden had some high-profile females competing in Athens; for example, in track and field, equestrian and soccer.

The most attention, by far, was granted to Swedish track and field gold medallist Carolina Klüft (see Table 3). She was the subject of more than twice as much space in cm^2 (15,354 cm^2 vs. 7,203 cm^2) than the combined coverage for the two male gold medal winners in track and field; high jumper Stefan Holm and triple jumper Christian Olsson. The extensive coverage of Klüft cannot be explained simply by the fact that she won a gold medal, because so did both Holm and Olsson. Klüft was the focus of 19 articles compared to only 8 for Holm and Olsson combined, and the Olympic coverage also featured 17 images of her versus a total number of 10 for the two male track and field athletes.

Table 3. The five most covered Swedish athletes based on article size

Sport	Name	Gender	Article (n)	Article size	Image (n)	Image size
Track & field	C. Klüft	Female	19	15,354	17	6,962
Soccer	Soccer team	Female	22	13,284	10	2,219
Track & field	Holm+Olsson[1]	Male	8	7,203	10	3,930
Kayak	Nilsson/ Oscarsson	Male	8	5,388	7	2,248
Table tennis	J-O. Waldner	Male	7	5,222	7	3,223

[1] Note that coverage of Holm and Olsson was combined into one count because they competed and won their gold medals on the same day, which meant that articles focused on them both simultaneously.

Coverage of Carolina Klüft constituted as much as one fourth (25.1%) of coverage in cm^2 for female athletes. Second most attention in terms of total article space in cm^2 was given to the female soccer team (21.8%), who finished in fourth place. In fact, when the article size for Klüft and the women's soccer team is combined, it adds up to 47% of the total amount of Olympic coverage for women. If coverage (3,413 cm^2) of the bronze-medal-winning sailing team of Therese Torgersson and Vendela Zachrisson is added, the number rises to 52.5%. However, the combined percentage for the three most-featured male athletes/teams (who were all gold medal winners), Holm, Olsson and the kayak team of Nilsson and Oscarsson, is only 21%. The fact that both the soccer team and Carolina Klüft, who competed in long jump as well as heptathlon, got added exposure because they competed during more days than many other Olympians, has to be considered. Still, this analysis does suggest that the equal numbers for coverage of female and male Olympians might not tell the whole story. Media coverage of women's sport is centred upon a small number of highly successful female athletes, whose successes contribute to national prestige. Hence, there might be a more narrow scope to the media interest in women's sport, while men's sport is seen as interesting in its own right (and not only when medals are expected or won).

This hypothesis is further reinforced by the fact that outside of Olympic coverage, the sport pages are heavily dominated by male sport (see Table 4). In day-to-day sport coverage, which in this study is categorized as non-Olympic sport, women tended to be severely under-represented and marginalised. The results hereby confirm previous research findings of the Olympics providing a rare opportunity for female athletes to get a lot of attention (see Figure 1).

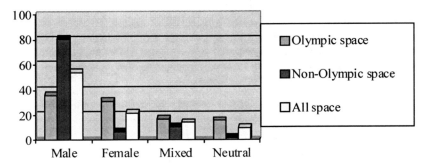

Figure 1. Percentage of media coverage of Olympic, Non-Olympic and All space by gender.

The non-Olympic coverage in *Dagens Nyheter* was found to focus upon, above all, men's soccer and ice-hockey. Male sport made up 80.56% of the number of non-Olympic articles, compared to just 6.76% for women's sports. When considering article space in cm^2, the figures were 65.68% for men and 7.91% for women. The large percentage for the mixed category in non-Olympic article space, 25.35%, was due to the fact that the results sections was counted as just one article and labelled 'mixed', since it always contained female as well as male results. This may have caused the mixed category to be misleading, since the results sections were actually highly dominated by male sports results. The dominance for male sports was, then, even bigger than results for article space indicate.

Table 4. Non-Olympic coverage in Dagens Nyheter during the 2004 Olympic Games

Measurement	Male	Female	Mixed	Neutral	Total
Space in cm^2	69,915	8,423	27,000	1,115	106,453
Percentage (%)	65.68	7.91	25.36	1.05	100%
Images in cm^2	23,612	4,147	1,094	331	29,184
Percentage (%)	80.91	14.21	3.75	1.13	27.41
Stories (n)	286	24	38	7	355
Percentage (%)	80.56	6.76	10.7	1.97	100%
Images (n)	95	15	4	2	116
Percentage (%)	81.90	12.93	3.45	1.72	32.68

As Tables 1, 2 and 4 show, a consistent tendency to over-represent women in images in comparison to their proportion of the text was found in Olympic as well as in non-Olympic coverage (23.67% of total coverage in cm^2 compared to 32.98% of images; 32.63% of Olympic coverage but 39.81% of images; 7.91% of non-Olympic coverage but 14.21% of images). This suggests, I would argue, that women were regarded as visually more interesting than men. Coverage of the bronze-medal winning equestrian jump-team is telling. The only female member of the team, Malin Baryard, is a woman who at the time was in her late 20s and has become something of a poster-girl for the sport. Baryard was the subject for 1,343 cm^2 of the 2,125 cm^2 total image space for the jump-team, which makes 63% of image coverage. Apart from several articles focusing exclusively on Baryard, images of her were repeatedly chosen to illustrate articles on the jump-team.

My own previous research of media coverage in the 1950s, 1960s and 1970s suggests that female Olympians often are not shown in sports activity in the same way that men are (Tolvhed, 2005). Instead, the image material represents them as passive and posing. For this reason, I have here taken a special interest in whether images show athletes in sport-related situations or not, and whether they are shown as physically active or not.

In Table 5, images are split into three categories: *doing sport/active* (an image that captures the athlete in physical activity), *sport-related/passive* (around the arena and/or dressed for sport) and *not sport*. Of a total of 97 images of women, 61 show the athlete/s in sport activity (62.9%), compared to 50 of 99 images of men (50.5%). Thus, in *Dagens Nyheter*, more women than men are shown during activity in coverage from Athens 2004. This is a rather surprising result, considering previous research, and could suggest that earlier stereotypical understandings of female bodies as passive and weak have lost their relevance in Swedish sport media.

Table 5. Image focus in Olympic coverage[1]

Image focus	Male (n)	Male cm^2	Female (n)	Female cm^2	Mixed (n)	Mixed cm^2
Doing sport/ active	50	14,776	61	22,818	1	450
Sport-related/ passive	27	10,801	21	6,915	3	1,187
Not sport	22	4,555	15	3,572	4	1,312

[1] This analysis focuses only on images: The focus of associated articles was not considered.

CONCLUDING REMARKS

Compared to previous findings about Swedish media coverage of female athletes, this study does seem to point to some positive tendencies. During the Olympics, female athletes were found to receive slightly more coverage in cm^2 compared to men. The results reflect some high-profile Swedish female athletes' increasing popularity in recent years, not least in sports that have historically been considered masculine, such as track and field and soccer. The most exposed athlete, by far, was a woman competing in heptathlon, a sport which shows an athlete's versatility: 'raw' strength and ability as well as technical skills are needed to succeed. In soccer, a sport that historically has been very closely tied to masculinity, the women's team was given a lot of attention. This suggests that the hypothesis based on previous research, stating that female athletes competing in sports more strongly linked to femininity or dressed in ways that highlight gender difference will receive relatively more coverage than those competing in sports more strongly linked to masculinity, was not accurate for the Swedish coverage of the 2004 Olympics. Regarding image focus, the study showed that more women than men were found to be represented during sport activity. In 2004, then, it was possible to publicly display women as possessing strength, activity and capability and doing sports that have historically been connected to masculinity and the male body. This might suggest that the concept of femininity is under negotiation.

At the beginning of this chapter, the lingering male dominance of Swedish sport organisations was discussed. Does the extensive coverage of female Olympians perhaps imply that the media take a more progressive stance on gender equality in sport than sport organisations do? Not unambiguously, in my opinion. The results are mixed in terms of gender equality in sports coverage. Olympic coverage is still, to a large extent, focused upon a small number of highly successful female athletes, and women tend to be severely under-represented and marginalised in non-Olympic sport. In non-Olympic coverage, female athletes received only a fraction of attention in comparison with male athletes (7.91% compared to 65.68% in cm^2, and 6.76% to 80.56% in number of stories). The results hereby suggest that national identity is the most important factor in Games coverage – and a factor that seems to override sport's usual logic of gender when it comes to prestigious events such as the Olympic Games, where women's contribution is vital for winning medals and national success. Outside of these major events, however, there is still a long way to go before women's sports are given the same status as men's in media coverage.

REFERENCES

Bernstein, A. (2002). Is it time for a victory lap? Changes in the media coverage of women in sport. *International Review for the Sociology of Sport, 37*(3), 415–428.

Hausmann, R., Tyson, L. D., & Zahidi, S. (2006). *The global gender gap report 2006*. Geneva: World Economic Forum. Retrieved January 15, 2007, from http://www.weforum.org/pdf/gendergap/report2006.pdf

Hjelm, J., & Olofsson, E. (2004). A breakthrough. Women's football in Sweden. In J. A. Mangan & F. Hong (Eds.), *Soccer, women, sexual liberation. Kicking off a new era* (pp. 182–204). London: Frank Cass.

Kane, M. J., & Greendorfer, S. L. (1994). The media's role in accommodating and resisting stereotyped images of women in sport. In P. J. Creedon (Ed.), *Women, media and sport: Challenging gender values* (pp. 3–27). London: Sage.

Koivula, N. (1999a). *Gender in sport*. Stockholm: University Print.

Koivula, N. (1999b). Gender stereotyping in televised media sport coverage. *Sex Roles, 41*(7/8), 589–603.

Kvinnor och män inom idrotten 2005 [Facts and figures on women and men in sport 2005] (2005). The Swedish Sports Confederation. Retrieved January 15, 2007, from http://www.rf.se/files/{A816F6F2-1065-435D-AD5A-6FCA9F039C5B}.pdf

Larsson, H. (2001). *Iscensättningen av kön i idrott*. Stockholm: HLS Förlag.

Lundquist Wanneberg, P. (2004). *Kroppens medborgarfostran. Kropp, klass och genus i skolans fysiska fostran 1919–1962*. Stockholm: Repro Print AB.

Olofsson, E. (1989). *Har kvinnorna en sportslig chans? Den svenska idrottsrörelsen och kvinnorna under 1900-talet. [Do women have a sporting chance? Organized sport and women in Sweden in the 20th century]* Umeå: University Print.

Sportspegeln. (2006, December 17). [Television broadcast]. Stockholm: Sveriges television (SVT).

Swedish gender equality and the Equal Opportunities Ombudsman. (2006). Presentation from the Swedish Equal Opportunities Ombudsman. Retrieved January 15, 2007, from http://www. jamombud.se/ inenglish/docs/presentationswedishequalopportunitiesombudsman.ppt

Tolvhed, H. (2005). Brassebönor, stålmän och svarta spöken. Idrottande kroppar i *Ses* bevakning av sommar-OS 1948–1980. *Kvinnovetenskaplig tidskrift, 26*(1), 41–64.

Verksamhetsberättelse 2005 med årsredovisningar. (2005). [2005 annual report from the Swedish Sports Confederation]. Retrieved January 15, 2007, from http://www.rf.se/files/{7873CF17-BFF2-417D-A986-B3A22FE92DA7}.pdf

Helena Tolvhed
Malmö University
Sweden

KELLY REDMAN, LUCY WEBB, JUDY LIAO
AND PIRKKO MARKULA

6. THE UNITED KINGDOM

Women's Representation in British Olympic Newspaper Coverage 2004

INTRODUCTION

There is a general consensus that women receive less sport media coverage than men. In this chapter we map women's representation in British sport media by analysing the amount of coverage women received in 2004 in two newspapers, the *Times* and the *Sun*. The gender gap in sport media is occasionally justified by appealing to women's lower participation in sport. Therefore, we will first examine women's current participation rates in sport and physical activity and then review the previous quantitative literature regarding media coverage of women athletes in Britain.

WOMEN AND SPORT IN BRITAIN

Britain prides itself on its success in many international sports fields. In addition, Britain is considered the birthplace for several popular sports including football and rugby. Sport being so eminent in the national psyche, we would expect the Britons to be avid participants on multiple levels of a whole variety of sports. In its report, Sport England (2002), using the data from the 2002 General Household Survey, analysed sport participation rates in England. In this report adults were asked about their participation in sporting activity over two reference periods: the previous 12 months (denoting occasional participation) and the previous four weeks (denoting regular participation). In this study, sport was understood loosely as encompassing any physical activity ranging from walking to games such as cue sports.

The results demonstrated that men were more likely to participate in sport or physical activity than women: 80% of men compared to 70% of women had taken part in at least one activity during the previous 12 months. Walking was the most popular activity for both men and women. After walking, women favoured swimming, keep fit/yoga and cycling. However, 53% of women compared to 65% of men took part in regular physical activity and only 11% of women participated in physical activity three times a week compared to 19% of men. While women seem to be physically less active than men, the differences are quite marginal. However, in terms of competitive sport, almost four times as many males as females

T. Bruce, J. Hovden and P. Markula (eds.),
Sportswomen at the Olympics: A Global Content Analysis of Newspaper Coverage, 73–88.

participated competitively: 20% of regular participants in competitions were male whereas only 5% were female participants. While this report discussed women's participation in different sports, there are no statistics regarding which sports women participated in competitively rather than recreationally. In addition, the survey demonstrated that the percentage of adults participating in competition decreased with age. Participation rates in such team sports as football, rugby, netball, hockey, basketball and volleyball fell significantly from those aged 16–19, although the survey did not include specific figures for women's participation. However, Donohoe (2004) reports that girls, particularly, have been put off by competitive sport: girls as young as seven years show signs of disliking sport. In addition, as many as 40% of girls drop out of sports activity by the time they reach 18. These statistics provide some alarming details considering that London has won the bid to host the 2012 Olympic Games.

Sportswomen in the British Media: Quantitative Findings

Considering the high profile and visibility of sport in the British media, there are surprisingly few studies that quantitatively record women's sport media coverage. In Britain, the Women's Sport Foundation UK has conducted a series of studies regarding women's sport coverage in the newspapers, and points to sport media coverage as one of the reasons for girls dropping out of sport and women's low participation rates. In their month-long study (20 August to 17 September, 1991) of British national newspapers, only 4% of articles and 2–10% of photographs were about women's sport (Women's Sports Foundation, 2003a, 2003b). In a follow up study during 1998, only 10.9% of sports articles in the *Times* were on women's sports and a dismal 0.5% of sports articles in the tabloid newspaper the *Sun* covered women's sports (Bernstein, 2002). More recently, the Women's Sport Foundation UK (2000) conducted a further study of sports coverage by tabloid newspapers. They found that women's sport received only 2.3% of coverage and there were only 36 photographs of women athletes compared to 1,564 photographs of male athletes. When they followed up this research in 2003, they found that the daily average space dedicated to women's sport was significantly stronger in the national broadsheets (7.1%) but across the board of tabloids and local newspapers the figure dropped to 2.65%. In addition, the study pointed out that there was an average of 10 days a month when women's sport received absolutely no mention at all (Donohoe, 2004). However, when the Women's Sport Foundation commissioned a telephone survey of 624 adults aged over 16, 88% of respondents felt that it was important to see more of Britain's successful sportswomen in the media. In addition, 45% would watch more women's sport if it was broadcast on television (Women's Sports Foundation UK, 2003a, 2003b).

There is even less research on how British women Olympians have been represented by the British media. In general, the research demonstrates that the British newspaper media tend to provide more coverage of women's sports during major events like the Olympic Games. The amount of coverage, however, remains unequal to the men's sport coverage. One of the earliest studies to report on newspaper presentation of British women athletes was Mathesen and Flatten's (1996) assessment of changes in the coverage of women athletes in six national and Sunday newspapers – the *Telegraph, Guardian, Independent, Express, Mail* and *Mirror* – by analysing coverage from 1–14 July in both 1984 and 1994. They began by comparing women's participation numbers in 1984 and 1994. They concluded that 39% of sports participants in 1987 and 42% in 1993 were women over 15 years of age.[1] In addition, they pointed out that of British Olympians (32% in 1984 and 39% in 1992), 39% were women. Therefore, there was a definite increase of sporting women in Britain. Consequently, we could expect an increase in women's sport media coverage.

Mathesen and Flatten's sample included the front pages, editorials and sport pages and counted the number of front page articles and photographs, the total number of articles and photographs and the text in cm^2. Mathesen and Flatten (1996) found that, in general, there was a dramatic increase in the quantity of sport newsprint over the decade. However, while men's broadsheet sport articles doubled, women's sport media coverage actually decreased. In 1984, women athletes received 11% of all the articles and 20% of all the photographic coverage. However, in 1994 these figures had dropped to 6.5% of the articles and 6% of the photos. While there were some differences between the broadsheets and the tabloid coverage, they were minor. Women were, therefore, under-reported compared to their participation rates and although their participation rates rose over the ten years, the media reported even less about women's sport. The researchers concluded that "the coverage for women in GB decreased between 1984 and 1994 by 5.2% for articles per day, 5.2% for square centimetres and 7.1% for photographs" (Mathesen & Flatten, 1996, p. 78). Consequently, they asserted, "British sport and press both need a 'culture change'. Only when such a culture change evolves can women expect the removal of barriers to their participation" (Mathesen & Flatten, 1996, p. 79).

One of the occasions to view women's sport in Britain is during the Olympic Games. Alexander (1994) examined how the British newspapers covered athletics during the 1992 Barcelona Olympic Games. Her study included the *Guardian, Independent, Telegraph, Express, Mail, Mirror* and *Sun* (three broadsheet and four tabloid papers). She found that female athletes received 24% of headlines, 22% of written lines and 27% of photos in reports regarding athletics. The pictures of the male athletes tended to be larger than those of female athletes. The differences between the different types of newspapers were nonsignificant. However, Alexander noted that some newspapers failed to mention women's events during some days of the competitions: For example, "on half the days following Olympic Games athletics competition, *The Sun* failed to include reports on women's events" (1994, p. 660).

Vincent, Imwold, Masemann and Johnson (2002) conducted an international comparison of newspaper representation of Olympic athletes in Canada, United States and Great Britain during the entire period of the Centennial Olympic Games, also dubbed the 'Games of the Women', from 9 July to 5 August, 1996. From Britain they selected the *Times* and *Daily Mail* for the content analysis because of their national prominence, their nationwide circulation and their extensive sport coverage. The researchers found that the newspapers "provided generally equitable coverage of female and male athletes" (p. 324). For example, 51% of articles with photos represented male athletes compared to 36% of women. Similarly, 51% of articles without photos were about men compared to 31% of women. Male athletes were pictured in 56% of the photographs whereas women athletes were pictured in 43%. Vincent et al. (2002) further divided the photographic representation into categories of female appropriate (archery, diving, equestrian, fencing, gymnastics, swimming, synchronised swimming, table tennis, tennis and volleyball) and female inappropriate sport based on classifications of women's sports by using a combination of Metheny's (1972) sport typology, Rintala and Birrell's (1984) sport category and Kane's (1988) sport classification for women. Based on this division, the results revealed that an approximately equal number of photographs showed female athletes competing in each category. Similarly, there was an equal amount of general coverage of female appropriate and inappropriate sports.

Vincent et al. (2002) also sought to determine whether the female athletes were portrayed qualitatively differently compared to male athletes. To examine this, the researchers looked for 'negative' and 'positive' portrayal of female athletes in terms of their 'physical appearance/attire', 'psychological characteristics', 'physical strength/athleticism' or 'family role'. They found that 'popular' newspapers such as the *Daily Mail* "contained over twice as many negative paragraphs as they did positive paragraphs describing female athletes' 'physical appearance/attire'" (Vincent et al., 2002, pp. 328–329) and had not eliminated 'trivialized' coverage of female athletes to the same extent as the 'serious' newspapers. On the other hand, "female athletes had over twice as many paragraphs describing positive attributes as negative attributes in relation to their 'physical strength and athleticism'" (Vincent et al., 2002, p. 329). In addition, female and male athletes were portrayed "qualitatively similarly in terms of the number of photographs depicting female and male athletes 'competing' or 'not competing' in their sport or event" (p. 329) and there were actually more posed photographs of male athletes than female athletes. The researchers found that although the British newspapers "devoted more negative paragraphs to male athletes in relation to their 'physical appearance and attire' than they did to female athletes" (p. 332), they nevertheless "had nearly twice as many photographs of male athletes compared with female athletes" (Vincent at al., 2002, p. 333). In addition, the researchers calculated that the British Olympic team for 1996 consisted of 300 athletes (182 males and 118 females) but the British female athletes won only one Olympic medal compared to 14 won by the male athletes. Therefore, compared to their success, the British female athletes appeared to obtain significant coverage in the newspapers. One must note, however, that this study did not include specific data for British coverage but presented combined results from the three countries. The researchers concluded that "female athletes receive more coverage when they compete in the unique format of major international sporting events…than they do throughout the regular sporting year" (Vincent et al., 2002, p. 333). The earlier study by Women's Sports Foundation (2003a) confirms this conclusion.

METHODS

In this chapter, we aim to expand these findings by analysing the sport media coverage of one broadsheet newspaper, the *Times*, and one tabloid newspaper, the *Sun*, during the Athens 2004 Olympic Games. The previous studies of British newspaper coverage of women's sport have typically included both a broadsheet newspaper and a tabloid newspaper (Alexander, 1994; Bernstein, 2002; Donohoe, 2004; Mathesen & Flatten, 1996; Vincent et al., 2002). Following Vincent et al. (2002), we included the *Times* because of its national prominence, nationwide circulation and its extensive sport coverage. We chose the *Sun* and its Sunday sister paper, the *News of the World*, because the *Sun* newspaper is the best-selling daily tabloid in the country, selling 3.9 million copies a day and representing a daily readership of approximately 10 million people. The *News of the World*[2] is the only paper that sells more with around 4.5 million copies sold every Sunday (Greene, 2004). The *Sun* has been described by Harris and Clayton (2002) as a publication aimed predominately at a lower-middle class readership with sport, and sporting celebrities in particular, being the key to the popularity of the newspaper.

The sample of newspapers was taken during the 2004 Olympic period. This period included a week prior to the opening ceremony through to the day after the closing ceremony (6 August 2004 to 30 August 2004). The quantitative analysis of this investigation stemmed from every section of the newspaper with exclusion only of the *Sun's* football supplement "Score" and its page dedicated to horse racing and betting. Our examination is based on five hypotheses, each of which is discussed below.

RESULTS

Hypothesis 1: Women Athletes Will Receive Relatively Equal Amounts of Newspaper Olympic Coverage with Male Athletes in Terms of Number, Size and Prominence of Articles and Photographs, but Less in the Non-Olympic Sport Coverage

Overall, this study found that during 2004 Athens Olympic Games women athletes received significantly less coverage than the male athletes in the British newspapers. In addition, there was little women's sport coverage outside the Olympic reporting. Tables 1 to 4 demonstrate that while women received about 11% of the overall sport coverage in the *Times* and in the *Sun*, they featured in less than 1% of the coverage outside the Olympics. Notably, although one newspaper was a tabloid and one a broadsheet, the percentages and gender distributions were very similar for both total and non-Olympic coverage.

Table 1. Total space and number of stories in the Times

Measurement	Male	Female	Mixed	Neutral	Total
Space in cm^2	254,366.33	40,150.32	66,570.61	37,443.59	398,530.85
Percentage (%)	63.83	10.08	16.70	9.39	100
Number of stories	977	96	154	477	1704
Percentage (%)	57.34	5.63	9.04	27.99	100

Table 2. Total space and number of stories in the Sun

Measurement	Male	Female	Mixed	Neutral	Total
Space in cm^2	348,121.79	64,194.39	87,178.88	39,362.42	538,857.48
Percentage (%)	64.60	11.91	16.18	7.31	100
Number of stories	1257	143	208	479	2087
Percentage (%)	60.23	6.85	9.97	22.95	100

Table 3. Non-Olympic space and number of stories in the Times

Measurement	Male	Female	Mixed	Neutral	Total
Space in cm^2	199,430.66	1,754.7	11,830.01	24,759.63	237,775.00
Percentage (%)	83.87	0.74	4.98	10.41	100
Number of stories	781	12	43	443	1279
Percentage (%)	61.06	0.94	3.36	34.64	100

Table 4. Non-Olympic space and number of stories in the Sun

Measurement	Male	Female	Mixed	Neutral	Total
Space in cm^2	260,874.07	2,019.26	14,923.28	22,548.04	300,364.65
Percentage (%)	86.85	0.67	4.97	7.51	100
Number of stories	986	12	54	434	1486
Percentage (%)	66.35	0.81	3.63	29.21	100

Tables 5 and 6 demonstrate that Olympic coverage received less than a third of the overall sporting coverage of the newspapers analysed. Although beyond the scope of this study, it was obvious during the analysis that English football remained the most featured topic despite exclusion of the football supplement of the *Sun* from the content analysis. In contrast, almost all female coverage (90% of stories, 95% of space) came from Olympics coverage. In the *Times* there were total of 521 Olympic story items and slightly more, 601, in the *Sun*. Tables 5 and 6 show the distribution of the Olympic media coverage between the genders. Women received about 20% of the story items and obtained about 25% of the space in cm^2 devoted to the Olympic coverage. The *Sun* had slightly more stories on women athletes than the *Times*.

Table 5. Olympic-only space and number of stories in the Times

Measurement	Male	Female	Mixed	Neutral	Total
Space in cm^2	54,935.67	38,395.62	54,740.60	12,683.96	160,755.85
Percentage (%)	34.18	23.89	34.03	7.90	100
Number of stories	196	84	111	34	521
Percentage (%)	46.12	19.76	26.12	8	100

Table 6. Olympic-only space and number of stories in the Sun

Measurement	Male	Female	Mixed	Neutral	Total
Space in cm^2	87,247.72	62,175.13	72,255.6	16,814.38	238,492.83
Percentage (%)	36.58	26.07	30.30	7.05	100
Number of stories	271	131	154	45	601
Percentage (%)	45.09	21.80	25.62	7.49	100

In general, women athletes received more photographic coverage than text coverage in both newspapers. The only exception was in the space measurements for the *Times*, where females received slightly more text. The *Sun* clearly highlighted women athletes in photographs as they were depicted in almost 37% of all photographs and occupied almost 40% of the image space.

Table 7. Olympic-only space and number of photographs in the Times

Measurement	Male	Female	Mixed	Neutral	Total
Space in cm^2	76,277.86	22,598.95	4,025.98	5,264.34	108,167.13
Percentage (%)	70.52	20.89	3.72	4.87	100
Number of photos	202	134	19	33	388
Percentage	52.06	34.54	4.90	8.50	100

Table 8. Olympic-only space and number of photographs in the Sun

Measurement	Male	Female	Mixed	Neutral	Total
Space in cm^2	40,519.69	31,653.62	39,88.93	4,051.98	80,214.22
Percentage (%)	50.52	39.46	4.97	5.05	100
Number of photos	258	174	19	26	477
Percentage (%)	54.09	36.48	3.98	5.45	100

The results, therefore, support hypothesis 1 in that sportswomen did receive significantly less coverage than sportsmen outside the Olympic coverage. However, while receiving much more Olympic coverage, women's coverage was not equal to men's Olympic coverage. Women were depicted in significantly fewer articles (21%) than the male athletes (46%). However, when measured by space, the difference was smaller, with male athletes receiving 35% and female athletes receiving 25% of the Olympic coverage. Women were also depicted in fewer photographs than men (53%), yet received more pictures (36%) than stories. Therefore, the results do not support the first part of hypothesis 1. There were, however, fewer female Olympians than male Olympians in the Great Britain team which might help explain these results.

Hypothesis 2: Female and Male Athletes Will Receive Coverage Relative
to Their Proportions of the Olympic Team

Although we did not calculate coverage just for British athletes and, thus, cannot directly compare the coverage of British athletes with their proportions on the Olympic team, the overall Olympic coverage for both male and female athletes was similar to the gender ratio of the Great Britain Olympic team. Table 9 shows the combined values for all male and female articles and photographs and excludes the results for the mixed and neutral categories.

Table 9. Olympic media coverage relative to Olympic team composition both newspapers

Gender	British team (n)	British team	All Olympic competitors (n)	All Olympic competitors	Olympic media items[1] (n)	Olympic media items	% difference compared to British team
Male	166	61.25%	6296	59.3%	927	63.93%	+2.68
Female	105	38.75%	4329	40.7%	523	36.07%	-2.68
Total	271	100%	10,625	100%	1,450	100%	

[1] Media items include number of articles and number of photographs combined. The data combines results from both the *Times* and the *Sun*.

The coverage was closer to the percentage of the British team than to the gender makeup of all Olympic competitors. Males received slightly more (+2.86%) coverage than the British participation rates while females received slightly less (–2.68%) coverage. In comparison to the proportions of all Olympic competitors, males received more coverage (+4.63%) and females received less (–4.63%). However, on both measures, the percentage difference was less than 5%. We next examine whether all women athletes in the team received equal amount of coverage.

Hypothesis 3: Women Athletes Will Receive Newspaper Coverage in Terms
of Articles and Photographs Relative to Their Participation
and Their Success

When we examined which female athletes received a share of the female coverage, the most featured athletes in both newspapers were Kelly Holmes and Paula Radcliffe (see Tables 10, 11 and 12). Between them, they dominated the female coverage in the *Times*, receiving one third of all coverage of women athletes, and gained just over one-fifth in the *Sun* (see Table 9). Holmes, who won two gold medals (in the 800m and 1500m) received more coverage than Radcliffe, who controversially did not finish the marathon. Of interest is that both Holmes and Radcliffe also received a higher percentage of the articles than photographs, which contrasts to the overall trends for female coverage.

Table 10. The two most featured female athletes, by percentage of female Olympic coverage

Athlete	Times articles	Times photos	Total Times	Sun articles	Sun photos	Total Sun
Kelly Holmes	19%	16%	17%	16%	9%	12%
Paula Radcliffe	16%	12%	13%	15%	6%	9%
% of female coverage	35%	28%	30%	28%	15%	21%

Some differences emerged in the other female athletes and sports featured in the two newspapers (see Tables 11 and 12). Thus, among the women who received the next most coverage were two – pentathlete Georgie Harland and archer Alison Williamson – who featured highly only in the *Times*, and two – judoka Kate Howey and heptathlete Denise Lewis – who featured highly only in the *Sun*. In the *Times*, after athletics, the women's sports that received the next most coverage were modern pentathlon, sailing and archery. Pentathlete Georgie Harland received 13.5% of female coverage (3.5% of articles, 10% of photographs) although the percentage for the sport of pentathlon rises to 17.5% if the three images of pentathlete Kate Allenby are also included. Sailing took 10% (3% of articles, 7% of photographs) and archery gained 8% (3% of articles, 5% of photographs). Equestrian featured quite strongly in the images with two different riders – Pippa Funnell and Jeanette Brackenell – receiving 9% of photographic coverage between them. Other female athletes who received 4% of the *Times* coverage included cyclist Nicole Cook and taekwondo exponent Sarah Stevenson (each with 3 photographs). In contrast, the *Sun* focused on judo, heptathlon and sailing. Heptathlon received 14.6% of overall coverage (6.3% articles, 8.3% photographs), followed by sailing (8.3% photographs) and judo (6.3% articles). The *Sun* coverage also included 4 photographs (5.6%) of mixed groups of female athletes.

Both the *Times* and the *Sun* devoted majority of their women's coverage to Kelly Holmes (2 gold medals) and Paula Radcliffe (unsuccessful). Both also featured the trio of women Yngling sailors (1 gold medal). Interestingly, Denise Lewis who did not complete her heptathlon event received the third most coverage in the *Sun*. Lewis was the defending gold medallist in this event from the Sydney Olympics 2000 which might explain some of the attention her performance received. Similarly, Kate Howey received a silver medal in Sydney and, therefore, she might have obtained media focus based on her previous success. Paula Radcliffe was the reigning marathon world record holder and her failure to finish her race most likely resulted in the significant media attention she received.

Table 11. Most featured female athletes[1] in Olympic articles in the Times and the Sun

Athlete, Sport (Olympic achievement)	Article Times (n)	Article Sun (n)	Article Times %	Article Sun %	Total articles (n)
Kelly Holmes, Athletics (gold 800m, gold 1500m)	16	21	19%	16%	37
Paula Radcliffe, Athletics (dnf[2] marathon; world record holder)	13	16	16%	12%	29
Kate Howey, Judo (no medal; 2000 Olympic silver medal)	-	6	-	5%	6
Denise Lewis, Athletics (dnf heptathlon; 2000 Olympic gold medal)	-	6	-	5%	6
Georgie Harland, Athletics (bronze pentathlon)	4	-	5%	-	4
Alison Williamson, Archery (bronze)	3	-	4%	-	3
Sarah Ayton, Sarah Webb & Shirley Robinson, Sailing (gold Yngling)	3	-	4%	-	3

[1] The *Sun* coverage included 7 articles (5.3%) and 4 photographs (2.3%) that featured mixed groups of female athletes
[2] dnf = did not finish

Table 12. Most featured female athletes in Olympic photographs in the Times and the Sun

Athlete Featured	Photo Times (n)	Photo Sun (n)	Photo Times %	Photo Sun %	Total photos (n)
Kelly Holmes	21	15	16%	9%	36
Paula Radcliffe	16	11	12%	6%	27
Georgie Harland	7		5%	-	7
Denise Lewis	-	6	-	4%	6
Sarah Ayton, Sarah Webb & Shirley Robertson	5	6	4%	4%	11

The sports in which women won the most medals were equestrian (mixed three-day event), rowing and athletics. Gold medals came in equestrian, athletics and sailing. Women in four sports – kayak, archery, heptathlon and pentathlon – each gained a bronze medal. Yet, in the *Times* coverage, women's rowing and equestrian each received only two articles in sports that won three medals each. No rowers featured within the list of women athletes receiving the most newspaper coverage, which might reflect the fact they did not win any gold medals. Kayaker Helen Reeves who won a bronze medal received only one small photograph during the Olympic coverage. It should be noted, however, that as all the three-day event medals (including the two individual medals by female riders Leslie Law and Pippa Funnell) were won in the mixed team event, females would have received coverage in the mixed articles covering this event. The three-woman Yngling sailing team received three articles for their gold medal. Sailing was also reported in mixed articles, where females were represented.

Table 13. Sports in which British women won medals at the 2004 Olympic Games

Sport	Gold	Silver	Bronze	Total
Equestrian	1	1*	1	3
Rowing		2	1	3
Athletics	2			2
Sailing	1			1
Badminton		1*		1
Kayak			1	1
Archery			1	1
Heptathlon			1	1
Modern Pentathlon			1	1
Total	4	4	6	14

Note: * indicates medal in a mixed event.

The *Times*, however, devoted a substantial amount of coverage to less visible sports such as women's modern pentathlon and archery. It must be pointed out that British women won bronze medals in these events. Kelly Holmes, the only British athlete to win two gold medals received a significant share of all the women's Olympic coverage. Therefore, the results support hypothesis 3 only partially: While some successful athletes such as Kelly Holmes received substantial media coverage, other women medallists, such the women rowers, were not represented nearly as visibly. Obviously, the media is drawn to report certain women's sports. Therefore, we examined next which women's sports received the most media coverage.

Hypothesis 4: Women Athletes in Sports Emphasising Power and Strength Will Receive Less Coverage than Sports Focusing on Endurance or Aesthetics

Clearly, the most popular women's sport in both newspapers was athletics with the *Times* dedicating 47% and the *Sun* 55% of its female coverage to the various athletics disciplines. As we know, the majority of the athletics coverage was devoted to Kelly Holmes' spectacular achievement of two gold medals and to marathon runner Paula Radcliffe whose unexpected failure was followed closely by the media. Of the *Times* coverage, for example, 16% was dedicated to the marathon. Therefore, women's middle distance and long distance running were featured strongly in the Olympic newspaper coverage.

The next most popular women's sports, modern pentathlon, equestrian, judo, sailing and swimming, received much less coverage compared to athletics (see Table 14). Modern pentathlon and judo are not considered stereotypically feminine sports as they are strength- and power-based sports. Sailing is difficult to classify, but it can be noted that the gold-medal women's sailing trio were all blond, traditionally feminine-looking women. Equestrian in Britain is traditionally considered an upper class women's sport and thus does not deviate greatly from acceptably feminine sports. While British women were very successful in rowing, the sport did not receive very much coverage in either newspaper. It is difficult to classify rowing clearly either as an endurance discipline or a power/strength discipline and, therefore, it is not clear why media coverage of rowing was relatively low. However, in general, a variety of women's sports received media coverage, such as cycling, triathlon, archery, shooting, beach volleyball and taekwondo which all received 4% of coverage in at least one newspaper, and it is not clear which types of sports, excluding women's running, dominated. The sports that can be argued to sexualise women by revealing their bodies to almost a full display to the spectators are athletics, triathlon, beach volleyball, swimming and gymnastics. Indeed, beach volleyball did receive quite an amount of coverage despite having no British competitors while athletics, as noted before, was one of the most popular sports in the British coverage. While women with skimpy uniforms appeared to be visible in the Olympic newspaper coverage, it is difficult confirm hypothesis 4 based on these results.

Table 14. All featured women's Olympic sports in the Times and the Sun by percentage of total female coverage

Sport Featured	The Times %	The Sun %
Athletics, including marathon & heptathlon	47%	55.2%
Modern pentathlon	7%	2.1%
Equestrian	6%	3.1%
Judo	4%	9.5%
Sailing	4%	4.3%
Cycling	4%	3.1%
Triathlon	4%	2.1%
Archery	6%	-
Beach volleyball	4%	-
Shooting	4%	-
Taekwondo	4%	-
Swimming	-	4.3%
Gymnastics	-	3.1%
Rowing	-	2.1%
Other[1]	6%	11.1%

[1] This category includes sports that received less than two articles or mixed groups of athletes representing more than one sport (3.1% of the *Sun* coverage).

Hypothesis 5: Women and Men Athletes Will Be Portrayed Similarly in Photographs

Our final hypothesis focused on the pictorial representation of women athletes. Both the *Times* and the *Sun* represented women and men in a very similar manner in their photographs. Most athletes, both men (80%) and women (80%), were pictured in sport settings and the majority were in sport action (60% for both genders) rather than featured in passive poses outside of sport. The *Sun* had slightly more women than men pictured in non-sport settings but, overall, the image focus in both newspapers was remarkably similar. Interestingly, the *Sun* pictured more women than men in medal ceremonies.

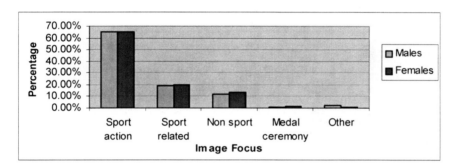

Figure 1. Distribution of image coverage over the range of image focus in the Times.

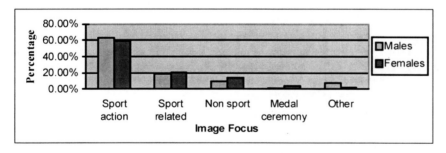

Figure 2. Distribution of image coverage over the range of image focus in the Sun.

The *Times* presented more athletes in colour photographs than the *Sun*. In addition, male athletes were depicted slightly more often in both black and white and colour photographs. In the *Sun*, however, women athletes appeared in more colour photographs (40%) than men (36%), but the black and white photographs of male athletes (51%) were the most numerous type of image.

Therefore, although there were slight differences how women and men were portrayed in photographs in the *Sun* and also slight differences between the two newspapers, hypothesis 5 was confirmed.

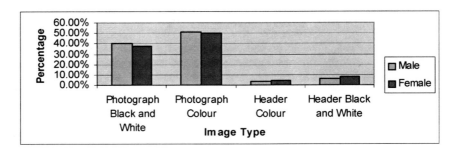

Figure 3. A comparison of image type distribution between males and females in the Times.

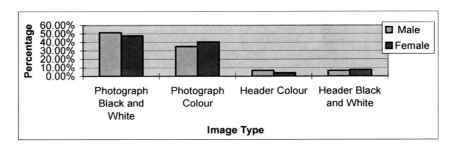

Figure 4. A comparison of image type distribution between males and females in the Sun.

CONCLUSION

Based on our results, women Olympic athletes received less newspaper coverage than men. The average amount of women's Olympic coverage was 25% of the articles and 36% of the photographs for 30.5% coverage overall. In this sense, these results differ from Vincent et al.'s (2002) results where the coverage was found to be equitable. However, similar to Vincent et al.'s study, there were no significant differences between how the tabloid newspaper the *Sun* and the broadsheet the *Times* represented the female athletes. This amount of coverage, however, is much higher than the average received by women athletes in Britain (2–6% of all sport coverage). Similar to Vincent et al.'s findings, the amount of coverage did not necessarily depend on the success of the female Olympians or the type of sport they represented. For example, Paula Radliffe's unsuccessful Olympic campaign received a huge amount of media attention whereas the British women rowers' medal success with 2 silver and 1 bronze was relatively invisible. The extensive media coverage on Radcliffe was possibly due to the great expectation of a gold medal performance. In addition, judoka Kate Howey and heptathlete Denise Lewis won medals in the previous Olympics in Sydney 2000 and were expected to perform well again. In this sense, the expected success of the female athlete seemed to guarantee at least some media exposure regardless of the actual performance in Athens. In addition, women's sports coverage did not follow the clearly defined line of 'acceptable' female sports. However, unlike Vincent et al. (2002), who concluded that there was an equal amount of coverage on female appropriate and inappropriate sports, we would like to draw attention to the difficulty of defining women's sports in such terms. Based on Metheny's (1965) original classification, from which Vincent et al. also derive their categories, only swimming, archery and volleyball of all the Olympic sports represented by the British newspapers could be deemed as acceptable for women. It might be timely to replace this classification with other ways of analysing women's sport.

In conclusion, it is evident that British newspaper coverage of women's sports remains low even during a major event like the Olympic Games. Despite such dismally low reporting, British women appear relatively active: 70% of women participate in some form of sport. In addition, women reported almost the same activity levels as men and favoured almost the same activities such as walking, swimming and cycling. Recreational forms of these activities are not reported in the newspaper sport sections, neither is keep fit or yoga, which are among women's favourite activities. It was obvious, however, that far fewer women (5%) than men (20%) participated in competitive sports. The most popular competitive sport for women, according to the Sport England survey, was netball which is not an Olympic sport and remains almost invisible in the British media. We observe that men's participation in competitive sport is also relatively low (20%), despite ever-increasing media exposure of men's sport. Therefore, we cannot draw a clear link between ample media coverage and participation in sports: the favourite participation sports do not receive any sport media coverage and the most represented sports do not have the most participants.

It is also striking how little research actually exists on the gender representation in British sport media coverage. In this article we only reviewed the quantitative media analyses and, while there is some qualitative research in this area, more examinations of the interface of sport, media and gender from different research perspectives are required.

NOTES

[1] Notably, the researchers excluded walking from the calculations as walking would not receive any sport media coverage.

[2] The data from the *News of the World* is included in the data from the *Sun*.

REFERENCES

Alexander, S. (1994). Newspaper coverage of athletics as a function of gender. *Women Studies International Forum, 17*, 655–662.

Bernstein, A. (2002). Is it time for a victory lap? Changes in the media coverage of women's sport. *International Review for the Sociology of Sport, 27*, 415–426.

Donohoe, H. (2004). Media blackout. *Sports Management, 8*(10), 26–28.

Greene, M. (2004). The land of the rising sun: Are ten million readers wrong? *Christianity and Renewal.* Retrieved November 8, 2004, from http://www.christianityandrenewal.com/ arcapr2003.htm

Harris, J., & Clayton, B. (2002). Femininity, masculinity, physicality and the English tabloid press: The case of Anna Kournikova. *International Review for the Sociology of Sport, 37*(3–4), 397–413.

Mathesen, H., & Flatten, K. (1996). Newspaper representation of women athletes in 1984 and 1994. *Women in Sport and Physical Activity Journal, 5*, 65–83.

Metheny, E. (1965). *Connotations of movement in sport and dance.* Dubuque, IA: WM. C. Brown.

Sport England. (2002). *Participation in sport in England: 2002.* Retrieved May 31, 2005, from http://www.sportengland.org

Vincent, J., Imwold, C., Masemann, V., & Johnson, J. T. (2002). A comparison of selected 'serious' and 'popular' British, Canadian, and United States newspaper coverage of female and male athletes competing in the centennial Olympic Games. *International Review for the Sociology of Sport, 37*, 319–335.

Women's Sports Foundation UK. (2003a). *Britain's best kept secrets.* London: Women's Sports Foundation. Retrieved May 31, 2005, from http://www.wsf.org.uk/media/wsf-research-report-media.pdf

Women's Sports Foundation UK. (2003b). *Women's Sports Foundations slams "appalling" media coverage of female sport in Britain.* Women's Sports Foundation News Release. Retrieved May 31, 2005, from http://www.wsf.org.uk/media/press_releases/20031119.htm

Kelly Redman and Lucy Webb
University of Exeter
United Kingdom

Judy Liao and Pirkko Markula
University of Alberta
Canada

EUROPE: WESTERN AND SOUTHERN EUROPE

JEROEN SCHEERDER, BERT MEULDERS, STEFANIE LAENEN,
KATRIN LINTERS AND BART VANREUSEL

7. BELGIUM

*Gendered Medals, Gendered Media? Coverage of Men and Women in
Belgian Printed Sports Media*

INTRODUCTION

Since the 1980s, Anglo-American scholars have developed a strong research
tradition in analysing the representation of men and women in the sports media.
The academic interest for this field of study can be situated within the considerable
and growing impact of gender and media studies over the last three decades.
Printed as well as audiovisual media are included in these analyses (see e.g.,
Bryant, 1980; Duncan, Messner & Williams, 1991; Duncan, Messner & Willms,
2005; Pedersen, Whisenant & Schneider, 2003; Reid & Soley, 1979; Theberge &
Cronk, 1984). Data on western sports media have shown a consistent pattern of
female under-representation. As a consequence, women's sports are extremely
under-reported. This trend is most visible in daily reporting on sport (Wensing &
Bruce, 2003). Some change, however, can be noticed, especially for major sporting
events, such as the Olympic Games, where a shift towards a more equal gender
representation in the media has been observed during recent years (Bernstein,
2002). These 'global' sport manifestations present an important platform for a more
balanced gender representation.

In Belgium, however, no equivalent tradition of research exists. For example,
the coordinating organisation in Flanders[1] for equal rights between men and
women, called the *Vrouwenraad* ('Women's Council'), published two special
issues of its journal on women and sport (Rowie, 2003) and media and gender
(Rowie, 2004) but no attention was paid to the topic of representation of men and
women in sports media. The same goes for the Dutch academic journal *Tijdschrift
voor Sociologie* with regard to its special issues on media (Mortelmans & Van den
Bulck, 2002) and gender (Spee, 2003). In contrast to the widespread international
findings, research into gender representation in sports media in Belgium is scarce,
and comparative data from a longitudinal perspective are not available. One
Belgian study analysed sport articles in five Flemish newspapers from November
1990 until February 1991. The results showed that only one out of 20 lines was
dedicated to women's sport (Adriaens, 1992). Another study was carried out in
2000 analysing photographs in sport articles from three Flemish newspapers
(Haepers, 2002). The findings from this study indicated that the number of

T. Bruce, J. Hovden and P. Markula (eds.),
Sportswomen at the Olympics: A Global Content Analysis of Newspaper Coverage, 91–102.
© 2010 Sense Publishers. All rights reserved.

photographs of men in the sport pages was much higher than the number of photographs of women. The ratio of male to female portraits was 11.3 to 1. The under-representation of female athletes not only turns up in the printed media like newspapers but also appears in the audiovisual media. In her content analysis of the newscasts of three Belgian television channels in 2001, Vandenbempt (2002) showed that performances of female athletes are generally under-represented in the news on television. Two exceptions, however, are put forward. With regard to track and field, men and women are treated alike whereas in tennis, female athletes dominate the reporting. This media attention has to be understood in light of the performances of three Belgian elite athletes: tennis players Kim Clijsters and Justine Henin (Zontrop, 2003) and sprint athlete Kim Gevaert. Due to their successes on the international sports scene, the representation of Belgian female athletes has increased in the Belgian media.

Since the 1990s, the number of Belgian female participants attending the Olympic Games, world championships and European championships has increased. For example, at the Games from 1948 to 1988, only 13% of the Belgian Olympians were females, whereas this percentage was 37% for the 1992–2006 Olympiads (www.olympic.be). Furthermore, at the Olympic Games from 1948 until 1988,[2] Belgian male athletes won 55 (95%) medals and Belgian female athletes only 3 (5%). At the Olympics from 1992 until 2006 this ratio shifted to 9 medals for male athletes (45%) versus 11 medals for female athletes (55%), indicating that performances of Belgian female athletes have caught up with their male counterparts from an international point of view. The female athletes of the Belgian Olympic delegations, representing about one third (37%) of the 1992–2006 Olympians, provided more than half (55%) of the 1992–2006 Olympic medals. Moreover, Belgian female athletes excelled in sports disciplines with strong international competition, including judo, tennis and track and field. Belgian female judokas, for example, won medals at the 1992, 1996, 2000 and 2004 Olympic Games. At the 2004 Olympic Games, only one medal was won by a Belgian male athlete, while Justine Henin won the gold medal in the single tennis competition and Ilse Heylen won the bronze medal in the under-52kg judo competition. In tennis, Kim Clijsters and Justine Henin, among other elite tennis players, can be considered as precious promoters of the Women's Tennis Association (WTA) competition and its ideology. As such, their contribution to the international marketing of women's tennis can hardly be overestimated. In track and field, Kim Gevaert (sprint) and Tia Hellebaut (high jump) became the first Belgian gold medalists at the European Championships in 35 years. Gevaert is also the first woman to win the European Championships sprint double (100m and 200m) since 1994. Moreover, during the 2007 European Athletics Indoor Championships held in Birmingham, a unique thing happened in the history of Belgian television broadcasting: for the first time the live transmissions of two popular classic male single-day cycle races[3] were interrupted to cover Gevaert's semi-final and final of the 60 metres and Hellebaut's winning high jump. Performances of other Belgian female athletes in gymnastics, track and field and triathlon also contributed to the growing media attention. At the international level, Belgian female athletes are also successfully competing in basketball, gymnastics and triathlon. It is remarkable, however, that Belgian female athletes, like their male counterparts, mainly excel in individual sports disciplines.

Along with the (inter)national breakthrough of Belgian female athletes, an increase in participation rates among women can also be noticed with regard to other forms of sport involvement. In recent years, female participation in sport has truly increased. For instance, between 1969 and 2005, the female adults' level of active leisure-time sports participation in Flanders multiplied by eight whereas their male counterparts' sports participation multiplied by less than four (Scheerder & Pauwels, 2006; Scheerder, Vanreusel, Taks & Renson, 2002). In the same period of time, the active membership of a sports club strongly increased among men (by 5 times) as well as women (by 6 times) (Scheerder & Pauwels, 2006; Scheerder et al., 2002). The involvement of women in the system of club-organised sports in Flanders also increased: between 1974 and 2005, the share of women with a management role within a sports club rose from 10% to 24% (Boeckx & Meuwissen, 2006; De Knop et al., 1991; Van Meerbeek, 1977). Over the last decade, some changes can also be detected regarding the sports audience: the number of female sports spectators slightly increased (31% in 1997 vs. 36% in 2003) while the number of male spectators almost remained the same (54% in 1997 vs. 55% in 2003) (Pauwels & Scheerder, 2004).

Despite the fact that more women are involved in sports than ever before, it is clear that the differences between the two sexes still significantly prevail (Scheerder Vanreusel & Taks, 2005; Taks, Vanreusel, Scheerder & Renson, 2002). In the 2000–2001 Belgian soccer competition, for example, the number of female referees equalled only 2.5% (Vandenbempt, 2002). Moreover, it is obvious that women are more under-represented in decision-making positions (managers, coaches, etc.) than in participating roles (Taks, Renson & Vanreusel, 1999). This under-representation is also manifest in the sports-related job market: since 1985, only 20% of the people employed in the Belgian sports sector are women (Taks, 2000). In 2006, for example, only 19 (4.2%) out of the 457 professional sport journalists in Belgium were female (BBS, 2006). Thus, a gender imbalance still persists in the sports system. No longer, however, can sports be considered as a merely male pastime. Once an exclusive male territory, the field of sport nowadays features growing numbers of female participants, spectators, coaches, managers and other sport professionals. The question is whether this growing representation of women in different sport roles is supported by a more equal representation in the sports media.

METHODS

The present study focused on a content analysis of the coverage of male and female athletes in Belgian print media at the occasion of the Olympic Games in Athens 2004. Content analysis is a research technique for the objective, systematic and quantitative description of the manifest content of communication (Hüttner, Renckstorf & Wester, 1995). In the analysis the focus was on the quantity of coverage in two Belgian daily newspapers, *Het Laatste Nieuws* and *Het Nieuwsblad*.[4] These dailies are the most popular newspapers in Flanders and can be considered representative for Flemish sport reporting. All editions of both newspapers from August 5, 2004 up to September 4, 2004 were examined,[5] covering the 2004 Olympic Games including the week before the opening ceremony of the Games and the week after the closing ceremony. This time frame allows for the inclusion of articles that appeared in the period running up to the Games and the articles which reported back on the Games and its impact afterwards. Articles appearing in the sports section of each paper as well as those appearing on the front page or other pages in the newspapers are coded and analysed. Team standings charts, statistical leaders' lists, box scores or other agate results are included in the study as well.

In total, 49 journal editions, 4,547 sport-related articles and 2,715 illustrations were coded and analysed (Table 1). About one third of the articles (n=1,573) relate to Olympic-only media coverage.

Table 1. Descriptive statistics of the two newspapers

Measurement	Het Laatste Nieuws	Het Nieuwsblad	Total
Number of newspaper editions (n)	25	24	49
Percentage (%)	51.0	49.0	
Number of articles (n)	2,121	2,426	4,547
Percentage (%)	46.6	53.4	
Number of illustrations (n)	1,512	1,203	2,715
Percentage (%)	55.7	44.3	
Space in cm² (total)	447,496.4	405,722.7	853,219.1
Percentage (%)	52.4	47.6	
Space in cm² (illustrations only)	142,360.9	138,244.3	280,605.2
Percentage (%)	50.7	49.3	

The data were collected by two research assistants who examined the two newspapers and recorded the data on the standardised coding sheets described in detail in Chapter 2 (Laenen & Linters, 2006). In order to maximise the inter-coder reliability, the two investigators jointly coded one edition of *Het Laatste Nieuws* (August 23, 2004). Potential inconsistencies in the coding practice were discussed to come to an agreement on a common interpretation of the variables on which further coding activities were based. In the next phase, the two researchers each coded all editions of one newspaper.

As mentioned before, the present study is aligned with the issue of gender representation in Belgian sports media. For this purpose, the following four hypotheses were tested:
1. In sports media coverage, textually as well as photographically, female athletes are under-represented compared to male athletes.

2. In coverage of the Olympics, female athletes receive relatively equal newspaper coverage compared to male athletes.
3. Female and male athletes receive media coverage relative to their proportions on the Olympic team.
4. In non-Olympic coverage, female athletes significantly receive unequal and less newspaper coverage compared to male athletes.

RESULTS

In the two Belgian newspapers analysed during the 2004 Olympic Games, as demonstrated in Table 2, in total coverage, articles about men (72.1%) outnumber the articles about women (13.1%) by far. Because no significant differences could be detected between the two newspapers no separate data for both dailies are included in this contribution. The ratio of men-only stories to women-only stories is 5.5 to 1. If stories about both men and women are counted along with women-only stories, the percentage of stories containing at least some information about women's sports is 26.1.

Table 2. Combined Olympic and non-Olympic coverage in two Belgian newspapers during the 2004 Olympic Games

Measurement	Male	Female	Mixed	Neutral	Total
Number of articles (n)	3,277	594	589	87	4,547
Percentage (%)	72.1	13.1	13.0	1.9	
Number of illustrations (n)	1,801	455	102	357	2,715
Percentage (%)	66.3	16.8	3.8	13.1	
Space in cm² (total)	635,837.4	114,257.6	89,663.9	13,460.2	853,219.1
Percentage (%)	74.5	13.4	10.5	1.6	
Space in cm² (illustrations)	203,489.9	49,153.2	23,827.3	4,134.8	280,605.2
Percentage (%)	72.5	17.5	8.5	1.5	

Similar disparities appear in case of space coverage and the use of portraits: almost 75% of all sports media surface, and about the same percentage of the portrait surface in particular, are devoted exclusively to men's sports. In 66.3% of all of the illustrations analysed, only male athletes are depicted. Women-only illustrations account for 16.8% of all illustrations. With regard to the illustration type, it is remarkable that out of 184 illustrations showing a coach, 179 exclusively depict a male coach. Only one photograph has a sole focus on a female coach. These findings confirm our hypothesis that women are under-represented in the sports media compared to men. Considerably more stories are written about soccer and cycle racing than any other sports discipline (Table 3). These two sports are predominantly practiced by men and boys at all levels of play, in Belgium and abroad. Male soccer stories in themselves account for 51.3% of all the men-only articles and 37.0% of all the stories published. When the number of men's soccer and men's cycle racing articles is subtracted from the total number of men's stories, men-only stories are still more frequent than women-only stories, outnumbering the latter by a margin of 1.9 to 1. On their side, women are mainly represented in articles covering track and field and tennis. In tennis, the number of women-only stories (51.6%) even surpasses the number of men-only stories (24.8%). With regard to the five most popular sports disciplines, only stories written about track and field represent sportsmen and sportswomen at almost the same level. Again, no significant differences can be found between the two newspapers.

Table 3. Combined Olympic and non-Olympic sports specific coverage in two Belgian newspapers during the 2004 Olympic Games

Sports discipline	Male		Female		Mixed		Neutral		Total
	(n=)	%	(n=)	%	(n=)	%	(n=)	%	(n=)
Soccer	1,660	97.8	16	0.9	17	1.0	4	0.2	1,697
Cycle racing	459	89.5	17	3.3	36	7.0	1	0.2	513
Track & field	172	42.7	154	38.2	71	17.6	6	1.5	403
Tennis	77	24.8	160	51.6	73	23.5	0	0.0	310
Basketball	82	78.1	7	6.7	16	15.2	0	0.0	105
Other sports	789	53.9	232	15.8	372	25.4	71	4.8	1,464
Total	3,239	72.1	586	13.0	585	13.0	82	1.8	4,492

Stories focusing only on men's sports account for 56.5% of the front page stories while stories about women-only make up 31.5% (data not included in table). Stories containing information about both male and female athletes are only 6.5% of the front page total, whereas less than 6% can be considered as neutral stories. Nevertheless, almost 6% of all the women-only articles are presented on the front page while this is only the case for less than 2% of all the men-only stories. Thus, regarding all the women-only stories, relatively more attention is given on the front page, compared to the men-only articles. Probably this gender difference with regard to the front page news can be explained by the remarkable performances of Belgian female athletes at the time of the present study.

When Olympic and non-Olympic reporting are considered separately, some serious changes in gender representation appear. Although gender inequalities still prevail, the difference in the quantity of men's and women's stories in the Olympic media coverage diminishes markedly. In the two Belgian newspapers (as indicated in Table 4), 40.0% of all of the Olympic-only stories are devoted to men and 30.4% to women, making the media coverage gap previously demonstrated between men and women much smaller. Measured in square centimetres, the ratio of men-only media coverage to women-only coverage is almost reduced to 1 (39.8% to 35.4%). Thus, in coverage of the Olympics, female athletes receive approximately equal newspaper coverage compared to male athletes. More and more, reports on outstanding sports performances are also published on the front page of newspapers. In this way, it is remarkable that articles focusing only on women's Olympic sports account for 58.8% of all of the front page Olympic sports stories whereas stories about men-only only make up 21.6%, resulting in a ratio of women-only stories versus men-only stories of almost 3 to 1 (data not included). The dominant position of women's Olympic sports coverage on the front page of newspapers also appears on the front page of the sports section (ratio = 1.5 to 1). In the sports section itself, however, again men-only stories outnumber women-only stories (ratio = 1.5 to 1). Once more, no significant differences between the two newspapers are observed.

Table 4. Olympic-only coverage in two Belgian newspapers during the 2004 Olympic Games

Measurement	Male	Female	Mixed	Neutral	Total
Number of articles (n)	629	478	397	69	1,573
Percentage (%)	40.0	30.4	25.2	4.4	
Space in cm²	108,609.9	96,662.2	55,141.9	12,300.3	272,714.3
Percentage (%)	39.8	35.4	20.2	4.5	

In the Olympic-only media coverage, one out of five stories is written about track and field (Table 5). Women-only track and field articles are more frequent (45.1%) than men-only track and field articles (38.7%). Also in the Olympic reporting on judo and tennis, women-only stories prevail. Articles on Olympic swimming and Olympic cycle racing, on the other hand, are predominantly male-oriented.

Table 5. Olympic-only sports specific coverage in two Belgian newspapers during the 2004 Olympic Games

Sports discipline	Male		Female		Mixed		Neutral		Total
	(n=)	%	(n=)	%	(n=)	%	(n=)	%	(n=)
Track & field	110	38.7	128	45.1	42	14.8	4	1.4	284
Tennis	19	14.6	95	73.1	16	12.3	0	0.0	130
Cycle racing	82	70.7	16	13.8	18	15.5	0	0.0	116
Swimming	45	50.6	25	28.1	18	20.2	1	1.1	89
Judo	8	11.3	50	70.4	13	18.3	0	0.0	71
Other sports	365	41.5	164	18.6	288	32.7	63	7.2	880
Total	629	40.1	478	30.4	395	25.2	68	4.3	1,570

A more in-depth analysis was carried out concerning the Olympic media coverage. The data in Table 6 demonstrate that men-only stories account for 56.8% of the Olympic stories, excluding the mixed and neutral articles. The percentage of women-only stories is 43.2. These percentages do not significantly differ from the figures indicating the number of male versus female athletes that belonged to the Belgian 2004 Olympic team. This confirms our hypothesis that female and male athletes receive media coverage relative to their proportions in the Olympic team.

Table 6. Male/female-ratio in the Belgian Olympic team vs. male/female-ratio in the Olympic-only coverage in two Belgian newspapers during the 2004 Olympic Games

Measurement	Male	Female
Number of athletes in the Olympic team (in %)	60.8	39.2
Number of Olympic articles (in %)	56.8	43.2
Number of Olympic medals (in %)	33.3	66.7

Note: at the 2004 Olympics Belgium won three medals, two gained by female athletes and one by a male athlete.

With respect to the non-Olympic coverage in sports media, the dissimilarity between men and women is overwhelming, as demonstrated in Table 7. Almost 90% of all of the published articles are devoted to exclusively men's sports. On the other hand, the number of women-only stories is below 5% in both of the Belgian newspapers and neutral stories are almost non-existent. The same pattern of media coverage also turns up when the surface of articles is taken into account. Based on these findings, our hypothesis that in non-Olympic coverage female athletes significantly receive unequal and lesser newspaper coverage compared to male athletes can be confirmed.

Table 7. Non-Olympic coverage in two Belgian newspapers during the 2004 Olympic Games

Measurement	Male	Female	Mixed	Neutral	Total
Number of articles (n)	2,648	116	192	18	2,974
Percentage (%)	89.0	3.9	6.5	0.6	
Space in cm²	527,227.5	17,595.4	34,522.1	1,159.8	580,504.8
Percentage (%)	90.8	3.0	5.9	0.2	

Given this significant general under-representation of female athletes in the non-Olympic media coverage, it is remarkable that with respect to tennis, women-only stories are more frequent than men-only stories (Table 8). Nevertheless, reporting about all of the other sports disciplines are predominantly male-oriented. If women-only stories are counted along with stories about both men and women, only with regard to track and field does the number of stories containing at least some reference to women's sports approximate the number of men-only stories.

*Table 8. Non-Olympic sports specific coverage in two Belgian newspapers during the
2004 Olympic Games*

Sports discipline	Male		Female		Mixed		Neutral		Total
	(n=)	%	(n=)	%	(n=)	%	(n=)	%	(n=)
Soccer	1,646	98.6	8	0.5	11	0.7	4	0.2	1,669
Cycle racing	378	95.0	1	0.3	18	4.5	1	0.3	398
Tennis	58	32.2	65	36.1	57	31.7	0	0.0	180
Horse riding	155	98.7	0	0.0	1	0.6	1	0.6	157
Track & field	62	50.8	29	23.8	29	23.8	2	1.6	122
Other sports	347	78.5	12	2.7	74	16.7	9	2.0	442
Total	2,646	89.2	115	3.9	190	6.4	17	0.6	2,968

IMPLICATIONS AND CONCLUSION

The aim of this study was to contribute to research on gender representation in
Belgian sports media. Two Belgian newspapers were analysed during a one-month
period of time from the beginning of August 2004 until the beginning of September
2004 covering the Olympic Games of Athens as well as other sport events taking
place during this time frame. Quantitative data were used to identify the coverage
of men and women in sports-related articles and illustrations. It is generally
acknowledged that women are under-represented in sports media coverage. This
pattern of gender stratification is confirmed in the present study. The results indicate
that there is a huge statistical difference in the coverage of men's and women's sports
in Belgian newspapers with regard to the quantity of articles, the size of articles, the
size of illustrations and the type of illustrations. Our results confirm the hypotheses
formulated previously and are consistent with other studies in Belgium documenting
the under-representation of women in the printed as well as audiovisual sports media.

Generally, women are significantly under-represented in the sports media
compared to men. Articles exclusively about men's sports outnumber women-only
articles by far. More than 70% of all of the sports stories are devoted to men's
sports only. A similar pattern can be found with regard to the article size and
illustration size. This under-representation of women's sport is even enlarged in the
non-Olympic reporting, resulting in the most obvious gender disparity. In the non-
Olympic media coverage, the number of women's sports is almost negligible. This
type of sports media coverage can still be identified as part of a strongly male-
oriented institution. One exception, however, can be made. In tennis, women-only
articles are clearly more frequent than men-only articles. It is supposed that this
media attention is strongly related to the performances of the Belgian elite tennis
players Kim Clijsters and Justine Henin (Zontrop, 2003). In Olympic-only reporting,
a more balanced pattern of newspaper coverage of women's sports can be detected.

Although men-only stories are still more frequent than women-only stories, it is clear that in the Olympic-only coverage female athletes receive a more equal media position. As such, it is encouraging that in Olympic reporting the gender differences diminish. The higher media exposure of Olympic women's sport indicates that in covering major sport events such as the Olympics, a more balanced media visibility between the two sexes can be generated. It is assumed that the successful performances of Belgian female athletes at the 2004 Olympics were probably an important factor in the difference in media attention compared to non-Olympic sports. The shift towards lesser gender inequalities is most clear with regard to the media coverage in relation to the male/female proportions within the Olympic team. The results indicate that Belgian female and male athletes receive media attention relative to their proportions on the Olympic team.

Although a shift in the coverage of women's sports and female athletes has occurred, it is clear that a blatant gender imbalance still persists. Sports media perform an important symbolic role in our society (Rowe, 2004). Research into the mechanisms of gender representation in sports media contributes to a global awareness of gender equity. Therefore, further research – in particular over a longer period of time – is needed to better understand the trends in media coverage and also to explore the impact of sports media on gender representations in general.

NOTES

[1] Although a federal government is in place in Belgium, this country is divided into two main regions; i.e., Flanders and Wallonia. These regions have considerable independence in specific matters such as education, cultural affairs and sport.

[2] Summer Games as well as winter Games.

[3] I.e., the *Omloop Het Volk* (March 3, 2007) and *Kuurne-Brussels-Kuurne* (March 4, 2007). In both of these cycle races, the Belgian 2005 World Road Race Champion Tom Boonen was participating.

[4] In 2004, all Flemish media groups of daily newspapers (*Concentra, Corelio* and *De Persgroep*) sold an average of 966,107 copies each day (De Ruyter, Van Puymbroek & Verhoeven, 2006). *Het Laatste Nieuws* and *Het Nieuwsblad/De Gentenaar* had a common market share of 51.6%. *Het Laatste Nieuws* (29.8% in 2004) is the most popular daily newspaper in Flanders; *Het Nieuwsblad/De Gentenaar* (21.8% in 2004) the second most popular one.

[5] With exception for the edition of *Het Nieuwsblad* of September 2, 2004.

REFERENCES

Adriaens, M. (1992). *Het geslacht van sport is vrouwelijk* [The genus of sport is female]. Torhout: Debeer.

BBS. (2006). *MeMento 2006*. Brussels: Belgische Beroepsbond van Sportjournalisten.

Bernstein, A. (2002). Is it time for a victory lap? Changes in the media coverage of women in sport. *International Review for the Sociology of Sport, 37*(3–4), 415–428.

Boex, T., & Meuwissen, E. (2006). *Studie van de genderrepresentatie in bestuurlijke functies in de sport* [Analysis of gender representation in management-related sport roles]. Unpublished master's thesis, Katholieke Universiteit Leuven, Leuven, Belgium.

Bryant, J. (1980). A two year investigation of the female in sport as reported in the paper media. *Arena Review, 4*(2), 32–44.

De Knop, P., Laporte, W., Van Meerbeek, R., & Vanreusel, B. (1991). *Analyse van de georganiseerde sport in Vlaanderen* [Analysis of the club-organised sport in Flanders] (Physical fitness and sport participation among young people in Flanders 2). Brussels: IOS.

De Ruyter, K., Van Puymbroek, J., & Verhoeven, R. (2006). *Media* (De Economie Vandaag 15; supplement to De Standaard; March 31, 2006). Groot-Bijgaarden: VUM.

Duncan, M. C., Messner, M., & Williams, L. (1991). *Coverage of women's sports in four daily newspapers.* Los Angeles, CA: Amateur Athletic Foundation of Los Angeles. Retrieved January 24, 2007, from http://www.aafla.org/9arr/ResearchReports/ResearchReport1.htm

Duncan, M. C., Messner, M. A., & Willms, N. (2005). *Gender in televised sports. News and highlights shows, 1989–2004.* Los Angeles: Amateur Athletic Foundation of Los Angeles. Retrieved January 24, 2007, from http://www.aafla.org/9arr/ResearchReports/tv2004.pdf

Haepers, K. (2002). *Studie van genderrepresentaties in de sport. Een inhoudsanalyse op basis van Vlaamse kranten* [Gender representations in sport. A content analysis of Flemish newspapers]. Unpublished master's thesis, Katholieke Universiteit Leuven, Leuven, Belgium.

Hüttner, H., Renckstorf, K., & Wester, F. (Eds.). (1995). *Onderzoekstypen in de communicatiewetenschap* [Types of research in communication sciences]. Houten: Bohn Stafleu Van Loghum.

Laenen, S., & Linters, K. (2006). *Gender en mediarepresentatie in de sport. Bijdrage tot het onderzoeksproject 'Sportswomen in the 2004 Olympics: An international project on media coverage'* [Gender and media representation in sports]. Unpublished master's thesis, Katholieke Universiteit Leuven, Leuven, Belgium.

Mortelmans, D., & Van den Bulck, H. (Eds.). (2002). *Tijdschrift voor Sociologie* [Special issue on Media], *23*(3–4).

Pauwels, G., & Scheerder, J. (2004). *Tijd voor vrije tijd? Vrijetijdsparticipatie in Vlaanderen: Sport, cultuur, media, sociale participatie en recreatie* (Stativaria 32) [Time for leisure-time? Leisure participation in Flanders]. Brussels: Planning & Statistics Administration.

Pedersen, P. M., Whisenant, W. A., & Schneider, R. G. (2003). Using a content analysis to examine the gendering of sports newspaper personnel and their coverage. *Journal of Sport Management, 17*(4), 376–393.

Reid, L. N., & Soley, L. C. (1979). Sports Illustrated's coverage of women in sports. *Journalism Quarterly, 56*(4), 861–863.

Rowe, D. (2004). *Sport, culture and the media. The unruly trinity.* Berkshire: Open University Press.

Rowie, A. (Ed.). (2003). *Vrouwenraad* [Special issue on Women and Sport], *13*(1).

Rowie, A. (Ed.). (2004). *Vrouwenraad* [Special issue on Media and Gender], *14*(3).

Scheerder, J., & Pauwels, G. (2006). Kortetermijntrends inzake sportparticipatie in Vlaanderen. Een analyse 1999–2005 [Short-term trends in sports participation in Flanders. 1999–2005 analysis]. In P. De Knop, J. Scheerder, & H. Ponnet (Eds.), *Sportbeleid in Vlaanderen. Trends, visies, cases en cijfers* [Sports policy in Flanders. Trends and data] (Vol. 1, pp. 63–74). Brussels: Publicatiefonds Vlaamse Trainersschool.

Scheerder, J., Vanreusel, B., Taks, M., & Renson, R. (2002). Social sports stratification in Flanders 1969–1999. Intergenerational reproduction of social inequalities? *International Review for the Sociology of Sport, 37*(2), 219–245.

Scheerder, J., Vanreusel, B., & Taks, M. (2005). Stratification patterns of active sport involvement among adults. Social change and persistence. *International Review for the Sociology of Sport, 40*(2), 139–162.

Spee, S. (Ed.). (2003). *Tijdschrift voor Sociologie* [Special issue on Gender], *24*(2–3).

Taks, M. (2000). *Sport en tewerkstelling* [Sport and employment] (Sport & Society 8). Brussels: King Baudouin Foundation.

Taks, M., Renson, R., & Vanreusel, B. (1999). Organised sport in transition. Development, structure and trends of sports clubs in Belgium. In K. Heinemann (Ed.), *Sport clubs in various European countries* (Series Club of Cologne 1) (pp. 183–223). Cologne: Hofmann & Schattauer.

Taks, M., Vanreusel, B., Scheerder, J., & Renson, R. (2002). Marketing and sponsoring of women's sport. In D. Sportbund (Ed.), *European women and sport* (Proceedings of the 5th European Women & Sport Conference) (pp. 35–44). Berlin: Deutscher Sportbund-EWS.

Theberge, N., & Cronk, A. (1984). Work routines in newspaper sports departments and the coverage of women's sports. *Sociology of Sport Journal, 3*(3), 195–203.

Vandenbempt, A. (2002). *Sport en geslacht. Vergelijking van de berichtgeving door de media wat betreft mannelijke en vrouwelijke sportprestaties* [Sport and gender. Comparison of the media coverage regarding men's and women's sport performances]. Unpublished master's thesis, Katholieke Universiteit Leuven, Leuven, Belgium.

Van Meerbeek, R. (1977). *Structurele analyse van de sportclubs in Vlaanderen* [Structural analysis of sport clubs in Flanders]. Unpublished master's thesis, Katholieke Universiteit Leuven, Leuven, Belgium.

Wensing, E. H., & Bruce, T. (2003). Bending the rules. Media representations of gender during an international sporting event. *International Review for the Sociology of Sport, 12*(38), 387–396.

Zontrop, V. (2003). *Receptie van de tennisvedetten Kim Clijsters en Justine Henin in de dagbladpers (2001–2002)* [Reception of the tennis stars Kim Clijsters and Justine Henin in daily press (2001–2002)]. Unpublished master's thesis, Katholieke Universiteit Leuven, Leuven, Belgium.

Jeroen Scheerder, Bert Meulders, Stefanie Laenen, Katrin Linters and
Bart Vanreusel
Katholieke Universiteit Leuven
Belgium

GRÉGORY QUIN, ÉLODIE WIPF AND FABIEN OHL

8. FRANCE

Media Coverage of the Athens Olympic Games by the French Press:
The Olympic Games Effect in L'Équipe and Le Monde

Based on the belief that major sporting events have an influence on male and especially on female coverage, this chapter aims to describe an Olympic Games effect in the French national press, focusing on two of its major newspapers, *L'Équipe* and *Le Monde*.

At the Olympic Games in Athens, for the first time in the history of competition, female athletes represented 40% of the athletes taking part. This has not always been the case. At the first Games in 1896 there were no female athletes competing, while only 22 (2.28% of the total athletes) competed at the 1900 Paris Games, and 328 (8.24%) took part in Berlin in 1936. The most significant changes took place during the 1970s where a real feminising of the national Olympic delegations was noticeable. Indeed, by 1976 in Montréal women represented more than 20% of the delegations.

In the 1970s, following the seminal works of Frenchwoman Simone de Beauvoir and the development of 'gender studies' in America, a more favourable context slowly arose for women in France. Feminist movements, fighting for laws and rights focused on equality and better social recognition, changed women's place in society as well as in the workforce. In France, as a result of increasing female enrolments in university courses and growth in university academic appointments for women, research about gender emerged in the 1980s. However, no French universities created women's or gender studies departments, largely due to their distrust of activist movements.

Throughout the 1970s and 1980s French sociology showed little interest in the topic of gender, which was seen only as a variable in analyses focused primarily on education and social class; it was never a major factor in the research. During this period, the discipline of sociology of sport started to institutionalise and a wide range of research appeared, partly thanks to the sociology of the media. Since its beginning, sport has been closely linked to the media, and these links have allowed both to develop in parallel. Sport is very mediated, and presents itself as a spectacle to be consumed by the public.

Since the pioneering studies of Gritti (1975), sociology of sport has been a creative area of studies of the intersections of gender and media. French research on the links between sport and gender increased, including work by Louveau (1986) using

T. Bruce, J. Hovden and P. Markula (eds.),
Sportswomen at the Olympics: A Global Content Analysis of Newspaper Coverage, 103–114.
© 2010 Sense Publishers. All rights reserved.

the sociological framework inspired by Pierre Bourdieu. Later, Menesson (2000) dealt with the theme of women taking part in men's sports, and Chimot (2003) studied the weak female participation within sporting organisations.

In relation to sport, Brocard (2000) and Guilloud and Ohl (2003) analysed the coverage of women athletes in major track and field events. Brocard's (2000) work on the track and field world championship showed that 21.6% of the media coverage was on women and 78.4% on men but if one considers the most popular competitions such as the 100m, the place of women decreased to only 6.9% of the coverage. Brocard (2000) also observed variations depending on the position of the newspaper in the media field. Specialized and intellectual newspapers gave more coverage to women. There were also qualitative differences between the track and field contests. Guilloud and Ohl (2003) observed that competition in conformity with the female aesthetic stereotypes, such as women high jumpers or sprinters, received more coverage, even when some French women were successful in other disciplines such as shot put.

Bourdieu's theories (1996, 1998) have also influenced work that has concentrated on the structuring of the sport media field. These studies emphasized the male domination of sports press at both the national (Marchetti & Dargelos, 2000) and regional (Ohl, 2000) levels. The under-representation of females in the field of sports journalism has also contributed to the maintenance of masculine hegemony and low media coverage of women athletes.

Rowe's (2004) analysis of media coverage distinguishes three interdependent areas for analysis: firstly, the production of texts, followed by their content or messages and, finally, their reception and interpretation by readers. Our purpose in this study was to examine the second area, focusing on the media coverage of women athletes which is expected to be greater in the Olympic Games period. We quantitatively analysed the media content in two of France's national daily newspapers, L'Équipe (a sports-only newspaper) and Le Monde.

Following a brief description of the methods and the content of the samples taken, we detail the effects that the event had on media coverage given to female athletes in the above newspapers, and highlight what we call the Olympic Games effect.

METHOD: PERIOD, SAMPLE, COLLECTION AND CODING

The Olympic Games of Athens lasted 16 days, from August 14 to 29, 2004. In order to investigate the specific ways in which the media covers women athletes during the Olympic Games, the study began one week before the Games and ended one week after the Games, from August 6 to September 5, 2004.

The sample consisted of 28 editions of Le Monde and 31 editions of L'Équipe. The reasons for selecting these newspapers include their large distribution and the particularity of their editorial views. On average during the 2004/2005 year, L'Équipe sold 357,731 copies per day and Le Monde sold 380,592, making them among the most read newspapers in France. During the week before the Olympic Games, the average circulation for L'Équipe was about 450,404 copies per day.

During the first week of the Games, circulation rose to 469,812 per day before dropping to 413,612 per day during the second week of the Games, and returning to 'normal' in the week following the Games, with 353,119 copies per day.

Variances were noted in the sports reporting, based on the position of each newspaper in the media field. Indeed, the way *L'Équipe* or *Le Monde* describe a sporting event differs. It depends as well on the journalist's point of view and on his (or her) relative autonomy in the media field. *L'Équipe* tends to be guided by consumer satisfaction and, thus, conforms its content to social stereotypes, especially gender stereotypes. The majority of its content focuses on motorsport, boxing, rugby and football, and *L'Équipe* remains, above all, a daily newspaper intended for male readers whose media consumption is traditionally sensitive to cars, sport, do-it-yourself, fishing and hunting. *L'Équipe* is a more commercial newspaper, dependent on sports coverage (it is part of the ASO company that also owns the Tour de France and other sporting events). It disputes *Le Monde's* legitimacy and domination of the market with regards to sports journalism (Marchetti & Dargelos, 2000).

On the other hand, the more intellectual *Le Monde* is not dependent on sport and has positioned itself as the referent for general news, meaning that its sports articles differ in terms of their style and representation of events. Rather than defending sport as a 'masculine' terrritory, *Le Monde's* articles and photographs show females and males. Moreover, the newspaper always offers an original point of view about female sport and marginal subjects such as the link between sports and politics. Although no in-depth research on readership has been done, we can assume that *Le Monde* readers are generally similar to readers of *L'Équipe,* from the middle to upper classes. Nevertheless, it seems that *L'Équipe* readers would be identified as having a stronger business orientation and more economic than cultural capital and *Le Monde* readers as having higher cultural capital (Bourdieu, 1979).

We have analysed all the sport articles in the 59 editions. These include the complete contents of *L'Équipe* and the sport section of *Le Monde*, including special issues focusing on the Olympic Games. It should be noted that the number of articles analysed from each newspaper was not the same due to the difference in editorial focus – one being a general source of news and the other reporting only sport news. Thus, overall, less than 20% of the articles came from *Le Monde* and most of these appeared in the special Olympic Games supplements (see Table 1).

Table 1. Distribution of articles by newspaper

Newspapers	Number of articles	% of the sample
L'Équipe	2,474	80.46
Le Monde	93	3.02
Le Monde special issue	508	16.52
Total	3,075	100

Each article was selected using a list of criteria, with 18 variables[1], which were part of the *Global Women in Sports Media Project*. The first screening was conducted on these basic variables. In the second analysis, the chosen articles were reassessed, using more variables, in order to isolate the Olympic Games period. While the main variable was 'gender', other variables such as 'article position' were pertinent to our quantitative interpretation.

THE OLYMPIC GAMES EFFECT

Overall, our results indicated a pattern of media coverage that we called the Olympic Games effect and which we discuss in more detail in the following sections. The first analysis identified an effect from the Olympic Games on the media coverage of both males and females. We were able to show an increase in media coverage of women athletes during the Olympic Games from 14–29 August (see Figure 1), although male athletes continued to receive more coverage than women. Nevertheless, we named this the Olympic Games effect because of the noticeable change in women's media coverage during those 16 days.

Overall, female athletes were represented in 10.2% and 12.6% of the sport articles in the weeks before and after the Olympic Games, and in 19.4% and 21.6% during the two Olympics weeks. However, the majority of the newspaper editions were still dominated by articles reporting on male events. The percentage of articles focusing on the male athletes was 69.7% and 65.6% in the weeks leading up to and following the Olympics, and 55.2% and 56.3% during the Olympics. The percentages of articles in the 'mixed' and 'neutral' categories were relatively stable throughout the study. An increase in the mixed category during the first week of the Olympics (15.3% compared to the 9.9% during the week before the Games) was due to articles dedicated to tennis and fencing which often showed men and women together.

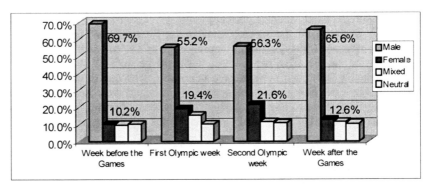

Figure 1. Combined results by week and gender.

DIFFERENCES BETWEEN THE TWO NEWSPAPERS

The Olympic Games effect was not the same in the two newspapers. For example, the Olympic supplements[2] in *Le Monde* put more women athletes forward than *L'Équipe* (see Figures 2 & 3). The same is true for the neutral category which received three times more coverage in *Le Monde* than in *L'Équipe*. On the one hand, the higher percentage of male coverage in the specialised sports newspaper *L'Équipe* (see Figure 2) can be explained by its priority on masculine and popular sports, especially football and rugby, not only outside the Olympic period but also during the Olympic Games, in parallel to Olympics events coverage.

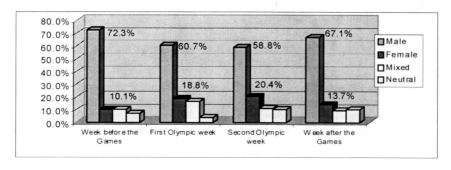

Figure 2. Results by week and gender for L'Équipe.

On the other hand, the non-specialised newspaper *Le Monde*, with its more analytical focus, presented higher percentages from both the mixed and neutral categories, especially during the week before the Olympic Games for neutral stories (descriptions of sporting facilities) and during the week after the Olympic Games for mixed stories (analysis of the Games, of the strengths and weaknesses of the French team, of what should be remembered for history, etc.). The neutral category is more important in *Le Monde's* columns but the decline in media coverage focused only on women in the week after the Games, which is visible in both newspapers, is even more obvious in *Le Monde* than *L'Équipe* (4.5% versus 13.7%).

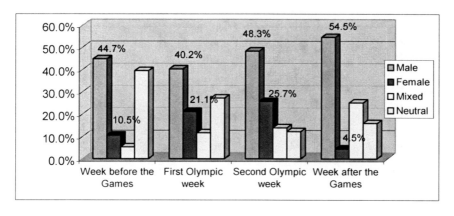

Figure 3. Results by week and gender for Le Monde.

This difference could be explained by the number of articles that assessed the overall outcome of the Games for the entire French delegation in the week after the Games; an editorial focus that raised the mixed category to 25% in *Le Monde* (see Figure 3). In such articles, the journalists discussed both men and women as they underlined the positive and negative results of the French team. However, despite the newspapers' differences in editorial focus, the Olympic Games effect was visible in both newspapers.

NON-OLYMPIC COVERAGE AND TEMPORAL SPECIFICITY OF THE OLYMPIC GAMES EFFECT

The Olympic Games effect is indeed emphasized by data about the specific Olympic coverage: In the Olympic articles, men represent less than the half of the sample and women around a quarter, while mixed (16.05%) and neutral (14.51%) coverage are also both more important in the Olympic sample (see Figure 4).

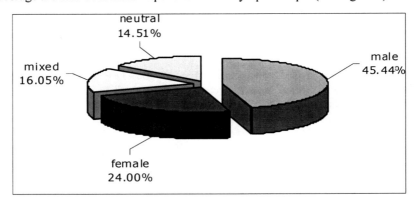

Figure 4. Olympic coverage by gender in both newspapers.

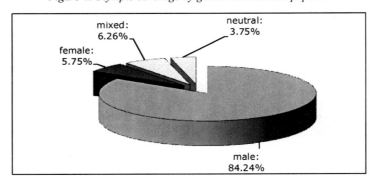

Figure 5. Non-Olympic coverage by gender in both newspapers.

However, the increase in coverage of women does not seem to last very long. Indeed, it is concentrated on the Olympic events. Figure 5 illustrates the narrowness of the Olympic Games effect. Outside the Olympic events (but also including non-Olympic coverage during the two Olympic weeks), women received just over 5% of the sport articles, while men dominated the non-Olympic articles with more than 80%.[3]

THE INFLUENCE OF ARTICLE POSITION AND SIZE

As discussed earlier, gender was not the only pertinent variable in our analysis. The Olympic Games effect visibly affected the media coverage given to female athletes in terms of the change to article size and position and the inclusion of colour photographs, thus drawing the attention of the reader to the articles. Focusing simply on the articles about Olympic events, in terms of article size, both genders were shown similarly: 79.4% of the articles about the male athletes were less than one quarter of a page, as were 76.6% about the women. The female athletes (23.5%) were a little further ahead of their male counterparts (20.6%) with regards to larger articles (see Table 2).

Outside of the Olympic stories, the female sport remained limited to brief articles with little analysis of the event. Of the non-Olympic coverage, 85.7% of the female sports stories were less than one quarter of a page whereas almost 30% (29.5%) of the articles on male sports were given more than one quarter of a page (see Table 3). Undeniably, the Games affected the coverage of women athletes. This finding supports an Olympic Games effect: the major sporting event, the Olympic Games, has generated increased media interest in the results of the female athletes.

Table 2. Gender and Olympic article length

Article length	Brief	Less than a 1/4 page	From 1/4 to 1/2 page	More than a 1/2 page	Total
Male	44.8%	34.6%	11.7%	8.9%	100%
Female	40.2%	36.4%	13.4%	10.1%	100%
Mixed	29.2%	40.9%	11.7%	18.1%	100%
Neutral	14.7%	61.6%	19.6%	4.1%	100%
Overall	36.8%	40.0%	13.3%	10.0%	100%

Table 3. Gender and non-Olympic article length

Article length	Brief	Less than a 1/4 page	From 1/4 to 1/2 page	More than a 1/2 page	Total
Male	25.2%	45.3%	13.3%	16.2%	100%
Female	46.0%	39.7%	6.3%	7.9%	100%
Mixed	40.5%	40.5%	16.2%	2.7%	100%
Neutral	34.1%	34.1%	19.5%	12.2%	100%
Overall	27.7%	44.3%	13.3%	14.7%	100%

PHOTOGRAPHIC COVERAGE

As the size of articles covering female Olympic sports increased, they tended to be accompanied with photographs. Of all the articles on Olympic sport published with a photograph, 30% were of female athletes (see Figure 6). In the non-Olympic articles, photographs of male sports made up 86.9% of the total images published in the newspapers. Photographs of female athletes were rarely seen.

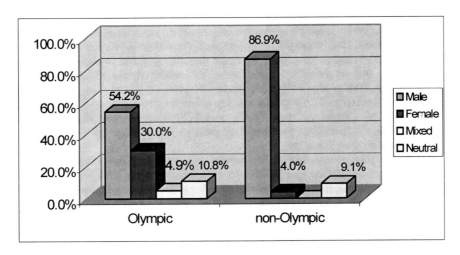

Figure 6. Gender differences in photographs in both newspapers.

DECLINE OF THE OLYMPIC GAMES EFFECT BASED ON SPORTING EVENTS

The characteristics of the Olympic Games effect can still be noticed when analysing gender and specific sporting events. It should be noted that Table 4 is not exhaustive but shows only those Olympic sporting events that have any significant percentages to analyse.

In three sports, females received more coverage than males – artistic gymnastics (51.1%), tennis (53.3%) and the female-only synchronised swimming events (100%). Women received more than 30% of the coverage in events such as handball, swimming, wrestling and athletics. Quite often the increase was attributable to the success of a French female competitor in that sport. In a sport such as wrestling, which is not deemed to be a female sport, the media attention was 33.3% which was more than the coverage given to the female competitors in the athletic events (see Table 4). The wrestling coverage could be linked to the two medals won by French competitors in an event making its debut at the Olympic Games.

Table 4. Gender differences in Olympic coverage by sport

Sport	Male	Female	Mixed	Neutral
Athletics	54.5%	32.7%	10.4%	2.4%
Basketball	77.3%	18.2%	2.3%	2.3%
Boxing	97.9%	0.0%	0.0%	2.1%
Equestrian	30.0%	10.0%	52.0%	8.0%
Fencing	44.6%	28.6%	25.0%	1.8%
Football	71.9%	28.1%	0.0%	0.0%
Gymnastics (Artistic)	40.0%	51.1%	6.7%	2.2%
Handball	55.8%	39.0%	3.9%	1.3%
Judo	41.5%	26.4%	24.5%	7.5%
Sailing	55.9%	14.7%	26.5%	2.9%
Shooting	60.0%	0.0%	40.0%	0.0%
Swimming	42.0%	38.7%	17.3%	2.0%
Synchronised swimming	0.0%	100.0%	0.0%	0.0%
Tennis	22.2%	53.3%	20.0%	4.4%
Wrestling	58.3%	33.3%	4.2%	4.2%

THE FRENCH OLYMPIC GAMES EFFECT

The ratio of male to female athletes representing France favoured the men, with only 114 (36%) of the 315 competitors being female. On the medals table, France was ranked seventh with 33 medals overall (11 gold, 9 silver and 13 bronze). France's female competitors won 16 of the 33 medals (3 gold, 6 silver and 7 bronze), achieving a higher overall success ratio in comparison to the male competitors. However, the female competitors only accounted for 29% of the sports articles on French competitors in both *L'Équipe* and *Le Monde*. Without making too many assumptions about the reasons for the low media coverage, we could suggest that the colour of the medals won by the French female competitors could have been a deciding factor. Indeed, the overall percentage of French female coverage was very close to the percentage of French gold medals (27%) they won.

THE FRENCH TEAM AND THE MEDALS EFFECT

The analysis of the Olympic articles showed that of the media coverage of French competitors, a relatively large portion reported on the female competitors (29%), whilst only 24% of the non-French coverage focused on female competitors from other nations. The increased coverage of female sports was largely due to the success of the French competitors.

Always on the look out for a scoop, the newspapers showed a tendency to favour the male athletes. However, although female competitors who were runners-up or silver medallists were less favourable topics for the newspapers to report, on the plus side, winning medals can lead to articles on events which do not usually get as much attention in the press. For example, French female competitors won two medals in wrestling, creating what we have called a *medals effect*, where their success led to an increase in media coverage of that sport. The medals effect also creates opportunities to challenge clichés about femininity because sports such as wrestling, which are far from traditional feminine sports, provide little opportunity for the media to produce traditional gender discourses.

The medals effect must also be considered in relation to national identity at an event like the Olympic Games. The media builds up the stakes for its readers, resulting in the French public craving the success of the national team. This creates a demand that enables the media to report on all events regardless of which gender is competing. As a result, journalistic discourse tends to erase gender with its insistence on national success. Such media build up is very effective when there is historical conflict and passion between the two competing countries, such as between England and France, or Australia and New Zealand.

CONCLUSION

A year after the Athens Olympics, on October 15, 2005, *L'Equipe* introduced a new supplement to its usual Saturday issue: *L'Equipe* magazine was now to be accompanied by *L'Equipe Féminine*, a sport supplement dedicated to women. In the editorial of the first issue, the editor in chief talked about *L'Equipe* as a newspaper focused on sport competition that is "*ni masculine, ni féminine*" [neither masculine nor feminine]. The newspaper would therefore claim to be representing gender in a similar way to *Le Monde* and other general newspapers. The fact that newspapers claim to be more interested in the question of gender is a sign of their concern about creating an evolution in the media treatment of sport. However, claiming is one thing, being equal is another. According to our results, equality is far from being delivered, either by *L'Equipe* or *Le Monde*.

The aim of this study was to assess whether a major sporting event, such as Athens 2004, would impact on the media coverage of female sports. The real effect of the Olympic Games is that women are shown more during Olympic events than outside those events. However, we suggest their higher representation during the Games is only a contextual effect. Indeed, because the Olympic Games offer similar numbers of sports for men and women, and women represent 40% of the national delegations, it is possible to represent women "*sans effort*" [without effort] because they are in the stadiums at the same time as men. This contextual effect can be verified when the percentage of female sports outside the Olympic period falls back under the 10% threshold in the two newspapers, whereas it had reached almost 30% during the Games coverage.

During the Olympics, women are also shown in less traditional sports, such as wrestling in this case. Also, we want to emphasize a medals effect which combines with a national effect. Indeed, journalists reserved much space for 'their' national champions, and these factors seem to be more important for women athletes, who need to win gold medals to appear on the first page.

Some additional qualitative analysis of the sample suggests that the great majority of articles do not represent a misogynistic view of gender. This trend indicates, as suggested in the 2005 *L'Equipe* editorial, some reflexivity and evolution in the media treatment of women. Nevertheless, if we consider the quantitative results, it can be seen that women are still under-represented. Further, even though women receive more media coverage during big sporting events like the Olympic Games, they are still shown in traditional ways that, for example, focus on the importance of motherhood or use males as the reference.

ACKNOWLEDGMENTS

We would like to thank Pierre-Edouard Chalet who played an important role in collecting the data and Toni Bruce for her editing role and her help for the English version of the paper. Nevertheless, the contents and analysis are our responsibility.

NOTES

[1] The variables included: Newspaper, Day, Sport, Olympic or not, Gender, Individual/team sport, Nationality, Article position, Article focus, Article type, Article size, Image size, Individual/team sport in image, Gender in image, Nationality in image, Image focus, Type of image, and Colour or black & white.

[2] On the whole, this was also true for *Le Monde's* classic edition.

[3] However, while this high percentage of male articles was the main trend in the non-Olympic coverage, the inclusion of *L'Équipe*, with its main focus on football, in our sample may have accentuated the trend. We suggest that a sample with more general newspapers could decrease the proportion of male coverage but would not change the overall trend. *Le Monde*, for example, also focused mainly on football outside the Olympic period.

REFERENCES

Bourdieu, P. (1979). *La distinction. Critique sociale du jugement*. Paris: Minuit.

Bourdieu, P. (1996). *Sur la télévision* [On television]. Paris: Raisons d'agir.

Bourdieu, P. (1998). *La domination masculine* [Masculine domination]. Paris: Seuil.

Brocard, C. (2000). Sport et différenciation sexuelle: Les performances sportives dans les commentaires journalistiques. *Regards sociologiques, 20*, 127–142.

Chimot, C. (2003). *La place des femmes dans les organisations sportives*. Paper presented at the *Colloque Femmes et Sport* (Mars 2003 à Grenoble) [Symposium on Women and Sport (March 2003 in Grenoble, France)]. Paris, CNOSF.

Gritti, J. (1975). *Sport à la une*. Paris: Armand Colin.

Guilloud, C., & Ohl, F. (2003, Juillet/Septembre). Femmes: Les déesses du stade? *Lunes, 24*, 70–77.

Louveau, C. (1986). *Talons aiguilles et crampons alu... Les femmes dans les sports de tradition masculine*. Paris: INSEP.

Louveau, C. (2000, Octobre). Au-delà des Jeux Olympiques de Sydney: Femmes sportives, corps désirables. *Le Monde diplomatique*. Retrieved from April 24, 2008, from http://www.monde-diplomatique. fr/2000/10/LOUVEAU/14322

Marchetti, D., & Dargelos, B. (2000). Les professionnels' de l'information sportive entre exigences professionnelles et contraintes économiques. *Regards sociologiques, 20*, 67–87.

Mennensson, C. (2000). 'Hard' women and 'soft' women: The social construction of identities among female boxers. *International Review for the Sociology of Sport, 35*(1), 21–35.

Ohl, F. (2000). Le journalisme sportif dans les quotidiens régionaux: Une production sous influence. *Regards sociologiques, 20*, 109–128.

Rowe, D. (2004). *Sport, culture and the media: The unruly trinity* (2nd ed.). Maidenhead: Open University Press.

Grégory Quin and Fabien Ohl
Faculté des SSP-ISSEP
University of Lausanne
Switzerland

Élodie Wipf
University of Lausanne
Switzerland, and
University Marc Bloch
Strasbourg, France

9. GERMANY

The 2004 Olympic Games in German Newspapers – Gender Equitable Coverage?

INTRODUCTION

As a part of the *Global Women in Sports Media Project*, the focus of this chapter is on media coverage of the Olympic Games 2004 in two German newspapers. The article is structured into three parts. First we present some general data about gender and sport in Germany focusing on the inclusion of men and women into physical activities and sport. The second part is devoted to a summary of the existing media studies of sport in Germany that deal with gendered coverage and reporting. Part three comprises the results of our research on the media coverage of the 2004 Olympic Games related to gender in the sports media.

GENDERED INCLUSION INTO PHYSICAL ACTIVITIES AND SPORT IN GERMANY

Historical Development

The development of the German sport system started with the formation of physical education and 'gymnastics' at the end of the 18th and the beginning of the 19th centuries. The patriotic goals of the gymnastic movement (Turnbewegung) and Friedrich Ludwig Jahn's emphasis on military preparedness predetermined the exclusion of girls and women. Physical education for girls was only gradually introduced into schools at the end of the 19th century and far later than the implementation of physical education for boys. In the early years of the 20th century, modern sport entered the German scene and particularly attracted the upper classes. Besides differences in the concepts of physical activities, gymnastics and sport, their central ideas were fitness and performance. This reference point became the general orientation of action of people involved in sport and of their central organisations, the clubs. Body-centered performance can be seen as the driving force to codify sporting activities, to establish rules of competition, to create associations, and to integrate these into national federations. At the end of the 19th and beginning of the 20th century, gymnastics and sports began to take the clear shape of a social system with its differentiated social and material structures (Hartmann-Tews, 1996, p. 60f).

T. Bruce, J. Hovden and P. Markula (eds.),
Sportswomen at the Olympics: A Global Content Analysis of Newspaper Coverage, 115–126.
© 2010 Sense Publishers. All rights reserved.

Profile of Inclusion in the 20th and 21st Centuries

In the late 20th century sport and physical activity have become increasingly more important. Growing prosperity and leisure time, and a growing concern about health and physical fitness led to a rising demand which in turn was accompanied and further pushed by a growing supply of infrastructure and organisations.

This process of increasing inclusion of people into sport is well reflected in general survey data and in membership statistics of sports clubs (Hartmann-Tews, 1996; Rulofs, Combrink & Borchers, 2002). This data allows the following conclusions to be drawn regarding gendered participation in sport. The traditional gender gap has been constantly decreasing over recent years and nowadays 67% of men and 60% of women participate in physical activities and sport on a regular basis (at least once a month), with men tending to participate significantly more often than women only in the younger age groups. Most active sportsmen and sportswomen (57% overall) perform their main sport in a non-organised form (i.e., outside of any kind of institution), about a quarter participate in sports clubs and about 12% in a commercial institution (Hartmann-Tews & Luetkens, 2003).

Inclusion into sports clubs has always been more gendered than participation in physical activities in general. The profile of sports clubs in the 1950s was that of a male and youth dominated field of competitive sports activities with a proportion of female membership of only 10%, whereas today there is a female membership of close to 40%. The traditional profile of sports clubs has changed over the past 50 years to a less youth, less male and less competitively oriented organisation (Hartmann-Tews, 1996).

The constantly growing proportion of girls and women in sport and physical activities is reflected in elite sport as well. In the 1992 Olympics in Barcelona, 35% of the German team were female athletes (168), in the 1996 Atlanta Games the proportion had grown to 41% (194), and in the 2000 Sydney Games as well as in the 2004 Athens Games, female athletes made up 44% of the German team (187 and 197 respectively) (NOK, 2005). At the same time, the success rate of German female athletes at the Olympic Games has been slightly higher than the success rate of their male colleagues. In Athens, the proportion between female and male participants in the German team was 44% to 56% and the relation of female and male medallists was 47% to 53%.

However, the German sports system is far from being a 'gender neutral' domain. This is obvious when taking a closer look at the situation of women in leadership and decision-making positions in the voluntary sport sector. Despite the substantial increase in female sport membership, there is no equivalent inclusion of women into decision-making positions and coaching. On average, only 20% of honorary decision-making positions are held by women. The proportion of women is highest within the Executive Board and Standing Committees of the national umbrella organisation (*Deutscher Olympischer Sportbund* [DOSB]) and lowest on the Executive Boards of the governing bodies of sports on the regional level (24% vs. 10%) (Hartmann-Tews & Combrink, 2005).

STUDIES ON GENDER, MEDIA AND SPORT IN GERMANY

Media studies have a long tradition within gender studies in countries like the USA, Canada and Britain. In contrast, there is no equivalent tradition in Germany. For a long time the only central reference study was a study of sport coverage in 1979 (Klein & Pfister, 1985; Klein, 1988, 1986). This study included four daily newspapers over a period of 12 months and reported findings that were similar to the findings of the Anglo-American research. In the late 1990s, more and more doubts were put forward about the relevance of this data for the present. It was argued that growing gender equity in society and sport, and changes in the interrelation between media and sport, have had a positive impact on the coverage of female athletes in the media (Anders & Braun-Laufer, 1999). Against the backgound of this discussion, we designed several studies to fill this gap in research and knowledge (Hartmann-Tews & Rulofs, 2005, 2003; Rulofs, 2003). One of them was a follow-up and quasi-longitudinal study, in order to gain comparative data about the coverage in 1979 and 1999/2000. Other studies focused on single sporting events (e.g., world championships in track and field, Olympic Games), including print media as well as television. The research design was complemented by studies of internet presentation of athletes, and interviews with managers and journalists in order to cover the whole process of media communication in sport (Rulofs & Hartmann-Tews, 2006).

The content analysis in 1979 (Klein, 1986) covered articles and photographs in three national daily newspapers (*Frankfurter Rundschau, Die Welt, Bild Zeitung*) and one regional daily newspaper (*Westdeutsche Allgemeine Zeitung*), and included all publishing days in the course of 1979. Our follow-up study was based on a random sample of three artifical weeks[1] between June 1999 and May 2000 of the same three national newspapers plus an additional national newspaper (*Frankfurter Allgemeine Zeitung*) which substituted for the regional paper. These four national newspapers are among the biggest in Germany and represent different political programmes.

Various international studies on the representation of women athletes in the media demonstrate two general themes. The first relates to the amount of coverage, revealing the under-representation of women athletes in the sports media. The second relates to the type of coverage, indicating various patterns of trivialization, marginalization and sexualization of women athletes. These topics structure the following more detailed presentation of the results of the two studies of German newspapers in 1979 and 1999/2000.

1. Annihilation – The Under-representation of Female Athletes

The most remarkable result of the original research in 1979 was the extreme under-representation of female athletes in the newspapers – a phenomenon that has not changed much over the past 20 years. In 1979, only 6% of the total space for sports in the newspapers (measured in cm² of each article) was devoted to women's sports; 20 years later this coverage had increased to only 10%. This finding confirms the consistent under-reporting of female athletes throughout all mass media in

Anglo-American research (e.g., Bernstein & Blain, 2002; Bishop, 2003; Flatten & Mathesen, 1997; Harris & Clayton, 2002; Knoppers & Elling, 2004; Koivula, 1999; Messner, Duncan & Cooky, 2003; Toohey, 1997).

However, quite different results were documented in an analysis of the 1999 World Championships in track and field: female athletes received 43% of the coverage in German newspapers (Rulofs, 2003). This almost equitable representation of women in the coverage of a single sporting event corresponds with the findings of other studies focusing on the media representation of a single event (e.g., Billings & Eastman, 2002; Capranica & Aversa, 2002; Eastman & Billings, 1999; Knoppers & Elling, 2004; Pemberton, Shields, Gilbert, Shen & Said, 2004; Tuggle & Owen, 1999; Vincent, 2004; Vincent, Imwold, Masemann & Johnson, 2002).

2. De-athletisation of Female Athletes

Results of the 1979 research indicated some qualitative differences in the coverage of female and male athletes and their sporting events. In 1979, the articles about women athletes included fewer references to sport and performances than the coverage of male athletes but, at the same time, more references to events and facts beyond their respective sporting lives. This finding was not confirmed in the follow-up research, as reporting about male and female athletes was similarly characterised by the description of their performances which were referred to in 88% of the articles about women and 85% of the articles about men.

However, out of the seven topics most often covered, three had gendered significance: non-sport-topics dealing with the private life of the athletes were more often referred to in articles about female athletes (29% vs. 20%), whereas information about medical aspects and commercialisation were more often referred to in the coverage of male athletes.[2]

3. Gender Stereotypes

The 1979 coverage presented traditional gender stereotyping, including the fact that media coverage emphasized the representation of women and men in so-called 'gender-appropriate' sports. This finding holds partly true 20 years later but interesting changes have taken place as well.

Looking at the findings of 1979 it is remarkable that the most often covered sports in the articles about female athletes were individual sports – ranking from 16% for track and field to 9% each for gymnastics and figure skating, both sports with a strong focus on the aesthetics of the performance. By far the most often covered sport in the articles about male athletes was soccer – 50% of the whole coverage of men dealt with soccer. The other sports were only marginal in comparison to soccer and, thus, the media representation of male athletes was very one-sided (Hartmann-Tews & Rulofs, 2005).

Our findings in the follow-up study 20 years later suggest, firstly, that the over-representation of women in individual sports has decreased. With a share of 33%, tennis – as an individual sport – leads the rankings but team sports such as soccer and handball have risen into the top five of most covered women's sports. Secondly, our findings show that newspaper coverage of male athletes sticks in a more rigid way to gender-appropriate sports by still strongly over-reporting soccer (32%) followed by tennis, track and field, boxing and Formula One.

In 1979, gender-stereotyping was also found with respect to the number of references to physical appearance, which occurred significantly more often in the coverage of female than of male athletes. Comments on physical appearance occurred in 22% of the articles about women and in 10% of the articles about men (Klein, 1986). This finding could only partly be confirmed 20 years later. Descriptions of the outward appearance occurred in 15% of the articles about women and in 9% of the articles about men, yet the difference did not prove to be significant. However, there was a difference in the intensity of the comments and descriptions; that is, the number of references within the articles about the body, its appearance and its shape. When the appearance of a female athlete was addressed it was done in a more elaborate way than reporting about male athletes, which means that more comments per article were made about the appearance of female athletes. Furthermore, the way the athletes' appearances were described was still gender stereotyped. General descriptors like beautiful, good-looking or pretty were used for women, whereas the comments about men's appearance referred to aspects of the men's bodies emphasising physical strength or height.

The results of our follow-up study indicated some changes in the coverage but the findings do not allow us to sum them up as equitable coverage – neither quantitative nor qualitative (Hartmann-Tews & Rulofs, 2005). It seems, however, that the construction of masculinity and femininity has become more subtle and less overt than in the 1980s.

GENDERED SPORTS COVERAGE IN THE 2004 OLYMPIC GAMES?

The newspaper articles and photographs analysed in this study were taken from two daily national newspapers in Germany, the *Frankfurter Allgemeine Zeitung (FAZ)*, as a representative of the daily broadsheet press, and the *Bild Zeitung* (BILD), the most important tabloid in Germany.

The *Bild Zeitung* has the highest circulation of daily national newspapers in Germany, selling 3.6 million papers a day. The newspaper has approximately 11.8 million readers across the age categories and across social strata, and 61% of the readership are men. Opinions about the BILD are diverse: advocates highlight the brevity and comprehensibility of the articles, the quality of entertainment and the large amount of sport coverage. Critics highlight the unbalanced reporting and register the high number of violations with respect to the code of ethics of the German Media Council.

The circulation of the *Frankfurter Allgemeine Zeitung* is 400,000 papers a day and the highest among the broadsheet newspapers in Germany. It has a high reputation in regard to the economy and sport sections. The editorial board of the sport section has received numerous awards for the best German editorial staff in sport (including the years 2004 and 2005). More than half of the readership are highly educated and 62% of them are men.

The period spanned by the 2004 sample is from August 7 to September 1 (26 days), including six days of pre-reporting and three days of post-reporting about the Olympic Games. The sample consists of all articles and photographs appearing on the front page and in the entire sports section dealing with the Olympic Games. All articles and photographs focusing on non-Olympic topics were excluded. For the following analysis we selected all articles and photographs that focused on athletes and teams, and excluded all articles and photographs not focusing on the central agents (i.e., reports on organisation, on the audience and on the infrastructure).[3]

Our initial data gathering produced 1,093 articles and 765 photographs. However, these numbers included 212 articles and 13 photographs that focused on female and male athletes together.[4] In our analysis we split these articles into two units in those cases where we could identify distinct paragraphs on male and female athletes, in order to analyse them separately. Photographs focusing on male and female athletes were split into two units as well, thus adding a further 152 text units and 13 photograph units to the overall total. Therefore, with this focus on narratives and pictures about the central agents of the Olympic Games, the number of text units analysed is 1,245 (532 BILD, 713 FAZ) and the number of photograph units is 778 (548 BILD, 230 FAZ).[5] These figures demonstrate the different profile of the two newspapers. The proportion of photograph units to text units is almost 1:1 in the BILD and 1:3 in the *FAZ*. Information about the Olympic Games in the tabloid newspaper, the *Bild Zeitung,* is equally based on visual communication and on written communication, whereas the more traditional broadsheet newspaper, *Frankfurter Allgemeine Zeitung,* is predominantly based on written communication.

The content analysis delivers data on the core variables of the *Global Women in Sports Media Project* and some additional variables that add to our previous studies (Hartman-Tews & Rulofs, 2003, 2005; Rulofs, 2003) and promises to produce answers to questions that are still unanswered for the German case.

AMOUNT OF COVERAGE

The results show fairly equitable coverage of female and male athletes regarding the number of text units and photograph units (see Table 1).[6] Further, the question of whether newspaper coverage was gender equitable or not can be answered with diverse reference points.

The first one is the objective fact of number of text units and photograph units. Female athletes were reported on in fewer text units (44% vs. 56%) and in fewer photograph units (45% vs. 55%) than their male colleagues. The two newspapers differ insofar as the unequitable visual communication was even more obvious in the *Frankfurter Allgemeine Zeitung* than it is in the *Bild Zeitung*.

The text units and photograph units varied as to their size. In the *Frankfurter Allgemeine Zeitung* both text units and photograph units were bigger in size than in the *Bild Zeitung*. The results also show that text units about female athletes were a little smaller than about male athletes (98cm² vs. 106 cm²) and that photograph units about female athletes were a little larger than about their male peers (148 cm² vs 142 cm²).

Table 1. Total number and percentage of German newspaper coverage by gender category in relation to 2004 Olympic Games participants

		Athletes		
		Male	Female	Total
		%	%	N
	Games participation – All athletes	59.3	40.7	10,910
	German athletes	56.0	44.0	384
BILD	Text units	55.5	44.5	532
BILD	Photograph units	53.1	46.9	548
FAZ	Text units	56.4	43.6	713
FAZ	Photograph units	59.6	40.4	230
Total	Text units	56.0	44.0	1,245
Total	Photograph units	55.0	45.0	778

The second reference point is the gender representation in the Olympic team: There were 10,910 participants with a relation of 40.7% female and 59.3% male athletes. Comparing the amount of coverage to the representation of female and male athletes in the Olympic team revealed that the proportion of coverage was in favour of female athletes (see Table 1). Both newspapers provided coverage of the athletes that slightly over-represented female athletes.

The third reference point is the gender representation in the German Olympic Team, which consisted of 56% male and 44% female athletes. With regard to this gender relation, the results show again that the media coverage of male and female athletes at the 2004 Olympic Games was almost equitable in the two newspapers (see Table 1).

The decision about 'newsworthiness' in the editorial process of the sports section is centrally based on the criteria of success, and a variety of studies have documented that reporting on sports focuses on successes, winners and record-holders (e.g., Hartmann-Tews & Rulofs 2003). At the Olympic Games in Athens 10,910 participants were competing for 929 medals in individual and team competitions; thus, the proportion of medallists in relation to participants was about 10%. The reporting on these athletes in text units was more than twice as much: 23.4% of all text units featuring a main agent[7] are concerned with medal winners.

Table 2 shows the male and female share of the medallists and the gender proportions in the coverage of medallist (both for the overall medallists and the German medallists). The figures reveal a modest over-representation of female medallists: Women won 43.0% of the Olympic medals and 49.1% of all articles about medallists depict female medallists. For the German team, 46.9% of the

German medals were won by women whereas the women's share of the total number of articles about German medallists is 54.5%. Overall, the findings indicate that female winners were slightly over-represented in the Olympic coverage of the German newspapers.

Table 2. Total number and percentage of German newspaper coverage by gender category in relation to 2004 Olympic Games medallists

	Athletes					
	Male		*Female*		*Total*	
	N	*%*	*N*	*%*	*N*	*%*
All medallists	546	56.9	413	43.0	929[1]	100
German medallists	26	53.1	23	46.9	48[2]	100
Text units about medallists[3]	148	50.9	143	49.1	291	100
Text units about German medallists	91	45.5	109	54.5	200	100

[1] A total of 929 medals were awarded. Of this, 30 medals were conferred upon team and mixed competitions (e.g., equestrian, sailing open class, badminton mixed). In this table these medals are allocated to male <u>and</u> female athletes in the gender-differentiated columns but counted only once in the total column.

[2] A total of 48 medals were awarded to German athletes. Of this, 1 medal was conferred upon a mixed competition (equestrian). In this table this medal is allocated to male <u>and</u> female athletes in the gender differentiated columns, but counted once only in the total of all medals.

[3] Only text units with a main agent were considered.

CONTENT OF COVERAGE

An additional focus of our research was the content of the written and visual communication conveyed in the newspaper texts and photographs. Analysis of the text units identified various thematical clusters (see Figure 1).

As expected, there was one dominant topic: 73.7% of all text units reported on the performances, successes or failures of the athletes. Beside this central topic of performances, all other topics seemed to be far less relevant. The second most often reported topic was ethics (14.5%; e.g., information on doping, unfairness) followed by the psychological constitution of the athletes (9.3%; e.g., information on the emotions of the athletes), non-sport topics (8.3%; e.g., information on the athlete's private life) and sport-related background information (7.7%; e.g., information on the athlete's training methods). There were only small differences with regard to gender category. Only the non-sport topics showed slightly biased coverage in favour of female athletes.

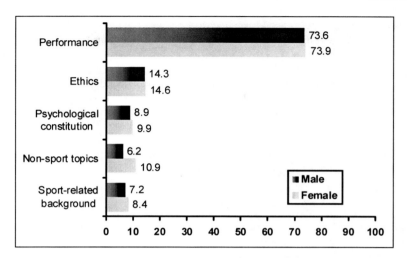

Figure 1. The five most covered topics in the German newspaper coverage of the 2004 Olympic Games by percentage. (Note that multiple topics are possible.) (N=1,245).

Differences in coverage between the two newspapers were more obvious than differences concerning the gender category. On the one hand, the *Frankfurter Allgemeine Zeitung* reported more on performances (80% vs. 66%), on ethics (18% vs. 9%) and on the psychological state of the athletes (14% vs. 3%) than the *Bild Zeitung*. On the other hand, the *Bild Zeitung* reported more on topics not related to sports (14% vs. 4%) and on sport-related background information about the athletes (11% vs. 7%).

The analysis of the 778 photograph units (45% female and 55% male athletes) was based on three categories of photographs: a) in action or competing; b) in a sporting context but not in action; and c) in a non-sport setting. Overall, most of the photograph units showed the athletes in a sporting context but not in action (51.7%); for example, sitting in the stadium or posing at the celebration ceremony. One third of the photograph units depicted the athletes in action and only 15.3% showed situations with the athletes in a non-sport setting (e.g., the athlete at home with family) (see Table 3).

Table 3. Content of photograph units in German newspaper coverage of the 2004 Olympic Games

Content	Athletes					
	Male N=(428)		Female N=(350)		Total N=(778)	
	N	%	N	%	N	%
Sporting context/not in action	216	50.5	186	53.1	402	51.7
In action/in competition	158	36.9	99	28.3	257	33.0
Non-sport setting	54	12.6	65	18.6	119	15.3

There were, however, gender-related differences in the visual communication of the athletes. Male athletes were more often depicted in action than female athletes (36.9% vs. 28.3%) who were more often depicted in non-sport settings than their male peers (18.6% vs. 12.6%).

Differences between the two newspapers indicate that this general finding was almost exclusively caused by a strong gender bias in the visual communication of the *Bild Zeitung*.[8] For example, 39.5% of all photograph units about male athletes in the *Bild Zeitung* depicted them in action and competition while this was the case for only 27.6% of all photograph units about female athletes. In comparison to this gender bias in the coverage of the BILD, there was only a marginal difference and negligible bias in the *Frankfurter Allgemeine Zeitung*.

DISCUSSION

Confirming Anglo-American findings about the coverage of a single event and especially the Olympic Games, our study shows that male and female athletes were almost equitably represented in the coverage of the 2004 Olympic Games. With a share of coverage of 44%, women were slightly over-represented in relation to their participation and the medals they won. In addition, the most common topics of the articles about the Olympic Games showed only marginal gender differences and confirmed the tendency towards more equitable coverage during high profile events and especially the Olympic Games. These findings about media representation of the Olympic Games form a strong contrast to our investigations of day-to-day mediasports, where the women's share of the total coverage was only 10%.

The almost equitable representation of women and men in the media depiction of the Olympic Games might be interpreted as a reflection of the ongoing process of acceptance of women's sport in Germany. At the same time it might be an effect of the rationale of the Olympic Games. National teams are competing with and against each other and competitions for male and female athletes are held at the same time. As performances, medallists and records are the most newsworthy incidences during the Games, it seems to be rational – and unavoidable – that journalists cover male and female events in the same manner, thus producing an almost equitable representation of women and men. Outside mega-events in day-to-day reporting, other aspects, especially the predominance of soccer, seem to be responsible for the strong under-representation of female athletes and the highlighting of men's sport in German newspapers.

NOTES

[1] Each day of the week is represented three times in our sample and, at the same time, these days are spread over 12 months from June 1999 to May 2000.

[2] "Medical aspects" were depicted in 21% of articles about men and 14% of the articles about women; "commercialisation" occurred in 21% of the articles about men and 12% of the articles about women.

[3] In other chapters in the book, these articles are categorised as neutral coverage.

[4] In other chapters in the book, these articles are separately categorised as mixed coverage.

[5]   The differentiation of so-called 'mixed' articles into male and female text units is based on other German studies (Klein, 1986; Rulofs, 2003). The term 'text unit' refers to 'article' but acknowledges that some articles have a focus on male and female competitors and thus have been further divided into both 'male' and 'female' text units. This method helps us to compare our results with previous German findings.

[6]   We do not provide statistical tests as our data comprises all articles and thus is a complete data collection of the coverage.

[7]   A main agent was defined as more than 75% of the text unit dealing with this agent.

[8]   The number of photographs in the sample is dominated by the 548 (70.4% of the total photograph units) in the BILD versus the 230 (29.6% of total) in the FAZ.

REFERENCES

Anders, G., & Braun-Laufer, E. (1999). Sportlerinnen in den Medien – Möglichkeiten und Grenzen (Dokumentation des Workshops am 10. Februar 1999). In Bundesintstitut für Sportwissenschaft (Ed.), *Wissenschaftliche Berichte und Materialien*, Bd. 14. Köln: Sport Buch Strauß.

Bernstein, A. (2002). Is it time for a victory lap? Changes in the media coverage of women in sport. *International Review for the Sociology of Sport, 37*(3–4), 415–428.

Bernstein, A., & Blain, N. (Eds.). (2003). *Sport, media, culture: Global and local dimensions*. London: Frank Cass Publishers.

Billings, A. C., & Eastman, S. T. (2002). Selective representation of gender, ethnicity, and nationality in American television coverage of the 2000 Summer Olympics. *International Review for the Sociology of Sport, 3*(34), 351–370.

Bishop, R. (2003). Missing in action – Feature coverage of women's sports in sports illustrated. *Journal of Sport & Social Issues, 27*(2), 184–194.

Capranica, L., & Aversa, F. (2002). Italian television sport coverage during the 2000 Sydney Olympic Games – a gender perspective. *International Review for the Sociology of Sport, 37*(3–4), 337–349.

Eastman, S. T., & Billings, A. C. (1999). Gender parity in the Olympics – Hyping women athletes, favoring men athletes. *Journal of Sport & Social Issues, 23*(2), 140–170.

Flatten, K., & Mathesen, H. (1997). Gender politics in sport newsprint: A longitudinal study of six British national newspapers. In *Proceedings of the 10th Scientific Congress of the International Association for Sports Information, 10–12 June, 1997* (pp. 326–332). Paris: INSEP Publications.

Harris, J., & Clayton, B. (2002). Femininity, masculinity, physicality and the English tabloid press – The case of Anna Kournikova. *International Review for the Sociology of Sport, 37*(3–4), 397–413.

Hartmann-Tews, I. (1996). *Sport für alle!? – Strukturwandel des Sports im internationalen Vergleich: Deutschland, Großbritannien und Frankreich.* (Schriftenreihe des Bundesinstituts für Sportwissenschaft, 91). Schorndorf: Hofmann.

Hartmann-Tews, I., & Combrink, C. (2005). Under-representation of women in governing bodies of sport – The significance of recruitment procedures and affirmative action. In G. Doll-Tepper, G. Pfister, D. Scoretz, & C. Bilan (Eds.), *Sport, women and leadership* (pp. 71–78). Köln: Sport und Buch Strauß.

Hartmann-Tews, I., & Luetkens, A. (2003). The inclusion of women into the German sport system. In I. Hartmann-Tews & G. Pfister (Eds.), *Sport and women – Social issues in international perspective* (pp. 53–69). London, New York: Routledge.

Hartmann-Tews, I., & Rulofs, B. (2005). "Goldmädel, Rennmiezen und Turnküken" revisted – A comparison of newspaper coverage of sports and gender representation in Germany 1979–1999. In A. R. Hofmann & E. Trangbaek (Eds.), *International perspectives on sporting women in past and present* (pp. 307–320). Copenhagen: Bookpartner.

Hartmann-Tews, I., & Rulofs, B. (2003). Sport in den Medien – Ein Feld semiotischer Markierung von Geschlecht? In I. Hartmann-Tews, P. Gieß-Stüber, M.-L. Klein, C. Kleindienst-Cachay, & K. Petry (Eds.), *Soziale Konstruktion von Geschlecht im Sport* (pp. 30–69). Opladen: Leske + Budrich.

Klein, M.-L. (1988). Women in the discourse of sports reports. *International Review for the Sociology of Sport, 23*(1), 139–152.

Klein, M.-L. (1986). *Frauensport in der Tagespresse. Eine Untersuchung zur sprachlichen und bildlichen Präsentation von Frauen in der Sportberichterstattung.* Bochum: Universitätsverlag Dr. N. Brockmeyer.

Klein, M.-L., & Pfister, G. (1985). *Goldmädel, Rennmiezen und Turnküken. Die Frau in der Sportberichterstattung der BILD-Zeitung.* Berlin: Bartels & Wernitz.

Knoppers, A., & Elling, A. (2004). "We do not engage in promotional journalism" – Discursive strategies used by sport journalists to describe the selection process. *International Review for the Sociology of Sport, 39*(1), 57–73.

Koivula, N. (1999). Gender stereotyping in televised media sport coverage. *Sex Roles, 41*, 589–604.

Messner, M. A., Duncan, M. C., & Cooky, C. (2003). Silence, sports bras, and wrestling porn – Women in televised sports news and highlights shows. *Journal of Sport & Social Issues, 27*(1), 38–51.

NOK. (2005). *Nationales Olympisches Komitee für Deutschland: Statistik.* Retrieved May 29, 2006, from http://www.nok.de/komitee/statistik/teilnehmer.htm

Pemberton, C., Shields, S., Gilbert, L., Shen, X., & Said, H. (2004). A look at print media coverage across four Olympiads. *Women in Sport and Physical Activity Journal, 13*(2), 87–99.

Rulofs, B. (2003). *Konstruktion von Geschlechterdifferenzen in der Sportpresse? Eine Analyse der Berichterstattung zur Leichtathletik-WM 1999.* Butzbach-Griedel: Afra.

Rulofs, B., Combrink, C., & Borchers, I. (2002). Sport im Lebenslauf von Frauen und Männern. In Henning Allmer (Hrsg.), *Sportengagement im Lebensverlauf* (Brennpunkte der Sportwissenschaft, 23, S. 39–60).

Rulofs, B., & Hartmann-Tews, I. (2006). Zur sozialen Konstruktion von Geschlecht in der medialen Vermittlung von Sport. In I. Hartmann-Tews & B. Rulofs (Eds.), *Handbuch Sport und Geschlecht* (pp. 230–244). Schorndorf: Karl Hofmann.

Toohey, K. (1997). Australian television, gender and the Olympic Games. *International Review for the Sociology of Sport, 32*(1), 19–29.

Tuggle, C. A., & Owen, A. (1999). A descriptive analysis of NBC's coverage of the centennial Olympics – The "Games of the Women"? *Journal of Sport & Social Issues, 23*(2), 171–182.

Vincent, J. (2004). Game, sex, and match: The construction of gender in British newspaper coverage of the 2000 Wimbledon championships. *Sociology of Sport Journal, 21*, 435–456.

Vincent, J., Imwold, C., Johnson, J. T., & Massey, D. (2003). Newspaper coverage of female athletes competing in selected sports in the 1996 centennial Olympic Games: The more things change the more they stay the same. *Women in Sport and Physical Activity Journal, 12*(1), 1–21.

Ilse Hartmann-Tews and Bettina Rulofs
Institute of Sociology of Sport
Gender Studies
German Sport University Cologne
Germany

MONTSERRAT MARTIN

10. SPAIN

'The Big Forgotten': The Search for the Invisible Sportswomen of Spain
An Analysis of Spanish Media Coverage during the Olympic Games

Spain joined the European Union in 1986, and since then has enjoyed a rising standard of living comparable to other Western European nations. However, it has not always been this way. It is not possible to give an account of women and sport in Spain without mentioning the differing political spheres that have affected Spanish society. Before 1936, during the Second Republic (1931–1936), Spain became one of the most forward-thinking places for women's politics in Europe (García, 1989). Radical ideas questioning the status quo between the genders originated during the Second Republic. A growth of feminist consciousness settled among the most progressive sectors and soon the consequences were far reaching. Women gained the right to vote in 1931, at the same time or even before some European countries. Divorce and the right to perform abortions was legalised in 1932 (García, 1989). However, progressive ideas and aspirations for equality amongst women and men came to an abrupt end on the 18th of July 1936 when a war broke out between fascist militias and the defenders of the democratically elected government. After three years of bloody conflict and executions, General Franco became the self-nominated chief (*caudillo*) of Spain in 1939 "by the grace of God" (as Franco arrogantly printed on the old Spanish peseta).

The 40 years of 'Francoism' that followed were a fatal setback to the modernisation and liberation enjoyed in the years prior to the Civil War. Freedom of thought and speech were completely eradicated and, with a return to a former set of morals, traditional female values and stereotyped gender relationships were again in place. The stereotypical passive role of women was mainly supported by the Catholic Church and the ultra conservative members of Franco's government. Within this period sport for women was mainly used as a tool to improve female biological and reproductive functions and to emphasize stereotyped femininity, such as submission and maternity (Puig, 1987). Sport was not used as a way to challenge ideas of traditional femininity, and was certainly not used to undermine the unequal relationships between men and women. Promoting women's sport competition and any sport that was suspected of masculinising women's bodies and not entirely supporting all traditional female values was seen as a betrayal of Franco's principles (Vázquez, 1987). Only individual sports, which clearly promoted women's health and aesthetics, such as gymnastics, swimming or even tennis, were

T. Bruce, J. Hovden and P. Markula (eds.),
Sportswomen at the Olympics: A Global Content Analysis of Newspaper Coverage, 127–138.

accepted as feminine but participation was only encouraged at a recreational level. Consequently, very little female sport competition was promoted by sport institutions during those decades after the Civil War (Nash, 1992).

Franco died in 1975 and in 1978 the Spanish democratic constitution that exists today was approved. Since then, Spanish society has undergone radical changes towards becoming a member of the developed West. As the growth of the economy quickened, the democratisation of politics and society became a reality, and the egalitarian process of gender relations took off for the first time since the Second Republic. Rates of women gaining access to higher education and employment increased rapidly (Nash, 1999). At the same time a real expansion of women's sport in Spain took place during the 1970s and 1980s (García, 1989). Spanish sportswomen started to participate in highly competitive national and international sport and the vast majority of Spanish sport unions began to gradually include women's sections and teams. Spanish women's participation in sport activities has notably increased in recent decades. According to a Spanish national survey that measures the sporting habits of the Spanish population, women's participation in sport has increased from 16% in 1980 to 27% in 2000 (García Ferrando, 2001). Following on from García Ferrando's (2001) results regarding sport participation according to gender, Puig and Soler (2003) assert that in general terms women have gradually gained access to sport but, far from reproducing masculine sport behaviour patterns that emphasize sport competition, women have modelled it according to other patterns.

Table 1. Spanish participation in sport

	Men	*Women*
Sport participation	48%	27%
Sport interest	73%	27%
Sport competition	28%	8%
Recreational sport	50%	82%
Most practiced sports	Football Swimming Indoor football Tennis Trekking	Swimming Gymnastics Aerobics Fitness Dance

Source: García Ferrando (2001).

Table 1 illustrates that a significantly lower percentage of women than men participate in sport at a competitive level and that a considerably greater percentage of women participate in recreational sport than men. Do these results echo gender stereotypes in sport or, on the contrary, do they show an alternative female way of practising and enjoying sport which challenges the traditional male view of sport as a primarily competitive pursuit?

The first time significant numbers of Spanish female athletes participated in the Olympic Games was in 1960 in Rome where 7.4% of the team were women (although 4 women did participate in Paris in 1924 [García, 1989]). The 1992

Spanish Olympic Games in Barcelona still saw low female participation in comparison to men's participation: 29% in contrast to 71%. However, the last Olympic Games in Athens 2004 represented the most equal percentage to date between Spanish female and male participants: 143 female (43.3%) and 187 male (56.7%). Almost half of the Spanish Olympic team that participated in Athens 2004 was female.

The main pursuit of this chapter is to consider if the egalitarian participation of Spanish athletes in Athens 2004 is similarly reflected in the printed press media coverage. However, before analysing in depth the quantitative results of female sport coverage in Spanish newspaper *El País*, a review of the data which shows the overall position of female sport in the Spanish printed press is necessary.

FEMALE SPORT IN THE SPANISH SPORTS MEDIA

According to sports journalists M. Eugenia Ibáñez and Manuela Lacosta, media coverage of sport in Spain is predominantly male-dominated. They describe the poor situation of Spanish women's sport information in the media as 'faceless', 'completely invisible' and 'the big forgotten' (Ibáñez, 2001; Ibáñez & Lacosta, 1998, 1999). The authors were both part of the journalistic team that covered the 1992 volleyball competition in Barcelona; a sport that both of them had played at competitive level. In addition, Ibáñez played in the Spanish female volleyball premiership for several seasons. During those 17 days they had the opportunity to confirm that female Olympic athletes received far less and more humiliating and derogatory coverage than men, regardless of their victories and sport performances. Enraged by their experience, they decided to corroborate their own findings by undertaking a review of the number of articles and photographs in the written press and, in doing so, hoped to confirm their views on the neglect of women's sport by the media. They chose three random weeks in 1995 – one in February, one in April and one in July. They analysed six Spanish newspapers: four sport sections of general newspapers, including *El País*, and two that specialised in sport. The results were shocking. From all the articles gathered, only 4% were devoted to women and more than 50% of those dealt only with tennis. This meant that no more than 2% of the coverage was dedicated to all the rest of female sports. It is worth noting that in 1995 two top-ranking international tennis players were Spanish women: Arantxa Sánchez-Vicario and Conchita Martínez.

Results from analysing the photographs did not improve the situation. Only 3.4% depicted women. In this case, 73% were related to tennis and these were mainly photos of Sánchez-Vicario and Martínez. Distressed by these results, and in the hope that 1995 may not have been a representative year for women's sport, Ibáñez and Lacosta carried out another study in 1999. This time they analysed only one week in April looking at two specialised sports newspapers. The results were again depressing, and Ibáñez (2001) described the phenomenon with a Marx Brothers' quote in mind: "the presence of female sport in the Spanish media has overcome poverty to reach the highest levels of misery" (p. 112).[1] The corresponding percentages from 1995 had dramatically decreased, with only 2% of sport articles and only 0.4% of sport photographs being dedicated to women. Women's sport information in the media came across as a clandestine activity. Apart from Arantxa Sánchez-Vicario and Conchita Martínez whose achievements were reported rigorously and correctly, the rest of the news was mainly anecdotal and without continuity. Ibáñez and Lacosta (1999) did not find any female sport, apart from tennis, that was well explained and followed, and, therefore, questioned who the potential audience could be for such fragmented and superficial reporting.

Joana Gallego (1999), a professor of journalism specialising in gender and the media, confirms that, like other international researchers (e.g., Bernstein, 2002; Daddario, 1994; Wensing & Bruce, 2003), female sport in the media has a subordinate presence. If both the male and female teams of any sport have beaten their opponents, the male team will always have priority, either being at the top of the page and/or having more space on the page. As Ibáñez and Lacosta (1998) conclude, "Female information? Look for it at the last paragraph" (p. 96).

According to Gallego (1999), the lack of interest by the media in female sport can be attributed to three facts: the non-acknowledgment of social changes; the non-acknowledgment of changing audience interests and ignoring the fact that half the population are women; and, lastly, the lack of political willpower for change. In an attempt to redress this imbalance, Pilar Castillo, the Minister of Education, Culture and Sport, in 2000 explicitly declared in Parliament that she wanted to strengthen the position and image of women's sport. Having made this declaration, she announced the newly appointed people to top positions and not a single high-ranking position was held by a woman (Ibáñez, 2001). With this manifest invisibility of sportswomen in the media, Ibáñez, disheartened, acknowledges that it is 'a miracle' that Spanish girls and women participate at all in sport. How long can this situation be maintained, and to what extent will Spanish sportswomen tolerate so little media presence and visibility?

METHODS

In the next section, I present the findings of my own analysis of women's sports in the media. I have used the Spanish newspaper, *El País*. Before continuing, a brief introduction to the newspaper and Spain is necessary. *El País* is one of the few general information newspapers that is sold throughout Spain. Spanish territory is characterised by having different nationalities and cultures, including three – Catalonia, Euskadi (Basque country) and Galicia – that also have their own languages as well as Castilian (Spanish) and are officially bilingual. Although the Spanish state is formed by 17 autonomous communities, each with their own government, there is a difference in the degree of autonomy within each community. For instance, Catalonia and Euskadi have a higher level of independence from central government than other regions. In these two regions the departments of Health and Education are autonomous and other departments such as Justice and Inland Revenue are in the process of decentralisation. As a consequence, it is hard to find newspapers that are sold in all of 17 communities. *El País* is one of the few and it is considered the most intellectual newspaper. However, like most of the newspapers, *El País* is not politically or ideologically neutral.

I analysed 30 days of the 2004 Athens Olympic media coverage in *El País*: 16 days during the Games (13 – 29 August); one week before the start of the Games; and one week after their conclusion. As a result, I gathered and analysed information from Saturday 7 August until Sunday 5 September 2004. Although the majority of the material was gathered from the sports section of the newspaper, some was also collected from the newspaper's front page. In order to be able to compare the Lacosta and Ibáñez (1998, 1999) results with those of 2004, I also counted and analysed all sports news other than the Olympic Games; the vast majority of which concerned male football and the preparation of the upcoming Spanish football premiership season. With reference to gender, I divided the articles into four categories: female, male, mixed and neutral. I considered an article female or male when the title and 75% of text was devoted to one of the genders. The mixed category corresponds to articles when both genders had almost equal importance in the text. For instance, the early articles about Spanish Olympic teams often belonged to this category. The neutral category corresponds to articles and photographs representing institutions, committees, politicians and equipment. Finally, I do not present the area covered by the articles and photographs but, instead, the number of items. Consequently, the overall total for the sport coverage is a result of combining the numbers of Olympic and non-Olympic articles and Olympic and non-Olympic photographs.

RESULTS FROM *EL PAIS*

My analysis finds that even though media coverage of female sport during Olympic Games improves considerably, the non-Olympic coverage remains the same. Primarily, the following results confirm that Spanish Olympic sportswomen were under-represented in the media in Athens 2004.

Nevertheless, it is interesting to note that the Olympic Games media tends to treat women's sport in a more egalitarian manner than the sports media in general. The different percentages between male and female articles and photographs are not as dramatic as in Ibáñez and Lacosta's (1999) report (see Table 2). The total amount of the sports media items (number of articles and photographs, Olympic and non-Olympic) coverage in *El País* is 1,174 items of which 885 were dedicated to Olympic coverage which makes up 75.4% of the total sport coverage in *El País* during the 30 days analysed. The total percentage coverage that female athletes received in *El País* during the 2004 Olympic Games was 14.5%, whereas male athletes received 66% (participation proportion was 43.3% female to 56.7% male athletes). In addition, if the mixed coverage percentage of 12.7% is added to the female coverage percentage, the total coverage which included female athletes was 27.2%, a far cry from the 66% of male athletes' coverage. Even though the findings are not as extreme as those of Ibáñez and Lacosta (1999), I found a percentage gap between female and male sport media coverage of 51.5 points. It is clear that there is still a long way to go to achieving equality in newspaper sports coverage. Spanish female athletes have not had their 'victory lap' in the media (Bernstein, 2002).

In a similar fashion to Gallego (1999), my analysis of *El País* in Athens 2004 showed that the male basketball team received priority coverage even when the women's team performed at a higher level. The male team ended in 8th position, whereas the female team ended in 7th. However, 16 articles were dedicated to the men's team and only 8 to the women's team. The position of the articles in the newspaper is also of significance. The men's team, with Pau Gasol as the main attraction, were on the front page of the newspaper once, and three times on the front page of the sports section. This was a position never afforded to women's basketball which always, without exception, came after the men's news.

Table 2. Total coverage of all sports by number of articles and photographs in El País during the 2004 Olympic Games

	Articles (n)	%	Photographs (n)	%	Total items	Total %
Female	73	11.1	97	18.7	170	14.5
Male	400	61.0	374	72.2	774	66.0
Mixed	122	18.6	27	5.2	149	12.7
Neutral	61	9.3	20	3.9	81	6.8
Total	656	100	518	100	1,174	100

Table 2 illustrates that the percentage of total photographs is higher for both genders in comparison to articles and decreases in the case of mixed and neutral categories. The differences in the percentages between female and male athletes with reference to articles and photographs are similar although, as discussed above, females are 51.5 points less represented in the media than their male counterparts.

When considering only the Olympic Games coverage (both Spanish and non-Spanish female and male athletes in *El País*), Table 3 shows that female and male percentages of coverage are different from the total coverage. The total number of Olympic articles was 481, of which 70 (14.6% of the total) were devoted to women and 235 to men (which represents 48.9%). The remaining 36.5% was shared between mixed gender articles and neutral articles.

The total number of Olympic photographs is 404 with women's photos numbering 94 and men's numbering 266. Both female and male photographs coverage saw an increase compared to the article coverage which was 70 for female and 235 for male. However, if we delve deeper into these figures we can see that in reality the percentage increase in photographs coverage is actually far greater for men than for women – the female representation in photographs is 23.3% of the total, as opposed to their male counterparts whose percentage is 65.8%. The difference in percentage terms of photographs coverage between men and women is 42.5% as opposed to the 34.3% differential in article coverage.

Table 3. Olympics-only coverage by number of articles and photographs according to gender in El País during the 2004 Olympic Games

	Articles (n)	%	Photographs (n)	%	Total items (n)	Total %
Female	70	14.6	94	23.3	164	18.5
Male	235	48.9	266	65.8	501	56.6
Mixed	118	24.5	25	6.2	143	16.1
Neutral	58	12.1	19	4.7	77	8.7
Total	481	100	404	100	885	100

Table 4. Non-Olympic coverage by number of articles and photographs according to gender in El País during the 2004 Olympic Games

	Articles (n)	%	Photographs (n)	%	Total items (n)	Total %
Female	3	1.7	3	2.8	6	2.0
Male	165	94.3	108	94.7	273	94.5
Mixed	4	2.2	2	1.7	6	2.0
Neutral	3	1.7	1	0.8	4	1.4
Total	175	100	114	100	289	100

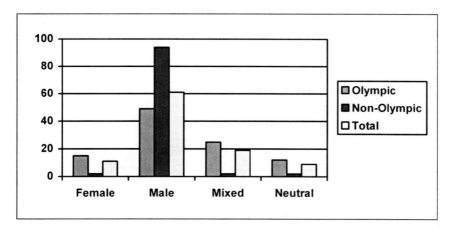

Figure 1. Percentage of total articles during the 2004 Olympic Games by gender.

The percentages of the female non-Olympic coverage (1.7% for articles and 2.8% for photographs) are similar to those found by Ibáñez and Lacosta in 1995 (4% for articles and 3.4% for photographs) and 1999 (2% for articles and 0.4% for photographs) (see Table 4 and Figures 1 and 2). Five years on, in non-Olympic coverage, it can be said that the situation of Spanish women's sport coverage is still as hopeless as ever and remains 'the big forgotten' by the media.

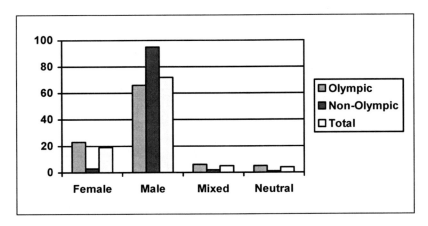

Figure 2. Percentage of total photographs during the 2004 Olympic Games by gender.

Spanish athletes went onto the podium 19 times in total, although Spanish sports institutions and the media had expectations of achieving more medals. This represents the second best performance of Spanish athletes in the Olympic Games. The best performance is still Barcelona 1992 where Spain obtained 22 medals. In Athens 2004 the medals were distributed by gender as follows: male athletes or teams won 3 gold medals, 7 silver and 3 bronze, whereas Spanish female athletes or teams only won 3 silver medals and 2 bronze. One silver medal was won by a mixed team. Whilst the percentages of participation and coverage according to genders are imbalanced, the percentages of medals won and coverage by gender is relatively equal (see Table 5 and Figure 3).

Table 5. Percentage of Spanish competitors and medals by gender in relation to the Olympic media coverage received

	Olympic competitors	Medals	Media coverage
Female	43.3%	26.3%	18.5%
Male	56.7%	68.4%	56.6%

With reference to participation, 143 women (43.3% of the total participants) received 18.5% of the Olympic coverage compared to 187 men (56.7% of total participants) who received 56.6% coverage. With reference to medals, 5 medals won by female athletes (26.3% of the total) received 18.5% coverage compared to men who won 13 medals (68.4%) and received 56.6% coverage.

As Table 6 shows, the three most reported female sports were athletics, swimming and basketball. One explanation for athletics receiving the most coverage may be due to the number of events that fell within that category. Furthermore, athletics is traditionally the main sport of the Olympic Games.

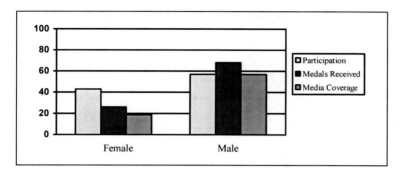

Figure 3. Percentage of Spanish competitors, medals and media coverage by gender.

Swimming and basketball also received a lot of coverage as great hopes were pinned on the female teams before the start of the competitions. In the case of gymnastics and synchronised swimming, two sports that are more generally associated with women and seen as primarily feminine sports, it is not known whether *El País* reporters covered these sports because of the female gymnasts' and swimmers' performances or because of the sports' feminine connotations.

Table 6. Most covered Olympic female sports as a percentage of female Olympic coverage

Sport	Articles (n)	Photographs (n)	Female Olympic coverage %
Athletics	17	19	22.0
Swimming	9	9	11.0
Basketball	12	6	11.0
Gymnastics	6	7	7.9
Shooting	5	7	7.3
Synchronised swimming	5	3	4.8
Total of top six sports	54	51	64.0

Comparing Tables 6 and 7 it can be seen that *El País* coverage within the various sports does not correlate with the number of medals won within each sport. For instance, the three silver medallist sports, shooting, sailing and tennis, did not get the most coverage. Shooting received the most coverage out of the female medal-winning sports although tennis is historically the most covered female sport in the Spanish printed press. Even though shooting is not seen as a popular Spanish sport, María Quintanal achieved the first Spanish medal of the 2004 Games and perhaps the media concentrated on this due to the lack of other Spanish medals at the time.

Table 7. Female medal winners' coverage as percentage of female Olympic coverage

Sport (athlete/s & medal)	Articles (n)	Photos (n)	Female Olympic coverage %
Shooting (María Quintanal, silver)	5	7	7.3
Gymnastics (Patricia Moreno, bronze)	2	4	3.7
Dressage (Beatriz Ferrer-Salat, bronze)	2	4	3.7
Tennis (Virginia Ruano/Conchita Martínez, silver)	2	3	3.0
Sailing (Natalia Via-Dufresne/ Sandra Azón, silver)	1	3	2.4
Medal Winners	12	21	20.1

In the analysis of photographs in the Olympic media, women and men are quite similarly portrayed (see Table 8 and Figure 4). For both men and women, most of the photographs portrayed the athletes either in sport action (42.9% for women and 48.3% for men) or in sport-related contexts (35.2% for women and 31.9% for men).

Table 8. Types of photographs of males and females by percentage

	Sport action (SA)	Sport related (SR)	Medal (M)	Non-sport (NON)
Female	42.9%	35.2%	7.7%	14.3%
Male	48.3%	31.9%	5.3%	7.6%

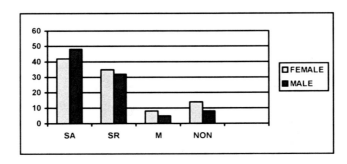

Figure 4. Types of photographs of males and females by percentage.

These figures show that men were slightly more often portrayed in sport action pictures than women. In contrast, women were more often portrayed in sport-related contexts than men; that is, female athletes were portrayed in their sport environment but not doing the actual sport. Furthermore, women had a slightly higher rate of photographs in the medal ceremony (7.7% for women and 5.3% for men) and in a non-sport environment than men (14.3% for women and 7.6% for men). Overall, a greater percentage of the photographs showed the athletes in a sporting context: sport action and sport-related results (78.1% for women and 80.2% for men).

CONCLUSIONS

Spanish female athletes are under-represented in international events such as the Olympic Games. Despite having gained more media visibility in comparison to non-Olympic sports reporting, this by no means implies that women achieve representative space or quality coverage in the sport media. Female sports events and performances are never a fundamental part of printed media. The sports media only seem to reveal the tip of the iceberg when it comes to female sport reporting.

El País did not proportionally cover female and male athletes with reference to their participation. Whilst Athens 2004 represented for Spanish athletes the closest parity between genders, the percentages of coverage according to gender were far from balanced. However, gender biased coverage is in favour (although not to a great extent) of female athletes with reference to medals received.

Despite the fact that Spanish female participants did not achieve a medal in any athletic event, it was the most covered female sport, receiving twice the coverage of the next most visible sports. Almost a quarter (22%) of the total female Olympic sport coverage in *El País* was devoted to it. Oddly, this would go against others' findings that suggest that female athletes competing in sport more strongly linked to femininity will receive relatively more coverage than those competing in sports more strongly linked to masculinity. The medal winning athletes and the sports they represented, with the exception of María Quintanal (shooting) and Patricia Moreno (gymnastics), were not in the list of most covered female sports. Singling out tennis and in comparison to Ibáñez and Lacosta (1998, 1999), their study showed that even within the "misery" of women's sport articles coverage (4% in 1995 and 2% in 1999), tennis was by far the most covered sport, whereas in Athens 2004, female tennis doubles achieved a silver medal and the coverage did not correlate to this achievement: In fact, tennis was not one of the most covered sports (see Table 6). There does not appear to be any pattern to the female media coverage, nor a determining factor for what is covered and what is forgotten. In summary, the situation in the Spanish media is that women's sport is alarmingly under-represented (although less so during the Olympic Games) and women's sport, described by Ibáñez (2001) as 'the big forgotten', remains as forgotten as ever, a forlorn case.

NOTES

[1] Where relevant, quotes from the original Spanish have been translated into English by the author.

REFERENCES

Bernstein, A. (2002). Is it time for a victory lap? Changes in the media coverage of women in sport. *International Review for the Sociology of Sport, 37*(3), 415–428.

Crolley, L., & Teso, E. (2007). Gendered narratives in Spain. The representation of female athletes in Marca and El Pais. *International Review for the Sociology of Sport, 42*(2), 149–166.

Daddario, G. (1994). Chilly scenes of the 1992 winter games: The mass media and the marginalization of female athletes. *Sociology of Sport Journal, 11*, 275–288.

Gallego, J. (1999, November). *Tratamiento hombre/mujer en los medios de comunicación. El deporte femenino en los medios de comunicación: el farolillo rojo.* Paper presented at the II Fórum Olímpico Las mujeres y el movimiento olímpico: Presente y futuro, Barcelona, Spain.

García, M. (1989). Inicis de l'esport femení. In *Dona i esport: Recull de ponències* (pp. 5–14). Barcelona: Centre de Documentació de la Dona.

García Ferrando, M. (2001). *Los Españoles y el deporte: Prácticas y comportamientos en la última década del siglo XX.* Madrid: Ministerio de Educación, Cultura y Deporte.

Ibáñez, M. E. (2001). Informació sobre esport femení: El gran oblit. *Revista Apunts d'Educació Física i Esports, 65*(2), 111–113.

Ibáñez, M. E., & Lacosta, M. (1998). Informació esportiva: només per a ells. In A. M. Bach (Ed.), *Génere i informació* (pp. 87–160). Barcelona: Institut Català de la Dona & Ajuntament de Barcelona.

Ibáñez, M. E., & Lacosta, M. (1999, November). *Tratamiento hombre/mujer en los medios de comunicación. Deporte femenino: el gran olvido.* Paper delivered at the II Fórum Olímpico Las mujeres y el movimiento olímpico: Presente y futuro, Barcelona, Spain.

Nash, M. (1992). *Les dones fan esport.* Barcelona: Institut Català de la Dona.

Nash, M. (1999). La construcción de los roles de género: Las mujeres en la España contemporánea. In M. Nash (Ed.), *Rojas. Las mujeres republicanas en la Guerra Civil* (pp. 35–85). Madrid: Taurus.

Puig, N. (1987). El proceso de incorporación al deporte por parte de la mujer española (1939–1985). In *Mujer y deporte (Serie Debate, 3)* (pp. 83–90). Madrid: Ministerio de Cultura, Instituto de la Mujer.

Puig, N., & Soler, S. (2003). Women and sport in Spain. In G. Pfister & I. Hartmann-Tews (Eds.), *Sport and women: Social issues in international perspective* (pp. 83–101). London: Routledge.

Vázquez, B. (1987). Educación Física para la mujer, mitos, tradiciones y doctrina actual. In *Mujer y deporte (Serie Debate, 3)* (pp. 55–64). Madrid: Ministerio de Cultura, Instituto de la Mujer.

Wensing, E. H., & Bruce, T. (2003). Bending the rules: Media representations of gender during an international sporting event. *International Review for the Sociology of Sport, 38*(4), 387–396.

Montserrat Martin
Universitat de Vic
Catalonia-Spain

EUROPE: EASTERN EUROPE

ANDREA GÁL, ATTILA VELENCZEI AND ÁRPÁD KOVÁCS

11. HUNGARY

An Unchanged Situation in a Changing Society: The Hungarian Case

INTRODUCTION

For both its size and population Hungary is considered a small country. However, the successes of its Olympic athletes made the country a true sports empire in the 20th century. Although elite sports always enjoyed priority treatment from the political leadership, objective and scientific research into social aspects of sport only really commenced in the 1960s. In terms of this chapter, we can only give an accurate description of any segment of Hungary's social life if we take a brief overview of the peculiar 20th century history of Central and Eastern European countries. Following World War II, the state-socialist system emerging in the Soviet block countries forced its Marxist ideology onto all areas of social life; ignoring fundamental human rights and freedoms and suppressing civil society. Various aspects of social life were operating under the control of the Communist Party and they received smaller or greater emphasis depending on what role they happened to play in the constant rivalry with capitalist systems. One of these sub-systems was top sports which, with its successes, were supposed to prove the endurance and competitiveness of the state-socialist system. Sport, therefore, received outstanding financial and moral support, and the top athletes, coaches and sports managers all enjoyed above average social prestige in a society that was levelled off in low living standards. An interesting irony characterises this situation, namely that women could gain advantages in top sports; an area which was said to be one of the most masculine domains of social life. Outstanding salaries, trips abroad, preferential treatment in getting a flat and/or a new car were advantages that only a few men and women outside the world of sports were lucky enough to have.

While academics generally agree about the social status of top athletes, there are differences in opinions about the general status of women. Female emancipation was given priority in the ideologies of Eastern European communist parties but it was a rather limited definition which concentrated on the integration of the female population into the labour market (Fodor, 2003). Although the enforced modernisation strategy of state-socialism 'lifted' generations of women up to the same level of education and paid work as men, the model of a woman managing well in both production and family life was planned from the top, and those affected experienced it as a situation they were forced into. Taking jobs that were

T. Bruce, J. Hovden and P. Markula (eds.),
Sportswomen at the Olympics: A Global Content Analysis of Newspaper Coverage, 141–151.

typically underpaid in addition to the unequal burden of unpaid housework preserved the patriarchal system (Asztalos-Morell, 1997; Neményi & Tóth, 1998). Actually, this 'one-sided' female emancipation made women in education, culture or even in politics almost equal but in private and family life, as well as in public life, the traditional method of shaping female and male roles remained virtually unchanged (Ferge, 1999).

It is also worth giving a brief outline of the media of the era, since prevailing ideologies are transmitted to the members of society through the mass media. Until nearly 1987–1988 in Hungary, the media system and the press were owned by the state party which operated, financed and controlled public information transmission (Tamás, 1997). Publishing and broadcasting were illegal without permission: only specific organisations approved by the state were entitled to apply for such permission. Censorship of the press operated through a complex system of formal and informal rules which applied not only to the generation and transmission of information but also with respect to the education and appointment of editorial staff and journalists as well as in connection with the allocation of resources. Overall, the press had little possibility for openly criticising the regime (Giorgi, 1995).

In 1989, state-socialism collapsed in Central and Eastern European countries, the one-party system was changed over to parliamentary democracy, and a market economy began to function instead of a socialist planned economy. Naturally, this double change rocked the foundations of and reshaped all segments of social life. Following these democratic changes, the aim of this study is to provide an insight into the status of women and, more precisely, female athletes today, by examining the media representation of female athletes in Hungary.

THE SOCIAL STATUS OF (SPORTS)WOMEN IN HUNGARY[1]

Since the 1989–1990 political system change, many articles written about the situation of Hungarian women have focused on how their social status has changed in the market economy. Of these, the key studies concentrate on the positions men and women hold in power and economic leadership (Laki, 1999; Lévai, 1999; Szalai, 1999), since these indicate best the extent of inequality between the genders. Research findings show that although the number of highly qualified female managers of state-owned companies as well as independent entrepreneurs has grown significantly, in the really successful fields leading positions are still typically taken by men (Sági, 1994).

Hungary's accession to the European Union in 2004 and the adjustment to the EU's policy in the field of equal opportunities for men and women gave new impetus to analyses of the social situations of the genders. However, certain areas have not been examined extensively. One of these areas is competitive sport, which was probably the most successful social sphere of the old state socialist system but, unfortunately, has become one of the losers in the political and economic system changes. Following the cessation of the opposition between the communist and capitalist world orders, the privileged status of sports was discontinued and decreasing state support was not replaced by private capital. Thus, sport funding was a problematic issue for a long time and no policy was developed that would have solved the economic problems that arose after 1989–1990. This situation has affected the social status of female athletes fundamentally. The 'semi-amateurs' of the state communist system (i.e., state-amateurs whose sports activity was illegally financed by public money but who participated in the Olympic Games as true amateurs) became the semi-professionals of the market economy – and they usually did not receive professional salaries and were not provided with a professional sport environment (Földesi, 1999). Rather than success, it is popularity, marketability and media visibility that largely influence the financial and moral rewards the athletes can enjoy. Team sports are in a position of greater financial security because of broadcasting royalties for matches and the income from advertising for clubs that do well in national and international championships and tournaments. Athletes whose sports are less suited for television or less popular with viewers are disadvantaged because they are less exposed to sponsors who can provide necessary financial support. Although female athletes of the previous era believed that male athletes enjoyed an advantage in terms of income and benefits (Földesi, 1984), women athletes today believe that rewards depend on achievement and media visibility of their sports rather than their gender. Therefore, top female athletes with less international success in sport or less financial support from the media have to start preparing for their civil life during their sports career. Although most female athletes would be glad to continue working as coaches or sports managers, they are aware that few will have a chance to do so. Despite this, more women study and graduate as sports specialists (e.g., sports coach, sports manager, recreational professional). Because of the large-scale expansion of higher education that started in the 1990s, they can choose from an increasing variety of programmes, especially part-time or distance study.

Naturally, most female athletes plan on establishing their family, which can substantially shorten the valuable period of their sports career. The age for getting married and having children has reached the early or mid-30s, so it is quite common for female athletes to have their first child at a later stage of their life. The pre-condition for female athletes who give birth during their sports career to return is the existence of a social net that assists them in their tasks as mothers as well as in childcare and can substitute for the mother in the family when she is away competing at international championships (Gál, 2008).

GENDER DIFFERENCES IN MEDIA COVERAGE IN HUNGARY

Media and 'gender' type research projects could only start in Hungary following the democratic changes. After that, however, they began to increase and, at the same time, the institutional system for the research work was also gradually created. Learning about the findings of media coverage of the genders in the Western literature gave motivation to specialists in social sciences, and they realised that only these types of research projects can foster finding an effective solution to the problems that stem from the inequality of the genders. Quantitative and qualitative analyses of media products suggest that the media have further aggravated the problems in the patriarchal Hungarian society that is already saturated with prejudice. However, despite the fact that Western media studies raised the interest of sports sociologists, so far there is only limited research that concentrates on the media coverage of male and female top athletes.

As a participant in the Global Media Monitoring Project,[2] the Hungarian Association for Fairness and Equality between the Genders (IgEN) examined the news items of one average weekday in February 2005 in various Hungarian media – press, radio and television – to get an overall picture of journalism (see Gallagher, 2005). The results of the research showed a devastating picture: Among the subjects of the news, women and men were represented in a proportion of 12% to 88%, respectively. Both quality and tabloid media focused on male public figures and covered news mainly about men. Women hardly ever made it to the headlines, and were represented in less significant news items. The tabloid media often did not go beyond representing women as housewives or as the subjects of male sexual desire. Based on the national sports paper, *Nemzeti Sport,* and the sports sections of the political daily paper, *Népszabadság,* which has the largest circulation in Hungary, it found that women were hardly represented in sports news (receiving only 4% of coverage), which means that sports news is clearly dominated by male sports and male athletes (96% of coverage). The researchers claimed that in sports (and other news topics such as health care, education or business life), the disproportionate representation of women does not reflect their true social roles and presence.

There is more research that focuses on the media representation of women generally. On the basis of the existing research, we can conclude that television and the press contribute to preserving the patriarchal traditions of the Hungarian society. Argejó (1998a) analysed the content of soap operas, weekly papers and news programmes in order to examine how the media represent women and the relationship between the genders. Presenters of news programmes as well as those appearing in the news were examined. It was found that men are over-represented among TV presenters, correspondents and reporters. The situation was even worse when it came to examining the topics female reporters covered in their interviews, since Argejó (1998b) found that spectacular, intellectually challenging or large-scale topics or interviews with high-profile people at the top of the social hierarchy were predominantly reserved for male communicators. In contrast, their female counterparts had to be satisfied with less significant (sometimes insignificant) topics or interview subjects. Regarding the people the news items were about, the picture regarding equality of the female gender was even darker, since 81% of the news items contained no exemplary female image. Those few who were represented were self-made women who reached top positions similar to men (e.g., politicians, business leaders, lawyers or chief physicians) or who spoke as mothers. Nevertheless, interpreting and solving the problems were nearly always left for male presenters. If men and women appeared on the screen together, men received longer speaking times, and in fact women often did not say a word but were only present as the 'background' setting for a masculine world. 'Power is male business' – this is the message of news programmes, and the genders are represented in line with the traditional male and female attributes: Women appeared on the screen less frequently, and they were depicted as passive, unimportant people while men were represented in open spaces being actively involved in actions. Analysis of the three most widely read women's weeklies highlighted the fact that women are mostly presented as mothers or as partners who provide the secure 'background' for their husbands' careers (Argejó, 1998a). This research concluded that in news programmes men do not allow women to step into 'their' world, while women's weeklies do not allow women to step out of their narrow space of life, and do not present any alternative life models that women could follow beyond their traditional roles.

METHODS

The aim of this chapter is to introduce the Hungarian findings of the *Global Women in Sports Media Project*, which suggest that the printed sports media also follow the general Hungarian trend of male-centred coverage. For data collection, we used the issues of the *Népszabadság*, the Hungarian daily paper with the highest circulation, (152,000 copies sold daily) published between 7 August and 5 September 2004. We analysed all the sport stories on the front page and in the sport section of 24 issues in total (the paper is not published on Sundays). In the period examined, on two occasions the daily paper was supplemented with a magazine containing articles exclusively on the Olympic Games and we included these in our analysis. In total 339 articles (including the photographs that went with the articles) were analysed, the aggregate size of which amounted to 66,646.3cm^2.

The articles were grouped into four categories: besides the categories dealing solely with males or females, there was a 'mixed' category including stories about females and males, and a 'neutral' category which included stories about non-gender specific issues such as ticketing, descriptions of facilities and security for the Games.

THE MAIN FINDINGS OF THE NEWSPAPER ANALYSES

Table 1 demonstrates the distribution of the articles between the categories and the aggregate space measurement of the articles (including photographs). The figures suggest that in respect of both numbers of articles and their space, males enjoy a significant advantage compared to females. The daily newspaper devotes much more space to men (28,196.2cm^2) than women (5,782.5cm^2).

Table 1. Combined Olympic and non-Olympic coverage in one Hungarian newspaper

Measurement	Male	Female	Mixed	Neutral	Total
Space in cm^2	28,196.2	5,782.5	24,822.2	7,845.4	66,646.3
Percentage (%)	42.3	8.7	37.2	11.8	100%
Number of articles	184	38	78	39	339
Percentage (%)	54.3	11.2	23.0	11.5	100%

Regarding the number of articles, it can be stated that the proportion of male sports depiction is also much higher (54.3%) than the under-represented female sports (11.2%). In the mixed category were 23% of the articles and 37.5% of the total space. Mixed category articles were used mainly for Olympics-only news by journalists as shown in Tables 2 and 3. For example, 43.7% of the Olympics space was mixed (Table 2) compared with only 5.9% of the non-Olympics space (Table 3). The trend was the same for the number of articles, with 34.3% of the Olympics articles dedicated to mixed coverage and only 4.0% of the non-Olympics articles. These mixed articles mostly focused on the gender that was more successful in the sports they actually reported on.

Table 2. Olympics-only coverage in one Hungarian newspaper by space and number of stories

Measurement	Male	Female	Mixed	Neutral	Total
Space in cm^2	18,132.7	5,303.6	24,142.1	7,626.9	55,205.2
Percentage (%)	32.8	9.6	43.7	13.8	99.9%
Number of articles	78	27	73	35	213
Percentage (%)	36.6	12.7	34.3	16.4	100%

In Olympics coverage, although the number and space measurement of articles dealing exclusively with female athletes (9.6% of space and 12.7% of articles) is far behind those dealing with males athletes (32.8% of space and 36.6% of articles), the large number of mixed articles (43.7% of space and 34.3% of articles) improves the presentation indexes of females. Overall, this means that 53.5% of space and 47.0% of stories included females.

As Table 3 suggests, in the case of non-Olympic (international, national or regional sport events) coverage, the representation of females is much worse. For example, only 8.7% of the articles deal with female sports compared to the 84.1% of articles dealing with males. Even with mixed coverage added to the female total, it only reaches 10.1% of total coverage.

Table 3. Non-Olympic coverage in one Hungarian newspaper by space and number of articles

Measurement	Male	Female	Mixed	Neutral	Total
Space in cm^2	10,063.5	479.0	680.1	218.5	11,441.1
Percentage (%)	88.0	4.2	5.9	1.9	100%
Number of articles	106	11	5	4	126
Percentage (%)	84.1	8.7	4.0	3.2	100%

Tables 4, 5 and 6 demonstrate the similarity of trends concerning photographs; for example, there continued to be a higher percentage of mixed photographs (29.3% of space, 35.3% number of images) in the Olympics coverage than in non-Olympics coverage (16.5% of space, 10.5% number of images). It is also true that women received a higher percentage of photos in Olympic coverage (13.3% of space, 14.7% number of photographs) than in non-Olympic coverage (5.5% of space, 5.3% number of photos). The most important conclusion is that although the trends are the same, the females received a higher percentage of photos than they did of articles – so they were more 'visible' in images.

Table 4. Combined Olympic and non-Olympic coverage in one Hungarian newspaper by space and number of photographs

Measurement	Male	Female	Mixed	Neutral	Total
Space in cm^2	4,203.3	1,322.5	2,981.8	2,278.3	10,785.9
Percentage (%)	39.0	12.3	27.6	21.1	100%
Number of photos	61	18	43	13	135
Percentage (%)	45.2	13.3	31.9	9.6	100%

Table 5. Olympics-only coverage in one Hungarian newspaper by space and number of photographs

Measurement	Male	Female	Mixed	Neutral	Total
Space in cm^2	3109,01	1245,2	2750,13	2278,3	9,382.7
Percentage (%)	33.1	13.3	29.3	24.3	100%
Number of photos	45	17	41	13	116
Percentage (%)	38.8	14.7	35.3	11.2	100%

Table 6. Non-Olympic coverage in one Hungarian newspaper by space and number of photographs

Measurement	Male	Female	Mixed	Neutral	Total
Space in cm^2	1 094,3	77,3	231,7	0,0	1,403.3
Percentage (%)	78.0	5.5	16.5	0.0	100%
Number of photos	16	1	2	0	19
Percentage (%)	84.2	5.3	10.5	0.0	100%

The analysis of photographs shows that there are differences in the depicting of male and female athletes concerning the focus of photos that were used in their representation. As Figure 1 shows, the sportsmen are depicted in various situations, but sportswomen are represented mostly in action (46.15%) and in sport-related (46.15%) situations. There were more female coaches portrayed in the photographs (7.69%) than male ones (4.26%).

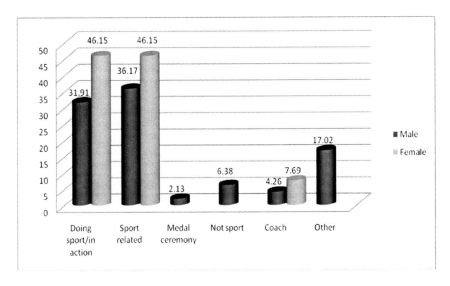

Figure 1. Focus of all photographs by percentage of space.

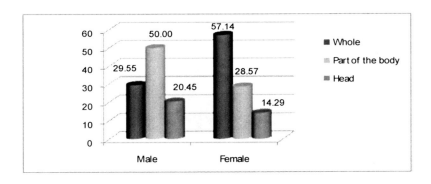

Figure 2. Parts of the body shown in all coverage by percentage of space.

In our analysis we also found a difference in the form of representation used in the photographs of male and female athletes. As Figure 2 indicates, while for males the partial imagery of the body and the image of the face are used mostly (50% the parts of the body, 20.45% only the head versus 29.55% the whole body), women are mainly shown in full figure photos (57.14% the whole body versus 28.57% the part of the body and 14.29% only the head).

The 2004 Hungarian Olympic team of 219 members comprised 129 male (58.9%) and 90 female (41.1%) athletes. In total, we received 8 Olympic gold medals, five of which were won by female athletes and three by males; two silver medals went to females and 4 to males, and our male athletes won our three bronze medals. Concerning all the medals, 10 of the 17 were won by men (58.8%) and 7 were won by women (41.2%). Male athletes participated in the awards ceremony on 10 occasions, and women on seven occasions. In summary we can conclude that the Olympic coverage of the two genders (32.85% of space in cm^2 and 36.6% of number of articles for male, 9.65% of space and 12.7% of number of articles for female) does not correspond to either their proportions in the Olympic team, or to the proportion of the Olympic medals they won. However, the non-correspondence is much worse for female athletes than for male athletes.

Few Hungarian female athletes participated in sports that are more strongly linked to femininity or where athletes are dressed in ways that highlight gender differences (like tennis, artistic and rhythmic gymnastics or synchronised swimming), and none of them managed to achieve outstanding results. Therefore, there was no opportunity to analyse whether these sports received more sports media attention compared to those sports that are more strongly linked to masculinity or where athletes are dressed in ways that do not highlight gender differences. With the exception of one silver medal in weight-lifting, Hungarian women won medals in Athens in sports – kayak-canoe, pentathlon, fencing and rifle shooting – that are traditionally successful in Hungary and that are, therefore, historically linked to national identity. Despite the fact that women won more gold medals (62.5%) than men (37.5%), they are under-represented in Olympic coverage: Consequently, it can be stated that nationalism did not seem to affect the coverage for females and nor did success.

DISCUSSION

In Hungary, the collapse of the Soviet type of state-socialist system in 1989–1990, then the emergence of parliamentary democracy and a market economy has exerted a different impact on the various subsystems and participants of society. Due to the end of the priority state support that top class competitive sport had received before, it is regarded by experts as a loser in the system changes, while the media became one of the winners as a result of the lifting of political censorship it had experienced previously. Opinions vary regarding the change in the situation of women; although the possibility to establish civil associations provided them with more chances of fighting for equal opportunities in many fields of social life, they are still at a disadvantage compared to their male counterparts. The Hungarian results of the *Global Women in Sports Media Project* demonstrate that the same is true for sports media: The quantitative analysis of the most read, traditional, political daily newspaper proved that male athletes are significantly over-represented. In the past one and a half decades, the former above-average status top athletes had enjoyed was shaken, which affected both men and women. However, due to the lack of previous research, it is impossible to establish to what extent the differences in their media representation at the 2004 Olympic Games are the result of a continuing tendency or an indication of the general status of women. Nevertheless, this analysis of printed sports media confirmed the findings of previous studies that consider the media a male world. Due to our particular history, however, the evolution of this male world has followed a different path in Hungary than in Western European societies. In the future, the quantitative and qualitative analysis of various forms of the media can provide additional data for the further description of the representation of athletes.

NOTES

1   See more about the same topic in Gál (2008).
2   To download a copy of the Global Media Monitoring Project report in English, Spanish or French, go to http://www.whomakesthenews.org/who_makes_the_news/report_2005

REFERENCES

Argejó, É. (1998a). Hímnem, nőnem: a médium nem semleges. In É. Argejó (Ed.), *Jelentések könyve* (pp. 173–179). Budapest: Új Mandátum.

Argejó, É. (1998b). Menekülés a túlélésbe. A devianciák a médiában. In É. Argejó (Ed.), *Jelentések könyve* (pp. 180–184). Budapest: Új Mandátum.

Asztalos-Morell, I. (1997). A nemek közötti egyenlőtlenségek az államszocializmus korszakában. *Szociológiai Szemle, 3*, 33–66.

Ferge, Zs. (1999). Hogyan hatott a rendszerváltás a nők helyzetére? In K. Lévai, R. Kiss, & T. Gyulavári (Eds.), *Vegyesváltó* (pp. 13–29). Budapest: Egyenlő Esélyek Alapítvány.

Fodor, É. (2003). A női emancipáció Magyarországon és Ausztriában, 1972–1992. *Szociológiai Szemle, 3*, 28–54.

Földesi, S. G. (1984). *Magyar olimpikonok önmagukról és a sportról.* Budapest: Közgazdasági és Jogi Könyvkiadó.

Földesi, S. G. (1999). *Félamatőrök, félprofik. Magyar olimpikonok (1980–1996).* Budapest: MOB.

Gál, A. (2008). Social status of Hungarian (sports) women before and after the 1989–1990 political system change. *European Journal for Sport and Society, 5*(2), 195–210.

Gallagher, M. (Ed.). (2005). *Who makes the news? Global media monitoring project 2005.* London: World Association for Christian Communication [WACC]. Retrieved April 18, 2008, from http://www.whomakesthenews.org/who_makes_the_news/report_2005

Giorgi, L. (1995). *The post-socialist media: What power the West? The changing media landscape in Poland, Hungary and the Czech Republic.* London: Avebury.

Laki, L. (1999). A tartós munkanélküliség, a nők és a család. In K. Lévai, R. Kiss, & T. Gyulavári (Eds.), *Vegyesváltó. Pillanatkép nőkről, férfiakról* (pp. 57–74). Egyenlő Esélyek Alapítvány.

Lévai, K. (1999). A nőpolitikától az esélyegyenlőségig és vissza. In K. Lévai, R. Kiss, & T. Gyulavári (Eds.), *Vegyesváltó. Pillanatkép nőkről, férfiakról* (pp. 30–37). Egyenlő Esélyek Alapítvány.

Neményi, M., & Tóth, O. (1998). *A nők társadalmi szerepének változásai az ezredfordulón.* Nemzeti Stratégiai Kutatások. Budapest: MTA.

Sági, M. (1994). Managerek. Az új gazdasági elit rekrutációja. (Managers' recruitment of the new economic elite). In R. Andorka, T. Kolosi, & G. y. Vukovich (Eds.), *Társadalmi Riport* (pp. 334–350). Budapest: TÁRKI.

Szalai, J. (1999). Közös csapda. In K. Lévai, R. Kiss, & T. Gyulavári (Eds.), *Vegyesváltó. Pillanatkép nőkről, férfiakról* (pp. 41–56). Egyenlő Esélyek Alapítvány.

Tamás, P. (1997). Hatalmi viszonyok átalakulása a szerkesztőségekben. In T. Terestyéni (Ed.), *Médiakritika* (pp. 92–104). Budapest: Osiris.

Andrea Gál
Faculty of Physical Education & Sport Sciences
Semmelweis University
Budapest
Hungary

Attila Velenczei and Árpád Kovács
National Institute for Sport Talent Care
Budapest
Hungary

IRENA SLEPIČKOVÁ

12. CZECH REPUBLIC

Czech Women in the Sports Media

INTRODUCTION

The Czech Republic has opened itself to the world in which globalization
penetrates all fields of the life of society. Czech sport appears to show the same
tendencies as anywhere else in the world. A question is to what extent such
tendencies mutually correspond in the field of female sport media coverage.
Media not only provide information on the sporting community but also create
and influence the views and attitudes of the general public regarding various
aspects of (not only) elite sport. They also have a potential to attract people to
play sports for other reasons than those typical for elite sport. During the
Olympics, sport broadcasts and news media coverage are followed avidly by
people, even those who show little or no interest in sports in the period between
Olympics (Slepička & Slepičková, 2002).

No major research examines the coverage of Czech female athletes in our
media. Only simple analyses, usually based on student work, are currently
available. While media gender issues in general have been analysed by numerous
Czech authors (e.g., Havelková & Vodrážka, 1998; Jirák & Köpplová, 2003), no
larger study covering the subject matter of gender in sports exists. Therefore, to
situate the current study in context I provide an introductory historical explanation
of cultural, social and political milestones in the development of Czech society and
sport as a social phenomenon. This is meant to facilitate the understanding of the
presentation of women's sports at the 2004 Olympic Games in Athens.

WOMEN'S SPORTS HISTORY AND DEVELOPMENT IN THE CZECH LANDS

Women's sports have had a very long tradition in the Czech lands, with the
beginnings of their organised forms dating back to the latter half of the 19th
century. In similar fashion to numerous other European countries, there were two
different lines of women's sports development in the Czech lands. The first of
them related to the physical education system of the Sokol organisation, while the
other one was connected with the development of competitive sport. The latter half
of the 19th century is known to have been a very dynamic period of European and
Czech history connected with economic progress, as well as political changes. The
emergence of a national revival as well as the pursuit of national identity were

T. Bruce, J. Hovden and P. Markula (eds.),
Sportswomen at the Olympics: A Global Content Analysis of Newspaper Coverage, 153–165.
© 2010 Sense Publishers. All rights reserved.

among the significant social development trends of that time. These trends took place concurrently with the development of modern sport quickly spreading across from the British Isles to the countries of the Euro-American cultural region.

The territory of the present-day Czech Republic was then part of the Austro-Hungarian Empire. By far the most developed in terms of economy, the region was politically controlled from Vienna. With the establishment of the voluntary Sokol organisation in 1862, sport became one important platform to strengthen the ideas of national consciousness. The views of the ideal woman and her place in society began to change. Educated and healthy women were needed to lead the nation towards self-awareness through the education of children (Bláha, 2003). In 1863, girls' physical education was introduced by Sokol, and the year 1866 was marked by the first public presentation of girls' physical exercising. In 1870, the Physical Activities Association of Prague Ladies and Girls obtained permission for running its activities. Gradually, women began to set up their own training programmes, overcoming the previous men's recommendations to perform only 'cautious and feminine' exercises. Obviously, even then, the issue of the appropriateness of different kinds of sports for women was discussed. In 1911, Sokol adopted equal membership conditions for both men and women.

It can be argued that the foundations of the traditional focus for Czech women's physical activities were laid in that particular period of time and further developed into the present, in many different forms which are based on the basic gymnastic exercises connected with various forms of dance as well as music. This kind of sport activity is very popular among women in the Czech Republic at present, which holds true for sport organisations[1] as well as private organisations offering paid services (mostly fitness centres that offer aerobics, spinning, etc.). This form of women's physical activity or 'sport' is also documented in the tradition of so-called 'mass performances'. In the period between the two World Wars, so-called All-Sokol Meetings with a significant female attendance reached maximum popularity. During the socialist era, the same festivals, which were well-known all over the world, took place under the name of Spartakiáda (or Spartakiads). Women's performances were always among the peak events of these sport festivals in terms of aesthetics, and were very important for women themselves.

The other line of women's sport development, competitive sport, must not be forgotten. Women had previously participated in various sports (ice-skating, swimming, etc.) for fun. At the very outset of sports clubs, bicycle, tennis and ski clubs in particular, the participation of women had a rather sociable character, rather than a strong focus on competition. Czech women joined tennis and cycling competitions for the first time in 1893 and 1894, respectively. In 1897, they took part in the first skiing competitions. With ball games promoted by physical education teachers, the first Czech handball club was founded in 1907. Its female members practiced also track and field sports. The first Czech female sports organisation, the Association of Handball and Women's Sports, was among the founders of La Féderation Sportive Féminine Internationale in Paris in 1921 (Schutová, 2003).

The end of WWI and the subsequent establishment of the independent Czechoslovakia[2] marked a milestone for Czech sports. Competitive sports were spreading internationally and the activities of sport federations thrived in the territory of Czechoslovakia as they did in other countries. This development was discontinued in 1948, three years after the end of WWII, when the new socialist political system was established.

The period of socialist Czechoslovak sport (lasting some 40 years until 1989) represented an important period of sport development. The politically motivated presentation of the achievements of both the state and the entire socialist block manifested itself in sport, too. The centralized management that created the crucial principles of the life of society had a clear impact on the development of competitive sport, female sport included. The involvement of the state in showcasing sports achievements brought in financial and organisational support and both males and females received methodical[3] support by teams of specialists.

The political changes since 1989 have resulted in the complete restructuring of the sport environment. This also changed the attitude of the state to the sport promotion.[4] Sport has become professionalised to a great extent (also at the level of voluntary organisations). The involvement of the state in elite sport has decreased. Sport in the present-day Czech Republic is organised in a similar manner to other European countries, where sports and athletes alike must seek financial resources from sponsors. Unlike many other European countries, however, Czech sport has not been strongly influenced by feminist movements, in part because of the rich and highly valued non-competitive female sport tradition. In addition, female competitive sport has never been significantly suppressed; on the contrary, it has been strongly supported at the elite level in the recent past.

OLYMPIC PARTICIPATION IN RELATION TO CHANGES IN CZECH SOCIETY

Czech participation in the Olympic Games has a long tradition, beginning at the very outset of the modern international Olympic movement. In 1894, Czech professor Guth-Jarkovský worked as a member of the team headed by Pierre de Coubertin, initiator and founder of the new history of the Olympic Games. In 1899, the Czech Committee for the Olympic Games Participation started the beginning of the Czech (and in 1919 the Czechoslovak) Olympic Committee and the Czech (and Czechoslovak) participation in the Olympic Games. Table 1 provides the basic overview of the participation of our male and female representatives. Note that athletes represented the Czech group of the Austro-Hungarian Empire from 1896–1912, Czechoslovakia from 1918–1992, and the Czech Republic from 1993 onwards.

Table 1 specifies the numbers of participating Czech male and female athletes. Nevertheless, it should be interpreted in the context of the development of both sports and the Czech social environment. In 1920, Czech athletes represented the independent Czechoslovakia at the Olympic Games for the first time. It was clear that female sport was just at the beginning of its development as Czech women made up only 1.8% of Olympic participants from 1920 to 1932; a total of 6 Czech

Table 1. Czech (Czechoslovak) participation in the summer Olympic Games

Year and Olympic venue	Men (n)	Men (%)	Women (n)	Women (%)	Total athletes
1896, Athens	0	0	0	0	0
1900, Paris	5	83.3	1	16.7	6
1904, St Louis	0	0	0	0	0
1908, London	21	100	0	0	21
1912, Stockholm	48	96	2	4	50
1920, Antwerp	122	99.2	1	.8	123
1924, Paris	124	96.9	4	3.1	128
1928, Amsterdam	68	98.6	1	1.4	69
1932, Los Angeles	7	100	0	0	7
1936, Berlin	166	92.7	13	7.3	179
1948, London	63	81.8	14	18.2	77
1952, Helsinki	91	85.5	15	14.2	106
1956, Melbourne	51	79.7	13	20.3	64
1960, Rome	105	87.5	15	12.5	120
1964, Tokyo	97	90.7	10	9.3	107
1968, Mexico City	94	77.0	28	23.0	122
1972, Munich	149	80.1	37	19.9	186
1976, Montreal	128	76.6	39	23.4	167
1980, Moscow	163	77.3	48	22.7	211
1984, Los Angeles	0	0	0	0	0
1988, Seoul	113	67.3	55	32.7	168
1992, Barcelona	141	70.9	58	29.1	199
1996, Atlanta	79	66.9	39	33.1	118
2000, Sydney	100	76.9	30	23.1	130
2004, Athens	80	56.3	62	43.7	142

Source: Havránková, Hladík, Kolář & Waic (1999), Vosečková (2005)

women compared with 321 men (98.2%). Greater female participation was reached in 1936, with 13 sportswomen (7.3% of Czech participants), mostly gymnasts, competing with more than 300 other women at the Berlin Olympics.

There was great development and support of elite sport in the period of socialist Czechoslovakia. Since the 1960s, sport has begun to be used worldwide as an important political tool (and understandably has become a subject of economic interests thanks to the first live TV broadcast from the Olympic Games in Rome). The elite sport system was built intensively in the socialist Czechoslovakia with a view to fulfilling this idea. It was at the Rome Olympics where the traditional Czechoslovak female sports, gymnastics and track and field (i.e., sports whose tradition lay in the overall development of female sport in our country), were joined by canoeing. Recreational river canoeing has been a very popular summer activity among Czech people for dozens of years. Czechoslovak female athletes became successful in other sports, too (e.g., team sports, rowing, tennis, etc.) but the previously very successful gymnastics came to a crisis that has not been overcome yet. The year 1989 (the end of the socialist regime – the Velvet Revolution) resulted in the split of Czechoslovakia into two independent states, the Czech Republic and the Slovak Republic. In 1992, Czech and Slovak athletes (141 males and 58 females) together represented a single state for the last time (see Table 1).

The total number of participants at each Games was impacted by which teams qualified; a fact particularly evident in regard to the male football team. In addition, participation has also reflected political tensions (such as at the 1980 Moscow and 1984 Los Angeles Games). The growing number of female Czech/ Czechoslovak Olympic competitors has corresponded with the development of female competitive sports and with the growing number of female disciplines included in the Olympic programme. Overall, it can be said that since the end of WWII, the ratio of our female and male Olympic competitors has been more or less equal to the ratio of female and male competitors taking part in the Olympic Games as a whole. However, the 2004 Olympic Games were the first in which the percentage of female athletes (43.7%) was close to the male percentage (56.3%).

RESEARCH AIMS AND METHODS

The principal aim of this study lies in the analysis of the Athens 2004 Olympic Games media coverage in one quality nationwide newspaper. The *Mladá fronta DNES* (MF DNES) daily newspaper was selected to represent the Czech Republic. This newspaper has had a long tradition. It used to be a daily aimed at the young and was government-controlled (by 1989) but has transformed into its present-day private form. A foreign company (Rheinisch-Bergische Druckerei und Verlagsgesellschaft mbH) owns 74% of this newspaper's stock now. DNES is published six days a week on some 20 pages including daily supplements (business, employment, health, etc.) with a circulation of 310,000. Its readership is approximately 1,200,000 people daily (Šmíd, 2006). The page size is 47 cm x 31.5 cm. The newspaper is printed in colour. It should be noted that it presents itself as a quality newspaper; nevertheless, as a private enterprise owned by a foreign company, it shows certain features of tabloids.

The analysis of this Czech daily paper covered the period from 7 August (one day before opening the Olympic Games) to 31 August (one day after the end of the Olympic Games). As the DNES is not published on Sundays, 21 issues were thus analysed. Every day during the period concerned, the MF DNES issued Olympic supplements, usually on 6 pages.

A quantitative analysis of different aspects of the published articles (space occupied by the respective articles and pictures, their locations within the layout, topics, presentation in terms of gender, etc.) was carried out. Simple statistics (frequency and percentage) were used as the basis for the evaluation of the Olympic Games coverage in terms of gender. In the following discussion, 'article' measurements include both text and photographs or other images. 'Photograph' measurements are a subset of 'article' measurements. These data are accompanied by a discussion that explains the findings in relation to the Czech sports environment, tradition of the Olympic Games participation and the respective Czech athletes' aspirations.

RESULTS

Czech Participation in the 2004 Olympic Games in Athens

Men and women were given equal participation conditions at these Olympic Games regarding the number of recogniseed sports. Czech athletes competed in a total of 21 different sports (see Table 2). Our 80 male and 62 female team members were given the opportunity to test their performance in 15 and 18 sports, respectively. The relatively large number of female athletes was a result of the Czech female basketball team; there was no collective representation of men, who did not participate in any team sports. However, it should not be omitted that the officials and support staff category was evidently dominated by men who held 88% of these positions.

Table 2. Czech participation in the Olympic Games 2004

Participation	Men (n)	%	Women (n)	%	Total sports
Sports	15	-	18	-	21[1]
Athletes	80	56.3	62	43.7	142
Officials and support staff	88	88.0	12	12.0	100

[1] The Total Sports column indicates the total sports participated in overall.

Table 3 specifies the achievements of Czech athletes at the Games. The Czech men won the gold medal in decathlon, silver medals in rowing and canoeing, and bronze medals in track and field, canoeing and modern pentathlon (i.e., traditionally masculine sports). Overall men won 62.5% of the medals including the only gold medal. A Czech woman obtained a silver medal in sailing which is particularly interesting as we are a land-locked country. This appears to be one of the proofs of the changes in society as the open borders and economic changes make it possible for our people (women included) to achieve success even in such sports. The second and third places in women's shooting are also very atypical in relation to the tradition of women's sport in the Czech Republic (although the father of the bronze-medal shooter is the 1968 Olympic winner in the same sport). As for the previously successful sport of gymnastics, our country was represented by no more than two female gymnasts who did not obtain medals.

Table 3. Medals won by Czech athletes at the 2004 Olympic Games

Medals	Men (n)	Women (n)	Total
Gold	1	0	1
Silver	1	2	3
Bronze	3	1	4
Total	5	3	8

Space Dedicated to the Olympic Games in the MF DNES

The newspaper presented information on the Olympics in a special sport supplement every day. Important information was also placed on other pages including the main news pages. The articles on sports included in the supplement and presented on other pages, however, did not refer exclusively to the Olympic events but included other sporting events too. Table 4 indicates that the Olympic Games accounted for almost three quarters of the sports news. The Games accounted for an even higher percentage of photographs (80.2% of photographs and 76.2% of space). A detailed analysis, however, revealed that disregarding the fact that it was the summer sporting season, unusually great attention was paid to professional Czech and foreign football and ice hockey. The Czech football league started at the beginning of August but there were several months left to the start of the ice hockey league. Numerous stories referred to the North American NHL, even though it was suspended at that time, dealing with a players' strike. This high level of coverage was surely caused by the popularity of these two sports in the Czech Republic. Both sports achieve the highest TV ratings and attendances at stadiums.

Minor sports – those with limited organised participation and not considered internationally important – were covered by DNES only sporadically; their presentation was found on less than 5% of the space reserved for sports. However, it should be pointed out again that for some sports this was a 'holiday period'. The number of photographs and other pictures (481) relating to the Olympic Games was almost equal to the number of articles (553) even though the summaries of results were included among articles. So, approximately one third of the coverage was taken up by photographs.

Table 4. Olympic and non-Olympic sport coverage in the MF DNES by number and size

Sport	Articles				Pictures			
	n	%	*cm²*	%	*n*	%	*cm²*	%
Non-Olympic	215	28	46,352	28.2	119	19.8	12,039	23.8
Olympic	553	72	117,895	71.8	481	80.2	38,489	76.2
Total	768	100	164,247	100	600	100	50,528	100

Gender on the Pages of the MF DNES

The following analysis focuses only on the Olympics coverage and includes news not relating to gender (the neutral category). It should be pointed out here that media attention was paid primarily to the Czech team at the Olympic Games. Articles on foreign athletes occurred only exceptionally.

Table 5. Gender in the Olympic Games coverage by number and space in cm²

	Articles				Pictures			
	(n)	%	*cm²*	%	*(n)*	%	*cm²*	%
Men	198	35.8	35,469	30.1	241	50.1	19,486	50.6
Women	127	23.0	21,029	17.8	151	31.4	11,105	28.9
Mixed	97	17.5	3,1325	26.6	28	5.8	2,696	7.0
Neutral	131	23.7	30,072	25.5	61	12.7	5,202	13.5
Total	553	100	117,895	100	481	100	38,489	100

Numerous mixed articles (17.5%) dealt with both men and women at the same time. Mixed articles took up more than one-quarter of the space (26.6%) but very few of the pictures (5.8%) or total space for pictures (7.0%) included mixed groups. Neutral articles did not deal with people but, for example, described the sport facilities, presented the history of Olympic Games or were focused on the city in which the Olympic Games took place. They accounted for approximately one quarter of the articles (23.7% of number of articles, 25.5% of space). The number of pictures relating to these neutral topics was also smaller; their number only slightly exceeded 10% of the total amount and space, suggesting that they may have been seen as uninteresting by the newspaper publisher. Men received the most coverage in terms of both number and space of articles and pictures. Almost twice as much area was dedicated to men compared to women for the space for articles, the number of pictures and the space for pictures. The relative comparison of the examined items gives a more objective view of the presentation of males and females. The coverage of the pages of the MF DNES with texts and pictures referring to men and women are considered in relation to numbers of Czech Olympic participants in each category.

Similarly to Table 5, the data summarised in Table 6 also favoured men. Comparing the percentage of athletes with the percentage of coverage, we find out that females receive 5 to 7 percentage points less and males receive 5 to 7 percentage points more than their participation rate. For females, this applies both to numbers and area values (space in cm^2). Thus, taking into account the proportion of men and women in the Czech team, the relative difference between males and females is far less significant than identified when the absolute values (males more than 60% of coverage; females less than 40%) are compared.

Table 6. Coverage by gender in relation to proportions on the Olympic team

	Men	Women	Total
Number of Czech Olympic Participants	80	62	142
%	56.3	43.7	100
Number of Articles	198	127	325
%	60.9	39.1	100
Space of Articles (cm^2)	35,469	21,029	56,498
%	62.8	37.2	100
Number of Pictures	241	151	392
%	61.5	38.5	100
Space of Pictures (cm^2)	19,486	11,105	30,591
%	63.7	36.3	100

Our research was also focused on the rates at which respective sports appeared in the coverage. A great number of articles and pictures referred to sports in which Czech (and other) athletes competed at the Olympic Games. See Table 7 for the specifications of the space covered with articles and pictures referring to sports in the four monitored gender categories. Concerning single sports, the readers were most often informed about track and field (117 articles), canoeing (30 articles), swimming (28 articles) and shooting (25 articles). These were the sports in which Czech athletes were (or were expected to be) successful. Track and field is the sport with the most disciplines and thus competitors as well. Czech male athletes won two medals, of which the gold in decathlon was widely celebrated. The achievements of our male athletes in track and field, as well as their number (20 men, 16 women) were reflected by the fact that a significantly greater number of articles with a significantly larger space referred to men (79 articles on men covering 18,964 cm^2, 18 articles on women covering 2,878cm^2). Two Czech females won medals in shooting and were referred to more often in texts and pictures (18 of 25 articles, 72%; 13 of 23 pictures, 56.5% for shooting in total). As for canoeing, Czechs have always been successful in this sport at the international level. Both male and female members of the national team aspired to win medals at the Games. However, these aspirations did not come true.

Table 7. Olympic space by number of sports represented in MF DNES

Gender	Articles (n=553)				Pictures (n=481)			
	of single[1] sports (n=342)		of multiple[2] sports (n=211)		of single sports (n=262)		of multiple sports (n=219)	
	cm²	%	cm²	%	cm²	%	cm²	%
Men	32,713	92.3	2,756	7.7	12,891	66.2	6,595	33.8
Women	20,600	98.0	429	2.0	8,143	73.3	2,962	26.7
Mixed	7,298	23.7	24,027	76.7	1,461	54.2	1,235	45.8
Neutral	3,397	11.3	26,675	88.7	849	16.3	4,353	83.7
Total	64,008	54.3	53,887	45.7	23,344	60.7	15,145	39.3

[1]   Single sports means articles/photographs about one sport, such as swimming.
[2]   Multiple sports means articles/photographs about several sports together, such as all the Czech athletes in the Olympic team.

Table 8. Coverage of key sports (important for Czech Olympic participation) in MF DNES

Sport	Czech Athletes (n)		Articles (n)					Photos (n)				
	M	W	M[1]	W	MI	N	TOT	M	W	MI	N	TOT
Track and field	20	16	79	18	14	6	117	59	30	5	1	95
Cycling	10	3	8	3	3	1	15	8	3	0	0	11
Canoeing	7	3	19	8	3	0	30	12	4	0	0	16
Shooting	6	2	5	18	0	2	25	5	13	3	2	23
Rowing	15	1	9	9	0	0	18	7	2	2	1	12
Swimming	5	9	16	5	3	4	28	15	3	4	0	22
Beach volleyball[2]	0	2	0	10	0	0	10	0	10	0	0	10
Basketball[2]	0	12	2	11	0	0	13	0	5	0	0	5

[1]   M = Men, W = Women, MI = Mixed, N = Neutral, TOT = Total coverage.
[2]   Only Czech women's teams participated in these events.

Evaluation of the coverage given to men and women by the press also needs to take into consideration their achievements at the Olympics. The most respected criterion (winning a medal) is appreciated and then published most often. Czech team members won a total of 8 medals in Athens (5 and 3 medals were won by men and women, respectively, see Table 3). When considering the first 8 places, men and women achieved such positions 15 and 8 times, respectively. Men were thus almost twice as successful as women.

The analysis of the types and focus of respective articles also turned out to be interesting. The most frequent types of articles were editorials referring to sport events (32%), information on previous events (20%), or event previews (17%). From our point of view, a surprisingly small number of articles described outstanding athletes (features, profiles), accounting for as little as 14% of all articles. Information on results covered almost 10% of the space. It appeared inadequate to specify the number of such articles as the results were often reported very briefly (e.g., on two or three lines). Another characteristic, the focus of the article, was defined as the subject matter dealt with by the article. Most articles dealt with athletes and teams (40%). One quarter of the articles dealt with sporting events and competitions, another quarter referred to specific topics (e.g., doping, impact of weather on performance, etc.) As for photographs, some two-thirds of them depicted both male and female athletes during, before or after their sport performances and some 8% of them presented athletes during medal and other ceremonies.

The articles published by the *Mladá fronta DNES* focused not only on prominent athletes, but presented a wide range of information on the Olympic Games events. Deeper analysis discovered relatively large space dedicated to the Czech team members who had been successful at previous Olympic Games. Most photographs (61%) presented males and females in situations when they were engaged in their sports (i.e., doing sport or in situations related to sport). No photographs that sexualised athletes (male or female) were found. Most of the coverage was positive, emphasising both men and women in accordance with the ideal of the healthy and beautiful body and a youthful look, as well as being good people, well-behaved, well-educated and of high social status. There was no sensationalism or tabloid-style coverage, perhaps because none of the Olympic team members were known as controversial or difficult athletes.

CONCLUSIONS

Our analysis allows us to draw several conclusions concerning newspaper presentation of the Czech athletes in Olympics 2004. It is necessary to point out two principal tendencies in this presentation. First, information in MF DNES was predominantly focused on the Czech Olympics athletes, who received 70% of text coverage and 80% of pictures. The next marked tendency concerns the trends in international research within which this study was realised. In contrast to some international research, the Czech study discovered that no really crucial discrimination of women was found on the pages of MF DNES. Considering these two main groups of findings, as well as the relations between them, the conclusion explains in more detail the overall newspaper presentation during the period of the 2004 Olympics.

MF DNES presents itself as a quality newspaper and the results support this presentation. Textual information clearly outweighed visual information which is characteristic of a quality newspaper. The dominant presentation of Czech Olympics athletes and of the most popular Czech sports – men's football and ice hockey (despite the absence of any Czech team in the Olympic football competition and ice hockey not being in the Games program) – shows a lot about the sport culture in the Czech Republic. However, in relation to the Olympics, the media coverage put a very strong accent on this international sport event and Czech participation in it. Stories about football and ice hockey are attractive mainly for male readers. It may also explain why almost no female non-Olympics sports appeared in the newspaper. A more qualitative analysis of the text implies that the issue of national identity is always more closely associated with male sports. For example, the Czech women's basketball team was not presented in this context as it usually is with male team sports. However, the reason may also lie in the fact that the women did not win a medal. Considering the fact that only a small number of our athletes won medals or placed among the top eight competitors, it was not possible to evaluate whether any preference was given to the traditional national sports in the Olympics coverage.

The leading motif of international research has been gender presentation during the Olympic Games. The data presented in this chapter showed that Czech women received less coverage than male athletes. However, the coverage was relatively 'fair' in terms of the female level of participation and level of success in winning medals at the Games. However, in numbers of articles and pictures as well as in space in cm^2 of the examined items, a small under-representation of female athletes was identified.

When analysing the presentation of both sexes in relation to the proportion of Olympic medals, two facts must be taken into consideration. The first one is the expectation of achievement or medal success by *former* Olympic winners (male or female), and the second is winning a medal in the *current* Games and becoming a champion. Considering these facts, it is difficult to decide whether or not the hypothesis that female and male athletes will receive coverage relative to their successes is supported. However, the Czech data showed that there was not discrimination against women. Also, the very small number of medals gained by Czech athletes does not allow us to make any 'strong' conclusions.

The international project has aspired also to consider the sexualisation of athletes in newspapers. We suggest that such an analysis is not easily supported by considering only the quantitative data. However, based on a more qualitative and subjective evaluation, we concluded there were no sexual implications in the textual or graphic presentations of male or female athletes. There was no stress on femininity nor were women presented like sexual symbols. In general, all athletes, female as well as male, were presented as symbols of health, having a nice body and being socially successful when they participated in such a big world event like the Olympic Games.

NOTES

[1] These include the Czech Association Sport for All *(Česká asociace sport pro všechny)* with two thirds of the members being women, the Czech Sokol Organization *(Česká obec sokolská)* with one half of its members being women, and various sport federations and associations of the Czech Sport Federation *(Český svaz tělesné výchovy)*.

[2] Czechoslovakia consisted of Bohemia, Moravia, Slovakia and Carpathian Ruthenia.

[3] In the Czech Republic, "methodical support" means based on scientific research which includes, for example, teams of specialists who develop, plan, record and evaluate training and recovery programmes and other activities required for sporting success.

[4] While elite sports support systems have been built in Western Europe since 1980s on the pattern of systems established by socialist countries, the same system in Czechoslovakia was almost liquidated in the period immediately following 1989.

REFERENCES

Bláha, F. (2003). Úloha "Tělocvičného spolku paní a dívek pražských" v emancipačním hnutí českých žen před první světovou válkou. In J. Schutová & M. Waic (Eds.), *Tělesná výchova a sport žen v českých a dalších středoevropských zemích: vznik a vývoj do druhé světové války* (pp. 7–27). Praha: Národní muzeum.

European Sport Charter. Retrieved October 10, 2006, from http://www.sportdevelopment.org.uk/ European_sports_charter_revised_.pdf

Havelková, H., & Vodrážka, M. (1998). *Žena a muž v médiích*. Praha: Gender Studies.

Hartmann-Tews, I., & Pfister, G. (2003). *Sport and women: Social issues in international perspective*. London: Routledge.

Schutová, J. (2003). Počátky ženského sportu v Čechách. In J. Schutová & M. Waic (Eds.), *Tělesná výchova a sport žen v českých a dalších středoevropských zemích: vznik a vývoj do druhé světové války* (pp. 5–59). Praha: Národní muzeum.

Slepičková, I. (2005). *Sport a volný čas*. Praha: Karolinum.

Slepička, P., & Slepičková, I. (2002). Sport z pohledu české společnosti II. *Česká kinantropologie, 6*(2), 7–21.

Šmíd, M. (2006). *Vliv vlastnictví médií na jejich nezávislost a pluralitu*. Retrieved September 10, 2006, from http://www.louc.cz/pril01/vlmed2004.doc

Tomlinson, A. (1997). *Gender, sport and leisure*. Aachen: Meyer and Meyer.

Havránková, H., Hladík, P., Kolář, F., Kössl, J., & Waic, M. (1999). *Český olympismus: 100 let*. Praha: Olympia.

Wensing, E. H., & Bruce, T. (2003). Bending the rules: Media representation of gender during an international sporting event. *International Review for the Sociology of Sport, 38*(4), 387–396.

Irena Slepičková
Charles University in Prague
Czech Republic

NORTH AMERICA

EMMA WENSING AND MARGARET MACNEILL

13. CANADA

Gender Differences in Canadian English-language
Newspaper Coverage of the 2004 Olympic Games

INTRODUCTION

Media sport is a prime site for the ideological construction of gender differences, forcing people to make comparisons between men and women and establishing male performance as the yardstick for *all* sport, including women's. (Hall, 2002, p. 212)

Feminist media research has been a rich and politically engaged scholarly project over the past 25 years (Gallagher, 2006). Since the 1970s, the 'symbolic annihilation' of women in media representations has been demonstrated by uncovering patterns of condemnation, absence, trivialisation (Tuchman, 1978), objectification, irrelevant sexualisation, infantalisation, domestication and victimisation (Graydon, 2001). Sport media researchers working in Canada have also coded for these patterns and expanded the list to examine frames of compulsory heterosexuality (e.g., Hall, 2002; Kidd, 1983; Lenskyj, 1987, 2003) and ambivalence (Wensing, 2005; Wensing & Bruce, 2003). This work has resulted in changes in media policy and production codes (McGregor, 2000; Robertson, 1994).

Gender differences in the amount and type of Canadian media coverage of the 2004 Olympic summer Games are examined in this chapter. This quantitative content analysis focused on a case study of the *Toronto Star* newspaper, the largest Canadian daily broadsheet. It revealed that female athletes were deemed sportsworthy in 2004 Olympic coverage, with patriotic codes of nationalism overshadowing codes of gender difference. Women in non-Olympic sports continued to be ignored in print media.

GENDER RELATIONS IN CANADA

Canadian girls and women enjoy a wide range of political rights, yet barriers to full participation in the workforce, politics, sport and other areas of social life continue to exist. Women in Canada were granted the same electoral rights as men in 1918 and legally declared 'people' in 1929. These rights have been further protected in the *Canadian Charter of Rights and Freedom*, ratified in 1981. Women represent 50.4% of the Canadian population (16.1 million women) (Stats Canada, 2005).

T. Bruce, J. Hovden and P. Markula (eds.),
Sportswomen at the Olympics: A Global Content Analysis of Newspaper Coverage. 169–182.
© 2010 Sense Publishers. All rights reserved.

Rising participation of women in the paid workforce has been a key social trend over the past 25 years: 58% of all women worked for pay in 2004 compared to 42% in 1976. However, women have been more likely than men to work part-time in low-paying jobs without benefits (27% vs. 11% respectively). Women continue to be concentrated in traditionally feminised occupations: 67% work as teachers, nurses, health care workers or in clerical and administrative roles. Moreover, the wage gap between women and men has changed little over the past decade: in 2003, women made an average annual salary of $24,400 or 62% of what men made (Stats Canada, 2003). While there have been remarkable advances in the status and lifestyles of women over the past century, Stats Canada (2005) has admitted that significant discrepancies in the experiences of women of different ages, socio-economic classes and abilities, and from aboriginal and racialised communities, have not been revealed in official census and trend reports.

CANADIAN WOMEN IN SPORT

There are three major turning points in the history of Canadian sport and gender relations according to Hall (2002). The first was the First World War, when first-wave feminists achieved the right to vote, and women migrated in great numbers to cities in search of wartime employment and new forms of recreation (Hall, 2002). The 1920s were dubbed the 'Golden Age of Women's Sport' when Canadian women enjoyed international success, university women tried non-traditional sports like ice-hockey, and grassroots urban sports opened up to women of all socio-economic classes (Cochrane, Hoffman & Kincaid, 1977; Kidd, 1996). World War II, the second major turning point, offered opportunities for women to work in the paid labour force and to use women's sport as a vehicle to fundraise for war-related causes, as a spectacle to entertain troops and as a health-promoting activity for girls and women (Hall, 2002). Hall has suggested that a third turning point occurred in the 1960s when feminists sought to deploy sport as a vehicle to expand the basic rights of women and to introduce gender equity policies and programs. In recent years, however, women's team sports have become increasingly professionalised, commodified and sexualised in ways that offset some gains in equity (Burstyn, 1999; Hall, 2002; Lenskyj, 2003, 2008). Further, as Parratt (1998) and Hall (2002) have noted, sport history research has tended to focus on white, middle class women and has excluded women with differing abilities, sexual orientations, religions, ethnicities and racialised identities. Likewise, sports media coverage and sport media research have failed to capture the history and issues facing diverse women participating in and spectating sport.

Women have long fought to become involved in sports leadership and have broken through some barriers, yet sport has continued to be a male-dominated institution in Canada. Women struggled to control their own sporting organisations as early as 1926 when sport opportunities developed within the context of suffrage victories during World War I (Kidd, 1994). While women in recent years have reached top positions, such as Nancy Lee becoming the Head of Sports for the Canadian Broadcasting Corporation between 1996–2006 (CBC, 2006), women have continued to be under-represented in coaching and administrative positions in

Canada. The first national survey about sport leadership, for example, found women relegated to clerical and program coordination roles, while men occupied management roles in amateur sporting organisations (Fitness and Amateur Sport, 1982). At the national level, this survey found that 30% of paid national team coaches and administrators and 26% of all volunteers were female. Despite advocacy work and gains in women's access to leadership positions, research from critical and feminist perspectives suggest that the Canadian government's focus on high performance sport, the masculinist and corporate-managerial cultures of sports administration, and the media have undermined equity initiatives in women's sport (Hall 1995, 2002; Lenskyj, 2003, 2008; McKay, 1997; Macintosh & Whitson, 1990).

Opportunities for girls and women to play popular sports, such as soccer and hockey, have significantly improved since the late 1980s. Soccer has enjoyed the highest registration of players for any organised team sport. The growth of women's soccer has almost doubled (43% growth) over the past decade. In 2006, females represented 43.8% of all junior players and 39.2% of all senior players in Canada (Canadian Soccer Association, 2006). Ice hockey has also witnessed very swift growth. In the 2006–2007 season, 73,791 females players were registered with Hockey Canada (13.5% of all players). A decade ago, there were only 2,872 registered female players (Hockey Canada, 2007). Over all sports generally, however, participation rates of adults fell and the gender gap widened between 1992 and 1998: 52.3% of men and 38.1% of women participated in sports in 1992, falling to 43.1% of men and 25.7% of women by 1998. This represented a drop of 9.2% of men and 12.4% of women (Canadian Heritage, 2005). Thus, while soccer and ice hockey have become popular among girls and women, the overall participation rates in sport and fitness activities have decreased in recent years.

MEDIA COVERAGE OF CANADIAN WOMEN'S SPORT

Sport media research has been pursued in Canada from a variety of perspectives and methodologies. Ethnographic and political economic research into the labour process has demonstrated that commercial considerations – especially the need for media to deliver an audience to their advertisers – have mediated many gendered choices during the production of sport (Gruneau, 1989; Jhally, 1989; MacNeill, 1996; MacNeill, Knight & Donnelly, 2001; Silk, Slack & Amis, 2000). Media producers and editors have argued that men's professional sports have dominated overall coverage because they have attracted male audiences desired by sponsors (Burstyn, 1999; Crossman, Hyslop & Guthrie, 1994; Lowes, 1999; MacNeill, 1996; Sparks, 1992; Theberge & Cronk, 1986). Further, the structure of the Canadian media industry has allowed broadcasters and press conglomerates to own shares in professional sports teams (Sparks, 1992), thereby ensuring the prominence and regular coverage of men's sport due to their economic interdependence (Burstyn, 1999). Despite the expansion in the range of women's sports and amount of coverage since the 1970s, the expansion of men's sport coverage on a daily level has increased at a much greater rate due to the creation and expansion of all-sports radio channels, sports websites, satellite programming and 24 hour per day cable sports channels (Prestedge, 2004; MacNeill, 2004).

The perceived lack of commercial appeal attached to female sports has widely been assumed to be the main cause of low levels of day-to-day coverage of women's sport (McGregor, 2000). Women's sport in recent years has historically received about 10% of newspaper sports coverage. Readers of papers, according to Theberge (1990), assume "that on a typical day in Canada, women's sport for the most part doesn't happen" (p. 391). To examine a typical non-Olympic period, van Beurden and MacNeill (2006) studied codes of sportworthiness in the *Toronto Star*. Dominant frames of sportworthiness – that is, socio-historically specific frames deemed worthy for inclusion in sports production (MacNeill, 2002) – included nationalism, professionalism, corporatism and heterosexism (van Beurden & MacNeill, 2006). They found 82.8% of sports coverage was dedicated to professional sport versus 17.2% to amateur sport coverage. Gender differences were significant as well: male athletes were the focus of attention in 90.6% of all sports articles, whereas women were the focus in 9.4% of total sports articles. Men's sports coverage was dominated by professional sports, including ice hockey despite the season being over. The *Star* was found to be a powerful gatekeeper favouring masculine corporate sport news and marginalizing women's amateur sport.

The main exception to the unequitable attention to women's sport by the media has typically occurred during the Olympic Games. Coverage of Canadian sportswomen during summer and winter Games has increased from a low of less than 15% (Lee, 1992) to slightly more than 30% (Vincent, Imwold, Masemann & Johnson, 2002). Still, women athletes have consistently been under-represented compared to male athletes in Olympic competition. Between 1924 and 1992, women received an average of 13.8% of coverage of the winter Games in the *Globe & Mail* newspaper (Urquhart & Crossman, 1999). Of newspaper coverage of the 1996 Atlanta Olympics in Canada, the UK and the USA, 34% focused on women, a rate proportionate to the percentage of female athletes on national teams (Vincent et al., 2002).

These trends have sent mixed messages to Canadians about what types of sports and physical activities have been acceptable for women to engage in (Theberge, 1990; Urquhart & Crossman, 1999). While greater attention has typically been paid to women's sports during the Olympic Games, the media has marked preferences for sports demonstrating hetero-normative gender codes. This has led to a focus on aesthetic traits, such as beauty and grace, and a focus on culturally appropriate sports for women (Lee, 1992). Lee (1992), for example, found a media preference for individual, female sports such as swimming, diving and gymnastics in newspaper coverage of the 1984 and 1988 Olympics. In winter Games, the Canadian media have paid the most attention to women competing in figure skating and downhill skiing (Urquhart & Crossman, 1999). Overall, the Canadian sports media coverage figures have been similar to other Western nations, such as the USA, UK, Australia and New Zealand (Wensing, 2005).

Feminist scholars and advocates have long criticised the media for its inattention to women's sport in non-Olympic coverage, for signifying men's sports as more important, and for reproducing a narrow range of hetero-normative physical activity options and characteristics deemed 'appropriate' for girls and women (Canadian

Association for the Advancement of Women in Sport [CAAWS], 1994; MacNeill 1988, 2004; Theberge, 1991). In a study of daily newspapers across Canada in the years 1990–1994, CAAWS (1994) found the amount of coverage dedicated to women's sports dropped in 13 of the 20 newspapers. Overall, women's sports have constituted an average of 5.5% of all print sports coverage in Canada (CAAWS, 1994). Thus, research designed to track the range of sports and deployment of gendered codes of sportworthiness continues to be useful for measuring, historically tracking and comparing manifest patterns of inequality.

METHODS

The Canadian case study within the *Global Women in Sports Media Project* examined Canada's largest local English-language daily broadsheet, the *Toronto Star*. The *Star* averaged a circulation of half a million daily papers in each edition during 2004 (*Toronto Star*, 2004). We analysed sports coverage within the *Star* from 7 August – 5 September 2004, extended from a week before the Athens Games to a week after. Content analysis included all sports-related coverage placed on the front page and first section, the sports section and pre/post Olympic sections. Coverage was divided into Olympic and non-Olympic sports coverage.

For Olympic coverage, the number of articles and their size (in cm^2) was recorded, as was the number and size of images (all figures presented in this analysis were rounded to one decimal point). Images were classified as any cartoons, graphics or photographs associated with the Games (the small reporter mug-shots[1] were excluded from analysis). Thus, image space was included in the space allocated to articles, as was headline and image caption space. Space occupied by banners/headers and Olympic results was also tracked, but has been excluded from the detailed analyses presented here. Four categories of Olympic coverage were tracked: male athletes, female athletes, 'mixed' coverage of both male and female athletes, and neutral coverage which focused on non-gendered issues surrounding the Games (e.g., security) or provided information (e.g., scheduling). Dedicated columns such as 'Digest' or 'Notebook' were included. The short reports, each with their own headline within these columns, have been counted as one article for the purpose of analysis. Only the space occupied by non-Olympic articles, rather than the number of articles, was tracked due to the large volume of professional men's sport coverage. However, when articles in the non-Olympic section were not about professional or male sport (i.e., were about females, or mixed sport) their individual size was noted. Our results are organised according to the *Global Women in Sports Media Project* guiding hypotheses.

RESULTS

Overall, male and female athletes were treated in an equitable manner in coverage by the *Toronto Star*. In total, 661,125.8 cm^2 of space was given to sports coverage in the *Star* during the analysis period. Olympic coverage accounted for 51.2% (338,384.5 cm^2 space or 825 individual articles).

1. Gender Equity in Olympic Coverage

Gender equity was achieved in Olympic coverage of the Athens Games. Hypothesis 1, that females will receive relatively equal coverage compared to male athletes in Olympic coverage, was confirmed. Articles about female athletes represented 22.7% of all Olympic articles (see Table 1).

Table 1. Number and space of Olympic articles by gender

Measurement[1]	Male	Female	Mixed	Neutral	Total
Space cm^2	83,564.9	73,607.8	46,198.3	88,462.6	291,733.5
Space %	28.6	25.2	15.8	30.3	100.0
Articles (n)	228	187	79	331	825
Articles %	27.6	22.7	9.6	40.1	100.0

[1] Calculation did not include Olympic results or headers but did include headlines, text and image space.

This proportion of coverage appeared lower than recent research in which females received 36% of the total number of articles (Vincent et al., 2002). However the apparent decline may be methodological – in this study we accounted for articles 'neutral' in gender whereas Vincent et al. (2002) did not. If neutral articles were to be discounted in our analysis, the proportion of articles focused on females would be 37.9% (n=494), a figure similar to Vincent et al. (2002). This adjusted result confirmed the continuation of the trend of women receiving greater levels of coverage during the Olympic Games, and suggested the proportion of coverage has been stable at approximately 35%. The most frequently reported sports for females were athletics (32 articles on track events), softball (16 articles) and diving (12 articles). Event reports were the most common type of coverage for female athletes (53 articles), followed by 'Digest' (49 summaries) and 'Notebook' (31 briefs). There were 22 articles previewing female teams/sports, and 16 feature articles on female athletes. Male athletes received slightly more coverage than females: 27.6% of all Olympic articles (see Table 1). Discounting the neutral category would result in male-focused articles of 46.2%, which is a lower but similar portion to Vincent et al.'s (2002) 51% of male articles during the 1996 Olympics. The most frequently reported sports for males were articles about baseball (22), rowing (19) and swimming (18). Event reports were also the most common type of coverage for male athletes (73), followed by 'Digests' (53) and 'Notebooks' (29). There were 32 articles previewing male teams/sports, and 20 feature articles on male athletes.

Track events were the most frequently reported sporting events for mixed coverage (9 articles). There were, however, 20 articles that addressed briefly a range of sports for both genders. Event reports (24) and previews of sports/teams (15) constituted the most frequent type of mixed coverage. The apparently large number of articles in the 'neutral' category was attributed to the *Star's* inclusion of 'information pieces' each day, such as TV coverage, weather and sporting rules (79 articles). In addition, issues such as security and IOC politics were often subjects of gender neutral 'Notebook' stories (64 articles) and features (40 articles).

In the *Star's* coverage of the Games, male and female athletes received fairly equal coverage. Consistent with trends in other Western nations (see Wensing, 2005), press coverage of Canadian women significantly increased during the Olympics period compared to regular non-Olympic sports reportage.

2. Gender Inequity in Non-Olympic Coverage

Non-Olympic coverage was dominated by articles on male and professional sports. Thus, hypothesis 2, that females will receive unequal and lesser coverage compared to males in non-Olympic coverage, was confirmed. Regular professional sports covered by the *Star* were augmented rather than supplanted by coverage of the Games. During the analysis period, a total of only 39 articles, comprising 2.8% of non-Olympic sports coverage space, were identified as not being 'professional' sport articles, results or box scores (see Table 2). Of these articles, 28 were about women's sports, particularly tennis and golf. Despite increased attention to female Olympians during the Games, regular coverage of men's professional sport was not disrupted. Coverage of women in non-Olympic sports reporting was extremely limited, both in terms of space allocated and range of sports covered. Indeed, we find the proportion of women's non-Olympic sports coverage has continued a trend of declining amounts of coverage for sportswomen in the Canadian press.

Table 2. Non-Olympic article space by gender

Gender	Space cm^2	Space %	Articles (n)
Professional male	208,103.1	64.5	-
Results/box scores male	105,349.5	32.6	-
Female	6,267.3	1.9	28
Mixed female and male	2,239.3	0.7	9
Neutral	782.3	0.2	2
TOTAL	322,741.3	100.0	

3. Gender Differences in Coverage Related to Proportional Participation

The 2004 coverage was relatively proportionate to male and female representation on the Canadian Olympic team. Hypothesis 3, that female and male athletes will receive coverage relative to their proportions on the Olympic team, was confirmed. Canada sent a team of 268 athletes to the Games, including those athletes participating in demonstration sports. There were 135 female athletes (50.4% of the Canadian team) and 133 male athletes (49.6%). Neither gender dominated the *Star's* coverage of the Olympics and neither gender dominated the composition of the Canadian team.

4. Coverage Proportionate to Medals Won

Canadian athletes won a total of 12 Olympic medals at the Athens Games, with females and males each winning six medals (see Table 3). The overall 2004 Olympic coverage was relatively proportionate to the number of medals won by each gender on the Canadian team. Hypothesis 4, that female and male athletes will receive coverage relative to the proportion of Olympic medals they win, was confirmed.

Male medal winners accounted for 57.0% of the number of articles about Canadian medal winners, and females for 43.2%. Males accounted for 64.2% of the number of images of Canadian medal winners, and females for 35.9%. Thus, the parity in distribution of coverage between males and females discovered in total coverage did not hold for the smaller sample of Canadian medal-winners.

Table 3. Number of Canadian Olympic medals by gender

	Gold	Silver	Bronze	Total
Men	2	3	1	6
Women	1	3	2	6
Total	3	6	3	12

5. Femininity and the Portrayal of Female Athletes

Historically, female athletes competing in traditionally feminine sports have received greater coverage than those females competing in sports tied to hegemonic masculinity (Kidd, 1983; Lenskyj, 2008; MacNeill, 1988). Hypothesis 5, that female athletes competing in sports more strongly linked to femininity or dressed in ways that highlight gender difference will receive more coverage than those competing in sports more strongly linked to masculinity or dressed in ways that do not highlight gender difference, was not confirmed, since feminine, gender neutral and masculine coded sports received relatively proportionate coverage. Sports covered by the *Star* were allocated to three categories in relation to their status in Canada (*indicates a gender-exclusive Olympic sport). *Feminine* sports included aquatics (synchronized swimming* and diving), field hockey, artistic gymnastics, rhythmic gymnastics*, trampoline, tennis, beach volleyball and indoor volleyball. *Neutral* sports included new sports (triathlon) or sports that have traditionally involved both men and women (e.g., track, swimming and rowing). *Non-feminine* sports were historically masculine, combative and/or demonstrated strength or muscularity: water polo, athletics (field), basketball, canoe, cycling, fencing, soccer, handball, judo, sailing, shooting, softball*, taekwondo, weightlifting and wrestling. It should be noted that softball has increasingly been considered a gender neutral sport by athletes but has been deemed masculine by sport media (MacNeill, 2004). Feminine sports received the smallest portion of coverage of all articles (26.5%) and of all space (22.8%) accorded female athletes (see Table 4). Overall, the *Star* provided the greatest attention to female athletes in non-feminine sports (38.9% of all female articles and 41.7% of all female space).

Table 4. Number and space of female articles by 'femininity'

Measurement	Feminine	Neutral	Non-feminine	Total
Space in cm^2	13,168.5	20,510.3	24,061.5	57,740.3
% space	22.8	35.5	41.7	100.0
Articles (n)	49	64	72	185
% articles	26.5	34.6	38.9	100.0

The relative sportworthiness of particular sports may have been influenced by a number of factors, such as the order and overlapping of events in the Olympic program and/or the chance of victory for Team Canada.

6. Equitable Gender Portrayal in Photographs

Gender portrayal in photographs was relatively equitable between males and females on Team Canada. Hypothesis 6, that female and male athletes will be portrayed similarly in photographs, was confirmed. The 2004 *Star* Olympic coverage contained a total of 505 photographs. While a greater proportion of both the number and space was allocated to male athletes, this was likely attributable to the high-profile appeal of international athletic stars and a focus on predicted medallists, such as diver Alexander Despatie (14 images). Male athletes were depicted in 254 photos: 176 colour photos and 78 black and white photos. Females were featured in 205 photos: 148 colour and 57 black and white photos (see Table 5). Female athletes received a smaller proportion of photos compared to males: most framed predicted medallists for Canada (hurdler Perdita Felicien, 28 images; diver Emilie Heymans, 8 images; cyclist Lori-Ann Muenzer, 5 images). These results suggested that high performing athletes tied to codes of national glory received greater amounts and more appealing photo coverage than athletes with lower performance profiles.

Table 5. Number and space of Olympic photographs by gender

Measurement	Male	Female	Mixed	Neutral	Total
Space in cm^2	52,504.2	48,606.4	47,26.5	8,839.3	114,676.3
Space %	45.8	42.4	4.1	7.7	100.0
Photos (n)	254	205	20	26	505
Photos %	50.3	40.6	4.0	5.2	100.1

More photographs of female athletes (12) appeared on the front page of the newspaper than did photographs of males (8). The 12 cover photos of women spanned eight different sports (diving, water polo, cycling, artistic gymnastics, trampoline, sailing, wrestling and athletics). The front page of the sports section slightly favoured images of males (44 photos) compared to females (38 photos). However, photos of females occupied a greater amount of space than the space dedicated to photos of males (7,534.5 cm^2 for females and 7,490.0 cm^2 for males). Sport action photos framing athletes engaged in sporting action accounted for the greatest proportion of all photos (44.0% overall; 46.1% of photos of males and 49.8% of photos of females) (see Table 6).

Table 6. Number of Olympic photographs by content and gender

Content	Male	Female	Mixed	Neutral	Total
Sport action	117	102	1	2	222
Sport-related	81	66	0	0	147
Non-sport	21	14	3	4	42
Medal	14	13	1	0	20
Other	21	10	15	20	64
Total	254	205	20	26	505

Previous research has shown that sports media coverage tended to sexualise images of female athletes. This Canadian case study found that sexualisation rarely occurred in the *Star's* coverage. In 2004, only 11 of the 205 photographs of Olympic women (5.4% of photos) were heterosexualised: for example, by focusing on the breasts of a Brazilian volleyball player or the crotch of a Canadian synchronised swimmer. Sexualised coding has decreased historically and, except for a small percentage of photos in this study, male and female athletes were portrayed similarly.

7. Gender, Success and National Identity

Hypothesis 7, that female athletes who win medals in sports that are historically linked to national identity will receive more coverage than female medal winners in other sports, could not be tested since Canadian women did not compete or win any medals in sports historically related to nationalism (ice hockey and curling are not offered on the summer Olympic programme and lacrosse is not an Olympic sport). However, codes of nationalism related to patriotism, international prestige and national celebration of sporting victories were evident (Gruneau, 1989; Knight, Donnelly & MacNeill, 2005; MacNeill, 1996). Before the Games, predicted medal winners in women's events – in track, triathlon and trampoline – attracted media attention. At the Games, Karen Cockburn won a silver medal in trampoline and received the most media attention in terms of space of all female medallists. However, it was the 'failure' of reigning world champion Perdita Felicien to win gold or any medal in the 100 metre hurdles that garnered the greatest amount of attention for any Canadian team member, male or female, in terms of numbers of articles and images and space (see Table 7).

Felicien was constructed as the 'hope of the nation'. Her 20 articles and 28 images (see Table 7) garnered 20.6% of the share of total coverage accorded all female athletes, and was double the amount given to any other single athlete. Disappointment storylines surrounding Felicien's tumble in the hurdles dominated coverage in the *Star* that day rather than a celebration of Muenzer's gold medal in cycling. Overall, representational codes of nationalism rather than gender mediated the *Star's* coverage of the Games.

Table 7. Coverage of selected Canadian athletes

Athlete (medal, sport)	Articles (n)	Article space cm^2	Images (n)	Image space cm^2
Perdita Felicien (medal hope, athletics)	20	15192.3	28	7871.0
Lori-Ann Muenzer (gold, track cycling)	7	3443.8	5	1296.0
Karen Cockburn (silver, trampoline)	6	4365.3	4	1432.0
Emilie Heymans/Blythe Hartley (bronze, diving)[2]	4	2470.5	2	1154.0

CONCLUSION

Content analysis of the *Toronto Star's* coverage of the 2004 Olympic Games demonstrated that Olympic women athletes were sportsworthy and received significant coverage during the Olympics while remaining symbolically under-represented in non-Olympic coverage. Males and females received a relatively proportionate amount of coverage compared to their membership on the Canadian team. While these figures were an improvement on past coverage, the 2004 coverage was not distributed evenly in photographic coverage of male and female medal-winners. Coverage of females tended to focus on female stars predicted to bring glory to the nation by winning. Ultimately, athletic success was not necessarily an indicator of amount of coverage a female athlete received since media at the Games may not have been present at sporting sites to cover unexpected winning performances. As earlier research has confirmed, the importance of nationalism to the media during international events, combined with the economic and logistical pressures to plan which athletes to focus on prior to the Games, accounted for why some successful medal winners were ignored. Sport has long been used as a tool of nation-building (Macintosh & Whitson, 1990), and sport stars – whether male or female – were valued for the reflected glory they were predicted to bring the nation of Canada in 2004.

Greater media attention and reductions in sexist representations in the 2004 Olympic coverage, compared to previous Olympiads, have occurred in concert with equity initiatives in Canadian sport organisations, media outlets and society. Changing societal values have improved the acceptance of women competing in a greater range of sports (Vincent et al., 2002). The expanding Olympic program for women has provided greater opportunities for media to report on a greater number and range of events (McGregor, 2000). Furthermore, the content of Olympic broadcasting and print coverage has been pressured to become more 'female friendly' to broaden the audience base (McGregor, 2000; Prestedge, 2004).

Content analysis of media gatekeeping has illuminated the distribution of *what* events, cultural codes and storylines have been deemed sportsworthy but could not uncover *why* particular codes of gender were deployed by media or *how* they were interpreted and deployed by audiences.[3] Other methods are needed to delve beyond content analysis of traditional gender coding to also examine the cultural and political economies of media coverage, production struggles, audience negotiation of meaning, and the intersections of gender, race, class, ability, age and sexuality. Still, content analysis continues to be useful as a basis for cultural comparisons and tracking manifest historical shifts in codes of sportworthiness.

NOTES

[1] Mug shots (or head shots) are small images of the face of the reporter which regularly appear with stories written by that reporter.
[2] This data only includes coverage related to the event in which they jointly won a medal. Each athlete also competed in individual events.
[3] See MacNeill (2009) for a postcolonial feminist analysis of these issues with regards to Canadian media coverage of female athleticism associated with the 2004 summer Olympics.

REFERENCES

Burstyn, V. (1999). *The rites of men: Manhood, politics and the culture of sport.* Toronto: University of Toronto Press.
Canadian Association for the Advancement of Women and Sport and Physical Activity. (1994, November 29). *Coverage of women's sport plummets despite strike, lockout.* Message posted to CAAWS News Release electronic mailing list. Retrieved from http://caaws.ca.html
Canadian Heritage. (2005). *Sport participation in Canada.* Ottawa: Department of Canadian Heritage and Ministry of Public Works and Government Services.
Canadian Soccer Association. (2006). *2006 demographics: Player registration.* Retrieved July 9, 2007, from http://www.canadasoccer.com/eng/docs/2006_demographics.pdf
CBC Sports. (2006, October 17). *Nancy Lee leaving CBC sports.* Retrieved October 17, 2006, from http://www.cbc.ca/news/story/2006/10/17/lee-nancy-cbc.html
Clarke, D. (1981). Second hand news. In L. Salter (Ed.), *Communication studies in Canada* (pp. 20–51). Toronto: Butterworths.
Cochrane, J., Hoffman, A., & Kincaid, P. (1977). *Women in Canadian life: Sports.* Toronto: Fitzhenry and Whiteside.
Crossman, J., Hyslop, P., & Guthrie, B. (1994). A content analysis of the sports section of Canada's national newspaper with respect to gender and professional/amateur status. *International Review for the Sociology of Sport, 29*(2), 123–131.
Ericson, R. V., Baranek, P. M., & Chan, J. B. L. (1989). *Negotiating control: A study of news sources.* Toronto: University of Toronto Press.
Fitness and Amateur Sport. (1982). *Women in sport leadership: Summary of national survey.* Ottawa: Fitness and Amateur Sport.
Gallagher, M. (2006). Feminist media perspectives. In A. N. Valdivia (Ed.), *A companion to media studies* (pp. 19–39). Oxford: Blackwell.
Graydon, S. (2001). The portrayal of women in the media: The good, the bad and the beautiful. In B. Singer (Ed.), *Communications in Canadian society* (5th ed., pp. 179-195). Toronto: Nelson.

Gruneau, R. (1989). Television, the Olympics and the question of ideology. In R. Jackson & T. McPhail (Eds.), *The Olympic movement and the mass media: Past, present and future issues* (pp. 23–34). Calgary, Alberta: Hurford Enterprises.

Hall, M. A. (1995). Women in sport: From liberal activism to radical cultural study. In L. Code & S. Burt (Eds.), *Changing methods: Feminists transforming practice* (pp. 270–281). Toronto: Broadview Press.

Hall, A. M. (2002). *The girl and the game: A history of women's sport in Canada*. Peterborough, Ontario: Broadview Press.

Hockey Canada. (2007). *About Hockey Canada: Player registration.* Retrieved July 9, 2007, from http://www.hockeycanada.ca/2/3/9/5/2/index1.html

Jhally, S. (1989). Cultural studies and the sports/media complex. In L. A. Wenner (Ed.), *Media, sports & society* (pp. 70–93). Newbury Park, CA: Sage Publications.

Kidd, D. (1983). Getting physical: Compulsory heterosexuality and sport. *Canadian Women's Studies, 4*(3), 62–65.

Kidd, B. (1996). *The struggle for Canadian sport.* Toronto: University of Toronto Press.

Kidd, B. (1994, Winter). The Women's Amateur Athletic Federation. *CAAWS Action Bulletin, 1*, p. 1.

Knight, G., Donnelly, P., & MacNeill, M. (2005). The disappointment Games: Narratives of Olympic failure in Canada and New Zealand. *International Review for the Sociology of Sport, 40*(1), 25–51.

Lee, J. (1992). Media portrayals of male and female Olympic athletes: Analyses of newspaper accounts of the 1984 and 1988 summer Games. *International Review for the Sociology of Sport, 27*(3), 197–219.

Lenskyj, H. (1987). *Out of bounds: Women, sport and sexuality.* Toronto: Women's Press.

Lenskyj, H. (2003). *Out on the field: Gender, sport and sexualities.* Toronto: Women's Press.

Lenskyj, H. (2008). Women's issues and gender relations. In J. Crossman (Ed.), *Canadian sport sociology* (2nd ed., pp. 99–117). Toronto: Thompson, Nelson.

Lowes, M. D. (1999). *Inside the sports pages: Work routines, professional ideologies, and the manufacture of sports news.* Toronto: University of Toronto Press.

Macintosh, D., & Whitson, D. (1990). *The game planners: Transforming Canada's sport system.* Montreal and Kingston: McGill-Queen's University Press.

MacNeill, M. (1988). Active women, media representations, and ideology. In J. Harvey & H. Cantelon (Eds.), *Not just a game: Essays in Canadian sport sociology* (pp. 195–211). Ottawa: University of Ottawa Press.

MacNeill, M. (1996). Networks: An ethnography of CTV's production of 1988 winter Olympic ice hockey tournament. *Sociology of Sport Journal, 13*, 103–124.

MacNeill, M. (2002, December). *Building bridges with media: Dealing with gendered coverage.* Panel presentation to the National Conference on Women, Sport and Physical Activity, Hamilton, Canada.

MacNeill, M. (2004, October). *Breaking barriers: Women in sport.* Panel presentation to the Roger's Sportsnet Workshop in Sports Journalism, Montreal, Canada.

MacNeill, M. (2009). Opening up the gendered gaze: Sport media representations of women, national identity and racialized gaze in Canada. In P. Markula (Ed.), *Olympic women in the media: International perspectives* (pp. 50–69). Hampshire: Palgrave Macmillan.

MacNeill, M., Knight, G., & Donnelly, P. (2001). Corporate training: Identity construction, preparation for the Sydney Olympic Games & relationships between Canadian media, swimmers and sponsors. *Olympika, X*, 1–32.

McGregor, M. (2000). Canadian sports editor's speech. In P. Donnelly (Ed.), *Taking sport seriously: Social issues in Canadian sport* (2nd ed., pp. 164–172). Toronto: Thompson Educational Publishing.

McKay, J. (1997). *Managing gender: Affirmative action and organizational power in Australian, Canadian, and New Zealand sport.* Albany, NY: SUNY Press.

Parratt, C. M. (1998). About turns: Reflecting on sport history in the 1990s. *Sport History Review, 29*(1), 4–17.

Prestedge, S. (2004, October). *Breaking barriers: Women in sport.* Panel presentation to the Roger's Sportsnet Workshop in Sports Journalism, Montreal, Canada.

Real, M. R. (1989). *SuperMedia: A cultural studies approach.* Newbury Park: Sage Publications.

Robertson, S. (1994, February 8). *Expanded survey reveals a modest upsurge in coverage of women's sports.* Message posted to CAAWS News Release electronic mailing list. Retrieved from http://CAAWS.ca/html

Silk, M., Slack, T., & Amis, J. (2000). Bread, butter and gravy: An institutional approach to televised sport production. *Culture, Sport, Society, 3*(1), 1–21.

Sparks, R. (1992). Delivering the male: Sports, Canadian television, and the making of TSN. *Canadian Journal of Communication, 17,* 319–342.

Stats Canada. (2003). *Women in Canada: Work chapter updates.* Ottawa: Stats Canada.

Stats Canada. (2005). *Women in Canada: A gender based statistical report* (5th ed.). Ottawa: Stats Canada.

Status of Women. (1995). *Setting the stage for the next century: The federal plan for gender equity.* Ottawa: Status of Women Canada.

Toronto Star. (2004). *Circulation.* Retrieved August 7, 2004, from http://www.thestarworks.ca/ circulation

Theberge, N. (1990, May). *Women and the Olympic Games: A consideration of gender, sport and social change.* Paper presented at the Sport...The Third Millennium conference, Quebec City, Canada.

Theberge, N. (1991). A content analysis of print media coverage of gender, women and physical activity. *Journal of Applied Sport Psychology, 3,* 36–48.

Theberge, N., & Cronk, A. (1986). Work routines in newspaper sports departments and the coverage of women's sports. *Sociology of Sport Journal, 3,* 195–203.

Tuchman, G. (1978). *Making news.* New York: The Free Press.

Urquhart, J., & Crossman, J. (1999). The *Globe and Mail* coverage of the Winter Olympic Games. *Journal of Sport and Social Issues, 23*(2), 193–202.

Valgiersson, G., & Snyder, E. E. (1986). A cross-cultural comparison of newspaper sports sections. *International Review for the Sociology of Sport, 21*(2/3), 131–140.

Van Beurden, C., & MacNeill, M. (2006, March). *Gatekeeping in the Toronto Star: Factors affecting professional and amateur sport coverage.* Paper presented to the Rosenfeld National Undergraduate Research conference, Toronto, Canada.

Vincent, J., Imwold, C., Masemann, V., & Johnson, J. T. (2002). A comparison of selected 'serious' and 'popular' British, Canadian and United States coverage of female and male athletes competing in the Centennial Olympic Games. *International Review for the Sociology of Sport, 37*(3–4), 319–335.

Wensing, E. H. (2005, May). *Representations of gender in media coverage of the Olympic Games: The Canadian context.* Paper presented at the 13th International Seminar on Olympic Studies for PostGraduate Students, Olympia, Greece.

Wensing, E. H., & Bruce, T. (2003). Bending the rules: Media representations of gender during an international sporting event. *International Review for the Sociology of Sport, 38*(4), 387–396.

Emma Wensing
Independent scholar
Australia

Margaret MacNeill
University of Toronto
Canada

NANCY E. SPENCER

14. UNITED STATES OF AMERICA

*Content Analysis of US Women in the 2004 Athens Olympics
in USA Today*

Women from the United States have played a prominent role in the Olympics since 1900 when they first competed in the modern games. Indeed, five of the first 11 female athletes to enter the Paris Olympics were from the US. In 2004, the United States Olympic team included 257 women, out of more than 4,000 total female athletes (Wallechinsky, 2004). Women comprised 48% of the total 531 athletes on the US Olympic team as well (Shevin, 2004).

The increasing number of US female participants in the modern Olympics may be attributed to two factors: the Cold War and passage of Title IX of the Educational Amendments Act in 1972. Prior to World War II, girls were rarely encouraged to play sports unless they were 'female-appropriate'. However, as tensions between the US and U.S.S.R. escalated during the Cold War, the Olympics became recognised as a symbolic site of contestation for global supremacy (Cahn, 1994; Rader, 2004). In 1960, a turning point occurred when Doris Duke Cromwell donated $500,000 dollars to the USOC to support training of female Olympians (Rader, 2004).

Women in the United States also benefited from the passage of Title IX which aimed to eliminate sex discrimination in education (Carpenter & Acosta, 2005). One unanticipated consequence of Title IX was the proliferation in sport participation opportunities for girls and women. During the 1990s, the benefits of Title IX became evident when US women attained unprecedented success and media attention in global sports. In 1996, women's Olympic teams won gold in basketball, gymnastics, soccer and softball at the Atlanta Olympics (Jones, Murrell & Jackson, 1999). Two years later, the women's hockey team captured the first gold medal ever awarded in hockey at the 1998 winter Olympics in Nagano (Longman, 2000). Perhaps the 'watershed moment' for US women's teams occurred when the US soccer team defeated China in the 1999 World Cup. The final that was viewed by 90,185 fans at the Rose Bowl remains the "largest crowd ever to watch a women's sporting event in the United States" (Longman, 2000, p. 3).

Even though US women athletes have obtained more participation opportunities and greater visibility on the international stage, they continue to lag behind in the political arena. Admittedly the political status of women in the US improved considerably after 1920, when they received the right to vote (Rowe-Finkbeiner, 2004). However, according to *the Global Gender Gap Report* released by the

T. Bruce, J. Hovden and P. Markula (eds.),
Sportswomen at the Olympics: A Global Content Analysis of Newspaper Coverage, 183–194.
© *2010 Sense Publishers. All rights reserved.*

World Economic Forum, United States women ranked only 22nd out of 115 countries (Hausman, Tyson & Zahidi, 2006). A significant wage gap persists as well, where females receive on average 60% of the wages earned by males (Hausman et al., 2006). The political status of US women is reflected by their media coverage in international sports.

UNITED STATES MEDIA COVERAGE OF WOMEN'S SPORT

Extensive scholarly literature has documented the quantity and quality of media coverage of US female athletes (Andrews, 1998; Billings & Eastman, 2003; Cahn, 1994; Daddario, 1994, 1997; Duncan, 1992; Eastman & Billings, 1999, 2000; Hardin, Chance, Dodd & Hardin, 2002; Higgs & Weiller, 1994; Higgs, Weiller & Martin, 2003; Jones et al., 1999; Vincent, Imwold, Masemann & Johnson, 2002). Numerous scholars have specifically explored coverage of female athletes during the Olympics (Chisholm, 1999; Eastman & Billings, 1999, 2000; Hardin et al., 2002; Higgs & Weiller, 1994; Higgs et al., 2003; Jones et al., 1999; Tuggle & Owen, 1999). The 1996 Atlanta Olympics were of particular interest since they were popularly referred to as the 'year of the woman' (Chisholm, 1999; Eastman & Billings, 1999, Tuggle & Owen, 1999). Studies that examined coverage of women's sports in the 1996 Atlanta Olympics revealed mixed results (Eastman & Billings, 1999; Higgs et al., 2003; Tuggle & Owen, 1999). For example, Eastman and Billings (1999) observed that televised coverage of women's sports was comparable to men's sports, although favoritism was still shown toward men. Tuggle and Owen (1999) reported that "women in sports that involved power or hard physical contact between athletes received almost no attention" (p. 171). Higgs et al. (2003) also found notable improvements in coverage of women in the 1996 Olympics, but noted disparities in programming with coverage skewed toward gymnastics.

While the coverage of women athletes in the Atlanta Olympics reflected positive gains, Tuggle and Owen (1999) suggested that the true test of equitability was how it translated into daily sports coverage. Regrettably, studies that measure coverage of male and female athletes continue to reveal disparities that are greatest during non-Olympic times (Duncan & Hasbrook, 1988; Higgs et al, 2003; Vincent et al., 2002). More specifically, analyses of non-Olympic coverage indicate that females rarely receive more than 20% of print or electronic media coverage and are more likely to receive around 5% (Adams & Tuggle, 2004; Bishop, 2003; Bryant, 1980; Duncan, Messner & Cooky, 2000; Duncan, Messner & Williams, 1991; Duncan, Messner & Willms, 2005; Duncan, Messner, Williams & Jensen, 1990; Eastman & Billings, 2000; Reid & Soley, 1979; Tuggle, 1997). Eastman and Billings (2000) also studied the power of gender bias in sportscasting and sports reporting and found that it was more prevalent in electronic media than newspapers. Whereas men's sport received 95% of coverage on ESPN's *SportsCenter* and 93% on CNN *Sports Tonight,* women's sport received 4% and 6%, respectively; however, print media provided slightly more equitable treatment (Eastman & Billings, 2000). In *USA Today* and *The New York Times,* women received 16.5% and 9% of space, respectively, and a slightly higher percentage of photographs than space in each newspaper (19% *USA Today,* 11% *New York Times*)

(Eastman & Billings, 2000). Overall, "men received almost 5 times as much space as women in *USA Today* and a staggering 10 times as much as women in *The New York Times*" (Eastman & Billings, 2000, p. 202).

Studies of sports magazines reveal similar results. For example, studies of feature stories in *Sports Illustrated* from 1956 through 1996 (Bishop, 2003; Reid & Soley, 1979) clearly demonstrate the marginality of women's sport. Bishop (2003) found that females averaged between 2.4% and 9.1% of the magazine's feature articles and between 4.4% and 12.1% of photographs; these results did not differ significantly from Reid and Soley's (1979) previous findings.

In contrast to non-Olympic coverage, studies of the Olympics reveal increased media attention to female athletes that sometimes exceeds 40% of coverage during the Games. Many of the recent studies have focused on television broadcasts (Eastman & Billings, 1999; Higgs & Weiller, 1994; Higgs et al., 2003; Tuggle & Owen, 1999). In a comparison of televised coverage of sports in which both men and women competed during the 1992 Games, Higgs and Weiller (1994) found that females received 44% and males 56%. In 1996, similar results occurred in overall coverage with women receiving 47% to the men's 53% (Tuggle & Owen, 1999). During the 1994 and 1998 winter Olympics, Eastman and Billings (1999) found that the clock-time of primetime coverage approximated a 3:2 ratio of men to women, whereas coverage of women's sports was nearly as prominent as men's during the 1996 summer Olympics.

Numerous studies also demonstrate that women's sports that receive the most coverage are strongly associated with traditional notions of femininity, or are viewed as 'female-appropriate' (i.e., gymnastics, swimming and diving). For example, gymnastics was the most covered female sport in 1992 (almost 5 hours)(Higgs & Weiller, 1994) and 1996 (between 7 and 8 hours) (Higgs et al., 2003; Tuggle & Owen, 1999). In 1996, women's gymnastics received more than twice as much coverage as the next most-covered sport, which was swimming with almost 3.5 hours. Other sports to feature highly in recent Games include basketball, volleyball, and track and field (Higgs & Weiller, 1994; Higgs et al., 2003; Tuggle & Owen, 1999).

Newspaper portrayals of the 1984 and 1988 summer Olympics revealed that males received over twice as much coverage as females in news items, space, number of photos and illustrations (Lee, 1992). Furthermore, Jones et al. (1999) examined coverage of US women's gold-medal winning teams in the 1996 summer and 1998 winter Olympics and discovered that print media sometimes devalued female athletes' performances by comparing them to their male counterparts. Such devaluations were more likely to occur when women participated in 'male-appropriate' sports (defined as soccer, basketball and ice hockey) or 'neutral' sports (softball), whereas comparisons were rarely made (only 8%) in the 'female-appropriate' sport of gymnastics. However, Vincent et al. (2002) also compared print coverage in Britain, Canada and the US during the Centennial Olympic Games and concluded that coverage of male and female athletes was generally equitable. How can we understand these seemingly conflicting findings relative to coverage of US female athletes at the 2004 Olympics?

METHODOLOGY

This chapter focuses on *USA Today's* newspaper coverage of US male and female athletes during the 2004 Athens Olympics. As previous literature suggests, media coverage of female athletes tends to be greater during the Olympics than during non-Olympic times (Eastman & Billings, 2000; Vincent et al., 2002). And yet, while findings reveal that coverage of female athletes has generally improved, some studies suggest that discrepancies persist even during the Olympics (Eastman & Billings, 2000; Higgs et al., 2003). This chapter explores whether discrepancies based on gender were evident in *USA Today* during the 2004 Olympics.

USA Today was selected for this study because it enjoys the widest circulation of any newspaper in the United States – 5 million ("Just the facts," 2007). Previous studies have examined gendered coverage in *USA Today* (Eastman & Billings, 2000; Jones et al., 1999; Vincent et al., 2002). Eastman and Billings (2000) noted *USA Today's* relevance since it "epitomizes more popular reporting and seeks a large women's as well as men's readership" (p. 196). Although it is published only 5 days a week, the wide circulation and Olympic Bonus sections made *USA Today* appropriate for this study.

USA Today began publication in 1982 and had become the most widely read daily newspaper in the United States by 1986 ("Just the facts," 2007). By 1991, *USA Today* was reported to have "nearly 6.6 million readers – an all-time high," solidifying its status as the most widely read daily newspaper in the USA. ("Just the facts," 2007, 53). *USA Today's* readership appeals to an upscale clientele: 67% are males, 33% females; the median age is 45, with a median income of $77,462; 74% are college educated and 77% own a home ("Just the facts," 2007). In 1988, the newspaper began to insert daily bonus sections that included "extensive coverage and scores for all Olympic events" ("Just the facts," 2007, 35). Later that year, coverage of the summer Olympics resulted in a circulation record during the Games, with "more than 60,000 sales and 100 ad pages" ("Just the facts," 2007, 42). Although survey reports for 2006 indicated declines in daily readership, that trend is not surprising since many readers now turn to the Internet and cable television for more up-to-date news.

The editions included in this study appeared between Monday, August 9, 2004 and Friday, September 3, 2004. This time period encompasses more than the dates of the Olympics to allow for comparisons between Olympic and non-Olympic coverage. The inclusion of 12 Olympic Bonus sections allows for examination of the contrast between regular sports sections and bonus sections that appeared on particular dates.

RESULTS

Considering only the overall space, it was clear that *USA Today* took the Olympics seriously as a sporting event; devoting 48.6% (255,363.19 cm^2) of its total sports coverage to the Games. Overall, males dominated coverage, with 60% of space; followed by mixed coverage of men and women at 16%, then female-only coverage at 14%. Neutral coverage received 11% (see Table 1). The results were similar to Eastman and Billings' (2000) earlier study of *USA Today* where women's sport also received only 14% of total sport coverage.

However, separating the coverage between Olympic and non-Olympic coverage revealed very different patterns – with non-Olympic coverage being lower and Olympic coverage higher for females. In non-Olympic coverage, the significant disparities identified in past research on non-Olympic coverage persisted (see Table 2). Females received only 1.8% of non-Olympic space and only 4.86% of all stories. These results clearly support the hypothesis that female athletes will receive unequal and lesser newspaper coverage compared to male athletes in non-Olympic coverage.

Table 1. Total space in USA Today in cm^2

Measurement	Male	Female	Mixed	Neutral	Total
Olympic space	103,165.40	66,180.54	51,975.62	34,041.63	255,363.19
Non-Olympic space	210,938.02	4,856.71	32,650.59	21,541.35	269,986.67
Total space	314,103.42	71,037.25	84,626.21	55,582.98	525,349.86
Total %	60%	14%	16%	11%	

Table 2. Non-Olympic space and number of stories in USA Today

Measurement	Male	Female	Mixed	Neutral	Total
Space in cm^2	210,938.02	4,856.71	32,650.59	21,541.35	269,986.67
Percentage (%)	78.13	1.80	12.09	7.98	100
Number of stories	752	47	104	65	968
Percentage (%)	77.69	4.86	10.74	6.71	100

USA Today's coverage of male and female Olympians is clearly not equitable (see Table 3), as males received 40.4% of space in cm^2 while females received only 25.92%. Nonetheless, *USA Today's* Olympics-only coverage is far more balanced than non-Olympic coverage.

Table 3. Olympic-only space and number of stories

Measurement	Male	Female	Mixed	Neutral	Total
Space in cm^2	103,165.40	66,180.54	51,975.62	34,041.63	255,363.19
Percentage (%)	40.40	25.92	20.35	13.33	100
Number of stories	328	244	195	151	918
Percentage (%)	35.73	26.58	21.24	16.45	100

As they did in overall and non-Olympic coverage, however, males dominated Olympics coverage. Disappointingly, the results are much lower than in the previous studies of *USA Today's* coverage of female athletes during Olympics. For example,

Vincent et al.'s (2002) cross-cultural study of the Atlanta Olympics that included *USA Today* reported more than a 30% share for female athletes while Kinnick (1998) reported 38%. Pemberton, Shields, Gilbert, Shen and Said (2004) studied *USA Today's* coverage of the Atlanta and Sydney Olympics to find that women athletes received 41% of the coverage. In this study, the most similar levels of coverage were in relation to photographs, where females received 32.84% of photographic space (compared to 43.32% for men) (see Table 7). However, the percentage of women's photos is still much lower than the 43.5% reported by Vincent et al. (2002).

As with previous Olympics, medal counts continued to occupy a central role in US team coverage. Before the Olympics, the USOC "set a goal of 100 medals for the 2004 Games" ("USA prepares," 2004, p. 3C). The US team exceeded their goal, taking home a total of 103 medals (see Table 4), of which almost 40% were won by women. In one sense, the emphasis on winning medals has been important for US female competitors, since the Cold War motivated the US to enhance its status in the world by improving the performance of female Olympians (Rader, 2004).

Table 4. US Olympic team medals won by gender in the 2004 Olympics

Gender	Gold (n)	Gold %	Silver (n)	Silver %	Bronze n	Bronze %	Total (n)	Total %
Males	23	65.7	23	57.3	13	46.4	59	57.3
Females	12	34.3	16	40.0	13	46.4	41	39.8
Mixed	0		1	205	2	7.1	3	2.9
Total	35	100	40	100	28	100	103	100

However, in this Olympics, female athletes brought home fewer medals (39.8%) than their percentage on the team (48%) (see Table 5), while men brought home more medals (57.3%) than their percentage on the team (52%). These differences in levels of success might partly explain the lower levels of coverage for female athletes in comparison to previous research; the coverage as a percentage of medals won is similar, although slightly favoring men (70.4% versus 64.3%).

Table 5. Comparison of participation, medals won and Olympic coverage by gender

Gender	% on Olympic team	% of medals	% of Olympics coverage	Coverage as % of medals won
Male	52	57.3	40.35	70.4%
Female	48	39.8	25.58	64.3%
Mixed	-	2.9	21.38	

The US won over half its medals in swimming (n=28) and track and field (n=24). This is not surprising since the athlete receiving the greatest hype going into the 2004 Olympics was swimmer Michael Phelps, who was predicted to break Mark Spitz' record of 7 gold medals in the 1972 Olympics. Although Phelps failed to match the record (winning 6 gold and 2 bronze medals), he received more print coverage than any other US Olympian, male or female (see Table 6). The coverage of Michael Phelps, while certainly newsworthy, overshadowed the accomplishments of US women swimmers Natalie Coughlin, who "quietly won five Olympic medals", and Jenny Thompson, who "won her 11th Olympic medal to equal the career total of Spitz" (Shevin, 2004, 5–6). Neither Coughlin nor Thompson ranked in the top 10 most-covered US athletes, while Phelps dominated, with the most articles (28) and space (16908.31 cm^2; 6.2% of all Olympics coverage and 15.4% of all male Olympic coverage). Nonetheless, six of the top 10 positions were held by female athletes. The top 10 coverage was evenly divided between males and females, with females receiving 52% (38,277.01 cm^2) of the total space, 49% of image space (19,624.02 cm^2) and 47% of the articles (56). Only one woman of African-American heritage, soccer goal-keeper Brianna Scurry, appeared in the top 10; all the other US women were white.

All but one of the women in the top 10 competed in sports in which the US won a gold medal (gymnastics individual all-around, softball, beach volleyball and soccer). The only exception was weightlifter Tara Nott Cunningham, who had previously won gold at the 2000 Olympics. The two soccer players – Mia Hamm and Brianna Scurry – both played important roles in the team's gold medal win; Hamm made key goals and assists in several games while Scurry played every minute of every game and made several key saves in the final.

Table 6. Top ten most mediated US athletes at the 2004 Olympics

Name	Gender	Sport	Article (n)	Article size cm^2	Image size cm^2
1. Michael Phelps	M	Swimming	28	16,908.31	7,305.88
2. Paul Hamm	M	Gymnastics	23	10,474.11	11,318.03
3. Carly Patterson	F	Gymnastics	17	10,275.17	4,147.32
4. Jennie Finch	F	Softball	10	7,213.65	4,286.86
5. Misty May/ Kerri Walsh	F	Beach volleyball	11	6,084.96	2,127.83
6. Mia Hamm	F	Soccer	6	5,426.32	2,624.58
7. Tara Nott Cunningham	F	Weightlifting	4	5,339.38	4,248.58
8. Adam Nelson	M	Shot put	5	4,609.10	888.2
9. Tim Duncan	M	Basketball	8	3,977.84	907.88
10. Brianna Scurry	F	Soccer	8	3,937.53	2,188.85

The fifth hypothesis in this study predicted that female athletes would receive relatively more coverage if they competed in sports more strongly linked to traditional femininity or if they dressed in ways that highlighted gender difference.

189

Since gymnastics typically conveys traditional notions of femininity, it is not surprising that a gymnast, Carly Patterson, received more print coverage (10275.17 cm^2) than any other US female athlete. Indeed, former Olympic gymnast Mary Lou Retton predicted that Patterson would become the "next queen of gymnastics" (Boeck, 2004, p. 2A). Softball pitcher Jennie Finch received the second most print coverage (7213.65 cm^2) and the most photographic space (4286.86 cm^2). Although softball is not usually linked to traditional notions of femininity, marketers made an exception for Finch, who was targeted for fame as "the next big thing" after the 2004 Olympics (Horovitz, 2004, p. 1A). Descriptors emphasized her appearance: "She has a golden face. At 6 foot 1, she has hazel eyes, blond hair and a smile that make her look more like a runway model than a runaway Olympic gold candidate" (Horovitz, 2004, p. 2A). ESPN's website named Finch the "world's 'hottest' sports personality, easily exceeding often-Googled tennis beauty Anna Kournikova" (Horovitz, 2004, p. 2A). Also included in top ten coverage were Misty May and Kerri Walsh, who participated in what is arguably one of the most highly sexualised sports, beach volleyball.

The importance of fitting stereotypical notions of femininity was perhaps most evident in the coverage of women's weightlifting. Tara Nott Cunningham, a 2000 Olympics gold medalist, ranked 7th in the top 10 of US athletes receiving coverage, and received the second most photographic coverage of any US female. A petite 5'1" and 105 pounds, and competing in the lightest women's weight category, she clearly fitted within expected female norms despite competing in a sport traditionally linked to masculinity. In contrast, Cheryl Haworth was described as "America's largest female Olympian...at 5'9" and more than 300 pounds" (Umminger, 2004, p. 11D). Despite having captured a 2000 Olympic bronze medal and being considered a candidate for gold in Athens, Haworth did not rank in the top 10 and received coverage that amounted to only one article (321.93 cm^2 of total space) and one image (64.98 cm^2).

Table 7. Types of Olympic photographs by gender

	Male	Female	Mixed	Neutral	Total
Sport action cm^2	28,846.57	22,201.92	9,413.40	397.61	60,859.50
%	47.40	36.48	15.47	0.65	100
Sport-related cm^2	11,288.50	10,996.58	7,030.17	4,636.83	33,952.08
%	33.25	32.39	20.70	13.66	100
Medal cm^2	1,388.23	119.77	294.18	710.65	2,512.83
%	55.24	4.77	11.71	28.28	100
Non-sport cm^2	2,598.98	134.41	272.23	1,528.05	4,533.67
%	57.33	2.97	6.00	33.70	100
Total by gender	44,122.28	33,452.68	17,009.98	7,273.14	101,858.08
%	43.32	32.84	16.70	7.14	100

The results of this study support the sixth hypothesis which predicted that female and male athletes would be portrayed similarly in photographs. Males received the highest percentage of all categories of coverage (see Table 7). However, both males (65.4% of male images) and females (66.4% of female images) were most often photographed in action, followed by sport-related images (males, 25.6%; females, 32.9%). These results are slightly different from Pemberton et al.'s (2004) earlier findings of *USA Today* Olympic coverage where women athletes were also most often pictured in action, but these images comprised only 30% of the photographic coverage of female athletes. What is surprising is the very low percentage of images of US women with medals (less than 1% of female images), given that the female athletes with the most coverage were almost all gold medalists. However, the percentage of images in this category was also low for males (at only 3.15% of male images). In contrast to research in the 1980s and early 1990s, female athletes were seldom represented in non-sport contexts (less than 1% of images). Pemberton et al. (2004) reported that 25% of female athletes were photographed in non-action in the earlier *USA Today* Olympic coverage.

The final hypothesis suggested that female athletes winning medals in sports historically linked to national identity would receive relatively more coverage than female winners in other sports. Although the US has not always been dominant in gymnastics, the "highly regarded" US women's gymnastics team that was said to be "vying to be the next golden girls" (Boeck, 2004, p. 2A) received 12.9% of total coverage given to females. That coverage ranked third behind track (14.52%) and soccer (14.11%). This finding does not fully support previous Olympic studies which found gymnastics to be the most covered women's sport (Higgs & Weiller, 1994; Higgs et al., 2003; Tuggle & Owen, 1999), despite gymnast Carly Patterson receiving more individual coverage than any other female athlete (10275.17 cm^2) and the third most coverage for all US athletes in the 2004 Olympics.

CONCLUSION

As previous studies suggest, female athletes rarely receive more than 10% of total sports coverage during non-Olympic times. This was evident when comparing bonus Olympic sections to regular sport sections in *USA Today*. Coverage of US female athletes in the Bonus sections alone (26%) clearly exceeded the 10% ceiling during non-Olympic times, and female Olympic coverage even spilled over onto front pages (and sports pages) of the entire newspaper.

Overall, the findings somewhat reinforced the media's tendency to focus on females in sex-appropriate sports. Prior to the 2004 Olympics, a *USA Today* poll revealed that softballer Jennie Finch (76.2%); swimmer Natalie Coughlin (39.7%), and gymnast Carly Patterson (34.9%) were among five potentially marketable US Olympians; only Michael Phelps (82.5%) exceeded them in terms of potential marketability (Horrow & Ward, 2004). Patterson and Finch received the most coverage of any US female athletes, and beach volleyball players featured as the third-most covered US female athletes. However, even though Coughlin had been considered "the cover girl for the US swimming team" (Dodd, 2004, p. 1C), she was overshadowed by Phelps, like other US women swimmers. Indeed, she did not even appear among the top 10 US athletes to receive coverage.

Documenting media coverage of female Olympians is a time-consuming, yet important process. In the future, changes in how news is reported will dictate how such studies will be undertaken. Already, *USA Today* has seen declines in its readership, decreases that are likely to continue as readers seek access to more immediately available information via the Internet and/or cable television. Moreover, with the coming of age of generations of youth who have become accustomed to accessing news and information primarily through 'new media' sources, newspaper coverage may become an endangered species. These trends may not make such studies obsolete but, rather, will challenge scholars to conceptualise more appropriate ways to assess equitability of treatment based on gender.

ACKNOWLEDGEMENTS

The author would like to thank graduate students Melvin Moss, Matt Rheinecker, Megan Valentine, and Jay Wiseman from Bowling Green State University for contributing countless hours to recording quantitative information from newspapers, and to doctoral students Susan Scott-Chapman from the University of Waikato and Judy Liao from the University of Alberta for their assistance with coding and analysing data. Especial thanks go to Dr. Nancy Boudreau, in Applied Statistics at Bowling Green State University, for invaluable statistical analysis.

REFERENCES

Adams, T., & Tuggle, C. A. (2004). ESPN's *SportsCenter* and coverage of women's athletics: "It's a boys' club." *Mass Communication & Society, 7*, 237–248.

Andrews, D. L. (1998). Feminizing Olympic reality: Preliminary dispatches from Baudrillard's Atlanta. *International Review for the Sociology of Sport, 33*, 5–18.

Billings, A. C., & Eastman, S. T. (2003). Framing identities: Gender, ethnic, and national parity in network announcing of the 2002 Winter Olympics. *Journal of Communication, 53*(4), 569–586.

Bishop, R. (2003). Missing in action: Feature coverage of women's sports in *Sports Illustrated. Journal of Sport & Social Issues, 27*, 184–194.

Boeck, G. (2004, August 13–15). U.S. gymnasts look bound for glory: Women's team hopes to vault back into contention after winless 2000 Games. *USA Today*, pp. 1A, 2A.

Bryant, J. (1980). A two-year selective investigation of the female in sport as reported in the paper media. *Arena Review, 4*, 32–44.

Cahn, S. K. (1994). *Coming on strong: Gender and sexuality in 20th century women's sport.* Cambridge, MA: Harvard University Press.

Carpenter, L. J., & Acosta, R. V. (2005). *Title IX.* Champaign, IL: Human Kinetics.

Chisholm, A. (1999). Defending the nation: National bodies, U.S. borders, and the 1996 U.S. Olympic women's gymnastics team. *Journal of Sport & Social Issues, 23*, 126–139.

Daddario, G. (1994). Chilly scenes of the 1992 Winter Games: The mass media and the marginalization of female athletes. *Sociology of Sport Journal, 11*, 275–288.

Daddario, G. (1997). Gendered sports programming: 1992 Summer Olympic coverage and the feminine narrative form. *Sociology of Sport Journal, 14*, 103–120.

Dodd, M. (2004, August 2). Poised for pedestal: Versatile Natalie Coughlin gets chance to shine brightest. *USA Today*, p. 1C.

Duncan, M. C. (1992). A great athlete... and a cute, sexy flirt, too. *Extra!*, *5*, 20–21.

Duncan, M. C., & Hasbrook, C. A. (1988). Denial of power in televised women's sports. *Sociology of Sport Journal*, *5*, 1–21.

Duncan, M. C., Messner, M. A., & Cooky, C. (2000). *Gender in televised sports: 1989, 1993, and 1999*. Los Angeles: The Amateur Athletic Foundation.

Duncan, M. C., Messner, M. A., & Williams, L. (1991). *Coverage of women's sports in four daily newspapers*. Los Angeles: The Amateur Athletic Foundation.

Duncan, M. C., Messner, M. A., Williams, L., & Jensen, K. (1990). *Gender stereotyping in televised sports*. Los Angeles: The Amateur Athletic Foundation.

Duncan, M. C., Messner, M. A., & Willms, N. (2005). *Gender in televised sports: News and highlight shows, 1989–2004*. Los Angeles: The Amateur Athletic Foundation.

Eastman, S. T., & Billings, A. C. (1999). Gender parity in the Olympics: Hyping women athletes, favoring men athletes. *Journal of Sport & Social Issues*, *23*, 140–170.

Eastman, S. T., & Billings, A. C. (2000). Sportscasting and sports reporting: The power of gender bias. *Journal of Sport & Social Issues*, *24*, 192–213.

Hardin, M., Chance, J., Dodd, J. E., & Hardin, B. (2002). Olympic photo coverage fair to female athletes. *Newspaper Research Journal*, *23*(2/3), 64–78.

Hausman, R., Tyson, L. D., & Zahidi, S. (2006). *The global gender gap report 2006*. World Economic Forum. Retrieved June 17, 2007, from http://www.weforum.org/pdf/gendergap/report2006.pdf

Higgs, C., & Weiller, K. (1994). Gender bias and the 1992 summer Olympic Games: An analysis of television coverage. *Journal of Sport & Social Issues*, *18*, 234–246.

Higgs, C., Weiller, K. H., & Martin, S. B. (2003). Gender bias in the 1996 Olympic Games: A comparative analysis. *Journal of Sport & Social Issues*, *27*, 52–64.

Horovitz, B. (2004, August 10). Softball's Jennie Finch ready to make her pitch. Olympian has golden arm, golden marketing potential. *USA Today*, pp. 1A, 2A.

Horrow, E. J., & Ward, S. (2004, August 20). Olympians with commercial appeal. *USA Today*, p. 1C.

Jones, R., Murrell, A., & Jackson, J. (1999). Pretty vs. powerful in the sports pages: Print media coverage of U.S. Olympic gold medal winning teams. *Journal of Sport & Social Issues*, *23*, 183–192.

Just the facts. (2007). *USA Today media kit*. Retrieved February 23, 2007, from http://www.usatoday.com/media_kit/pressroom/pr_justfacts_usatoday.htm

Kinnick, K. N. (1998). Gender bias in newspaper profiles of 1996 Olympic athletes: A content analysis of five major dailies. *Women's Studies in Communication*, *21*, 212–237.

Lee, J. (1992). Media portrayals of male and female Olympic athletes: Analyses of newspaper accounts of the 1984 and the 1988 summer Games. *International Review for the Sociology of Sport*, *27*, 197–222.

Longman, J. (2000). *The girls of summer: The U.S. women's soccer team and how it changed the world*. New York: Harper Collins.

Rader, B. G. (2004). *American sports: From the age of folk games to the age of televised sport* (5th ed.). Upper Saddle River, NJ: Prentice Hall.

Reid, L. N., & Soley, L. C. (1979). *Sports Illustrated's* coverage of sports. *Journalism Quarterly*, *4*, 861–863.

Rowe-Finkbeiner, K. (2004). *The F-word, feminism in jeopardy: Women, politics, and the future*. Emeryville, CA: Seal Press.

Shevin, C. (2004, August 31). *U.S. Women shine at Olympics, thanks to Title IX*. National Organization for Women Website. Retrieved May 25, 2007, from http://www.now.org/issues/title_ix/083104olympics.html

Pemberton, C., Shields, S., Gilbert, L., Shen, X., & Said, H. (2004). A look at print media coverage across four Olympiads. *Women in Sport & Physical Activity Journal*, *13*, 87–99.

Tuggle, C. A. (1997). Differences in television sports reporting of men's and women's athletics: ESPN *SportsCenter* and CNN *Sports Tonight*. *Journal of Broadcasting and Electronic Media*, *41*, 14–24.

Tuggle, C. A., & Owen, A. (1999). A descriptive analysis of NBC's coverage of the Centennial Olympics: The "Games of the Woman?" *Journal of Sport & Social Issues, 23*, 171–182.

Umminger, A. (2004, August 18). Women do heavy lifting in pursuit of gold. *USA Today*, p. 11D.

USA prepares for major medal haul. (2004, August 2). *USA Today*, p. 3C.

Vincent, J., Imwold, C., Masemann, V., & Johnson, J. T. (2002). A comparison of selected 'serious' and 'popular' British, Canadian, and United States newspaper coverage of female and male athletes competing in the Centennial Olympic Games. *International Review for the Sociology of Sport, 37*, 319–335.

Wallechinsky, D. (2004). *The complete book of the summer Olympics (Athens 2004 edition)*. Wilmington, DE: Sport Media Publishing.

Nancy E. Spencer
Bowling Green State University
USA

ASIA: WEST ASIA

CANAN KOCA AND BENGU ARSLAN

15. TURKEY

Turkish Media Coverage of the 2004 Olympics

GENDER RELATIONS IN TURKEY

The dissolution of the Ottoman Empire and the establishment of the modern Turkish Republic in 1923 provided ideological and legal bases for the modernisation process in Turkey. Within this modernisation project, the new state replaced the Islamic civil code with a secular or republican code adopted from the Swiss code, which introduced gender equality in marriage, divorce and matters of inheritance. In 1930, Turkish women were granted the right to vote in local elections and, in 1934, the right to vote for and to be elected to public office in national elections. Republican gender ideology in general expected women to follow a particular form of education and act as visible ambassadors to challenge the backward image of Muslim women in the world as well as in Turkey (Kandiyoti, 1989). However, these reforms for recognising women as individuals did not in reality bring equality to women. In the new state, the women continued to be described according to their traditional female roles and this prevented the development of a perception of women as being equal partners of men (Arat, 1994; Kandiyoti, 1987). As Arat (1994) argues, Turkish women are emancipated but unliberated. Keeping mind all these modernisation movements and legal changes which are focused on women, it seems contradictory, as Muftuler-Bac (1999) has argued, that Turkish women are still oppressed by the patriarchal system. However, a whole year of intensive lobbying and widespread campaigning by the women's movement throughout 2001 has resulted in reforms which have drastically changed the legal status of women in the family and in the promulgation of the new Turkish Civil Code, which was passed by the Turkish Grand National Assembly on November 22, 2001 (WWHR, 2002). The new Code sets the equal division of the property acquired during marriage as a default property regime, assigning an economic value to women's hitherto invisible labour for the well-being of the family household.

Nowadays, the primary engine of the Turkish modernisation project has been Turkey's ongoing attempt to gain entrance into the European Union (EU). Within this ongoing project, Turkey signed the United Nations Convention on Elimination of All Forms of Discrimination Against Women (1979), and the Declaration on the Elimination of Violence Against Women (1993). A 2007 European Parliament report notes that the political participation by women in Turkey is too low and that there is an absolute need for female role models in positions of power and

T. Bruce, J. Hovden and P. Markula (eds.),
Sportswomen at the Olympics: A Global Content Analysis of Newspaper Coverage, 197–208.

decision-making. Regarding gender equality in access to education and the labour market, UNICEF estimates that each year between 600,000 and 800,000 girls are either prevented by their families from going to school or do not attend because of logistical difficulties. The Turkish female employment rate is just under 25%, compared to the average EU-25[1] women's employment rate of 55%. Members of the European Parliament therefore called on the Turkish government to ensure gender equality in access to education and the labour market, especially in the south-eastern regions (European Parliament, 2007).

GENDER RELATIONS IN SPORT

Although gender issues in sport have been studied extensively worldwide since the 1980s, they have been studied in Turkey for only a few years. The increasing rates of women's participation in both elite and recreational sport have led researchers to investigate the sport and exercise environment as an important arena of gendered cultural practices in Turkish society (Koca & Asci, 2005; Koca & Bulgu, 2005; Koca, Asci & Kirazci, 2005). In these studies it has been argued that although, like many other Western societies, patriarchy is still one of the most important characteristics of Turkish society and female athletes have been faced with various forms of patriarchal oppression, there have been some changes in the status of Turkish women in sport, particularly in urban areas. For example, Fasting and Pfister (1997) also concluded that at least some parts of Turkey were changing, and that not only was the younger generation more active in sport but parents also encouraged their children to enjoy sport, especially girls, because sport was considered as something positive. Relative to the situation of women in elite sport, although most of the elite female athletes are competing in volleyball and track and field, there have been increasing numbers of female athletes in martial sports such as taekwondo and judo and, recently, in weightlifting and wrestling. For recreational sport, increasing numbers of women have been participating in physical activity in their leisure time as a result of broader social transformations during recent years in Turkey. Factors such as continuing modernisation movements, rapid urbanisation and the growing attention from the municipalities towards physical activity for women have all motivated women in Turkey to participate in physical activity in different types of sport and exercise clubs (Koca, Bulgu & Asci, 2007).

In recent years, there has been a significant increase in the number of women in sports and in female athletes' participation and achievements in international sports competitions (e.g., having medals in World and European Championships and Olympics). According to information from the General Directorate of Youth and Sport, while the number of elite female athletes (330,258) is less than elite male athletes (856,572), there has been a five-fold increase in women's involvement in sport since 2002 (www.gsgm.gov.tr). Regarding the statistics, the number of female athletes was about 66,000 in 2002 and this number increased to about 350,000 in 2007. In addition, the highest participation of Turkish female athletes in the Olympics was at the 2004 Games, where Nurcan Taylan became the first Turkish female athlete to win a gold medal in the Olympics.

PREVIOUS RESEARCH ON GENDER DIFFERENCES IN MEDIA COVERAGE

The presentation of women in the media has gained a renewed interest by several scholars from different disciplines in Turkey and many researchers have pointed to the under-representation of women in Turkish media and the fact that, when women are represented, the coverage reinforces existing stereotypical norms such as housewives or mothers, and women as sexual objects (Gencel-Bek, 2001; Gencel-Bek & Binark, 2000; Hortacsu & Erturk, 2003). On the other hand, physical, sexual and psychological violence against women has been increasingly visible within the general community, including rape, sexual abuse and sexual harassment in family, work and educational institutions and, therefore, there are some other studies which investigated the media coverage of violence towards women. For example, Alat (2006) analysed the Turkish news coverage of violence against women. She found the following patterns in news stories: a victim blaming attitude, questioning perpetrators' mental status and women's adherence to gender norms, scrutinising the victim's intention for reporting the crime, and turning sexual assault into pornographic stories. These issues have been explored in a sport context by Bulgu and Koca (2006) who examined the presentation of a case of sexual harassment in the national women's weightlifting team in Turkish daily newspapers and found that, in order to protect the national popularity of weightlifting, the print media presented the case in ways that suggested they did not really believe the sexual harassment took place.

Although there have been many international studies of media coverage of women's sport in Western countries, there has been a limited number of studies about this subject in Turkey. One recent study (Öktem, 2004) analysed the media coverage of Süreyya Ayhan who is one of the most successful and famous Turkish track and field athletes and found that the achievements of women are disregarded and, further, that her success has been reflected as an extraordinary and unusual event in the media. In another recent study, Arslan and Koca (2007) examined gender stereotypes in both written and visual texts of female articles in Turkish newspapers. One of the findings of their study is that the number of female articles (6.05%, n=220) was significantly lower than male articles (87.02%, n=3,166) and, although the data revealed that there were gender stereotypes in media coverage of female athletes, particularly in visual texts of newspapers, the overall amount of these gender stereotypes remains low. For example, 13.9% of female athletes received photographic coverage as glamorous or sexy, and with reference to their heterosexual familial roles as wives, mothers and daughters. Semra Aksu, a former Turkish track and field athlete, was pictured with her baby on the blocks in a position ready for the start. In this study, which included both Olympic and non-Olympic periods, most of the articles were about female weightlifters, who have previously had the highest athletic achievement (such as medals in several World and European Championships) of female athletes in Turkey and, therefore, were great expectations for medals in the 2004 Olympic Games (Arslan & Koca, 2007). Female weightlifters are visibly strong and muscular (attributes long viewed as being unfeminine) and they certainly do not conform to stereotypes of femininity. Thus, it should come as no surprise to realise that, in the Turkish media, female weightlifters were mostly represented by their athletic performance rather than in relation to normative stereotypes of femininity (Arslan & Koca, 2007).

METHODS

Three Turkish daily newspapers, appealing to different audiences, were chosen. *Hürriyet, Cumhuriyet* and *Zaman* are three of the mass-circulation newspapers in the country. *Zaman* is a conservative newspaper and has the highest circulation (over 500,000 copies per day). The *Cumhuriyet* (Republic) has the highest circulation (about 50,000 per day) of the newspapers with social democratic views, and the *Hurriyet* (Liberty) has a circulation about 490,000 per day and supports liberal economic views.

The sample was collected from 13 – 29 August 2004 and consists of 1,132 sports-related articles. The data collection period starts from the date of the opening ceremony and ends with the date of the closing ceremony of Olympics. In the present study, media coverage refers to the number of articles reported in newspapers. Stories were analysed from the sport and news sections of each daily newspaper. Therefore, all articles related to both Olympics and non-Olympic sports in all sections of each newspaper were initially counted. The result sections were also counted. Then they were coded into categories with respect to gender; namely female articles, male articles and mixed. The researchers categorised articles as female articles that referred to events related only to females, and as male articles that referred to events related only to males. Articles that referred to events related to both females and males were coded as mixed articles. The articles that were related to general Olympics (e.g., philosophy and history) were not included in the content analysis: however, there were few such articles in each newspaper. The results from all three newspapers have been combined.

THE RESULTS OF THE CONTENT ANALYSIS

At the 2004 Olympic Games in Athens, 45 men and 20 women competed for Turkey. Turkish athletes won a total of 10 medals (in weightlifting, boxing, wrestling, taekwondo and track and field). Only one medal (gold) was won by a female – weightlifter Nurcan Taylan.

Men Dominate Media Coverage

The analysis of this project included both Olympics and non-Olympic coverage of newspapers. Although the analysis included just the dates of Olympics, the overall proportion of newspaper coverage devoted to Olympics was low (30.1%, see Table 1).

Table 1. Total coverage dedicated to Olympics and non-Olympics articles

Measurement	Olympics	Non-Olympics	Total articles
Number of stories	341	791	1,132
% of total coverage	30.1%	69.9%	100%

This high overall proportion of newspaper coverage devoted to non-Olympics is also likely to have influenced the total proportion of coverage for females which reached only 10.1% (see Table 2).

Table 2. Total coverage by gender

Measurement	Male	Female	Mixed	Total
Number of stories	883	114	135	1,132
% of total coverage	78%	10.1%	11.9%	100%

Females Receive Little Non-Olympic Coverage

The findings of this study indicated that in non-Olympic coverage, female athletes received only 2% of the newspaper coverage whereas male athletes received 95.6% (Table 3). Thus, our results indicate that female athletes received much less newspaper coverage in non-Olympic coverage compared to male athletes. Football (93%) had the most coverage in non-Olympic sport for males. On the other hand, track and field (37.4%) had the highest coverage in non-Olympic sport for females. The other stories concerning female athletes in non-Olympic sport were tennis (18.8%), handball (18.8%), volleyball (12.5%) and basketball (12.5%).

Table 3. Non-Olympic coverage by number of stories in Turkey Newspapers during the 2004 Olympic Games

Measurement	Male	Female	Mixed	Total
Number of stories	756	16	19	791
Percentage	95.6	2.0	2.4	100%

Females Receive Higher Levels of Olympic than Non-Olympic Coverage

This study found that female athletes received 28.74% of all Olympic coverage whereas male athletes received 37.24%. Although the percentage of female athletes in the Olympic coverage (28.74%) is much more than the percentage of female athletes in non-Olympic coverage (2%), female athletes still received less newspaper coverage than male athletes. The percentage of mixed coverage (34.02%) is higher than the percentage of female athletes in Olympic coverage (28.74%). The percentage of mixed coverage in Olympic sports is also higher than the percentage of mixed coverage in non-Olympic sports (2.4%). The reason for this difference can be explained by the mixed nature of the Olympics. There are both female and male sports in Olympics; therefore relatively more coverage was devoted to mixed stories in Olympic coverage than in non-Olympic coverage. Another reason for this difference could be the inclusion of the results sections that consisted of both male and female results. The content of the mixed articles was mostly male with a little female coverage. This finding should be attributed to the high number of male athletes in Turkish Olympic team. Thus, our results do not support the hypothesis that female athletes will receive relatively equal newspaper coverage compared to male athletes. The frequencies and percentages are shown in Table 4. Overall, most of the female coverage (86%; 98 of 114 articles) was from the Olympics, as was the majority of the mixed coverage (85.9%; 116 of 135 articles). However, the opposite was true for males: only 14.4% of all male coverage was devoted to the Olympics with 756 of 883 articles (85.6%) being focused on non-Olympic events.

Table 4. Olympics-only coverage by number of stories in Turkish newspapers during the 2004 Olympic Games

Measurement	Male	Female	Mixed	Total
Number of stories	127	98	116	341
Percentage	37.24	28.74	34.02	100%

Differences in Coverage Relative to Proportion on the Olympic Team

The findings of this study did not fully support the hypothesis which argued that female and male athletes will receive coverage relative to their proportions on the Olympic team (see Table 5). Male athletes received less coverage (37.24%) than their participation rate (69.7%), whereas female athletes' coverage was clearly much closer to their participation proportion (only 1.6% less). Thus, the coverage of female athletes (28.74%) was relative to their proportion (30.3%) on the Turkish Olympic team, while the male coverage was not.

Table 5. Olympic coverage of Turkish female and male athletes and their proportions on the Turkish Olympic team

Measurement	Male		Female	
	n	%	n	%
Olympic stories	127	37.24	98	28.74
Olympic team	46	69.7	20	30.3
Medal winners	9	90	1	10

The results also did not support the hypothesis that female and male athletes will receive coverage relative to the proportion of Olympic medals they win (see Table 5). Our findings showed that male athletes received less coverage than the proportion of Olympic medals they won, whereas female athletes received more coverage than their proportion of medals. Women athletes won only 10% of Turkey's medals but received 28.74% of the coverage; while males won 90% of medals and received 37.24% of coverage. It should be noted, however, that almost one-third of the coverage was mixed stories, which focused on both male and female athletes (see Table 5). Almost half of the mixed stories consisted of winners in the Olympics.

Females Who Were Expected to Win Medals in Olympics Had the Highest Coverage

Nurcan Taylan, a weightlifter, was the only Turkish female medal winner in the 2004 Olympic Games. Weightlifting is one of the sports that are historically linked to Turkish national identity and the highest achievement of Turkish athletes during the 2004 Olympics was in weightlifting (two gold medals and one bronze for males and one gold medal for females). Regarding the fifth hypothesis that female athletes who win in sports historically linked to national identity will receive more coverage than female winners in other sports, the 27.6% of articles related to Nurcan Taylan and other female weightlifters in the Turkish Olympic team is only the second highest percentage in the female articles and less than half the percentage for the most covered sport of track and field (see Table 6). Therefore, this study disproves the fifth hypothesis.

However, our findings support the hypothesis in another way. For example, the biggest expectation for female medals in the 2004 Olympic Games was from two well-known track and field athletes, Süreyya Ayhan and Elvan Abeylegesse. Ayhan was the 2002 European 1500m champion and had won the silver medal in the 2003 world championships. Abeygelesse held the world record in 5000m (14.24.68). Therefore, the high level of coverage is not unexpected, although they did not win any medals. Although track and field is not historically linked to national identity in Turkey, medal expectations are related to national identity and, therefore, these athletes received relatively more coverage than female medal winners in other sports. Therefore, the reason the hypothesis is not supported is that winning is the most important thing, rather than an association with sports that have historical links to national identity. Indeed, almost 85% of female coverage was of women who won, or who were expected to win. Although weightlifting, swimming and archery have similar numbers of athletes competing, weightlifting got much more coverage (27.6%) than swimming (5.1%) and archery (2%). The reason for this is highly related to the big expectation for medals in the 2004 Olympic Games from Nurcan Taylan who won the gold medal. She received 20.5% of the 27.6% weightlifting coverage. Similarly, Elvan Abeylegesse and Süreyya Ayhan received 50.1% of the 57.2% track and field coverage. Because of an injury, Süreyya Ayhan did not compete in 2004 Olympics, withdrawing shortly before the Games began. Therefore, Abeylegesse had more coverage (40.9%) than Ayhan (9.2%) of the 57.2% track and field coverage. Most of the coverage about Ayhan was related to her injury. In addition to this, the rest of the track and field coverage was devoted to female athletes from other countries.

Table 6. Olympic coverage of Turkish female and male athletes and their proportions on the Turkish Olympic team

Sport in order of total articles	Male				Female			
	Articles		Athletes on Olympic team		Articles		Athletes on Olympic team	
	(n)	% of male coverage	(n)	% of males on Turkish team	(n)	% of female coverage	(n)	% of females on Turkish team
Track and field	14	11.0	5	10.9	56	57.2	8	40
Weightlifting	25	19.7	6	13.0	27	27.6	4	20
Wrestling	30	23.6	12	26.0	-		-	-
Boxing	23	18.1	8	17.4	-		-	-
Taekwondo	8	6.3	1	2.2	-		-	-
Swimming	3	2.4	5	10.9	5	5.1	4	20
Judo	2	1.6	2	4.3	1	1.0	1	5
Shooting	2	1.6	1	2.2	-		-	-
Sailing	4	3.1	5	10.9	-		-	-
Archery	-		1	2.2	2	2.0	3	15
Other countries	16	12.6	-	-	7	7.1	-	-
Total	127	100	46	100	98	100	20	100

Our findings also disproved the hypothesis that female athletes competing in sports more strongly linked to femininity or dressed in ways that highlight gender difference will receive relatively more coverage than those competing in sports more strongly linked to masculinity or dressed in ways that do not highlight gender difference. Female athletes competing in track and field (57.2%) and weightlifting (27.6%) received more coverage than female athletes who competed in other sports (Table 6). Thus, this finding did not support this hypothesis since track and field is accepted as a gender-neutral sport and weightlifting as male-appropriate sport. On the other hand, these two sports are not stereotypically feminine sports. The uniforms worn by Abeylegesse and Ayhan, who had the most coverage, were not revealing and did not highlight femininity.

Males Receive Higher Levels of Olympic Photographic Coverage than Females

The analysis of this project included Olympic photographic coverage in the newspapers. This study found that male athletes received 39.8% of all Olympic photographic coverage whereas female athletes received 33% (Table 7). Consistent with the percentage of male athletes (37.24%) in Olympic coverage, male athletes had similar percentage in Olympic photographic coverage (39.8%). Female athletes' Olympic photographic coverage was clearly closer to their Olympic coverage proportion (only 4.26% less), whereas mixed coverage had fewer photographs (27.2%) than their proportion in Olympic coverage (34.02%).

Table 7. Total Olympics photographic coverage by gender

Measurement	Male	Female	Mixed	Total
Number of photographs	88	73	60	221
Percentage	39.8%	33%	27.2%	100%

Table 8. Olympic photographic coverage of Turkish female and male athletes

	Female		Male	
Sport in order of total articles	(n)	% of female coverage	(n)	% of male coverage
Track and field	40	54.8	10	11.4
Weightlifting	20	27.4	22	25.0
Boxing	-	-	18	20.5
Wrestling	-	-	17	19.4
Taekwondo	-	-	8	9.1
Swimming	1	1.4	1	1.1
Judo	-	-	1	1.1
Shooting	-	-		-
Sailing	-	-	1	1.1
Archery	-	-		-
Other countries	12	16.4	10	11.3
Total	73	100	88	100

Female track and field athletes had the highest photographic coverage (54.8% of female coverage) since they were expected to win medals in the Olympic Games (Table 8). The highest photographic coverage went to the three athletes most expected to win medals: Abeylegesse (39.7%), Taylan (15.9%) and Ayhan (5.7%). The Olympic photographic coverage for these three Turkish female athletes was close to their percentage of female Olympic articles: Abeylegesse (40.9%), Taylan (20.5%) and Ayhan (9.2%). For males, weightlifting (25%), boxing (20.5%) and wrestling (19.4%) had the highest coverage. Male athletes' Olympic photographic coverage also showed a similar percentage to their Olympic articles: weightlifting (19.7%), boxing (18.1%) and wrestling (23.6%).

Females Receive Photographic Coverage Relative to their 2004 Performance

Olympics photographs in each newspaper were also analysed based on two main categories: (a) relevance of performance and (b) gender stereotypes. Photographs that depicted female athletes actively participating in their own sports or shown in sports-related settings were coded as relevant performance, and photographs that depicted female athletes in non-sport settings were coded as non-relevant performance. Additionally, photographs that depicted female athletes with stereotypical female characteristics such as beauty, sexuality, physical appearance or femininity were coded as gender stereotyped.

Our findings indicated that 78.1% of female athletes' photographs were related to performance (Table 9). For instance, Elvan Abeylegesse and Nurcan Taylan were presented during their actual athletic performance in the 2004 Olympic Games. The vast majority of female athletes' photographs (91.8%) were not gender stereotyped. However, 8.2% of female athletes received glamorous, sexy and still shots. Turkish female athletes' photographic coverage was focused on performance rather than gender as defining their representation. Gender stereotyped coverage appeared only for female athletes from other countries. For example, the *Cumhuriyet* for August 18 included several inside photographs of tennis player, Venus Williams, showing her posing seductively for the camera in her off-court wear.

Table 9. Content of female athletes' Olympic photographic coverage

Female photographs	Relevance of performance			Gender stereotypes		
	Yes	No	Total	Yes	No	Total
Number of photographs	57	16	73	6	67	73
Percentage	78.1	21.9	100	8.2	91.8	100

CONCLUSIONS

Based on 1,132 sports-related articles from three different Turkish daily newspapers, this study indicates that male athletes received higher coverage than female athletes in both Olympic and non-Olympic articles. However, female athletes had relatively higher coverage in Olympic articles than non-Olympic articles. The findings show that females who compete in the Olympics appear to be of more interest to the media (28.74% of coverage) than those who do not (only 2% of non-Olympic coverage). The coverage of female Olympic athletes was also much closer to their proportion on the Turkish Olympic team than the coverage of male athletes. Females also received much more coverage than their percentage of medals won. Overall, most of the female coverage was from the Olympics, whereas most of the male coverage was devoted to non-Olympic events.

The increased coverage of female athletes in Olympic coverage might be attributed to the increasing number of Turkish female athletes who are participating and achieving in international competitions and, therefore, their increasing popularity in recent years. Besides, it should be also noted that Olympic Games seem to be important in publicising female athletes' sport achievements. Therefore, we can argue that the higher coverage of female athletes might relate to the strong nationalistic fervour ignited by the Olympics in Turkey. National identity can be fostered by reports from the media by representing national athletes' achievements in Olympics rather than athletes from other countries. Certainly our study shows that the Turkish media were most interested in Turkish athletes. For example, only 10.2% of all male and female Olympic stories (23 out of 225) were about athletes from other countries (see Table 6). This means that 89.8% of this coverage focused on athletes from Turkey.

The findings of this project indicate that winning is more important than an association with sports that have historical links to national identity. Almost 85% of female coverage was of women who won or who were expected to win. The athletes who win Olympic medals are celebrated as heroes/heroines in Turkey. In addition to this, winning was the most important since it did not matter how female athletes were dressed (feminine or not, revealing or not), it was the winners or expected winners who got coverage.

Overall, our study demonstrates that although males had relatively more coverage in both Olympic and non-Olympic events, most of the male coverage was devoted to non-Olympic events. Olympic coverage was only 30.1% of all the sports media coverage during this period; and males received 95.6% of the non-Olympic coverage. This study also found that male athletes received more Olympic photographic coverage than female athletes.

Female track and field athletes had the highest photographic coverage since they were expected to win medals. Our findings also indicated that most of the female athletes' photographs were related to their actual performance and most did not receive any gender stereotypes. Not only were female athletes who received gender stereotyped coverage (in glamorous, sexy and still shots) from other countries but almost all the female athletes from other countries received this kind of coverage. It seems important to note that because most of the female Olympic coverage focused on female athletes from Turkey, the media overall highlighted the athletic achievements of females. This finding might also support the view that the nationalistic fervour ignited by the Olympics leads the Turkish media to present Turkish female athletes in terms of their athletic achievements rather than emphasising gender stereotypes.

NOTES

[1] EU-25 is the 25 member states of the European Union.

REFERENCES

Alat, Z. (2006). News coverage of violence against women. *Feminist Media Studies, 6*(3), 295–314.
Arat, Y. (1994). *1980'ler Türkiye'sinde kadın hareketi: Liberal Kemalizmin radikal uzantısı* [Women's movement in Turkey in the 1980s: A radical extension of liberal Kemalism]. In N. Arat (Ed.), *Türkiye'de kadın olgusu* [The issue of women in Turkey] (pp. 71–92). Istanbul: Say Yayınları.

Arslan, B., & Koca, C. (2007). An examination of female athletes-related articles in Turkish daily newspapers regarding gender stereotypes. *Annals of Leisure Research, 10*(3/4), 310–327.

Bulgu, N., & Koca, C. (2006, July). *Media coverage of sexual harassment in sport in Turkey.* Paper presented at the third European Association for Sociology of Sport conference, Jyväskylä, Finland.

European Parliament. (2007). *Report on women's role in social, economic and political life in Turkey* (No: 2006/2214(INI)). Committee on Women's Rights and Gender Equality. Retrieved August 21, 2006, from http://www.europarl.europa.eu/oeil/file.jsp?id=5378852

Fasting, K., & Pfister, G. (1997). *Opportunities and barriers for sport for women in Turkey: A pilot study.* Unpublished manuscript.

Gencel-Bek, M. (2001). *Medyada cinsiyetçilik ve iletişim politikası. İletişim 2001 Kadın Yaz Çalışmaları [Sexism in media and communication policy. Communication 2001 Summer Women Studies],* 213–132.

Gencel-Bek, M., & Binark, M. (2000). *Medyada cinsiyetçilik [Sexism in media].* Ankara Üniversitesi, Kadın Sorunları Araştırma ve Uygulama Merkezi (KASAUM), Ankara.

Hortacsu, N., & Erturk, E. M. (2003). Women and ideology: Representations of women in religious and secular Turkish media. *Journal of Applied Social Psychology, 33*(10), 2017–2039.

Kandiyoti, D. (1987). Emancipated but unliberated? Reflections on the Turkish case. *Feminist Studies, 13*(2), 317–338.

Kandiyoti, D. (1989). Women and the Turkish state: Political actors or symbolic pawns? In N. Yuval-Davis & F. Anthias (Eds.), *Women-nation-state* (pp. 126–149). London: Macmillan.

Koca, C., & Aşçı, F. H. (2005). Gender role orientation in Turkish female athletes from different types of sport and female non-athletes. *Women in Sport and Physical Activity Journal, 14*(1), 86–94.

Koca, C., & Bulgu, N. (2005). Spor ve toplumsal cinsiyet: Genel bir bakış [Sport and gender: A general evaluation]. *Toplum ve Bilim [Society and Science], 103,* 163–184.

Koca, C., Aşçı, F. H., & Kirazcı, S. (2005). Gender role orientation in athletes and non-athletes in a patriarchal society: A case of Turkey. *Sex Roles, 52*(3/4), 217–225.

Koca, C., Bulgu, N., & Aşçı, F. H. (2007). *Analysis of Turkish women's physical activity participation regarding gender and social class.* Paper presented at the 4th World Congress of ISSA in conjunction with the 10th World Congress of ISHPES, Copenhagen, Denmark.

Muftuler-Bac, M. (1999). Turkish women's predicament. *Women's Studies International Forum, 22*(3), 303–315.

Öktem, M. G. (2004). *Sporcu kadının Türk yazılı basınındaki temsili: Süreyya Ayhan örneği* [Representation of Turkish female athletes in print media: The case of Süreyya Ayhan]. Paper presented at the Multidisciplinary Symposium of Women Studies, Yeditepe Üniversitesi, İstanbul, Turkey.

WWHR. (2002). *The new legal status of women in Turkey.* Istanbul: Women for Women's Human Rights. Retrieved February 2008, from http://www.wwhr.org/id_736

Canan Koca
Hacettepe University
Turkey

Bengu Arslan
Baskent University
Turkey

ASIA: EAST ASIA

PING WU

16. CHINA

Has Yin [Female] got the Upper Hand over Yang [Male]?

INTRODUCTION

This study concentrates on media coverage of Chinese male and female athletes during the Athens Olympic Games between 11 and 30 August 2004. The status of the relationship between gender and elite sport in China will first be discussed. Secondly, the statistics for media coverage of Chinese male and female athletes will be analysed. Thirdly, a case study will be presented to fill in the gap left by the statistics.

THE STATUS OF GENDER AND ELITE SPORT

Regarding gender equality, there is a very famous saying in China: "Women hold up half the sky [*funü neng ding banbiantian*]". The saying is so famous that it sounds like a cliché for the Chinese people. However, in the domain of Chinese elite sport, the saying actually needs to be revised because Chinese female athletes have proved in the six Olympic Games in which they have competed that they are more capable than just holding up half the sky. "The females get the upper hand over the males [*yin sheng yang shuai*]" is another famous saying commonly used by the Chinese news media to describe 'gender inequality' in terms of sporting achievements of Chinese female and male athletes.

In contemporary China, the relationship between elite sport and gender is very different from the Western model. Compared with most of the countries in the world, China shows great uniqueness in women's participation and achievement in elite sport. This uniqueness results from several factors, among which the Chinese government plays a determining role.

The People's Republic of China (PRC) was established in 1949 and this so-called 'New China' is a communist state under the leadership of the Communist Party of China (CPC). As Rai (1992) points out, class struggle and social liberation were rated by the CPC as its major missions before 1978.[1] Most of the progress in the emancipation of women in the PRC was made by government initiatives. Before the Chinese government started to carry out economic reform in 1978, the status of women was that generally in urban areas the vast majority of women were allotted a 'formal [*zhengshi*]' job by the government and paid the same wages as their male colleagues or fellow workers who were of the same administrative rank

T. Bruce, J. Hovden and P. Markula (eds.),
Sportswomen at the Olympics: A Global Content Analysis of Newspaper Coverage, 211–223.

[*xingzheng jibie*]. Chinese elite sport, as one of the institutions in Chinese society, was no exception. Thus, by 1978, after about 30 years of striving for women's emancipation, the government and the general public both believed that gender equality had been achieved in China. Today, although the great reform has fundamentally changed the nature of the Chinese economy (from a planned economy to a market economy) and the way in which Chinese people get their jobs (from being allotted a job to looking for a job themselves), it is still a generally taken for granted belief that women are equal to men in China.

In 1979 China renewed its membership of the IOC and in 1984 China returned to the Olympic arena after a long absence of 32 years. The Chinese Olympic delegation surprised the world, not only because it came fourth in the gold medal league but also because of its male-female composition. In the Los Angeles Olympic Games 46% of the Chinese athletes who participated were female and this was the highest percentage of women among all the teams (Riordan & Dong, 1999). Moreover, the Chinese female athletes won 7 gold medals, accounting for 46.7% of the gold medal haul of China. China suffered a setback in the 1988 Olympic Games in terms of overall medals won, but the Chinese female athletes started to overtake their male compatriots by winning 3 of the 5 gold medals China pocketed in Seoul. Remarkably, since 1992 Chinese sportswomen's Olympic performance has surpassed that of Chinese sportsmen (see Table 1).

Table 1. Gold medals won by Chinese male and female athletes at the summer Olympics, 1984–2004

Summer Olympics	Male gold medals (n)	Male gold medals %	Female gold medals (n)	Female gold medals %	Total medals won (n)
1984 Los Angeles	8	53.33	7	46.67	15
1988 Seoul	2	40.00	3	60.00	5
1992 Barcelona	5	31.25	11	68.75	16
1996 Atlanta	7	43.75	9	56.25	16
2000 Sydney	11.5	41.07	16.5	58.93	28
2004 Athens	12.5	39.06	19.5	60.94	32

Source: The 'Olympics Database' at the *Sohu* Website (www.sports.sohu.com).
Note: The .5 indicates a medal in a mixed event.

The better performance results from the hard work and diligence of Chinese female athletes and the 'women priority' policy carried out by the Chinese sports authority, which believes that by pouring more investment into women's sport, China will have a better chance of winning more gold medals in the Olympics. As Riordan and Dong point out, the rationale underlying the policy is "Chinese first and women second" (1999, p. 169). It is a solution suggested by pragmatic calculation rather than a 'sweet fruit' of consciousness of gender equality. Of greater significance is the sporting scene outside the Olympic theatre. In contrast to their overwhelming dominance in the Olympic Games, Chinese female athletes are training and living in an environment where male hegemony is presented without any equivocation. Within the training and administrative system of Chinese elite sport, the vast majority of professional coaches and sports officials are men (Dong, 2003). No sport may be a better example than table tennis, which is regarded as 'the national ballgame' [guo qiu] in China. Since China participated in the World Table Tennis Championships for the first time in 1953, none of the successive head coaches [zhu jiaolian] of either the men's team or the women's team has been female. Although the Chinese men's team has never established the same level of dominance as that of the Chinese women's team on the international stage, the post of 'chief coach' [zong jiaolian], which is of a higher administrative rank than head coach, has always been held simultaneously by the incumbent head coach of the men's team.[2]

MEDIA COVERAGE OF CHINESE SPORT

As for media coverage of Chinese women's sport, the picture becomes even gloomier. Despite the lack of empirical research, it is clear that the Chinese news media devote more coverage to men's sport than to women's sport. The major reported subject in both sports-devoted newspapers and the sports pages of normal newspapers in China is men's football, with both international and domestic dimensions. However, such a reporting policy reflects lack of choice in terms of news sources rather than a biased attitude reflecting gender inequality. In general, a Chinese normal daily newspaper has 3 sports pages every day, at least 2 of which are 'football pages'. The Chinese Men's Football Super League and the major European men's football leagues such as the *Premiership* in England and the *Serie A* in Italy are extensively reported because these leagues regularly 'supply' the Chinese news media with news materials and therefore are reliable news sources. The pressure of filling vast space on sports pages or TV schedules means the Chinese news media have no choice but to rely on coverage of men's football. China also has a women's football league but its very limited influence and scale is 'negligible' for the Chinese news media. Little attention is paid to women's football as a sport, let alone the domestic league, by the media and the general public unless the Chinese women's team is participating in an international tournament.

Media coverage of women's sport has drawn attention from some Chinese researchers. The relevant studies fall into two main categories: textual analysis of how the Chinese media portray women's sport and female athletes (e.g., Yan, 2004; Zhang & Ren, 2006) and quantitative analysis of the lack of media coverage of women's sport (e.g. Mi & Zhang, 2003; Li, Li & Mi, 2006). However, the number of the relevant quantitative studies is rather small. Based upon the data collected from 5 Chinese newspapers in 2002, Mi and Zhang (2003) argued that men's sport received a significantly higher level of media coverage (48.20% of the overall sports news reports space) than women's sport (15.52%). Another quantitative study based upon the data collected from 3 Chinese newspapers in 2005 found that men's sport received 49.10% of the overall sports news reports space and women's sport received only 20.77% (Li et al., 2006).

The above is the current status quo of the relationship between elite sport, media and gender in China. The results of this study of media coverage of Chinese male and female athletes during the 2004 Athens Olympics reflect this status quo on the one hand and show the limitation of statistics on the other. Therefore, after having presented the statistical analysis, I also present a case study to show a wider and more complete picture of media coverage of women's sport in China.

METHODS

Sample Selection

The first choice that had to be made in this study was between 'national' and 'provincial'. The most politically prestigious national newspaper in China is the *People's Daily*. It is the party organ directly controlled by the Central Committee of the CPC. In the late 1970s, the *People's Daily* experienced its golden era with a circulation of more than 7 million. However, its influence on ordinary readers in China has kept on declining since the mid-1980s. Today, although the *People's Daily* is still one of the 10 largest newspapers in the world with a circulation of 2.5 million,[3] almost all of its subscription relies on government spending. Very few Chinese people subscribe to or buy the *People's Daily* individually with their own money. The actual reading rate of the paper is rather low. In addition, compared with all the other Chinese newspapers, the reporting style of the *People's Daily* is the most conservative and definitely out-of-date. Each of the other national daily newspapers targets a specific smaller readership with limited circulation. For example, the readers of the *Brightness Daily* are well-educated intellectuals and the circulation is about 330,000,[4] while the *China Youth Daily* is targeting young readers and has a circulation of 540,000.[5] Except for the *People's Daily*, all the other national daily newspapers are less popular than most of the provincial daily newspapers either in terms of circulation or actual influence.

Currently, the most influential 'normal' newspapers in China are members of the 'City Paper Series'. Almost every province in China, except Tibet and Inner Mongolia, has its own 'city daily' newspaper and each city daily is subsidiary to an organ of a provincial party committee and circulated within a certain province. All these city daily newspapers regard themselves as members of the City Paper Series and the readership of this series is the largest in China at present, compared with that of other types of newspapers such as the party organs and municipal dailies which are only circulated within the cities where they are based. These city daily newspapers resemble each other in terms of page arrangement, editorial style, operational system and marketing strategy. Therefore, conclusions drawn from data collected from one typical city daily newspaper can be generalized to other city daily newspapers. Thus, research on one provincial city daily newspaper is as convincing as that on a national one.

The newspaper selected was the *West China City Daily* (WCCD), which is circulated within the Sichuan Province of China. Launched in January 1995, the WCCD was the first 'city paper' in China. All the other city daily newspapers are, to a certain extent, 'copies' of the WCCD. It was the first Chinese newspaper that orientated itself as a 'tabloid for citizens' without any ambiguity. Such an orientation is very different from the traditional 'mouthpiece of the Party' orientation of Chinese newspapers. That is one of the reasons why the city daily newspapers have become so popular in China. Now, more than 700,000 copies of the WCCD are circulated every day. In 2004, the advertising income of the WCCD reached 610 million *yuan* [nearly US$74 million]. Currently, the WCCD is one of the top 20 Chinese newspapers with one of the largest circulations in China.[6]

In addition, a case study was conducted to expand on the statistics and 4 Chinese newspapers were chosen for this case study. They were the WCCD, the *People's Daily*, the *Titan Sports Weekly* and the *China Sports Daily*. The *Titan Sports Weekly* is the best-selling and most influential sports-devoted newspaper in China. The *China Sports Daily* is the organ paper of the national sports governing body, the General Administration of Sport.

Data Collection

The data were collected during the Athens Olympic Games from 11 to 30 August 2004. The page size of the WCCD is 38.5 cm × 54.5 cm. It normally has 16-20 pages from Saturday to Wednesday and 40 pages on Thursday and Friday. There are 2 or 3 sports pages every day. During the Athens Olympic Games, the overall number of pages did not increase but the sports pages increased to 6-8 pages every day. The vast majority of the sports stories during this period appeared on the sports pages, but the data collected also included all the other sports-relevant stories on other pages. In most of the findings, only the 'Olympic news reports' are discussed (see Table 2). The other 3 types of coverage were not further broken down by gender in this study for several reasons. Firstly, the newspaper published only one piece of Olympics-related editorial on each day during the period of data collection. Each editorial was a kind of comprehensive evaluation of the performance of the Chinese athletes, both male and female, on the previous day. Therefore, all of the editorials belonged to the category of 'mixed'. Similarly, very few column pieces concentrated on a particular athlete or a particular sports team (either male or female). Some of the column pieces could be easily categorized as 'neutral', while most of the others were 'mixed'. Secondly, the definition of 'Other' meant that the vast majority of stories in this category were either 'neutral' or 'mixed', and a breakdown of this type of coverage by gender would contribute little to the analysis. Thirdly, the 'non-Olympics news reports' accounted for only 0.22% of the overall sports coverage, and a further breakdown of this coverage by gender would not make any statistical difference because of its rather small data scale in terms of either space or number of stories.

THE OLYMPICS DOMINATED THE SPORTS PAGES

During the period of data collection, the overall coverage of sport was 233,293.72 cm^2, only 0.22% of which was not related to the Athens Olympic Games, with the other 99.78% being Olympics-related (see Table 2). Table 2 also shows that 99.92% of the sports-related images appearing on the sports pages during the period were Olympics-related. The non-Olympics news reports were mainly of football.

Table 2. Total coverage of sport and sports-related images between 11 and 30 August 2004 by space and percentage in the West China City Daily

Type of coverage	Coverage space cm^2 [1]	Percentage %	Images space cm^2	Percentage %
Olympics news reports	125,152.57	53.65	54,804.86	92.74
Olympics columns/editorials	31,287.81	13.41	4,241.64	7.18
Non-Olympics news reports	512.69	0.22	50.56	0.08
Other[2]	76,340.65	32.72	0	0
Total	233,293.72	100	59,097.06	100

[1] Coverage space included text, images, journalist's by-line, logos, cartoons, etc.
[2] Other included advertisements on the sports pages, TV guides to the Olympics live broadcasts and letters from the readers.

In Olympics news reports, sportswomen received more coverage (34.46%) than sportsmen (31.88%), with a difference of 3,225.46 cm^2. However, more images of sportsmen (44.63%) than of sportswomen (41.52%) were attached to the Olympics news reports, with a difference of 1,704.03cm^2 (see Table 3, Figure 1).

Table 3. Total space and images by gender in Olympics news reports between 11 and 30 August 2004 in the West China City Daily

Gender	News reports space	Percentage %	News reports images space	Percentage %
Male	39,898.23	31.88	24,457.31	44.63
Female	43,123.69	34.46	22,753.28	41.52
Mixed[1]	20,725.08	16.56	2,333.91	4.26
Neutral[2]	21,405.57	17.10	5,260.36	9.59
Total	125,152.57	100	54,804.86	100

[1] Mixed included stories and images about both males and females.
[2] Neutral included stories and images about non-gender specific issues such as security, ticketing, facilities and transportation.

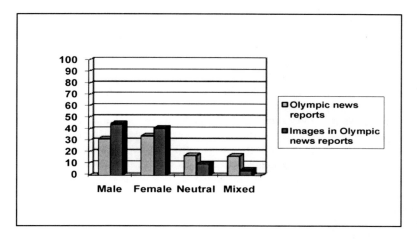

Figure 1. Total coverage and images in the Olympics news reports by gender and percentage.

Table 2 shows that the overwhelming majority (92.74%) of the sports-related images were attached to the Olympics news reports. The breakdown by gender in this category would determine the features of gendered breakdown of all the sports-related images. For this reason, the images attached to the Olympics columns and editorials and non-Olympics news reports, which accounted for only 7.18% and 0.08% of all the sports-related images respectively, were not further broken down by gender or further analysed.

The statistics showed that the WCCD devoted more news reports coverage to sportswomen (34.46%) than to sportsmen (31.88%) during the 2004 Athens Olympic Games. Thus, the overall results support the hypothesis that in coverage of the Olympics, female athletes will receive relatively equal newspaper coverage compared to male athletes. However, the unique features of Chinese elite sport should be taken into consideration before any further conclusions can be drawn.

THE CHINESE GOLD MEDAL FOCUS OR GENDER EQUALITY?

Out of the 407 Chinese athletes who participated in the Athens Olympic Games, 269 (66.10%) were female and 138 (33.90%) were male. This meant that the Chinese female athletes who participated in the Athens Olympic Games were twice as many as their male counterparts, with the proportion of sportsmen to sportswomen being 1:1.95. Out of the overall 63 medals China won in Athens, 39.5 (62.70%) were contributed by females and 23.5 (37.30%) by males. Out of the 32 gold medals China won, 19.5 (60.94%) were contributed by females and 12.5 (39.06%) by males. Out of the overall 17 silver medals China won, 11 (64.71%) were from women's sports and 6 (35.29%) from men's sports. Out of the overall 14 bronze medals China won, 9 (64.29%) were from women's sports and 5 (35.71%) from men's sports. In addition, among the most influential team sports, such as football, basketball, volleyball, handball and field hockey, which normally draw more media interest during the Olympics, the only Chinese men's team that made the Athens Olympic Games was the Chinese men's basketball team. By contrast, the Chinese women's teams participated in all these sports.

Another key factor that should be considered is the reporting policy employed by the Chinese news media when they cover the Olympics. Did they emphasize gender equality or did they focus on gold medals? The author of this chapter was a professional sports journalist in China between 1997 and 2003, and was sent as a special correspondent of the *Titan Sports Weekly* to Sydney to cover the Olympic Games in 2000. According to her reporting experience, the Chinese news media have never enlisted gender equality as one of the reporting principles by which they should abide. When they cover important sporting events such as the Olympics, the focus is always on the Chinese gold medallists. After the Athens Olympic Games, the author interviewed a sports editor and several sub-editors who worked in the sports departments of several normal and sports-devoted newspapers. It was clear that the reporting policy employed by these newspapers was definitely the traditional 'Chinese gold medal focus' policy (Wu, 2007).

The above analysis reveals two key facts: Chinese newspapers normally employ the 'Chinese gold medal focus' policy during the Olympics and the Chinese female athletes won more gold medals in Athens than the Chinese male athletes did. Thus, the higher level of media coverage received by women's sport is, in the first place, a 'natural' result of the 'Chinese gold medal focus' policy rather than intentional effort made by the Chinese media, if there was any, to emphasize gender equality. Very naturally, the next question would be – did the Chinese media try to emphasize gender equality while they were employing the 'Chinese gold medal focus' policy? Or, what was the real attitude of the Chinese media towards gender underlying the 'Chinese gold medal focus' policy? In order to answer this question, the author considered the hypothesis that female and male athletes will receive coverage relative to the proportion of Olympic medals they win. Further, if the 'Chinese gold medal focus' policy is accurate, a newspaper would be reckoned to have treated men's sport and women's sport equally if the difference of media coverage received between sportsmen and sportswomen accurately reflected the difference of *gold* medals won between sportsmen and sportswomen. To draw a valid comparison between the aforementioned differences in two different categories, the proportions of male to female in terms of gold medals won (1:1.56) and media coverage received (1: 1.08) were calculated.[7]

The results mean that theoretically, when the Chinese sportsmen managed to win one gold medal in Athens, their female counterparts won 1.56 gold medals at the same time. However, when men's sport received 1 unit of media coverage, women's sport only received 1.08 units. The proportion of male to female in terms of number of athletes was 1:1.95 and in terms of medals was 1:1.68, both significantly larger than 1:1.08 (see Table 4 and Figure 2). Although the statistics did show that Chinese female athletes received more media coverage (34.46%) than Chinese male athletes (31.88%), it was clear that the Chinese news media did not give female athletes fair coverage. The Chinese female athletes won 60.94% of the gold medals China pocketed in Athens, but the level of media coverage they received was far too low to reflect their sporting achievements in the Athens Olympic Games accurately. Thus, the hypothesis was not proven and Chinese sportswomen did not receive equal media treatment even though the Chinese media did employ the 'Chinese gold medal focus' policy in their coverage of the Athens Olympics.

Table 4. Contributions made by Chinese sportsmen and sportswomen in the 2004 Athens Olympics

Type of contribution	Total (n)	Male (n)	Percentage %	Female (n)	Percentage %	Male to female proportion
Athletes	407	138	33.90	269	66.10	1:1.95
Medals	63	23.5	37.30	39.5	62.70	1:1.68
Gold medals	32	12.5	39.06	19.5	60.94	1:1.56

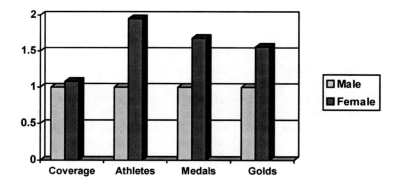

Figure 2. Contrast between media coverage and contribution by gender based on proportion of male to female in the 2004 Athens Olympics.

CASE STUDY: LIU XIANG *vs* XING HUINA

There are some other factors affecting media coverage during the Olympic Games that might help explain the statistical findings, such as the number of gold medals generated within a certain day, the different stages of the Olympic Games, the popularity of a certain sport or a certain sports star, the suspense of a certain match, the deadline reporters and editors have to meet, and the time difference. In order to fill in the gap left by the statistics and draw a more complete picture, a relevant case was studied. On the same day, 27 August 2004 (Athens time), two Chinese athletes, male 110m hurdler Liu Xiang and female 10,000m runner Xing Huina, won gold medals, the only two gold medals China gained from athletics in the Athens Olympics. For people in China (Beijing time), the two finals took place on the early morning of 28 August 2004 and the *People's Daily* did not report the results until the following day because of the limitation of the printout deadline, while the other three papers all reported the two finals in time. Table 5 shows the news reports space and images space these two athletes received in the *Titan Sports Weekly* (TSW), the *China Sports Daily* (CSD) and the WCCD on 28 August and in the *People's Daily* (PD) on 29 August.

Table 5. News reports and images of Liu Xiang and Xing Huina in four newspapers in cm²

Newspapers	News Reports on Liu Xiang	News Reports on Xing Huina	Images of Liu Xiang	Images of Xing Huina
TSW	1,101.80	525.15	562.92	198.02
CSD	1,679.64	867.46	547.70	206.41
PD	902.59	403.20	545.30	314.37
WCCD	1,418.65	420.50	1,204.00	433.64

Note: the News Reports space included text, images, journalist's by-line, logos, cartoons, etc.

Obviously, the statistics draw a picture very different from those discussed above. Figure 3 shows that Liu Xiang, the male athlete, received significantly higher levels of media coverage than Xing Huina, the female athlete, in all of the four newspapers whether in terms of news reports space or images space. In order to illuminate the difference more clearly, the proportions of the news reports and images space Liu Xiang received to those of Xing Huina in the four newspapers were calculated and presented in Table 6. The results meant that the Chinese news media treated these two athletes, who won gold medals on the same day in the same sport (athletics), very differently.

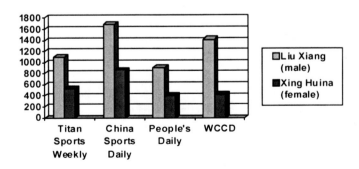

Figure 3. News reports coverage on Liu Xiang and Xing Huina in cm².

Two of the four newspapers are sports-devoted and the other two are normal newspapers. The *Titan Sports Weekly* and the WCCD are market-oriented, while the *People's Daily* and the *China Sports Daily* put more emphasis on political correctness. However, none of them treated Liu Xiang (male) and Xing Huina (female) equally. Only in the *China Sports Daily* did Xing Huina receive news reports space slightly more than half (52%) of that of Liu Xiang. The media coverage she received in the other 3 newspapers accounted for less than half (48%, 45% and 30% respectively) of that of her male counterpart.

Table 6. The proportions of news reports and images space Liu Xiang received to those of Xing Huina in the four newspapers

	Proportion of news reports space	*Proportion of images*
TSW	1: 0.48	1: 0.35
CSD	1: 0.52	1: 0.38
PD	1: 0.45	1: 0.58
WCCD	1: 0.30	1: 0.36

CONCLUSION

The data collected from the WCCD between 11 and 30 August 2004 showed that women's sport received more media coverage (34.46% of the overall Olympics news reports space) than men's sport (31.88%) during the 2004 Athens Olympics. However, this was more likely to be a result of the so-called 'Chinese gold medal focus' reporting policy, which was employed by the Chinese media during the Olympics, rather than the Chinese media's consciousness of gender equality. In fact, the gold medals won by the Chinese female athletes in Athens were 1.59 times as many as those won by their male counterparts but the media coverage they received was only 1.08 times as much as that of their male counterparts. Obviously, the level of media coverage of Chinese female athletes was not high enough to reflect their real sporting achievements accurately. Thus, the analysis suggested that although women's sport did receive more media coverage during the Athens Olympics, such a reality was still underpinned by a biased attitude towards gender held by the Chinese media in favour of men's sport.

To a certain extent, the findings of the case study reflect this biased attitude of the Chinese media towards gender more clearly. The media coverage received by a Chinese female athlete was less than half of that of the Chinese male athlete who won gold on the same day as she did. The four newspapers studied are representative of other Chinese newspapers. Therefore, the findings can be reckoned to represent a phenomenon commonly existing in the Chinese media.

In order to get a thorough understanding of the relationship between sport, gender and media coverage in China, we need to know what a wider picture outside the Olympics arena looks like. During the non-Olympics time, men's sport, men's football in particular, unequivocally dominates the sports pages of Chinese newspapers. However, this dominance does not solely result from the biased attitude of the Chinese media towards gender. Another key, and probably more determining, factor is the pressure of guaranteeing a stable supply of news material.

ACKNOWLEDGEMENTS

The author wishes to thank Professor Fan Hong, University College Cork, Ireland, for collecting sample newspapers and useful advice, and Professor Wang Hanjian, Guizhou University, China, for his supportive assistance in statistics.

NOTES

[1] Economic reform started in China in 1978, and the CPC's main mission has been 'economic construction' since then.

[2] This information was collected from an interview with a senior staff member of the Chinese Table Tennis Association on 26 March 2007.

[3] This information was collected from the official website of the *People's Daily*: www.people.com.cn

[4] This information was collected from the official website of the *Brightness Daily*: www.gmw.cn

[5] This information was collected from the official website of the *China Youth Daily*: http://zqb.cyol.com

[6] This information was collected from the official website of the *West China City Daily*: www.wccdaily.com.cn

[7] Percentage is not appropriate to be employed in this study to draw the comparison because the 'gold medals' category, as well as the 'athletes' and the 'medals', was broken down by gender into only *two* areas, male and female, but the 'media coverage' category was broken down by gender into four areas, male, female, mixed and neutral. That meant the percentages of male and female in the gold medals' category added up to 100%, but the percentages of male and female in the 'media coverage' category added up to less than 100%.

REFERENCES

Dong, J. (2003). *Women, sport and society in modern China*. London and Portland: Frank Cass.

Li, W., Li, J., & Mi, J. (2006). Ye lun baozhi de nvzi tiyu baodao [On female sports eports in newspapers]. *Zhonghua nvzi xueyuan xuebao* [*Journal of China Women's University*], *18*(1), 68–72.

Mi, J., & Zhang, C. (2003). Baozhi de nuzi tiyu baodao yanjiu [Study into female sports reports in newspapers]. *Tianjin tiyu xueyuan xuebao* [*Journal of Tianjin Institute of Physical Education*], *18*(3), 69–71.

Rai, S. (1992). 'Watering another man's garden': Gender, employment and educational reforms in China. In S. Rai, H. Pikington, & A. Phizacklea (Eds.), *Women in the face of change* (pp. 20–40). London: Routledge.

Riordan, J., & Dong, J. (1999). Chinese women and sport. In J. Riordan & R. Jones (Eds.), *Sport and physical education in China* (pp. 159–184). London and New York: E & FN Spon.

Wu, P. (2007). *Co-operation, confrontation and conflict: An investigation of the relationship between the news media and sports administrative organisations in contemporary China*. Unpublished PhD dissertation, De Montfort University, Leicester, United Kingdom.

Yan, J. (2004). Tiyu baodao zhong de xingbie pianjian [The sexual bias in the sports reports]. *Henan shehui kexue [Journal of Henan Social Sciences]*, *12*(2), 106–109.

Zhang, J., & Ren, X. (2006). Tiyu baodao zhong de nuxing shiyu zheng [On the silence for females in sports news reports]. *Hubei tiyu keji [Journal of Hubei Sports Science]*, *25*(5), 497–499.

Ping Wu
University of Bedfordshire
United Kingdom

TAKAKO IIDA

17. JAPAN

Japanese Case Study:
The Gender Difference Highlighted in Coverage of Foreign Athletes

GENDER IN JAPAN

More than a decade has passed since the *Basic Law for a Gender-Equal Society* was issued and enacted in 1999. After that, local government laws were enacted according to it in every prefecture and city. Recently, however, there has been a backlash against gender equality by conservative authorities. Thus, although Japan is said to be an advanced country, there is much gender discrimination everywhere. For example, on the United Nation's human development index Japan ranks eighth, whereas it only ranks 54th on the gender empowerment index (UNDP, 2007/2008).

GENDER IN JAPANESE SPORT

In 2000, the *Basic Plan for the Promotion of Sport* was developed as a result of the increasing importance of sports in modern Japanese society. Although the promotion of sports has been part of the government's policy goal to increase health, education, welfare and the economy, gender discrimination is still prevalent in the world of sports. Much injustice and inequity still exists, especially for women.[1]

The number of female executives in Japanese sport organisations in 2007 exemplifies this gender bias. Firstly, in the area of competitive sports, the Japan Olympic Committee was made up of 24 male members and 2 female members.[2] The percentage of female executives in the committee was therefore 8.3% (Japan Olympic Committee, 2007). As for the Japan Sports Association, females occupied only 7.0% of executive positions (Japan Sports Association, 2007).

There are many leaders called Physical Education Commissioners in each prefecture who provide support for lifelong physical activity and sport. The total number in 2007 amounted to 38,639 males and 16,295 females. Females thus account for 29.7% of the total. However, among executive position members, the inequality between the two genders is even more obvious. Males occupied 20 posts whereas females occupied only 2 posts, meaning that the female percentage was only 9.1% (Physical Education Commissioners, 2007a, 2007b).[3]

Gender inequality is also obvious in Japanese academic sports societies. For example, the Japan Society of Physical Education, Health and Sport Science, which is Japan's largest organisation in this field, had no female executives in 2007 (Japan

T. Bruce, J. Hovden and P. Markula (eds.),
Sportswomen at the Olympics: A Global Content Analysis of Newspaper Coverage, 225–236.
© *2010 Sense Publishers. All rights reserved.*

Society of Physical Education, Health and Sport Science, 2007).[4] Females made up 15.4% of the Japan Society of Sport Sociology executives (Japan Society of Sport Sociology, 2007) and only 8.3% of the executives in the Japanese Society of Physical Education Sociology (Japanese Society of Physical Education Sociology, 2008).

These results indicate that the status of females in decision-making fields in the Japanese sports world is still low. However, to change the male hegemony in the Japanese sports world, the Japan Society for Sport and Gender Studies was established in 2002. The percentage of female executives in this society is 80.0%.

RESEARCH INTO GENDER DIFFERENCES IN SPORTS MEDIA COVERAGE

As women's studies developed in the 1980s in Japan, the representations of gender stereotypes and sexualized descriptions of women in media, drama, images and literature have been criticised continuously by feminist researchers. On the other hand, because gender perspectives were introduced into the academic field of sport much later, there is little research about gender in the sports media. In the next section, I discuss the five studies of gender in sports print media in chronological order. Mabuchi (1995) analysed 23,665 headlines about sports in magazines that were published from 1945 to 1988. Mabuchi found the percentage of headlines about women totalled only 7.3%. Of this 7.3%, one quarter dealt with women who were uninvolved with sports except indirectly; for example, as wives of sporting figures.

Kumayasu (2000) analysed the number of articles on physical education and sports clipped from various newspapers from 1990 to 1999, excluding the results of professional sports.[5] Kumayasu found that the percentages of the articles about women remained constant around 10%, whereas the percentages of articles about men increased from 31% to 44% during those 10 years. If these newspaper clippings had included the results of professional sports, such as professional baseball and soccer, the differences in coverage between women and men would have been even bigger.

Sano (2004) counted the number of photographs in the *Asahi* newspaper in 1996, 1998, 2000 and 2002. Sano found that the total number of photographs increased year by year, but these were photographs depicting men's sport. The number of women's photographs did not increase and their percentage remained in the 15% – 25% range.

Iida (2002) examined three Japanese daily newspapers' sports coverage of the 2000 Olympic Games. This study found that female athletes (44.2%) received relatively equal newspaper coverage to male athletes (43.0%). However, the sports that ranked from first to tenth in coverage included gender-stereotyped sports, such as softball, synchronized swimming, artistic gymnastics, beach volleyball and rhythmic gymnastics in women's sports, and soccer, baseball and wrestling in men's sports. Overall, the photographs covered more than 50% of coverage in beach volleyball.

Iida (2003) analysed newspaper descriptions of a female medallist in the 1996 and 2000 Olympics and the World Judo Championships. This research indicated that her athletic abilities were trivialized in the articles. The newspapers described her achievements as always being encouraged by her father and her husband. Moreover, the newspaper articles praised her not only for her skill in Judo but also as a housewife. Through these articles an image of a woman who has no objection to patriarchy was constructed.

METHOD

The sample in this study is taken from the *Yomiuri*, which is the largest newspaper in the world. The circulation of the *Yomiuri* newspaper is 10,080,000. The period of analysis is from August 7th to September 5th, 2004. I analysed all of the sports articles in the papers. In this analysis, the measured article size includes photographs. The category of photographs does not include cartoons (0.6%), graphics (1.3%), logos (1.6%) or head shots (1.1%). Head shots were excluded because the lack of caption and their size made it difficult to determine gender. Thus, the photograph category includes 95.4% of the graphic space.

In addition to analysing the coverage in the *Yomiuri* newspaper, further analysis was conducted on the Olympics photographs published in the three largest serious newspapers in Japan – the *Yomiuri*, the *Asahi* and the *Mainichi*. In addition to the original categories for the broader project, the Olympic photographs were classified and analysed according to whether the subjects were Japanese or foreigners.

RESULTS

Overall the Olympics received almost twice the coverage (65.4%) of non-Olympics (34.6%) (see Table 1). However, there were notable differences by gender. For example, almost all the female space (96.3%) was in Olympics coverage, a trend that was similar for the mixed (82.7%) and neutral (78.5%) categories as well. In contrast, more space was dedicated to males in non-Olympic coverage (53.2%)

Table 1. Space dedicated to Olympic and Non-Olympic coverage in the Yomiuri newspaper August 7 to September 5, 2004

	Olympic coverage (OC)			Non-Olympic coverage (NOC)			Total coverage (TC)	
Gender	cm^2	% of total OC	% of TC	cm^2	% of total NOC	% of TC	cm^2	%
Male	105,407.1	39.9	46.8	119,782.4	85.7	53.2	225,189.5	55.7
Female	84,507.1	32.0	96.3	3,227.7	2.3	3.7	87,734.8	21.7
Mixed	56,688.9	21.4	82.7	11,869.8	8.5	17.3	68,558.7	17.0
Neutral	17,738.6	6.7	78.5	4,860.8	3.5	21.5	22,599.4	5.6
Total	264,341.6	100.0	65.4	139,740.8	100.0	34.6	404,082.4	100.0

than in Olympic (46.8%) coverage. Overall, males received 55.7% of the total coverage during the Olympic Games, more than twice as much as females who received 21.7%. Adding mixed coverage (17.0%) to the female coverage means that at least 38.7% of the coverage included information about female athletes. Olympic coverage in cm^2 was relatively similar for males (39.9%) and females (32.0%). However, there was a huge percentage difference between male (85.7%) and female (2.3%) non-Olympic coverage. In addition, there is also a high level of mixed coverage during the Olympics but very little in non-Olympic coverage. It is interesting that if you combine the mixed (21.4%) and female (32.0%) coverage, this means that more than half of the Olympics space (53.4%) actually included females.

Table 2 indicates the number of articles and percentage for male athletes, female athletes, mixed, and neutral in Olympics and non-Olympics. The results about the number of articles in the *Yomiuri* denoted the same tendency as those about the space.

Table 2. Number of articles dedicated to Olympics and Non-Olympics in the Yomiuri newspaper August 7 to September 5, 2004

Gender	Olympics coverage (OC)			Non-Olympics coverage (NOC)			Total coverage (TC)	
	(n)	% of total OC	% of TC	(n)	% of total NOC	% of TC	(n)	%
Male	321	37.7	43.4	418	74.0	56.6	739	52.2
Female	260	30.6	90.3	28	5.0	9.7	288	20.3
Mixed	180	21.2	65.2	96	17.0	34.8	276	19.5
Neutral	90	10.6	79.6	23	4.1	20.4	113	8.0
Total	851	100.0	60.1	565	100.0	39.9	1,416	100.0

Table 3 indicates photograph size and percentage by gender in Olympics and non-Olympics. The Olympics received almost three times as much photographic coverage (73.6%) as non-Olympics (26.3%). The percentage of photographic coverage focused on female, mixed and neutral was 95.6%, 92.7% and 77.0% respectively and, therefore, most coverage of the female, mixed and neutral categories was in the Olympics. There was a remarkable similarity between female and mixed Olympic photo coverage. On the other hand, male Olympic photo coverage was 59.1% and non-Olympic photo coverage was 40.9%. In photo coverage, Olympics received more coverage than non-Olympics.

Overall, male athletes received 58.3% and female athletes received 32.0% of all photo coverage during the period of analysis. Adding mixed photo coverage (7.1%) to the female photo coverage means that at least 39.1% of all photo space included information about female athletes. Olympic photo coverage in cm^2 was relatively

Table 3. Space dedicated to Olympic and Non-Olympic photographic coverage in the
Yomiuri newspaper August 7 to September 5, 2004

Gender	Olympic photographs (OP)			Non-Olympic photographs (NOP)			Total photographs (TP)	
	cm^2	% of total OP	% of TP	cm^2	% of total NOP	% of TP	cm^2	%
Male	38,182.9	46.8	59.1	26,444.5	90.5	40.9	64,627.4	58.3
Female	33,910.4	41.5	95.6	1,547.6	5.3	4.4	35,458.0	32.0
Mixed	7,334.2	9.0	92.7	581.1	2.0	7.3	7,915.3	7.1
Neutral	2,215.8	2.7	77.0	662.8	2.3	23.0	2,878.6	2.6
Total	81,643.3	100.0	73.6	29,236.0	100.0	26.4	110,879.3	100.0

similar for males (46.8%) and females (41.5%). However, there was a big difference
between non-Olympic male (90.5%) and female photo coverage (5.3%). Similarly,
while mixed Olympic photo coverage was very high, the non-Olympic mixed
photo coverage was very low. If you combine the mixed (9.0%) and female
(41.5%) coverage, this means that half of the coverage (50.5%) actually included
females.

Table 4 indicates number of photos and percentage for male athletes, female
athletes, mixed and neutral coverage in Olympics and non-Olympics. The results
about the number of photos in the *Yomiuri* denoted the same tendency as those
about the space.

Table 4. Number of photographs dedicated to Olympics and Non-Olympics in the Yomiuri
newspaper August 7 to September 5, 2004

Gender	Olympics photographs (OP)			Non-Olympics photographs (NOP)			Total photographs (TP)	
	(n)	% of total OP	% of TP	(n)	% of total NOP	% of TP	(n)	%
Male	257	47.3	52.0	237	87.1	48.0	494	60.6
Female	233	42.9	93.2	17	6.3	6.8	250	30.7
Mixed	37	6.8	82.2	8	2.9	17.8	45	5.5
Neutral	16	2.9	61.5	10	3.7	38.5	26	3.2
Total	543	100.0	66.6	272	100.0	33.4	815	100.0

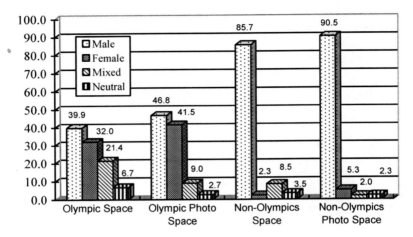

Figure 1. Media coverage during the 2004 Olympic Games by gender and space in cm^2 in the Yomiuri newspaper.

The results in Figure 1 show that, in Olympics coverage, the article size for male athletes occupied 39.9% and the photograph size for male athletes occupied 46.8%. The article size for female athletes occupied 32.0% and photograph size for female athletes occupied 41.5%. The article size for male athletes is larger than that of female athletes by 8%, and the photograph size for male athletes is larger than that of female athletes by 5%. The coverage was relatively similar for males and females, although males received more space and photographs overall. As well, photographic coverage was more focused on male and female athletes than the text; and while males received larger stories and photographs, the difference was smaller for photographs. Female athletes receiving more photo coverage than male athletes means the female athlete is treated as a sex object, and this result supports the previous research (Iida, 2002).

In non-Olympics, the article size of male athletes occupied 85.7% and photograph size of male athletes occupied 90.5%, whereas the article size of female athletes occupied only 2.3% and photograph size of female athletes occupied 5.3% (see Figure 1). The reason for this discrepancy is that there are some popular all-male professional sports, such as baseball, soccer and sumo, which dominate non-Olympic coverage while there are few female professional sports. In addition to these professional sports, articles about Japanese male athletes who play in foreign countries have appeared every day in newspapers recently. Moreover, the Japan high school baseball championship was held at the same time as the Olympics; a championship that involves only boys. The article size of all baseball occupied about 85% of the male non-Olympic coverage. If the analysis was conducted at another time, it is likely that female athletes would receive more coverage than in this study. It is also likely, however, that there would continue to be great differences in amounts of coverage between males and females (see Kumayasu, 2000; Sano, 2004).

The Olympics are seen as important by the Japanese media, and especially the focus on female athletes, because there are few high level sports events for female athletes compared to male athletes. The reason why the Olympics have media value seems to be related more to commercialism than nationalism recently.

In the next section, I discuss the results of further analysis conducted on the Olympics photographs published in the three largest serious newspapers in Japan – the *Yomiuri*, the *Asahi* and the *Mainichi*. When the 1,650 Olympics photographs were classified according to whether subjects were Japanese or foreigners, the results showed that the focus was overwhelmingly on Japanese athletes: Japanese photographs (1,019, 61.8%), foreigner photographs (402, 24.44%), photographs including both Japanese and foreigners (194, 11.8%), and other photographs (35, 2.1%). For the results presented in Table 5, although photographs including both Japanese and foreigners were identified, they were categorized into photographs for Japanese, because these photographs mainly focused on the Japanese athletes.

Table 5 indicates photograph size and percentage, and number of photographs and percentage for female athletes, male athletes, mixed and neutral classified into Japanese and foreigners. In Japanese athlete photographs, the numbers were relatively similar for males (570) and females (566) and the space was also relatively similar for males (48.7%) and females (44.5%). In comparison, in foreign athlete photographs, the number of male athletes is 210 (52.2%), and the number of female athletes is 168 (41.8%), and there is a big difference between male and female athletes. The percentages of photograph coverage were 54.3% for male and 38.7% for female foreign athletes.

The identification of whether the article concerned individuals or teams as well as items such as article position/location, article focus and article type were taken into account in the article analysis, while items such as photograph focus, type of photograph and photograph colour (colour or black and white) were examined in the photograph analysis for both Olympics and non-Olympics. Gender difference did not reach significance in any of these items so they are not discussed here.

Table 5. Olympic photographic space and numbers divided between Japanese and foreigners in three newspapers

Gender	Japanese				Foreigners			
	cm^2	% of TC^1	(n)	% of TN	cm^2	% of TC	(n)	% of TN
Male	80,763.5	48.7	570	47.0	25,477.3	54.3	210	52.2
Female	73,713.1	44.5	566	46.7	18,157.7	38.7	168	41.8
Mixed	9,568.1	5.8	66	5.4	2,904.3	6.2	21	5.2
Neutral	1,713.8	1.0	11	0.9	421.2	0.9	3	0.7
Total	165,758.4	100.0	1,213	100.0	46,960.5	100.0	402	100.0

[1] TC = total coverage by space; TN = total number of articles.

In the 2004 Olympics, 171 female athletes and 141 male athletes participated from Japan. The number and percentage (54.8%) of female athletes was more than that of male athletes for the first time since Japan first participated in the 1912 Olympics. As to the number of medals, female athletes won 9 gold medals, 4 silver medals and 4 bronze medals, while male athletes won 7 gold medals, 5 silver medals, and 8 bronze medals. Although the total number of female medals is less than that of the male medals, females won more gold medals than males (see Table 6).

Table 6. Medals won by Japanese athletes at the 2004 Olympics

Medals	Male		Female		Total
	(n)	%	*(n)*	%	
Gold	7	43.8	9	56.2	16
Silver	5	55.6	4	44.4	9
Bronze	8	66.7	4	33.3	12
Total	20	54.1	17	45.9	37

Figure 2 indicates the relationship between the photograph coverage for sports ranked from first to tenth in the three biggest newspapers and the results at the Games. It follows, therefore, that the Olympic photograph coverage does not directly reflect the results of the Japanese athletes in the Games. In the case of women's sports, synchronized swimming, where Japanese athletes won 2 silver medals, ranks above wrestling, where Japanese athletes won 2 gold medals, 1 silver medal and 1 bronze medal. Moreover, rhythmic gymnastics and artistic gymnastics, where Japanese athletes did not get medals, rank eighth and tenth respectively in terms of photograph coverage. Volleyball did not include beach volleyball. As Japanese beach volleyball could not make the cut at the 2004 Olympics, the photo coverage was very low. In contrast, as Japanese beach volleyball at the 2000 Olympics came 4th, the photo coverage that ranked in the top 10 was higher than taekwondo where Japan won 1 bronze medal (Iida, 2002).

In the case of men's sports, baseball, where Japanese athletes won 1 bronze medal, ranks above Judo, where Japanese athletes won 3 gold medals and 1 silver medal. In addition, soccer and basketball, where Japanese athletes did not get a medal, ranked sixth and ninth respectively. Japanese soccer was expected to win a medal but could not make the cut. On the other hand, Japanese basketball could not participate in the Olympics.

The top 10 sports photographed were divided into Japanese and foreign categories (these Tables do not appear in this paper). Consequently, it turned out that in the case of Japanese athlete photographs, all the female sports that ranked above tenth in the Olympic photograph coverage won medals and, in the male case, the sports that ranked above tenth all won medals except for soccer.

Female

1st	Judo	G	G	G	G	G	S				
2nd	Athletics	G	5th	7th							
3rd	Synchronized swimming	S	S								
4th	Swimming	G	B	B	4th	4th	5th	5th	6th	8th	
5th	Wrestling	G	G	S	B						
6th	Soccer	7th									
7th	Softball	B									
8th	Rhythmic gymnastics										
9th	Volleyball	5th									
10th	Artistic gymnastics										

Male

1st	Athletics	G	4th	4th	5th	6th					
2nd	Swimming	G	G	S	B	B	5th	6th	7th	8th	8th
3rd	Baseball	B									
4th	Artistic gymnastics	G	S	B	B	4th	5th	6th	6th	7th	8th
5th	Judo	G	G	G	S						
6th	Soccer										
7th	Wrestling	B	B	5th	5th	7th					
8th	Cycling	S									
9th	Basketball										
10th	Archery	S	8th								

Note: G Gold   S Silver   B Bronze

Figure 2. The photograph coverage of sports ranked from first to tenth in the three biggest newspapers and the results of the Olympic Games.

In the case of foreign athlete photographs, the top five female Olympic sports were athletics, rhythmic gymnastics, artistic gymnastics, soccer and synchronized swimming, while the top five male Olympic sports were athletics, soccer, swimming, baseball and basketball. Furthermore the number of male photographs was larger than that of female photographs (see Table 5). In other words, the Olympic photograph coverage of Japanese athletes reflects their results in the Games, whereas in the case of foreign athletes, gender stereotypes can be perceived both qualitatively and quantitatively. In women's sports, among the top five in Olympic photograph coverage of foreign athletes are three sports – rhythmic gymnastics, artistic gymnastics and synchronized swimming – which have often been regarded as 'female-appropriate' sports. These sports consist of the elements of beauty, balance and flexibility and, therefore, have contributed to the reproduction of the image of the woman's body as 'beautiful' which also indicates 'feminine'. For coverage of foreign athletes, this finding supported the broader research project hypothesis that female athletes competing in sports more strongly linked to femininity or dressed in ways that highlight gender difference will receive relatively more coverage than those competing in sports more strongly linked to masculinity or dressed in ways that do not highlight gender difference.

Among the top five sports for foreign males is athletics, which has been one of the traditional sports since the ancient Olympics. The next two that follow it are soccer and swimming, which are popular all around the world. Baseball and basketball come next, which are popular with American people. Baseball is the most popular sport in Japan, but basketball is not as popular as baseball. Japanese media appear to be influenced by American trends, similar to the American influence on Japanese government policy. Compared with the top five sports for foreign females, the men's sports are mostly team sports and consist of elements of strength and power and, therefore, help reproduce the image of men's bodies as strong, which can be linked to 'masculinity'. Moreover, these sports constitute the mainstream of sports where there is often monopolization of control and power by men.

Thus, overall, plain gender bias is not to be seen in the Olympic photographs for Japanese athletes, but the newspapers are making the gender representation cleverly by using foreign athlete photographs.

DISCUSSION

When this study's results were examined according to the hypotheses that framed the broader project, the study proved consistent with them. Thus, this study found: 1) that female athletes received relatively equal amounts of Olympics coverage to male athletes; as well as 2) unequal and lesser amounts of non-Olympic coverage; and 3) that males and females were represented similarly in photographs. In relation to the hypotheses that females would receive coverage relative to their proportion on the Olympic team and to the proportion of Olympic medals they won, the results support this hypothesis for Japanese athletes. As discussed above, the hypothesis that female athletes competing in sports more strongly linked to femininity or dressed in ways that highlight gender difference would receive relatively more coverage was found to be true for foreign athletes. Also, the hypothesis that female athletes who won medals in sports historically linked to national identity would receive more coverage was found in the focus on Judo.

Although there are few previous studies of newspaper coverage in Japan, this study generally supports the trends identified in them. For example, the results of studies that did not include the results of professional sports (Kumayasu, 2000) were similar to the findings of non-Olympic coverage in this study. Where the previous research found 10% in the number of female articles, this study found females received 5.3% of photo coverage and 2.3% of overall coverage. The non-Olympic photographs (6.5% for number; 5.3% for space) were much lower than Sano's (2004) findings of between 15% and 25% of photographs for females but this finding may be balanced by the high visibility of females in the Olympic coverage. In relation to the Olympic coverage, there were strong similarities in the types of sports which received the most coverage. Softball, synchronised swimming, artistic and rhythmic gymnastics as well as two forms of volleyball (volleyball in 2004 and beach volleyball in 2000) appeared in the top ten sports in both 2000 (Iida, 2002) and 2004.

The non-Olympic female sports coverage is still at the level of 'symbolic annihilation' and does not reflect females' recent activities in sports. The reason is that newspapers run articles only concerning high performance by top athletes. Commercialism and the inclination toward high performance both in sport and the media will be an issue in the future.

On the other hand, in coverage of Olympics, female athletes received relatively equal newspaper coverage compared to male athletes. However, the gender power structure of sport and the gender stereotypes were seen in foreign athletes' photographs as mentioned above. Thus, I conclude that the representation of gender in the newspaper is not likely to disappear easily. These representations of sport by the media have contributed to the production of the traditional paternalistic image of women among the public and have become an obstacle to the realisation of gender equality and equity.

NOTES

[1] The revised edition of the Basic Plan for the Promotion of Sport was issued in 2006. In addition to elderly people and disabled people, consideration for women practicing in sports was included in it.
[2] Data for the Japan Olympic Committee, Japan Sports Association, Japan Society of Physical Education, Health and Sport Science, Japan Society of Sport Sociology, and the Japanese Society of Physical Education Sociology is as of April 1, 2007.
[3] This data is as of June 30, 2007.
[4] I got this data from the office of Japan Society of Physical Education, Health and Sport Science on June 3, 2007.
[5] These newspaper clippings did not include articles giving the everyday results of professional sports.

REFERENCES

Gender Equality Bureau, Cabinet Office. (1999). *The basic law for a gender-equal society.* Retrieved July 31, 2007, from http://www.gender.go.jp/english_contents/index.html
Iida, T. (2002). Sport and gender studies: Women sports and media. *Journal of Physical Education,* 50(4), 73–75.

Iida, T.(2003). How have female athletes been gendered in newspapers? A case study: Change in identity from Miss Noriko Sugawara to Mrs. Noriko Narazaki. *Journal of Sport and Gender Studies*, *1*, 4–14.

Japan Olympic Committee. (2007). *The executives of the JOC*. Retrieved July 31, 2007, from http://www.joc.or.jp/english/executive.html

Japan Society for Sport and Gender Studies. (2007). *Organization*. Retrieved July 31, 2007, from http://www.jssgs.org/English/e-index.htm

Japan Society of Sport Sociology. (2007). *JSSS Board of Directors (2007–2008)*. Retrieved July 31, 2007, from http://jsss.jp/english/jssseboard07.html

Japan Sports Association. (2007). *Board members*. Retrieved July 31, 2007, from http://www.japan-sports.or.jp/about/pdf/yakuinmeibo.pdf

Kumayasu, K. (2000). Newspaper headlines about sports and gender: Monthly clipping of physical education and sports (1990–1999). *Journal of Human Sciences* (Ningen Kankei Ronshu), *17*, 145–163.

Ministry of Education, Culture, Sports, Science and Technology. (2000). *Basic plan for the promotion of sports*. Retrieved July 31, 2007, from http://www.mext.go.jp/english/news/2000/09/000949.htm

Ministry of Education, Culture, Sports, Science and Technology. (2006). *Basic plan for the promotion of sports* (revised). Retrieved April 16, 2008, from http://www.mext.go.jp/a_menu/sports/plan/06031014/001.htm

Physical Education Commissioners. (2007a). *The board members*. Retrieved July 31, 2007, from http://www.disclo-koeki.org/02a/00239/2.pdf

Physical Education Commissioners. (2007b). *The numbers of Physical Education Commissioners*. Retrieved July 31, 2007, from http://www.disclo-koeki.org/02a/00239/a.pdf

Sano, T. (2004). *The study on sports photographic coverage in newspaper*. Unpublished undergraduate thesis, Faculty of Human and Cultural Studies, Tezukayama Gakuin University, Japan.

Tabuchi, Y. (1995). Sports journalism and women. *Bulletin of Kwansei Gakuin University* (School of Sociology), *73*, 110–132.

United Nations Development Programme [UNDP]. (2007/2008). *Human development report 2007/2008 – Country fact sheets – Japan*. Retrieved April 16, 2008, from http://hdrstats.undp.org/countries/country_fact_sheets/cty_fs_JPN.html

Yoda, M., Nogawa, H., & Kitamura, K. (2008, March, Spring). The results of election. *Japan Society of Physical Education Sociology Newsletter*, p. 7.

Takako Iida
Tezukayama Gakuin University
Japan

EUNHA KOH

18. SOUTH KOREA

Media Portrayal of Olympic Athletes:
Korean Printed Media During the 2004 Athens Olympics

WOMEN IN KOREAN SOCIETY

Gender inequality and discrimination have been witnessed in every society. In Korea, however, the traditional gender role formed by Sung Ri Hak, a sect of Confucianism that originated from China, has influenced Korean society for several hundreds of years since the Chosun Dynasty (1392–1897). Sung Ri Hak strictly divided the social and domestic roles of men and women and spread the notion of the predominance of men over women, defining womanhood as subordinate to manhood. The norms and rules of Confucianism not only restricted women's opportunities in education and social activities but also produced the female 'docile body', to use Foucault's term, by presenting detailed standards for bodily actions and behaviors (Koh, 2002). Although it has been more than 100 years since Korea opened its gates to Western countries at the end of 19th century, traditional gender stereotypes and discrimination still remain in social values.

Recently South Korea ranked 26th in the United Nations Human Development Index. However, it reached only 64th out of 93 countries in the Gender Empowerment Measure (UNDP, 2007). Despite the government's recent gender equality policy, including the establishment of the Ministry of Gender Equality and enforcement of related laws and regulations, women's status in Korean society is still lower than in other countries with similar economic and political status. As noted in a recent South Korean TV news story, it is fair to say that Korean women "earn low income and have less power" (SBS TV, 2008).

KOREAN WOMEN IN SPORT

Since modern sport was first introduced to Korean society at the end of 19th century, sport has been a male domain, as it has been in most countries. Moreover, Confucianism in early 20th century Korean society also worked to hide the female body from public view, including in sport scenes. It is deliberate promotion and support of specific sports for specific international events by the government rather than a natural growth of girls' and women's participation in sport that has developed women's sport in post-War South Korea. The 14th Olympics held in London marked the first participation by Korean women. Taking place in 1948, after the liberation of

T. Bruce, J. Hovden and P. Markula (eds.),
Sportswomen at the Olympics: A Global Content Analysis of Newspaper Coverage, 237–254.
© *2010 Sense Publishers. All rights reserved.*

Korea from Japanese occupation in 1945, the London Olympics were the first in which Korea participated as an independent nation. Of the total 63 athletes, coaches and executives who took part, there was only one woman participant, who was a track and field athlete. In the 1960s the South Korean government began to promote elite sport as means of enhancing international prestige and encouraging national integration. Up to the year of 1960, the number of Korean participants only increased by a small portion, and there were only one or two women athletes who competed in track and field and gymnastics. After the 1960s, however, the number of Koreans participating in the Olympics grew substantially, and so did the number of women participants. The increase in women's participation in the Olympics is not only closely related to the growth of women's sport in general but also to the improved status of women and the enhancement of women's rights in society. The percentage of women in the Korean Olympic team steadily rose from 1.59% in 1948 to 11.66% in 1964, 18.06% in 1976 and 24.88% in 1988 (Koh, 2004). During the 2004 Athens Olympics, the number of women participants reached 137, accounting for 36.44% of the total Korean team.

From the 1980s, Korean women started to participate in various Olympic sports, such as shooting, archery, handball, swimming, judo, cycling, tennis and fencing, in addition to basketball and volleyball which were the previous focus. Between the 1988 Seoul Olympics and 2000 Sydney Olympics, Korean female athletes started to take part in such sports as field hockey, badminton, table tennis, weight lifting and Taekwondo. An increasing number of athletes began to participate in swimming, track and field and gymnastics. The sports in which Korean female athletes have been receiving outstanding results are archery, handball and field hockey, among others. Female athletes did not do as well as male athletes during the initial years of participation in the Olympics. However, their performance in the Olympics improved considerably, resulting in 56 medals overall (see Table 1).

As Korean women started to participate in the Olympics in earnest in 1960s, ordinary women's participation sport started to grow. There is no detailed document on participation in sports by the general female population back then. However, it is clear that in the elite sports sector, professional athletes were developed, with a focus on Olympic sports such as volleyball and basketball. The 1980s is when sports gained much attention from the general public in Korea. Demand for sports activities increased in tandem with an increase in leisure time and improvement in income levels resulting from rapid economic growth. This demand grew stronger with the hosting of the Seoul Olympics in 1988. The sports that were engaged in became diverse, moving away from less organised sports activities, such as free gymnastics and rope-skipping, to include ball games, swimming and aerobics. Since the 1990s, new areas of sports have been enjoyed such as inline skating and scuba diving. Accordingly, there is a continuous rise in the number of Koreans participating in sports. Although fewer women take part in sports activities than men, women's participation has been steadily increasing. The percentage of Koreans who exercise regularly at least two to three times a week increased from 19.4% in 1986 (Male, 28.9%; women, 12.4%) to 44.1% in 2006 (Male, 48.4%; female, 40%) (Ministry of Culture & Tourism, 2006).

Table 1. Medals won by Korean athletes during the summer Olympics

	Gold		Silver		Bronze		Total	Medals	
Year	M	F	M	F	M	F	M	F	Total
1948					2		2		2
1952					2		2		2
1956			4		1		5		5
1960									
1964			2		1		3		3
1968			1		1		2		2
1972			1				1		1
1976	1		1		3	1	5	1	6
1984	5	1	4	2	6	1	15	4	19
1988	8	4	8	2	10	1	26	7	33
1992	7	5	3	2	10	2	20	9	29
1996	3	4	9	6	2	3	14	13	27
2000	4	4	7	2	7	4	18	10	28
2004	6	3	7	5	5	4	18	12	30
Total	34	21	47	19	50	16	131	56	187

However, there needs to be more active participation by Korean women in sport as well as in roles as decision-makers in domestic and overseas sports organisations. At present, only 12 of the 82 Korean Olympic Committee members are women. Only three of the 13 vice-chairpersons and only one of the 14 executive members on the senior board of directors are women. Among the 55 presidents of national sport federations subscribed to the Korean Sport Council, 53 are men, with the exclusion of dance sports and orienteering (Korea Sports Council, 2008). This clearly shows that female representation in South Korean sports is considerably lower than at the international level.

MEDIA COVERAGE OF WOMEN'S SPORT

Since the 1980s many international studies on the relations between media and sports have focused their attention on how ideologies such as sexism, racism, nationalism and commercialism are reproduced or reinforced through sports media (Koh & Kim, 2004). The most remarkable trend was that the media reproduces or reinforces gender relations and gender discriminative ideology in sports, so that arguments were made that media sport influences the audience to take for granted that the male is superior to the female (Duncan, Messner, Williams & Jensen, 1994).

Many sport sociologists criticised the way that the media has marginalised the success of female sports and, therefore, played an important role in keeping sports as a men's domain (Hargreaves, 1994; Kane & Greendorfer, 1994). The most significant criticism was about how female sports are portrayed.

South Korean studies (Lee & Kim, 1996; Nam, 2004; Nam & Kim, 2003) support international research that has found, regardless of printed or broadcast media, that reports emphasize socially allowed femininity, highlight gender disparity, are limited to sports considered appropriate for females, and often trivialise, marginalise and sexualise female athletes.

Another important approach to analysing gender bias in media sport is to compare the space allocated to male and female sports. Until recently, many studies reported that despite the increase in sport coverage in various media, relatively small amounts of pages or air-time have been dedicated to female athletes. Again, research carried out in Korea supports the international findings that the amount of coverage of women's sports is far less than that of men's sports (Kim, 1998; Kim & Koh, 2004). A longitudinal study conducted in Korea analysing the daily average space of gender-related images during non-Olympic periods from 2000 to 2003 found that 20.9% of images were of female athletes, 68.5% were of males and 10.6% were mixed-gender (Kim & Koh, 2004).

Moreover, although some studies (King, 2007; Pfister, 1987; Vincent, Imwold, Masemann & Johnson, 2002) found that media coverage of women's sport increased significantly since 1980s, it is hard to conclude that international media became more favorable towards women's sport and thus produced more gender-balanced coverage. We should note, regardless of country, there is a tendency that while the coverage of domestic female sports is insignificant during ordinary times, the coverage increases significantly during international sports events like the Olympic Games (Kim & Koh, 2004). A study conducted during the 2003 Daegu Summer Universiade (Nam, 2004) showed that five major Korean dailies allocated 36.5% to 41.7% of Universiade-related photo space to women's sports while men's sports and mixed-gender photos took 42.0% to 57.3% and 3.4% to 18.0% of the space respectively. Meanwhile, another South Korean study conducted during one year of a non-mega event period (Cho & Cho, 1998) showed that two major Korean dailies which were included in Nam's (2004) study posted only 19.9% and 20.1% of women's sport photos while men's sport photos were 80.1% and 79.9% of total photo numbers.

South Korean researchers have explored a range of other sports media issues, including newspaper sport coverage trends during the 20th century (Ha & Yang, 1991; Jun, 1989), journalism in sport media (Choi & Chung, 2003; Kwon & Won, 1998; Song, 1998), ideologies and values delivered in Korean TV sport coverage texts (Kim, 1994, Lee, 2003; Yoon, H-J, 1998; Yoon, T-J, 1998), the portrayal of sport heroes and celebrities (Kim & Kwon, 2005; Yoon & Lee, 2005), the influence of sport media consumption on sport event attendance (Seo, 2000) and how sport media gender bias influences high school students' perceptions (Kim & Lee, 2006).

METHOD

This study aimed to investigate the South Korean printed media's reporting of the Olympic Games by identifying the coverage of male and female athletes in a major Korean daily newspaper during the 2004 Athens Olympics. More specifically, the study tried to identify whether the newspaper maintained traditional media practices that have been labeled unfair; that is, whether it allocated more space to men's sports while focusing on the appearance or daily lives of female athletes rather than on their performances, or whether more space was given to women's sports than before, according to the increase in media sports coverage and growth of women's sports in the Olympics.

DongA Ilbo was chosen for analysis out of 9 local daily newspapers with nationwide distribution. According to Vincent et al. (2002), the choice of a daily newspaper as the subject of analysis is determined by national prominence, national circulation and extensive sports coverage. *DongA Ilbo* is recogniseed as one of the 3 major newspapers along with *Chosun Ilbo* and *ChoongAng Ilbo* (Korean Association of Newspapers, 2008), and their national prominence, national circulation and extensive sports coverage are almost identical. As *DongA Ilbo* is known to be more conservative than the others, it was considered to be the best candidate to identify gender bias in sports coverage in Korean dailies. The period of analysis was 27 days from August 7 to September 8, 2004, which started 6 days prior to the opening ceremony and ended 7 days after the closing ceremony of the 2004 Athens Olympics, excluding Sundays when the daily was not published.

The research method used is the one that was universally selected by the *Global Women in Sports Media Project*. The method involves measuring of the number and size of all articles and images in all newspaper pages including front page and sports pages, and coding and analysing them using MS Excel based on Article/Image Size, Gender of Article/Image, Relevance to the Olympics, Article/Image Location, Article/Image Focus and Article/Image Type. In the analysis, Images are included in the Article data (i.e., they are a sub-section of Articles). In order to minimise the potential for undermining the study's validity that may occur during the classification of data (Padgett, 2001), observer triangulation and peer review methods were adopted. Observer triangulation is a method where multiple observers participate in data classification and analysis to exclude subjectivity and error that may interfere with the interpretation of the data, and ultimately come to an intersubjective agreement. For this study, two research assistants participated in the entire data analysis process including measurement, coding, review and correction of coding result and data analysis. As for peer review, researchers from the countries working on the joint project have discussed the standard data classification on the project webpage during the data gathering period.

ARTICLES AND IMAGES BY GENDER

For the period prior to, during and after the 2004 Athens Olympics, the quantity of total articles and images allocated to sports categorised by gender is illustrated in Table 2. This table suggests that while men's sports make up close to half of the total number of articles and images, female coverage falls significantly short. The quantity of female sports articles (18.6% of space, 15.6% of articles) is far smaller than the quantity of female images (30.9% of space, 25.3% of images). In both cases, the percentages were lower than for men (41.2% of article space, 43.5% of articles; 45.7% of image space, 48.7% of images).

Table 2. Total sport articles and images by gender

Gender	Article				Image			
	(n)	%	cm²	%	(n)	%	cm²	%
Female	86	15.6	26,067.3	18.6	105	25.3	16,803.6	30.9
Male	239	43.5	57,707.2	41.2	202	48.7	24,854.6	45.7
Mixed	104	18.9	30,204.2	21.6	41	9.9	6,162.2	11.3
Neutral	121	22.0	25,944.5	18.5	67	16.1	6,566.2	12.1
Total	550	100	139,923.2	100	415	100	54,387.3	100
F/M ratio[1]	1:2.78		1:2.21		1:1.92		1:1.48	

[1] F/M Ratio stands for female to male ratio. In the Article (n) column above, the ratio indicates that for every female article, there are 2.78 male articles.

Close observation identified many cases where the article was focused on men's sports with an eye-catching, often sexualised, female athlete photo. Moreover, in some cases, reports on women's sport were minimised to captions attached to related photos; that is, they were posted without any relevant article. The percentage of space allocated to female athlete photos is higher than the number of articles, as it was often the case that *DongA Ilbo* posted large images focusing on female appearance for the 'pleasure of the readers'. However, as has been found by other studies carried out in the context of the joint project, the percentage difference between numbers and space of articles and images is not significant. Thus, for convenience, the majority of the following quantitative analysis uses only the number of articles and images.

Tables 3 and 4 are the result of comparison between Olympic and non-Olympic sport to identify the change in sports coverage caused by the Olympic Games. Table 3 shows that 67.8% of all articles and 83.4% of all images were allocated to Olympic coverage. Meanwhile, non-Olympic coverage of international and domestic sports was much less (15.1% and 17.1% of the total articles; 11.3% and 5.3% of the total images). Almost all the mixed coverage was related to Olympic sport, with both articles and images exceeding 90%. The trend towards higher Olympic coverage was stronger for females (73.3% articles, 86.7% images) than for males. Table 3 shows that male articles were relatively evenly divided between Olympic and non-Olympic sport.

Table 3. Gender breakdown between Olympic and non-Olympic coverage

Division between Olympic and Non-Olympic		Article					Image				
		F	M	Mix	Neu	Total	F	M	Mix	Neu	Total
Olympic	% of total	73.3	55.2	92.3	67.8	67.8	86.7	78.6	92.7	86.6	83.4
Non-Olympic	% of total	26.7	44.8	7.7	32.2	32.2	13.3	21.3	7.3	13.4	16.6
Total %		100	100	100	100	100	100	100	100	100	100
Non-Olympic international[1]	% of total	22.1	23.8	3.8	2.5	15.1	10.5	14.9	4.9	6.0	11.3
Non-Olympic domestic	% of total	4.7	20.9	3.8	29.8	17.1	2.9	6.4	2.4	7.5	5.3

[1] The non-Olympic coverage is further divided into International and Domestic coverage. Minor differences in percentage totals are due to rounding.

Table 4. Coverage of Olympic and non-Olympic articles and images by gender

Olympic relevance		Article					Image				
		F	M	Mix	Neu	Total	F	M	Mix	Neu	Total
Total	(n)	86	239	104	121	550	104	202	41	67	414
Olympic	(n)	63	132	96	82	373	90	159	38	58	345
	%	16.9	35.4	25.7	22.0	100	26.1	46.1	11.0	16.8	100
Non-Olympic	(n)	23	107	8	39	177	14	43	3	9	69
	%	13.0	60.5	4.5	22.0	100	20.3	62.3	4.3	13.0	100
Non-Olympic international	(n)	19	57	4	3	83	11	30	2	4	47
	%	22.9	68.7	4.8	3.6	100	23.4	63.8	4.3	8.5	100
Non-Olympic national	(n)	4	50	4	36	94	3	13	1	5	22
	%	4.3	53.2	4.3	38.3	100	13.6	59.1	4.5	22.7	100

In Table 4, it is notable that mixed-gender articles and images are more frequent in the Olympic coverage (25.7% of articles, 11.0% of images) than non-Olympics coverage (4.5% of articles, 4.3% of images). This is considered to be the result of a significant increase in articles and images covering multiple Korean athletes due to the special focus on their performance or medal winning during the Olympics. Meanwhile, international or domestic coverage shows a more distinctive tendency than the Olympics coverage to favor men's sport. For women's sports, the change in the amount of coverage due to the Olympics was relatively small, with a slightly higher frequency in Olympic coverage (Olympic articles 16.9%, images 26.3%; non-Olympic articles 13.0%, images 20.3%).

The results partially support the findings of previous studies that the coverage of female sports increases during the Olympics (e.g., Kim & Koh, 2004). That is, during the Olympics, the media focus on Olympic sports at the expense of professional sports and, therefore, unusually high attention is paid to female sports. On the other hand, the increase in women's sports coverage during the Olympics is significant only in the number of articles; overall, it is still far less than men's coverage. However, these results are significantly different from Nam's (2004) study of the 2003 Daegu Summer Universiade. The difference is believed to result from a different definition of gender classification (Nam made no distinction between mixed-gender and neutral categories) as well as the fact that Korean photographers took all the pictures of the 2003 Daegu Summer Universiade whereas Olympic photos were taken by both Korean and international media. As shown in Table 5, female athletes received a higher percentage of coverage when measured by space than by number of articles or images. This trend was only true for female articles; for all other measures the highest percentage was related to number.

Table 5. Olympic articles and images by gender

Gender	Article				Image			
	(n)	%	cm²	%	(n)	%	cm²	%
Female	63	16.9	20,896.2	18.1	90	26.1	14,096.8	30.0
Male	132	35.4	42,810.6	37.2	159	46.1	20,615.4	43.8
Mixed	96	25.7	29,356.5	25.5	38	11.0	5,999.8	12.8
Neutral	82	22.0	22,074.7	19.2	58	16.8	6,321.8	13.4
Total	373	100	115,138.0	100	345	100	47,033.8	100
F/M Ratio	1:2.1		1:2.05		1:1.77		1:1.46	

LOCATION FOCUS OF OLYMPIC ARTICLES AND IMAGES

Major gender differences in Olympics coverage can be witnessed not only in the amount of coverage but also in the location, focus and type of articles and images.

The location of an article is directly related to its importance. Table 6 shows that the Olympic articles and images appeared mostly in the sports section (84.7%). Although during ordinary coverage, sports stories rarely make it to the front page, Olympics articles are handled as important stories and 8.6% of the total Olympic

Table 6. Location of Olympic articles[1]

Gender	Front Page (A)			Sports		Editorial		Other		Total (B)	
	(n)	%	A/B%	(n)	%	(n)	%	(n)	%	(n)	%
Female	6	18.8	9.5	55	17.4	1	8.3	1	7.7	63	16.9
Male	15	46.9	11.4	113	35.8	1	8.3	3	23.1	132	35.4
Mixed	7	21.9	7.3	84	26.6	2	16.7	3	23.1	96	25.7
Neutral	4	12.5	4.9	64	20.3	8	66.7	6	46.2	82	22.0
Total[2]	32	100	8.6	316	100	12	100	13	100	373	100
Page Type %			8.6		84.7		3.2		3.5		100
F/M Ratio			1:2.5		1:2.05		1:1		1:3.0		1:2.1

[1] The number of articles includes the number of images.
[2] Minor differences in percentage totals are due to rounding. The total percentage reflects the results of the original data.

stories appeared on the front page. Men's coverage was most frequent (46.9%) and, when combined with mixed-gender sports (21.9%), made up around two-thirds of all front page Olympic articles. A relatively smaller amount of women's sport (18.8%) was posted on the front page, suggesting that women's sports were seen as less significant. As a percentage of total coverage by gender, however, there was no significant difference among men's (9.5%), women's (11.4%) and mixed (7.3%) front page coverage. This means that the difference in front page coverage may result from the different amount of overall Olympic coverage by gender.

Of the 32 articles that appeared on the front page, 22 (68.8%) were on Korean athletes who won or were trying to win medals, suggesting that the Olympic coverage had direct relations with the nation's success. Excluding the daily 'today's medal forecast' (which had head shots of two Korean athletes trying to win a medal every day), a total of 14 medal-related articles on Korean athletes appeared on the front pages, of which 8 belonged to men's sports, 6 to women's sport and 2 were mixed. In addition to the size and location of the articles and images, another factor that determines the significance of an article or image is its focus and type. Table 7 shows the result of classification by focus and gender of the subject of 373 Olympic articles. The most common articles were those reporting on events (48%) or on specific athletes or teams (26.5%). Articles about female athletes or teams received more than twice the coverage (25.1%) of women's sports events. This is believed to be related to the worldwide trend in newspaper sports coverage that the media focus more on the personal life stories of female athletes than their performance.

Table 7. Focus of Olympic articles

Gender	Sporting event (1)		Athlete/team (2)		Facilities/ organisations (3)		Issue (4)		Total	
	(n)	%	(n)	%	(n)	%	(n)	%	(n)	%
Female	10	10.1	45	25.1	0	0.0	8	8.6	63	16.9
Male	25	25.3	92	51.4	0	0.0	15	16.1	132	35.4
Mixed	36	36.4	37	20.7	0	0.0	23	24.7	96	25.7
Neutral	28	28.3	5	2.8	2	100	47	50.5	82	22.0
Total[1]	99	100	179	100	2	100	93	100	373	100
% Article Focus	26.5		48.0		0.5		24.9		100	
F/M Ratio	1:2.5		1:2		-		1:1.9		1:2.1	

[1] Minor differences in percentage totals are due to rounding (see Table 6, note 2).

Table 8 shows that almost a quarter of the total images are of actual sport action, of which most focus on males (55.3%) and more than one-third focus on females (36.5%). The ratios between men and women athletes were similar for sport-related images such as athletes warming up, for medal-related images such as award ceremonies or athletes posing with medals, and for the non-sport category that focused on athletes' daily lives. This result confirms that the Olympics coverage is more generously allocated to males, although the disparity is slightly smaller in photographic coverage than in stories.

Table 8. Focus of Olympic Images

Gender	Sport Action (n) %	Sport-related (n) %	Medal (n) %	Non-Sport (n) %	Coach (n) %	Other (n) %	Total (n) %
Female	(31) 36.5	(16) 35.6	(19) 33.9	(13) 30.2	(0) 0.0	(11) 10.3	(90) 26.1
Male	(47) 55.3	(27) 60.0	(32) 57.1	(20) 46.5	(9) 100	(24) 22.4	(159) 46.1
Mixed	(7) 8.2	(2) 4.4	(5) 8.9	(10) 23.3	(0) 0.0	(14) 13.1	(38) 11.0
Neutral	(0) 0.0	(0) 0.0	(0)0.0	(0) 0.0	(0) 0.0	(58) 54.2	(58) 16.8
Total[1]	(85) 100	(45) 100	(56) 99.9	(43) 100	(9) 100	(107) 100	(345) 100
% Image Focus	24.6	13.0	16.2	12.5	2.6	31.0	100
F/M Ratio	1:1.52	1:1.69	1:1.68	1:1.54	1:9	1:2.18	1.1.77

[1] Minor differences in percentage totals are due to rounding (see Table 6, note 2).

COVERAGE OF OLYMPIC ARTICLES AND IMAGES BY SPORTS

One of the remarkable characteristics in the Olympic coverage is that it includes a large number of non-popular sports that are not often featured by the media; a trend which is closely related to the sudden increase in female sports coverage during the Olympic Games. *DongA Ilbo* reported on all 28 sports of the summer Olympics. The gymnastics category was further divided into artistic and rhythmic gymnastics, and the swimming cateogory was divided into swimming, synchronized swimming, diving and water polo for analysis, which increased the number of sports to 32, as there were significantly different reporting patterns according to sub-discipline (see Figure 1). Note that the gymnastics category in Figures 1, 2 and 3 relates specifically to artistic gymnastics.

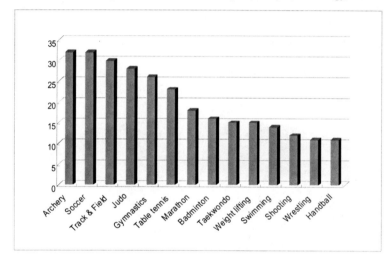

Figure 1. Sports featured in Olympic articles.

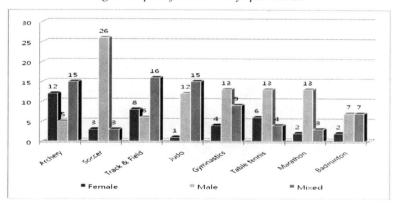

Figure 2. Sport items featured in Olympic articles by gender.

As illustrated in Figure 1, the 12 sports with highest number of articles are archery and soccer (32) followed by track and field (30), judo (28), artistic gymnastics (26), table tennis (23), marathon (18), badminton (16), taekwondo and weight lifting (15), swimming (14) and shooting (12), and wrestling and handball (11). Six of these sports coincide with the areas where Korean players won gold medals (archery, judo, table tennis, badminton, taekwondo, wrestling).

The contrast in Olympic coverage by gender is shown in Figure 2 which illustrates the top eight sports by gender. While the three top women's sports were archery, track and field and table tennis, five male sports – soccer, judo, gymnastics, table tennis and marathon – received as much as or more coverage than any women's sports. Sports with high levels of mixed coverage included archery, track and field and judo.

The female sport with the most articles and images, archery, is a sport at which Korean women are exceptionally good and readers' attention was focused on this sport during the Olympics. Korean women won three archery medals: Sung Hyun Park and Sung Jin Lee won gold and silver in the individual event, respectively, and took gold in the team event along with Mi Jin Yun.

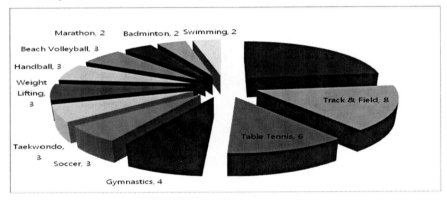

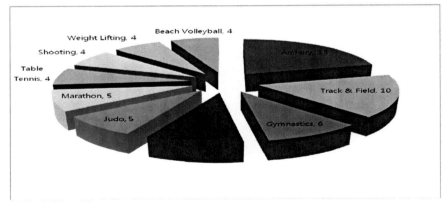

Figure 3. Female sport items featured in Olympic articles (above) and photographs (below).

Articles on table tennis were mainly due to Korean women winning two medals: Eun Sil Lee and Eun Mi Seok took the silver medal in doubles and Kyung Ah Kim won the bronze medal in singles. Coverage of such men's sports as artistic gymnastics, table tennis, judo, badminton, wresting and archery is also considered to be the result of Koreans winning medals. Marathon is often referred to as 'the essence of the Olympics' and usually covered more than once. However, it was covered exceptionally frequently in both articles and images in 2004 due to the incident where an audience member pushed the first-placed male Brazilian runner and the second-placed Italian won the gold medal. Track and field is a sport that attracts high levels of interest during the Games and thus had a large amount of coverage despite the fact no Korean athletes won medals. The analysis suggests that sports coverage is subject to not simply the gender preference of the newspaper but also to complex factors such as the popularity of sports during the Olympic period or in general and Korean athletes winning medals.

Figures 4 and 5 illustrate the amount of photographic coverage by sports and gender. The tendency for the printed media to favor sports that are popular in non-Olympic periods (Kim & Koh, 2004) was confirmed in the Olympic coverage. The sport that received highest media attention was soccer (24 photographs, 32 articles), followed by archery (23 images, 32 articles) and judo (22 images, 28 articles). High numbers of images were found for marathon (19), table tennis and track and field (18 each), artistic gymnastics (15), swimming (12) and badminton, shooting, weight lifting and taekwondo (10 each). These were sports where Korean athletes won medals or sports such as track and field and swimming with traditionally high coverage.

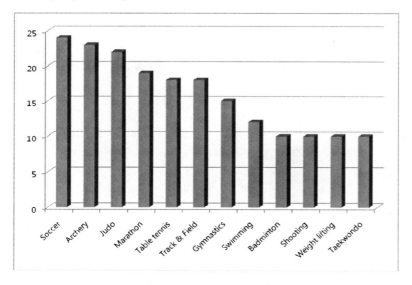

Figure 4. Sport items featured in Olympic-related photographs.

Women's sports with most photo coverage were archery and track and field (see also Figure 3). In both these sports, women received more photographs and articles than males. The tendency for Korean newspapers' Olympics coverage to have a higher percentage of archery photos was noted in a previous study (Kim & Koh, 2004). While swimming and marathon are key Olympic sports regardless of gender and thus considered to receive high media coverage, all photos of beach volleyball were confirmed to be close-up shots of specific body parts of female athletes or to focus on the revealing uniform. That is, photographic coverage was initiated not by the pure interest in the sport itself but by the intention to draw readers' attention to the female bodies that are likely to be marginalised and sexualised.

Meanwhile, men's sports with more coverage than females included soccer, marathon, judo and table tennis. Despite the dominance of the Olympic Games, the popularity of men's professional soccer led to multiple soccer photos, of which men received 75%, along with 81% of soccer articles. In addition to judo, table tennis, archery and artistic gymnastics, where Korean men won medals, photos of marathon, athletics and swimming were often featured as these sports received the highest attention during the Olympic period.

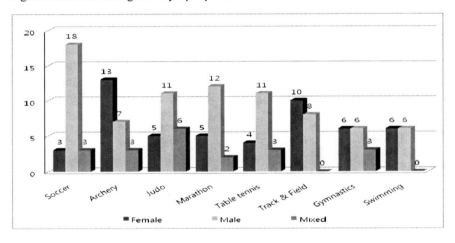

Figure 5. Sport items featured in Olympic photographs by gender.

CONCLUSION

Today, the sports media, or the 'media-sports-culture-complex' (Miller, Lawrence, McKay & Rowe, 2001), is leading the popular culture of post industrial society, ranging from the traditional print media to broadcasting media and the internet or 'new media' (Wilson, 2007). Sport sociologists have focused on the way that media coverage of sports has a continuous influence on the public conception of sports and society by reproducing or reinforcing existing ideologies. This study observed how *DongA Ilbo* newspaper, the most traditional media with wide public influence, reported the Olympics within the cultural context of Korea, with special attention to gendered ideology. The coverage of global mega sports events like the Olympics, where worldwide attention is given without the audience being at the scene of the events, is worthy of special attention in that how the media select, edit and report has enormous influence on the public conception of sports and athletes.

This study found that the sports coverage of a Korean newspaper prior to, during and after the 2004 Athens Olympics showed the same gender preference found in previous media sports analyses. Men's sports took around 40% of total coverage in terms of the number of articles and images, while female sports had 15.6% of total articles and 25.3% of total images, which is around one half of male articles and two-thirds of male images. Analysis specifically on the Olympic coverage showed a similar trend of greater discrepancies in number of articles than in number of images. Women received only half the number of Olympic articles about men's sports, and almost 60% of the number of male images. Non-Olympic sports coverage showed the same trend but an even larger gender discrepancy. Women received just over 20% of the number of male articles and just under one-third of the male images. The difference in the amount of coverage by gender supports the result of previous studies in Korea and internationally (Kim, 1998; Kim & Koh, 2004).

When we discuss the gender bias of media reports, we need to note that there are differences in the number of men's and women's sport events, as well as in their popularity as spectator sports. That is, outside global sports events such as the Olympics, we should not overlook the fact that there are relatively fewer women's sports events that demand media attention in comparison to the number of games and popularity of men's sports such as professional soccer and baseball. This partly results from, and at the same time led to, the phenomenon that the media prefer male sports which, in turn, undermines the growth of women's sports.

On the other hand, as today's Olympics have similar numbers of events for both genders, and as many media focus their attention on the performance of their country's athletes, the difference in media coverage by gender during the Olympics can be attributable to a large degree to gender bias. As for Korea, while female and male athletes showed similar performances in the 2004 Athens Olympics, with female athletes winning 12 medals from 8 sports and male athletes winning 18 medals from 10 sports, women's sports coverage during the Olympics was only around half of men's sports coverage. Such differences in coverage by gender can be also witnessed in the number and size of articles on the front page, the number and size of articles and images on games and matches, types of articles related to games and matches, and the number of color images. The biggest reason for such differences can be explained as being the result of the gender difference in the amount of overall Olympics coverage with slight variations by area of analysis.

The sports mainly handled in the Olympics coverage of the Korean newspaper were sports in which Korean athletes won medals – archery, judo, taekwondo, table tennis, badminton, artistic gymnastics and weightlifting – and sports that have received constant attention in the Olympics regardless of country – athletics, marathon and swimming. The trend of gender-biased reporting based on 'feminine appropriateness' of sports was not particularly evident, for the Olympics media coverage carries a nationalistic character and was, therefore, influenced by medals won by the country rather than the features of a sport. The result reinforces Koh and Kim's (2004) findings that female sports portrayed in the Korean media have played the role of icons who recreate nationalism since the 1970s. Meanwhile, media attention on other women's sports was noticed in beach volleyball where focus was placed on the appearance and the outfits of Western female players. The sudden increase of media coverage in the sport was a temporary occurrence related to marginalisation and sexualisation of female athletes, but this was restricted to Western women as Korean female athletes are often regarded as national icons during international sport events like the Olympics.

In conclusion, while the Korean newspaper favoured men's sports for Olympic coverage, the gender disparity was less evident than in ordinary times. This is because determination of which sport to cover and how it is covered is strongly influenced not only by gendered ideology but also by nationalism in the Korean media in particular, and in Korean society in general. That is, while Korean athletes winning medals is a key factor determining the content of media coverage, the appearance and outfits of Western female athletes that may attract readers' attention also works as one of the complex factors. In the future, a longitudinal study is required of multiple Olympics to identify which factors remain constant and which are changing over time, while comparative study between summer and winter Olympics may provide meaningful results. At the same time, qualitative studies on various printed, broadcasting and/or internet media texts are needed to further explore the discourses in Olympics coverage.

ACKNOWLEDGMENTS

An earlier version of this study appeared in Volume 21(1) of the *Korean Journal of Sociology of Sport* (pp. 205–227) in March, 2008. The data used in this study were reviewed and recoded by a second peer-reviewing process and may be slightly different from the earlier version. The author would like to thank Sook Kim, Yoonso Choi and Taeyoung Kim for their efforts in measuring, coding and reviewing data.

REFERENCES

Cho, S.-S., & Cho, K.-M. (1998). The marketing strategies for the photographic coverage of athletes by gender. *Korean Journal of Sport Management, 3*(2), 229–247.

Choi, B.-H., & Chung, C.-S. (2003). TV sport journalism deployment with the change in Korean broadcasting environment. *Korean Journal of Physical Education, 42*(6), 129–140.

Duncan, M. C., Messner, M. A., Williams, L., & Jensen, K. (1994). Gender stereotyping in televised sports. In S. Birrell & C. L. Cole (Eds.), *Women, sport and culture* (pp. 249–272). Champaign, IL: Human Kinetics.

Hargreaves, J. (1994). *Sporting females: Critical issues in the history and sociology of women's sport.* London: Routledge.

Jun, S.-D. (1989). *The trend of sport coverage in Korean newspaper since the liberation of Korea.* Unpublished master's thesis, Seoul National University, Seoul, Korea.

Kane, M. J., & Greendorfer, S. (1994). The media's role in accommodating and resisting stereotyped images of women in sport. In J. P. Creedon (Ed.), *Women, media and sport: Challenging gender values* (pp. 28–44). Thousand Oaks, CA: Sage.

Kim, B.-C., & Kwon, S.-Y. (2005). Gender and media sport: A content analysis of media portrayal of Se Ri Pak. *Korean Physical Education Association for Girls and Women, 19*(1), 89–101.

Kim, H.-J., & Koh, E. (2004). Photographic coverage of women's sport in daily newspaper: Donga Ilbo, from 1948 to 2003. *Korean Journal of Physical Education, 43*(4), 101–114.

Kim, I.-H., & Lee, K.-M. (2006). The influence of gender bias of media sports on students' gender role attitude and gender equality in high school. *Journal of Korean Physical Education Association for Girls and Women, 20*(4), 203–216.

Kim, Y.-J. (1994). Influences of mass media on values in sports. *Korean Journal of Physical Education, 33*(2), 2156–2169.

Kim, Y.-R. (1998). A study on the media coverage of male and female athletes and audience's satisfaction. *Korean Journal of Physical Education, 37*(3), 64–78.

King, C. (2007). Media portrayals of male and female athletes: A text and picture analysis of the British national newspaper coverage of the Olympic Games since 1948. *International Review for the Sociology of Sport, 42*(2), 187–199.

Koh, E. (2002). The rise of women's sport and the reconstruction of gender identity in South Korea. *International Institute for Asian Studies Newsletter, 28*, p. 7.

Koh, E. (2004). Olympic and women's sport. *Sport Science, 87*, 22–28.

Koh, E., & Kim, H.-J. (2004). Gender and nationalism in sport pages: Photographic coverage of women's sport in a Korean daily newspaper. *Korean Journal of Sport Science, 15*(4), 172–183.

Korea Sports Council. (2008). *Members.* Retrieved July 1, 2007, from http://www.sports.or.kr/eng/ksckoc.eng

Korean Association of Newspapers. (2008). *Statistics in newspaper business.* Author. Retrieved July 1, 2008, from http://www.presskorea.or.kr

Kwon, W.-D., & Won, Y.-S. (1998). Sport journalism and culture on Korean newspaper: From 1920 to 1992. *Korean Journal of Sociology of Sport, 10*, 31–44.

Ha, N.-G., & Yang, D.-G. (1991). An analysis of the effects and trend of sports reports through mass media. *Korean Journal of Physical Education, 30*(2), 2023–2033.

Lee, J.-O., & Kim, S.-G. (1996). Gender discourses in mediasport. *Journal of Korean Physical Education Association for Girls and Women, 10*(1), 123–134.

Lee, K.-W. (2003). Ideological practices of media sport texts. *Korean Journal of Sociology of Sport, 16*(1), 171–188.

Miller, T., Lawrence, G., McKay, J., & Rowe, D. (2001). *Globalization and sport: Playing the world.* London: Sage Publications.

Ministry of Culture & Tourism. (2006). *National sport participation survey.* Seoul: Ministry of Culture & Tourism.

Nam, S. (2004). Content and meaning analysis of female athletes' photographs on sports section in daily newspaper. *Korean Journal of Physical Education, 43*(4), 101–114.

Nam, S., & Kim, J. (2003). Analysis of photographic image of female athletes in daily newspapers. *Korean Journal of Sociology of Sport, 16*(2), 456–477.

Padgett, D. K. (2001). *Qualitative methods in social work research* (T. Woo, Trans.). Seoul: Nanam. (Qualitative methods in social work research: Challenges and rewards. London: Sage Publications, 1998).

Pfister, G. (1987). Women in the Olympics (1952–1982): An analysis of German newspapers (Beauty awarded vs. gold medals). In R. Jackson & T. McPhail (Eds.), *The Olympic movement and the mass media.* Canada: Hurford Enterprises Ltd.

SBS TV. (2008, March 7). *Korean women, low income and far from power.* Author.

Seo, H.-J. (2000). The influence of sport media on professional sport event spectating. *Korean Journal of Sociology of Sport, 13*(2), 253–262.

Song, H.-R. (1998). Sport journalism in Korea. *Korean Journalism Review, 26*(1), 42–52.

UNDP. (2007). Human Development Report 2007/2008. Retrieved July 1, 2008, from http://hdr.undp.org/en

Vincent, J., Imwold, C., Masemann, V., & Johnson, J. T. (2002). A comparison of selected 'serious' and 'popular' British, Canadian, and United States newspaper coverage of female and male athletes competing in the Centennial Olympic Games: Did female athletes receive equitable coverage in the 'Games of the women'? *International Review for the Sociology of Sport, 37*(4), 319–335.

Wensing, E. H., & Bruce, T. (2003). Bending the rules: Media representations of gender during an international sporting event. *International Review for the Sociology of Sport, 38*(4), 387–396.

Wilson, B. (2007). New media, social movements, and global sport studies: A revolutionary moment and the sociology of sport. *Sociology of Sport Journal, 24*(4), 457–477.

Yoon, H.-J. (1998). Meaning structure of TV sport coverage. *Korean Journalism Review, 26*(1), 66–76.

Yoon, T.-J. (1998). Non-professionalism and ideologies in sport coverage. *Korean Journalism Review, 26*(1), 52–60.

Yoon, Y.-K., & Lee, I.-H. (2005). Reporting sports heroes in Korean journalism and perception of the audience. *Journal of Communication Science, 5*(3), 373–410.

Eunha Koh
Korea Institute of Sport Science
South Korea

AFRICA

SUSAN SCOTT-CHAPMAN

19. SOUTH AFRICA

South African Newspaper Sports Coverage of the 2004 Olympic Games

INTRODUCTION

Since the collapse of apartheid, the post-1994 multiracial Government of National Unity has vocally emphasized the desire for an impartial and democratic constitution for *all* South Africans (Burnett, 2002; Cock & Bernstein, 2001; Hargreaves, 1997, 2000; Pelak, 2005). A part of this process of democratic change has been to actively promote women's rights, advance women's issues in the constitution and to encourage women to become more active within all aspects of life. Cock and Bernstein (2001) highlight that "in the 'new South Africa,' a bill of rights guarantees women equality before the law" (p. 146). However, to what extent this egalitarianism is genuine and how women are being supported and equipped to access the opportunities that the new legislation offers is unclear.

SOUTH AFRICA AND GENDER RELATIONS

Four years before the end of apartheid, the African National Congress National Executive Committee had voiced its concern that gender equality needed to be confronted independently, and highlighted that:

> The experience of other societies has shown that the emancipation of women is not a by-product of a struggle for democracy. It has to be addressed in its own right within our organization, the mass democratic movement and in society as a whole. (cited in Cock & Bernstein, 2001, p. 142)

Thus, the ANC caucus, made up of a number of women, already realised that eradicating racial discrimination would not necessarily or simultaneously eliminate gender discrimination. However, although the end of apartheid may have provided a 'racial victory' for the majority of South Africans, it has done little to eliminate the political, social and economic inequity of women (Burnett, 2001a, 2002; Cock & Bernstein, 2001; Hargreaves, 1997; Morrell, 2002; Pelak, 2005). Morrell (2002) describes the new constitution as "among the most progressive in the world" yet argues that "the new policies and laws have not overthrown patriarchy or removed men from their domination of public life, politics, and earnings" (p. 309). In almost all aspects of South African life, men firmly maintain control of businesses and political organisations.

T. Bruce, J. Hovden and P. Markula (eds.),
Sportswomen at the Olympics: A Global Content Analysis of Newspaper Coverage, 257–271.
© *2010 Sense Publishers. All rights reserved.*

Further, there is little similarity between the lives and experiences of White and African[1] women. In considering the implications and constraints for women, Pelak (2005) argues that "South African women do not form a homogeneous unified group that experiences gender inequalities in the same way" (p. 67). Much of the social research carried out since 1994 highlights that although women in general are discriminated against and remain marginalised, it is African women who not only bear the brunt of gender discrimination but also face racial, cultural and tribal subjugation (Burnett, 2002; Cock & Bernstein, 2001; Hargreaves, 1997; Morrell, 2002; Pelak, 2005). The majority of African women live in rural areas where traditional customary practices continue to be exercised through strict patriarchal control which allows women little personal or free time outside of their domestic responsibilities (Burnett, 2002; Cock & Bernstein, 2001; Hargreaves, 1997). Many African women still live in poverty, without education or a means for a better life. Cock and Bernstein (2001) point out that "overall, African women in rural areas are particularly powerless, voiceless, and dependent. Almost 65 percent of African rural women cannot read or write" (p. 149). Yet as women strive for greater access, respect and freedom, many men feel fearful of the progress that women are making (Morrell, 2002).

Since the 1994 elections, encouraged by women's watchdog groups, a number of studies have examined how the media incorporates women or women's views and supports gender equity (Cock & Bernstein, 2001; MISA & Gender Links, 2003; Pelak, 2005). MISA and Gender Links (2003) maintain that it "is one of the most important yet challenging areas of work for advancing gender equality" (p. 14). A concern raised in the MISA and Gender Links (2003) study is the lack of women's voices or female perspectives in media news reporting. They argue that there are "31 percent women in parliament and a similar proportion in cabinet. Yet women constitute only eight percent of the politicians quoted in the media monitored" (MISA & Gender Links, 2003, p. 10). Male politicians are thus able to voice their political opinions more often, despite frequently being junior to their female counterparts who are being ignored. The researchers further suggest that despite "potentially having a huge role to play in this 'liberation of the mind', the media has more often than not been part of the problem rather than of the solution" (MISA & Gender Links, 2003, p. 14).

SPORT AND WOMEN IN SOUTH AFRICA

In examining the extent of the new constitution that legislates for gender equality, Hargreaves (1997) highlights that "the anti-racist anti-sexist philosophy of the Government of National Unity has been applied to different areas of political, social and cultural life, including sport" (p. 192). The importance of sport in South Africa cannot be underestimated: even Nelson Mandela used sport to encourage national unity when he wore the Springbok rugby jersey to encourage sports fans of all races to support the men's national World Cup rugby team in 1995 (Hargreaves, 1997, 2000). However, Hargreaves (1997) argues that Mandela's "notion of unity in that context is a partial one which masks the gendered nature of South African sport and of South African society" (p. 199). Recent research contends that the main obstacle for advancing girls' and women's sporting opportunities has been the ongoing focus on boys and male sports (Burnett, 2001a, 2001b, 2002; Hargreaves, 1997). Additionally, Pelak (2005) argues that, "in post-apartheid South Africa, the legacies of colonialism and apartheid still shape women's access to sports" (p. 59). Thus, issues of race and gender continue to play a major part in shaping the sporting opportunities and experiences of many women.

Sports administrators, the media, sponsors and national sporting bodies focus on men's sport both at national and international levels (Burnett, 2002; Cock & Bernstein, 2001; Hargreaves, 1997; MISA & Gender Links, 2003; Pelak, 2005; Serra, 2005). As a result, women who participate in sport have to organise and finance their own sporting activities. In her analysis of women's soccer, Pelak (2005) highlights that "financial subsidies for transportation from football governing bodies and corporate sponsors are almost exclusively given to boys and men's soccer programs. Without adequate funds for transportation aspiring [female] athletes simply cannot participate" (p. 62). Not being adequately resourced to participate in sports at grassroots level has a major ripple effect on the number of women actively engaged in amateur and professional sports.

This gender imbalance in sport is clearly evident in the disproportionately low number of female athletes representing the country at such prestigious events as the Olympic Games. Table 1 reflects the gender ratio of South African athletes who participated at the most recent four Olympic Games from 1992 to 2004. On average, there were twice as many male athletes as female athletes who represented the nation. In 2004, although the total number of females increased only marginally from 2000, these athletes represented the highest proportion (38%) of females to represent South Africa at an Olympic Games.

Little appears to have changed over the last 14 years that South African athletes have been able to participate in international sports, following the lifting of sporting sanctions. Although racial and gender policies have been developed in respect of equitable sports participation, few changes have physically materialised and sportswomen, regardless of colour and ability, remain marginalised. Furthermore, although focus is being given to gender inequality within sport, the resulting number of participants needs to be carefully considered to take racial inequalities into account. Thus gender and racial imbalance in sport remains a serious concern for South African elite athletes (Bruce & Chapman, 2006; Burnett, 2001b, 2001a, 2002; Hargreaves, 1997; Pelak, 2005; Serra, 2005). Burnett (2001b), in describing the disproportionately small number of women of colour within the South African team sent to the 2000 Sydney Olympics, stated that "only two delegates (0.01%) represented this category – one hockey player (who did not play at the tournament) and one hockey official" (p. 309). Racial distinctions within sport are also an issue for women of Colour (non-African) who also felt the effects of apartheid discrimination yet are given less recognition than African women within the new regime, and continue to feel marginalised (Burnett, 2001a; Cock & Bernstein, 2001; Hargreaves, 2000; Pelak, 2005).

Table 1. The South African Olympic team makeup by gender at each Olympic Games from 1992 to 2004

Event	Male Athletes	Female Athletes	Total
	Number (%)[1]	Number (%)	Number (%)
1992 Barcelona Olympics	59 (69%)	27 (31%)	86 (100%)
1996 Atlanta Olympics	65 (76%)	20 (24%)	85 (100%)
2000 Sydney Olympics	93 (71%)	38 (29%)	131 (100%)
2004 Athens Olympics	67 (62%)	41 (38%)	108 (100%)
OVERALL TOTAL	284 (69%)	126 (31%)	410 (100%)

[1] All percentages are rounded to whole numbers.
Source: Numbers for 1992, 1996 and 2000 from Burnett (2001b, 2002); numbers for 2004 from the *Cape Argus* and Olympic Games-related websites.

SPORTS MEDIA COVERAGE

Although sports play a major role in South African society, little research has been done to establish what role the media play in conveying sport to an extensive, diverse, multicultural and multi-lingual society. The only known quantitative study analysed a six-month period from 1 April – 30 September 2004, a period that also included the 17 days of the 2004 Olympic Games (Serra, 2005). Serra's (2005) study incorporated an Afrikaans-medium newspaper, a traditional African newspaper and an English-medium newspaper to provide a broad overview of sporting coverage. In addition to examining a range of issues across racial, ethnic, social and language variation, Serra (2005) analysed the gender of media workers and athletes, the range of sports events that occurred and the media's placement of text and images. Serra's (2005) findings revealed that the overall coverage was "greatly biased towards male sport coverage" with men receiving 86.5% compared with 13.5% for females (p. 74). Males also received more praise (91.4%) for their "potential and budding career" than females who received only 8.6% of such praise (Serra, 2005, p. 66). Males dominated coverage in each of the three newspapers, and preference was given to sports that Serra (2005) argued reflected traditional racial sporting interests; soccer and boxing for the majority of African and Coloured newspaper readers, and rugby, cricket and soccer for the White and Coloured readership. Her study, thus, illustrated that the South African sports media focused attention on male athletes and those masculine sports traditionally linked to a sense of national and cultural identity such as rugby, cricket and soccer. Serra (2005) also found that media workers believed that the public were more interested in male sports, to the detriment of female athletes and those readers interested in women's sports and gender equality. For example:

One journalist mentions that the sport section must portray the new society of South Africa and its continuing metamorphosis. Yet, political restructuring and/or policies in the sporting world measured as the lowest theme covered in newspapers. Upcoming female sport stars are hardly reported on and when a story is covered, it is usually a story that trivialises the achievements and importance of women's sport. (Serra, 2005, p. 84)

METHOD

This South African study analysed the *Cape Argus* newspaper, an English-medium newspaper primarily targeted at a middle class Western Cape White and Coloured readership, with a circulation of approximately 405,000. The data collection extended from 7 August to 4 September 2004, incorporating the Olympics and a week prior to the opening ceremony and a week after the closing ceremony. Non-Olympic coverage incorporated all content not related to the 2004 Olympics, including all local, national and international sporting activities. The Olympic data included the media's pre-Olympic build-up and wrap-up of the actual sporting activities. The article size combines both the text and images. The newspaper sports pages as well as the front page and any sports supplements were analysed and measured in square centimetres.

This study not only examined how individual male and female athletes were reported on in the newspaper, but also identified mixed coverage of both male and female athletes in a single report or image, and neutral coverage relating to general issues and non-gender specific media content.

FINDINGS

Of the 108 South African athletes competing at the 2004 Olympics, 67 (62%) were male and 41 (38%) were female. Examining the racial background of the female athletes and describing them in South African racial classifications, 34 were White (83%), 1 was African (2.4%), 5 were Coloured (12%) and 1 was Indian (2.4%). Of the 6 medals won by the South African team (1 gold, 3 silver and 2 bronze), only one medal was won by a female, Hestrie Cloete, a White athlete who gained a silver medal in the high jump.

1. Media Focused Little Attention on Female Athletes Outside of Olympics

The non-Olympic coverage revealed that there were considerably more articles on male athletes and male sporting activities (69.5%) than there were for female athletes (11.3%). As seen in Table 2 below, the articles about male athletes were longer and allocated more space, taking up 76.3% of the total space and averaging 231cm^2, whereas articles on sportswomen were shorter and only occupied 4% of sports space (averaging 75cm^2 per article).

Table 2. Non-Olympic coverage by gender in one South African newspaper

Measurement	Male	Female	Mixed	Neutral	Total
Article space in cm^2	93,651.50	4,969.50	11,387.50	12,791.00	122,799.50
Percentage (%)	76.3	4	9.3	10.4	100%
Number of articles	405	66	58	54	583
Percentage (%)	69.5	11.3	10	9.2	100%

In analysing the data to establish what types of reference were made to individual sportswomen, the main finding revealed that when sportswomen were discussed in the 'mixed' category of coverage, they were more often included in articles that featured male athletes more prominently. Additionally, the lower percentage of space compared to the number of articles points to the fact that more often sportswomen featured individually in short articles, the sports briefs and the results section of the newspaper than sportsmen. This finding supports the hypothesis that female athletes will receive unequal and lesser coverage in non-Olympic coverage; as sportsmen not only receive substantially more newspaper space but also a far greater numbers of articles.

2. The Media Give Greater Prominence to Female Athletes During Major Sports Events

The Olympic coverage findings reveal a remarkable reversal of fortune for female athletes compared with the non-Olympic data. There were 811 Olympic articles, of which 400 related to male athletes, 224 to females, 95 to mixed coverage and 92 were of neutral reporting. Thus the overall Olympic coverage reflected in Table 3 highlights that males still received the greater percentage of articles (49.3%), compared with females (27.6%), mixed (11.7%) and neutral (11.3%). However, although the total articles for male athletes reduced only slightly between non-Olympic and Olympic coverage (5 less Olympic articles) the number of female, mixed and neutral articles increased dramatically. Female articles more than tripled from 66 in non-Olympic coverage to 224 in Olympic coverage; and the proportion of articles more than doubled from 11.3% to 27.6%. The trend was similar but more pronounced when comparing the amount of space; with the proportion of female coverage increasing five times from 4% to 21.2%. Although the findings show increased Olympic coverage for females, the results do not support the hypothesis that female athletes will receive relatively equal newspaper coverage to males during a major international sporting event. Clearly, media coverage still concentrated greatest emphasis on male athletes.

Table 3. Olympics-only coverage in one South African newspaper

Measurement	Male	Female	Mixed	Neutral	Total
Article space in cm^2	32,022.33	14,504.43	10,508.50	11,343.31	68,378.57
Percentage (%)	46.8	21.2	15.4	16.6	100%
Number of articles	400	224	95	92	811
Percentage (%)	49.3	27.6	11.7	11.4	100%

The substantial increase in coverage given to sportswomen is reflected not only in the number of articles but also in the newspaper space allocation. In both the Olympic and non-Olympic coverage, articles about sportswomen remained similar in size – 65cm^2 and 75cm^2 respectively. Yet during the Olympics the average article size for sportsmen decreased substantially from 231cm^2 to 80cm^2.

Thus, Olympics article sizes for males and females were much closer than during the non-Olympics coverage. In addition, an assessment of the media content revealed that there were a higher number of mixed articles during the Olympics; 95 as opposed to 58 during the non-Olympic coverage. These mixed articles focused on groups of medal winners, teams of athletes participating in the opening and closing ceremonies, and previews and wrap-ups of sports in which both males and females took part. This sort of mixed reporting does not often occur in non-Olympic media coverage. During the Olympic coverage, the results reveal that sportswomen were given more attention, regardless of their sporting success (see Tables 2 and 3). These findings for sportswomen were illustrated both within the increased allocation of space and the number of articles. Although the total coverage for sportswomen increases when combining the non-Olympic and Olympic activities, from 4% to 10.2%, this combined space allocated to female is a sixth of the space allocated to sportsmen, and less than the mixed or neutral coverage (see Figure 1).

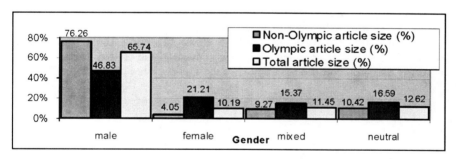

Figure 1. Percentage of space by gender of Non-Olympic, Olympic and Total Coverage.

3. Photographs of Female Athletes are Given a Minor Place Compared to Males

During the Olympics the space and number of photographs shown in Table 4 reflect that female athletes received approximately 30% of photographs. Yet photographs of male athletes were almost double that of females; 231 as opposed to 120. Although there was more space and greater number of images of male athletes, the average size of the photographs was similar for males ($58cm^2$) and females ($64cm^2$).

Table 4. Olympics-only photographic coverage

Measurement	Male	Female	Mixed	Neutral	Total
Photograph space in cm^2	13,414.41	7,694.5	63	4,834.75	26,006.66
Percentage (%)	51.6	29.7	0.2	18.6	100%
Photograph number	231	120	1	53	405
Percentage (%)	57	29.6	0.3	13.1	100%

Although this study focuses on Olympic coverage, the findings in relation to the non-Olympic photographs provide a glaring illustration of newspaper emphasis given to male athletes outside of major events. Table 5 exposes the considerable attention devoted to sportsmen, who had 19 times the number of images of sportswomen.

Table 5. Non-Olympics photographic coverage

Measurement	Male	Female	Mixed	Neutral	Total
Photograph space in cm^2	26,963.94	1,999.25	783	104.25	29,850.44
Percentage (%)	90.3	6.7	2.6	0.4	100%
Photograph number	171	9	2	5	187
Percentage (%)	91.4	4.8	1.1	2.7	100%

When assessing the types of images that were captured during the total coverage period, Table 6 reveals that female athletes were captured more in 'sport-related' photographs (66.7%) than in 'action' shots (31.7%). These sport-related photographs reflect a more passive sporting image of the athlete. However, there was only one non-sport image of a woman during the period of analysis.

Table 6. Types of photographs by gender of total coverage

Image	Male (n)	%	Female (n)	%	Mixed (n)	%	Neutral (n)	%	Total (n)	%
Sport Action	125	31.1	41	31.7	1	33.3	5	8.6	172	29.1
Sport-related	223	55.5	86	66.7	0	0	2	3.4	311	52.5
Medal Photos	7	1.7	1	0.8	0	0	1	1.7	9	1.5
Non Sport	47	11.7	1	0.8	2	66.7	50	86.2	100	16.9
Total	402		129		3		58		592	100

The findings indicate that male athletes had three times the number of action photographs as women (125 versus 41), and 2.6 times the number of sport-related photographs (223 versus 86). Overall, female athletes appeared in 21.8% of the 592 photographs, whereas photographs of male athletes accounted for 67.9% of the total. With minor variations, however, the results support the hypothesis that female and male athletes will be portrayed similarly in types of photographs; both males and females were most represented in sport-related settings, followed by sport action. These two categories dominated the coverage, with males receiving

86.6% and females 98.4% of images in these categories. However, what needs to be taken into consideration is that at the commencement of the Games, the newspaper issued two newspaper supplements containing photographs, mostly small headshots, of each of the Olympic athletes. These accounted for 127 male sport-related photographs, and 77 female sport-related photographs. Excluding these photographs, as shown in Table 7 below, negatively impacts on sportswomen as they had proportionately more (37.7%) supplement photographs. After discounting the supplement, the focus on sportsmen during actual participation in the Olympics increased from 67.9% to 70.9%, whereas for sportswomen it decreased from 21.8% to 13.4%.

Table 7. Total Coverage of photographs including and excluding the Olympic supplement

Photographs	Male	Female	Mixed	Neutral	Total
Including supplement (n)	402	129	3	58	592
Excluding supplement (n)	275	52	3	58	388
Including supplement %	67.9	21.8	0.5	9.8	100
Excluding supplement %	70.9	13.4	0.8	14.9	100

4. At Major Events, Athletes Expected to Win Medals Get More Media Focus

The media focused greater attention on potential winners and record breakers competing at the Olympics. The prospect of success provided more articles and photographic space for the winning athletes. Table 8 highlights the amount of space and number of photographs that reflect South African medal winners.

What needs to be considered when examining this data is that of the 108 national athletes competing at the Games, South Africa secured only 6 medals (five by males, one by a female). Although male athletes received 5 medals in total, only one male athlete received more focus than the other winners; Roland Schoeman, who won 3 medals in total. Additionally, not all medal winners were recognised in the same way. For example, during the Olympics, there were *no* action photographs of the 800m track silver medal winner, Mbulaeni Mulaudzi, the only African medal winner. On the day of his track event there was a preview article about Mulaudzi and fellow runner Hezekiel Sepeng underneath a large action photograph of Hestrie Cloete who was also competing on the same day. After Mulaudzi and Cloete both won silver medals, the next newspaper edition dedicated the majority of the main sports page to a large photograph of Cloete with the South African flag, celebrating her achievement. On the inside page there was an article about all six medal winners and other athletes who had done well, but only one and a half sentences ($9.75cm^2$) were about Mulaudzi's win. The negligible coverage of the only African athlete to win a medal perhaps highlights the racial composition of the readership of the *Cape Argus,* yet still appears at odds with the emphasis that was given to the other national and international medal winners.

Table 8. Space allocated to South African medal winners by gender and coverage size

Gender	Article space	Photo space	Photo (n)	Medal type	Medal winning athletes and events
Male	5,044.8	1,795.5	9	Silver & Bronze	Roland Schoeman – swimming, 100 m & 50 m freestyle
Male	2,915.8	1,184.0	9[1]	Gold	Roland Schoeman, Lyndon Ferns, Darian Townsend, Ryk Neethling, 4x100 m freestyle relay
Female	2,509.5	1,674.8	7	Silver	Hestrie Cloete – athletics, high jump
Male	125.0	43.0	4	Bronze	Donovan Cech, Ramon Di Clemente – rowing, pairs
Male	45.0	20.0	2[2]	Silver	Mbulaeni Mulaudzi – athletics, 800 m

[1] Includes 4 images only of Ryk Neethling (11% of photo space for this team).
[2] Both photographs were headshots in the supplement before the start of the Olympics.

When examining how the media represented South African medal winners, findings reveal that they received a disproportionately large amount of the total Olympic coverage. As shown in Table 9 below, both the article and photographic space allocated to winning athletes was considerable, when bearing in mind how few athletes actually won medals. In addition, the sole South African female medal winner, Hestrie Cloete, received more than a quarter (25.4%) of all female Olympic photographic coverage, and 17.3% of the female Olympic article space (see Table 9).

Table 9. Media coverage of South African Olympic medal winners

Type	Articles		Photographs	
Gender	Male	Female	Male	Female
% of Olympic space	11.9%	3.7%	11.7%	6.4%
% of gender-specific Olympic space	25.4%	17.3%	24.8%	25.4%

The media coverage for Cloete, a White high jumper, began with pre-Games narrative that identified her as South Africa's most likely gold medallist. The pre-Games supplement front-page article was headlined "Pure Gold: The Athletes Carrying SA's medal hopes" and the first third of the article was dedicated to discussing her winning chances. Despite 41 other South African females competing at the Games, Cloete clearly dominated the coverage; receiving 46.3% of the space given to South African females (see Table 10). Cloete's photographic dominance becomes more pronounced if the Olympic supplement with 77 female photographs are excluded (three of which were of Cloete), resulting in there only being 43 other photographs of females; of which only seven depicted other members of the South African team, while one focused on a local Cape Town hockey referee who would be officiating at the Olympics.

Table 10. Photographic coverage of the female South African Olympic team[1]

Athlete (sport) & article focus	Article size	Female SA space	Photo size	Female SA space	Photo type
Hestrie Cloete (high jump) medal prospect/silver medal	2,464.5	46.3%	1,498.0	48.3%	SA (3) SR (1)
Marsha Marescia (hockey) Natal player of colour	733.5	13.8%	447.3	14.5%	SA (2)
Marelize De Klerk (hockey) local Cape referee	611.0	11.5%	308.0	9.9%	SR
Sharne Wehmeyer (hockey) goal scorer	451.5	8.5%	72.0	2.3%	SA
Kirsten Lewis (archery) only SA competitor	430.0	8.1%	400.0	12.9%	SA
Jenna Dreyer (diving) local reaches semi-finals	403.0	7.6%	360.0	11.6%	SA
Michelle Edwards (badminton) local at 1st Olympics	225.5	4.2%	17.5	0.6%	SR
TOTAL	5,319.0	100%	3,102.8	100%	

[1] This table does not include the headshots from the Olympic supplement.

These results, although South Africa only had one female medal winner, support the hypothesis that athletes expected to win medals are given more focus by the media.

5. Winning women are given more media coverage

In addition to examining the emphasis given to national medal winners by the sports media, the data reflected in Table 11 illustrate that female media coverage of the Olympics was extensively developed around elite international athletes expected to win, break records or those involved in controversy during the Games.

Unsurprisingly, elite international athletes with past successes and the potential for medal wins were highly profiled. Yet what was surprising was that the Olympic coverage focused more attention on international female athletes (55.6%) than on national sportswomen (44.4%). The international female photographs revolved predominantly around medal winners, prospective medal winners and controversy.

In addition, the emphasis given to international female athletes was also evident in photographs in the non-Olympic coverage. Of the nine non-Olympic photographs, five were large images of the central female athletes at the US Open tennis championship (82.3% of the photographic space), and four featured local Cape Town athletes competing in local events (17.7% of the photographic space). There was total disregard for any of the other national or international sporting activities in which South African female athletes were competing during this time, such as the Spar National Netball Championships or the National Under-21 Hockey Tournament.

Furthermore, these findings highlight that success appears to be an overriding factor of newsworthiness during international sporting events where the main focus, especially for international athletes, is the ability to win medals. However, at the same time, the results also supported the hypothesis that female athletes competing in sports more strongly linked to femininity or dressed in ways that highlight gender difference will receive relatively more coverage than those competing in sports more strongly linked to masculinity or dressed in ways that do not highlight gender difference. In particular, the photographs of international female athletes were aligned with 'female-appropriate' sports, such as athletics, swimming, gymnastics and beach volleyball, and most of the women were depicted wearing figure-hugging sports gear such as swimming costumes, gymnastics uniforms, bikinis or tight-fitting athletic attire.

Table 11. Coverage of international Olympic female athletes

Athlete/s	Sport; Country	Article focus	Article size	Photo size	Photo type
Merlene Ottey	Track; Slovenia	Medal prospect	1,824.0	217.0	SR (2)
Carly Patterson	Gymnastics; USA	Gold medal	1,026.0	520.0	SA
Kelly Homes	Track; Britain	Gold medal	596.8	95.0	SR
Petra Cada	Table Tennis; Canada	Medal prospect	513.0	486.0	SA
Perdita Felicien & Irina Shevchenko	Hurdles; Canada and Russia	Controversy & medal prospect	636.50	412.8	SA (5)
Kristy Coventry	Swimming; Zimbabwe	Gold medal	440.8	162.8	SA
Karen Cockburn	Gymnastics; Canada	Silver medal	360.0	328.0	SA
Fanny Blankers-Koen	Track; Netherlands	Women's history at Olympics	324.0	126.0	SA
Amanda Beard	Swimming; USA	Gold, 2 silver medals	241.5	220.5	SA
Holly McPeak	Beach volleyball; USA	Bronze medal	173.3	152.3	SA
Fan Ye	Gymnastics; China	Medal prospect	160.0	144.0	SA
Relay Team	Swimming; Australia	Gold medal	120.0	96.0	SA
Svetlana Khorkina	Gymnastics; Russia	Silver & bronze medals	90.0	75.0	SA
Natalie Coughlin	Swimming; USA	2 gold, 2 silver & 1 bronze medal	75.0	65.0	SA
Yelena Slesarenko	High jump; Russia	Gold medal	42.5	42.5	SR(1) M (1)
Katerina Thanou	Track; Greece	Drug scandal	34.0	34.0	SA
TOTAL			6,657.35	3,176.75	

CONCLUSION

Sport in South Africa plays an important part in many people's lives. Daily, the newspapers highlight those sports and athletes that are considered to be newsworthy. The findings of this study reveal that when major international sports events such as the Olympics occur, those female athletes with the potential to win medals are given greater media focus, even if they are international athletes. Yet, when comparing Olympic coverage of all athletes, males received more than twice as much space about their endeavours (46.8%) than female athletes (21.2%). Similar results were established from the number of photographs of Olympic athletes, where 47.1% depicted sportsmen and 25.4% were of sportswomen.

However, when sportswomen participate in non-major sporting events they are marginalised and often totally ignored. The findings of this study for the non-Olympic analysis revealed that the space allocated to sportsmen equated to 76.3%, whereas for sportswomen it was only 4%. Even when combining the total coverage of all male and female athletes regardless of the events they participated in, sportswomen still received significantly less focus (10.19%) than their male counterparts (65.74%), regardless of performance. The increase in media coverage of sportswomen during major events appears to relate to an attempt to cover more female medal winners rather than to gender equality. These results support findings from Serra's (2005) six-month South African newspaper study that revealed that sportswomen were "significantly under-represented" compared to sportsmen (p. 54). Although similar trends emerged out of these two 2004 Olympic studies, Serra's findings highlighted greater coverage for both sportswomen (13.5%) and sportsmen (86.5%).

Burnett (2001b) argues that in South Africa, "mainstream sport could be read as 'male-stream' sport, as patriarchal values are perpetuated by decision-making that entitles men to exclude women's participation and marginalise women's ('Cinderella') sports, such as netball or synchronized swimming" (p. 71). The results of this analysis highlight that although the new South African constitution and Government of National Unity are emphatic about wanting to level the playing field for women, this is clearly not happening in the area of media coverage, particularly outside of major events such as the Olympics. South African sportsmen are still receiving the majority of media focus, both outside of *and* during major events. As suggested by Hargreaves (1997), "sport has different significance for different women, but in general South African women link sport with notions of liberation and enrichment" (p. 205). Yet sports coverage of a major international event focused more on international female athletes because their medal wins appeared to make them more newsworthy than national sportswomen who did not succeed. In addition, photographs of the international athletes all revealed a more stereotypical portrayal of lithe, feminine and sparsely-clad sportswomen who competed in sports commonly described as 'female-appropriate'. There was no coverage or photographs of women succeeding in 'female-inappropriate' sports such as weightlifting or judo. Although only one South African female athlete won a medal she was given extensive focus, more than half of that given to other national female team members and a quarter of all

Olympic female coverage. However, media emphasis remained tightly fixed on male athletes, especially in respect of non-Olympic events, where the number of photographs of sportsmen amounted to 29 times the number recorded for sportswomen. Thus, South African women still remain disadvantaged in sports and the media help to trivialise and marginalise their sporting achievements by retaining a focus on sportsmen. Denise Jones (2003) argues:

> What is clear is that a universal truth about South African women and sport does not exist ... Common goals need to be sought while simultaneously valuing diversity and constantly being sensitive to the way race, gender and class combine with structural constraints, social stereotypes and cultural norms to restrict the ability of women and girls to develop their potential as sporting females. (p. 141)

Her apt subtitle of her overview of female sport in South Africa, "Shaped by history and shaping sporting history", appears true of the sports media analysed in this study: Despite a small increase during the Olympics, South African media coverage appears to be repeating the disadvantages of the past rather than embracing the advantages that appeared to be offered with the end of apartheid and the Bill of Equal Rights.

NOTES

[1] In this discussion, the racial distinctions – White, African, Coloured, Indian – are those commonly used in South Africa and reflect the history of racial classifications during apartheid.

REFERENCES

Bruce, T., & Chapman, S. (2006, July). *Media representation of New Zealand and South African sportswomen during the 2004 Olympic Games.* Paper presented at the World Congress of Sociology, Durban, South Africa.

Burnett, C. (2001a). Sport as an engendered space in South African society: Feminist praxis and reality. *African Journal for Physical, Health Education, Recreation and Dance, 7*(2), 304–315.

Burnett, C. (2001b). Whose game is it anyway? Power, play and sport. *Agenda, 49,* 71–78.

Burnett, C. (2002). Women, poverty and sport: A South African scenario. *Women in Sport & Physical Activity Journal, 11*(1), 23–48.

Cock, J., & Bernstein, A. (2001). Gender differences: Struggles around "needs" and "rights" in South Africa. *NWSA Journal, 13*(3), 138–153.

Hargreaves, J. (1997). Women's sport, development, and cultural diversity: The South African experience. *Women's Studies International Forum, 20*(2), 191–209.

Hargreaves, J. (2000). *Heroines of sport: The politics of difference and identity.* London: Routledge.

Jones, D. E. M. (2003). Women and sport in South Africa: Shaped by history and shaping sporting history. In I. Hartmann-Tews & G. Pfister (Eds.), *Sport and Women: Social issues in international perspective* (pp. 130–144). London: Routledge.

MISA, & Gender Links. (2003). *The gender and media baseline study* [Electronic Version], 1–72. Retrieved August 15, 2005, from http://www.misa.org/Gender/baseline-study.pdf

Morrell, R. (2002). Men, movements, and gender transformation in South Africa. *Journal of Men's Studies, 10*(3), 309.

Pelak, C. F. (2005). Negotiating gender/race/class constraints in the New South Africa: A case study of women's soccer. *International Review for the Sociology of Sport, 40*(1), 53–70.

Serra, P. (2005). *The construction and deconstruction of gender through sport reporting in selected South African newspapers.* Unpublished master's thesis, University of Johannesburg, Johannesburg, South Africa.

Susan Scott-Chapman
University of Waikato
New Zealand

OCEANIA

TONI BRUCE AND SUSAN SCOTT-CHAPMAN

20. NEW ZEALAND

Intersections of Nationalism and Gender in Olympics Newspaper Coverage

INTRODUCTION

New Zealand prides itself on being a world leader in terms of gender equality. Evidence to support this claim includes its record as the first self-governing country to give all women the vote in 1893, the fact that women have recently held many of the top political positions, including Prime Minister, and the status of having the lowest gender gap (just over 5%) in median earnings for full-time workers in 22 OECD countries (Dixon, 2000; OECD, 2006). This real shift in power relations has engendered some backlash against women's political success and criticism of the apparent feminization of the nation; a backlash that Fountaine (2005) argues may "harm the terrain of gender relations in New Zealand" (p. 3). However, in world terms, New Zealand women enjoy significant freedom to pursue successful careers and to have their voices and experiences heard and taken into account.

WOMEN IN SPORT

As a result of European colonisation, competitive sport in New Zealand developed as a particularly male-dominated arena, in large part because the majority of migrants were men (Thompson, 2003). Thus, for the past 200 years, women have "struggled against ideological beliefs defining competitive sport as extremely highly valued male terrain" while, at the same time, enjoying access to a wide variety of non-competitive physical recreation activities (Thompson, 2003, p. 253). As in other Western nations, women were directed into sports considered suitable for females – netball and field hockey in New Zealand's case – and were "fiercely resisted" when they expressed interest in sports strongly associated with men such as rugby union and cricket (Thompson, 2003, p. 253). Indeed, it was only in the 1990s that New Zealand women were 'allowed' to play rugby union, the sport most strongly linked to national (and masculine) identity. However, across a variety of sports, females have participated successfully. For example, Ferkins (1992b) reports that between 1980 and 1992, New Zealand produced more female (57) than male (56) world-ranked, world record holder, Olympic medal or Commonwealth Games gold medal athletes. Top female athletes have become visible public figures and regularly feature on national surveys of the most trusted

T. Bruce, J. Hovden and P. Markula (eds.),
Sportswomen at the Olympics: A Global Content Analysis of Newspaper Coverage, 275–287.

New Zealanders (e.g., "Who do", 2007). A range of participation surveys between 1981 and 2001 suggest that many females are active in sport, although men tend to take part in more activities and maintain their involvement in competitive sports for much longer (Middleton & Tait, 1981; SPARC Facts, 2007). Cameron (1992) revealed that 69% of sport memberships were held by men and 31% by females although the gender breakdown was highly variable, ranging from 99% female membership in the premier women's sport of netball to 1% in the male-dominated sport of rugby union.

Research on sport leadership demonstrates widespread male dominance and recent research has done little to challenge Cameron's (1992) conclusion that "sport in New Zealand is controlled by men" (p. 17). Across a number of studies, the proportion of females involved as national volunteer administrators or board members has remained relatively static at around 20% (Cameron, 1992, 2000; Shaw & Cameron, 2008). Thus, as Cameron (2000) points out, despite females making up one-third of sports participants, they are less visible in the power structures of sport where, overall, they make up only one-fifth of sport managers. Women tend to have higher levels of representation as administrators in female-dominated sports such as netball (Cameron, 1992), and the percentage of women on the New Zealand Olympic Committee has risen from 17% to 37% in the past 15 years (Shaw & Cameron, 2008). Thus, although women are active and successful as sports participants, it appears that the management of sport remains a predominantly male domain, with men making most of the decisions that impact female participation.

MEDIA COVERAGE OF WOMEN'S SPORT

When it comes to media coverage, the picture is also far from rosy. Despite the cultural rhetoric of equality, and significant success on the world stage, female athletes are markedly under-represented in newspaper and television coverage. The first published studies appeared in the early 1980s and analyses of sports media coverage have continued with regularity. Thus, there is a significant body of quantitative research tracking the ongoing failure of the New Zealand sports media to recognise and highlight female athletic achievement (e.g., Alexander, 2004; Aston, 1987; Atkinson, 1994; Carpinter & Mackay, 1994; Chapman, 2002a, 2002b; Cooper, 1981; Ferkins, 1992a, 1992b; Fountaine & McGregor, 1999; McGregor, 1993; McGregor & Fountaine, 1997; McGregor & Melville, 1993, 1995; O'Leary & Roberts, 1985; Scott-Chapman, 2007; Scratchley, 1988; Shanks, 2005; Wensing, 2003; Whitaker, 1993). Covering a range of time periods and mass media formats, the trends identified in this research are robust and consistent.

One key trend is the existence of differences between 'everyday' coverage and 'major event' coverage; a finding that echoes international research which suggests that coverage of female athletes increases markedly during major events such as the Olympics or Commonwealth Games which are strongly tied to nationalism (see Wensing & Bruce, 2003). What is clear is that analyses of everyday coverage – which constitutes the bulk of sports media reporting – reveal the overwhelming dominance of male sport in the sports pages and on New Zealand television screens. Over a 25-year period, males have garnered the lion's share of media coverage (on average 83%) while women's sport has struggled to reach 10% (see Table 1). In no study of everyday coverage has female coverage surpassed 15% and in only one has male coverage dropped below 70%. Thus, even with female coverage at its best and male at its worst, men still receive more than 4.5 times the coverage of females (Bruce, 2008).

New Zealand researchers have taken the sports media to task for the everyday results, engaging in public debate aimed at increasing awareness of such discrepancies and promoting change (see Fountaine & McGregor, 1999; McGregor, 2000). However, as Fountaine and McGregor (1999, p. 113) have found, "such studies are persistently rejected as irrelevant ... often ignored or trivialised by news management and journalists" who are, overwhelmingly, male (see Ferkins, 1992b; Short, 2005, 2006). Despite criticisms from sports media workers, Fountaine and McGregor (1999) argue that the longitudinal research has confirmed "the structural rigidity of the gender inequality of press coverage" (p. 124).

Females have, however, gained some prominence on television as news readers and sports commentators – all three national nightly news shows have featured female sports news readers in the 2000s and several former athletes appear on general sport or rugby television shows – although this does not appear to have influenced the amount of female sports news which has consistently dropped over time from 13% in 1984 to 3% in 2005 (O'Leary & Roberts, 1984; Shanks, 2005).

Table 1. Averages and ranges for everyday and major event coverage in New Zealand

Type of coverage (period of analysis)	Male average		Female average		Mixed/ Neutral average	
	%	Range	%	Range	%	Range
Everyday (1980–2007)	83	69 – 95	9	3 – 14	8	2 – 18
Olympics only (1992)	55	52 – 58	24	17 – 30	22	12 – 31
Commonwealth Games only (2002, 2006)	34	28 – 36	41	30 – 66	23	0 – 38

However, it should be noted that major events, such as the Olympics and Commonwealth Games, shine a bright light on female athletic accomplishment, particularly when New Zealand women win medals. Female coverage reached almost one-quarter of total coverage during one analysis of the summer Olympics – an almost 250% increase over the everyday average (see Table 1). Thus, it would appear that the Olympics offer the potential for significantly increasing the public visibility of female athletes. The Commonwealth Games, at which New Zealand athletes win many more medals than at the Olympics, appear to offer even stronger potential for gender equity in media coverage. In stark contrast to existing research, studies of the 2002 and 2006 Commonwealth Games consistently found that female coverage exceeded male coverage (e.g., Bruce, Falcous & Thorpe, 2007; Chapman, 2002b; Wensing, 2003). These remarkable increases in coverage for female athletes are likely to be tied to issues of national identity and success (see Bernstein, 2002; Bruce, 2009; Wensing & Bruce, 2003) with female athletes having demonstrated similar if not superior success in winning medals. Indeed, an in-depth analysis of the 2002 Commonwealth Games identified nationalism as a key focus of media coverage, with 73.2% of all images featuring New Zealand athletes, officials, supporters or facilities (Wensing, 2003). A focus on athletes who succeeded for the nation was also evident, with 65% of New Zealand images highlighting medal winners (Wensing, 2003).

Across a number of studies, the proportion of coverage within the major event appears to reflect the success of the national team, by gender. For example, during the 1992 Olympics males won 60% of all medals and received 55% of all Olympics coverage (Whitaker, 1993); in the 2002 Commonwealth Games women won 56% of medals and received 54% of all New Zealand images, as well as 35% of overall coverage which was more than the men at 28% (Wensing, 2003); and women won 52% of all medals and gained more coverage than males (33% versus 29%) during the 2006 Commonwealth Games (Scott-Chapman, 2007). We should also not underestimate the media success of netball. Although newspaper coverage for netball remains well below that of rugby union and rugby league, it is gradually increasing (Alexander, 2004; Fountaine & McGregor, 1999; McGregor, 1994; McGregor & Melville, 1995; O'Leary & Roberts, 1985). Live coverage of netball on free-to-air television has recently gained large audiences and regularly ranked in the top 20 most-watched national broadcasts. For example, in the last few years, ratings for specific matches have outranked international rugby union and Olympics coverage.

However, while female invisibility is moderated during certain events, it is clear that these increases are unusual rather than leading to broader changes. Increased levels of coverage for women during major events are matched by ongoing low levels of coverage outside the event; a pattern that has remained constant over time.

METHODS

The New Zealand analysis included the largest daily newspaper, the *New Zealand Herald*, which has a circulation of 211,490 out of a population of 4 million people. All space was measured in cm^2 and all articles and photographs were counted from one week prior to one week after the opening and closing ceremonies – incorporating all editions between 7 August and 4 September 2004. All stories and results in the sports section, on the front page and all dedicated Games pages or special supplements were included in the analysis. For example, the *Herald* regularly dedicated page 2 to Games coverage, with gold medal wins highlighted on the front page of the newspaper. Overall, the *Herald* dedicated 53% of its sports coverage to the Olympic Games, thus highlighting it as an important sports event.

New Zealand won five medals at the Games. Of the three gold medals, female athletes won two, in cycling and double sculls rowing. Males won gold and silver in triathlon and silver in kayaking.

In the following discussion, article space and numbers include the headline, text and any images associated with an article. Photograph space is, thus, a subset of article space. In tables and figures, all percentages have been rounded to one decimal point. Coverage was divided into four categories: male coverage; female coverage; mixed coverage in which both male and female athletes were featured; and neutral coverage which did not refer specifically to gender, such as stories describing stadia, preparations for the Games and explanations of doping regulations.

We used the *Global Women in Sports Media Project* guiding hypotheses to organise our data analysis and, where appropriate, we address whether our results support or challenge the expected findings.

MAJOR EVENTS MEAN HIGHER LEVELS OF COVERAGE FOR FEMALE ATHLETES

The results for all coverage during the analysis period indicate that female athletes were more visible than usual – claiming 16.1% of total space (see Table 2). Male coverage was much lower than usual, dropping to 64.4% of space. This pattern was similar for number of articles (19% for females; 59.4% for males) and photographs (21.4% for females; 64.5% for males), thus indicating that the general trend was robust whether space or numbers were counted. The slight difference in percentages between space and number of articles indicates that stories about female athletes were generally shorter than articles about men, meaning that male sport was covered in more depth.

Table 2. Total space and number of stories in the Herald

Measurement	Male	Female	Mixed	Neutral	Total
Space in cm^2	190,352.47	47,728.65	29,224.40	28,517.80	295,823.32
Percentage (%)	64.4	16.1	9.9	9.6	100
Number of stories	944	302	151	192	1589
Percentage (%)	59.4	19.0	9.5	12.1	100

A closer analysis shows that media attention to female athletes was not divided evenly between Olympics and non-Olympics coverage. Almost all coverage of female athletes was related to Olympic coverage, in which women gained 26.5% of coverage compared with 45% for men (see Table 3); a result that supports previous research. If mixed and female coverage are combined, females were visible in almost 40% of coverage. Although female coverage clearly increased from previous studies of 'everyday' coverage, the results do not support the hypothesis that female athletes will receive relatively equal newspaper coverage to male athletes in Olympics coverage.

Table 3. Olympics-only space and number of stories in the Herald

Measurement	Male	Female	Mixed	Neutral	Total
Space in cm^2	70,993.17	41,806.00	20,725.40	24,258.90	157,783.47
Percentage (%)	45.0	26.5	13.1	15.4	100
Number of stories	405	247	93	150	895
Percentage	45.3	27.6	10.4	16.8	101

FEMALES REMAIN ALMOST INVISIBLE OUTSIDE MAJOR EVENT COVERAGE

Table 4 demonstrates that female athletes were almost invisible in the 47% of coverage that was not related to the Olympic Games. Females received only 4.3% of total space and only 7.9% of the total number of stories; a result that matches New Zealand's previous worst results of 4.4% of space in 1996 (McGregor & Fountaine, 1997). This finding supports the hypothesis that female athletes will receive unequal and lesser coverage compared to male athletes in non-Olympics coverage.

Table 4. Non-Olympic space and number of stories in the Herald

Measurement	Male	Female	Mixed	Neutral	Total
Space in cm^2	119,359.30	5,922.65	8,499.00	4,258.90	138,039.85
Percentage (%)	86.5	4.3	6.2	3.1	101
Number of stories	539	55	58	42	694
Percentage (%)	77.7	7.9	8.4	6.1	101

The overall differences in levels of coverage are particularly visible in Figure 1. Although males dominate Olympic, Non-Olympic and Total space, the level of dominance is much reduced in the Olympics coverage which demonstrates higher levels of female, mixed and neutral coverage.

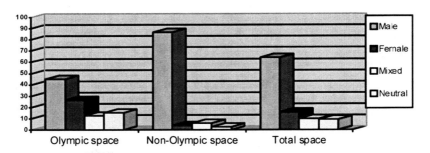

Figure 1. Media coverage of the 2004 Olympic Games by gender in the New Zealand Herald.

MALES AND FEMALES ARE PHOTOGRAPHED SIMILARLY

The hypothesis that males and females would receive equivalent photographic coverage by types of photographs was supported (see Table 5), with both genders showing the same trends in photographic type.

Table 5. Types of Olympic photographs by gender

Type of Image	Male	Female	Mixed	Neutral	Total
Sport action (n)	93	60	25	2	180
%	51.7	52.6	39.7	1.9	38.9
Sport-related (n)	58	30	16	7	111
%	32.2	26.3	25.4	6.6	24.0
Medal (n)	9	11	3	2	25
%	5.0	9.7	4.8	1.9	5.4
Non sport (n)	20	13	19	95	147
%	11.1	11.4	30.1	89.6	31.7
Total	180	114	63	106	463
% by gender	38.9	24.6	13.6	22.9	100

Overall, Olympic photographs emphasized the sporting context, with 82% of male and female images showing athletes in action (52%) or in a sport-related setting (30%) such as warming up for an event. Unlike the findings of previous international research, few photographs of women showed them in non-sport settings.

GENDER DIFFERENCES IN RELATION TO OLYMPIC PARTICIPATION

The New Zealand media did not provide coverage that was relative to the proportions of male and female athletes on the Olympic team (see Table 6). Both males and females received less coverage than their participation rates would suggest; although these results are moderated by the high levels of mixed coverage (see Table 3). However, despite only a 10% differential in participation numbers, New Zealand male athletes received almost 20% more media coverage than New Zealand female athletes. Thus, our results disprove the hypothesis that athletes will receive coverage relative to their proportion on the Olympic team; although the male coverage is clearly much closer (9% less) to participation proportions than female coverage (18.5% less).

Table 6. Coverage in relation to proportion on the Olympic team

Gender	Olympic participants (n)	% of Olympic participants	% of Olympic coverage
Male	83	55	45.0
Female	57	45	26.5

SUCCESS FOR THE NATION INCREASES COVERAGE

The results clearly demonstrated that winning for the nation results in higher levels of coverage. The women and men who won medals for New Zealand received the most coverage (see Table 7). The five New Zealand medal winners clearly dominated the coverage of New Zealand athletes, receiving more than one-fifth (21.4%) of all Olympics coverage. The percentage rises to almost one quarter (24.2%) when the other most featured New Zealand athletes are added to the total. While neither Valerie Adams (now Vili) nor Barbara Kendall won medals, they were expected to do well: Adams was the 2002 world junior shot put champion and Commonwealth Games silver medallist and was among the first women ever to compete at Olympia, site of the ancient Olympics; and Kendall had won windsurfing medals in three previous Olympics (gold in 1992, silver in 1996 and bronze in 2000). All five female competitors were well-known athletes who, in various ways, were popularly understood to represent key New Zealand characteristics such as modesty, hard work and a down-to-earth attitude.

Table 7. Most featured New Zealand athletes in the Herald

Athlete (sport) & achievement	Gender	Space cm^2	% of Male Olympics coverage	% of Female Olympics coverage
Sarah Ulmer (cycling) gold/world record	Female	9,295.25		22.2%
Ben Fouhy (kayak) silver	Male	7,013.50	10.0%	
Hamish Carter & Bevan Docherty[1] (triathlon) gold & silver	Male	5,765.50	8.1%	
Caroline & Georgina Evers-Swindell (rowing) gold	Female	2,065.25		4.9%
Valerie Adams (shotput) 9th	Female	1,820.90		4.4%
Barbara Kendall (windsurfing) 5th	Female	1,308.50		3.1%
Total cm^2		27,268.90	70,993.17	41,806.00

[1] Almost all triathlon stories included both Carter and Doherty so they have been combined in this Table.

The results disprove the hypothesis that female athletes competing in sports more strongly linked to femininity or dressed in ways that highlight gender difference will receive more coverage. Cycling, rowing, shotput and windsurfing are not stereotypically feminine sports; they all require muscular strength and physical stamina for success and do not highlight sexual difference in clothing.

In appearance, shotputter Valerie Adams challenged traditional New Zealand ideals of femininity via her ethnic background (Tongan heritage), imposing size (height, 1.96m/6'5"; weight, 120kg/264lbs) and muscularity. However, while clearly muscular and physically fit, the remaining four were blondes of European descent whose looks and body types more closely matched Western notions of feminine beauty. Notably all four also recently ranked in the top 10 of most trusted New Zealanders in a national poll ("Who do", 2007).

In the New Zealand context, the hypothesis that female athletes who win in sports historically linked to national identity will receive more coverage than female winners in other sports is difficult to assess. Given the relatively few medals that New Zealand wins at Olympics Games, nationalism appears to outweigh other considerations and the coverage appeared to reflect a combination of success and expected success – with all five women having been highlighted before the Games as potential winners and, between them, taking up more than one-third (34.7%) of female Olympics coverage. However, it is notable that the three international male athletes who received high levels of coverage were multiple medal winners in two of the 'glamour events' of the Olympics – swimming and athletics. Swimmer Michael Phelps (USA), track athlete Hiram El Guerrouj (Morocco) and swimmer Ian Thorpe (Australia) received the fourth, fifth and sixth most Olympics coverage overall, respectively. Phelps became one of only two athletes to win eight medals during a single Games, while Thorpe won four medals. El Guerrouj, after two failed Olympic attempts, finally won the 1500m gold to match his world record and became the first man since 1924 to win the 1500m and 5000m double. Each of these male international athletes received more coverage than any New Zealand female except Sarah Ulmer.

NATIONAL SUCCESS IS MORE IMPORTANT FOR FEMALE ATHLETES

One key finding is that female coverage is strongly linked to medal success. New Zealand female medal winners clearly received a higher proportion of female Olympics coverage (27.2%) than male winners did of male Olympic coverage (18.0%). It is also notable that no international females gained high levels of coverage. Further, the almost complete absence of female coverage outside the Olympics meant that female success garnered a much higher proportion (23.8%) of the total female coverage than male Olympic success did of total male coverage (only 6.7%). In addition, in percentage terms, photographs of female athletes showed them with their medals almost twice as often as males (9.7% versus 5%).

Analysis of coverage only of New Zealand medal winners shows that the amount of space dedicated to females (11,360.5 cm^2) was similar to that for males (12,779 cm^2); a finding that somewhat challenges the hypothesis that male and female athletes will receive coverage relative to the proportion of Olympic medals they receive (see Table 8). In fact, female winners received 47.1% of the New Zealand medal coverage; more than their proportion of overall medals (40%) while the males received less coverage (52.9%) than their proportion of medals won (60%).

Table 8. Coverage in relation to medals won

Gender	Medals (n)	% of Medals	% of Medal coverage
Male	3: 1 gold, 2 silver	60	52.9
Female	2: 2 gold	40	47.1

These results all point to the importance of success if females are to gain coverage. Thus, on three different measures – proportion of Olympic space, photographic space and coverage in relation to medals won – the women who won New Zealand's gold medals were much more visible than other female athletes.

HIGHLIGHTING ONE FEMALE: SARAH ULMER

The general trend of focusing on successful females is, however, complicated by the *Herald's* overwhelming focus on New Zealand cyclist Sarah Ulmer who was by far the most visible athlete of the Games – male or female. She received almost 6% of all Olympic coverage and, despite being only one of five medallists, her 23 articles and 20 photographs gave her close to half (44%) the New Zealand medallists' coverage. The *Herald* clearly focused most of its female coverage on Ulmer who won back her world record after another competitor broke it twice in qualifying rounds, and then broke the world record again while winning the gold in the 3000m individual pursuit. In terms of female Olympic coverage, the *Herald* dedicated 22% of space and 26% of photographic space to Ulmer (a percentage that dipped by only 2% to 20% of all female coverage and 24% of all photo space when total coverage was analysed). Ulmer received one-third more coverage than the other featured female athletes combined (see Table 7).

In some ways, the level of coverage is not unexpected. Ulmer was the world champion and expected to dominate her main event. By the 2004 Olympics, she was a well-known and popular athlete who had won four medals at three Commonwealth Games (1994, 1998, 2002) and was part of a high-profile advertising campaign for McDonalds. She was the New Zealand team captain and carried the national flag at the 2002 Commonwealth Games opening ceremony. However, the difference in coverage dedicated to Ulmer and to the Evers-Swindell twins is notable, given that they were both world champions and their events were conducted over several days. Although Caroline and Georgina Evers-Swindell received the second highest number of photographs (12) behind Ulmer and were the second most covered female athletes at the Games, they received only 5% of Olympic female space, and only 1.3% of all Olympic space, ranking them 7th overall, behind New Zealand's male gold and silver medallists and three male international multiple gold medallists. In total, they received 4.5 times less coverage than Ulmer, indicating that performance alone does not account for why particular athletes receive more coverage.

CONCLUSIONS

Overall, our results suggest that the Olympics provide an important chance for fans of women's sport to enjoy and celebrate female success and ability. Clearly, nationalism moderates the usual under-representation of female athletes, although they remain almost invisible outside of the major event coverage. In New Zealand, females who either win or are expected to win medals receive the most coverage. We suggest that our findings support Wensing and Bruce's (2003) contention that "coverage during international sports events...may be less likely to be marked by gendered...discourses or narratives than reporting on everyday sports, at least for sportswomen whose success is closely linked to a nation's sense of self (p. 393).

However, the focus on a limited number of females – where only five women received almost 35% of all female coverage and one athlete alone received 22% – operates to the detriment of potential coverage of a wide range of female athletes. Further, and perhaps more importantly, it reinforces the underlying ideology that sport is primarily a male domain. The much wider range of male coverage (including the 86.5% of non-Olympic space and the fact that three international men ranked ahead of all but one New Zealand female in the overall Olympic coverage) suggests that the sporting exploits of males are assumed to be of interest to a wide audience and worthy of extended attention even if they are not competing for the nation, whereas women's sporting performances are primarily of interest only when they contribute to nationalism. Thus, we conclude the 'equality' in Olympics coverage is more strongly linked to ideologies of nationalism than to gender; a finding that provides some explanation for the patterns of coverage identified in multiple studies of the New Zealand sports media in which women who win for the nation are acknowledged and celebrated but their everyday sporting exploits remain under-reported and ignored.

ACKNOWLEDGMENTS

The authors would like to thank the School of Education at the University of Waikato which provided financial assistance for this research and for sabbatical leave for Toni Bruce.

REFERENCES

Alexander, M. (2004). *The representation of professional and gender-based sports in the New Zealand print media.* Paper prepared for SPLS 304, University of Waikato, Hamilton, New Zealand.

Aston, S. (1987). *Sportswomen in the media eye – A fair share?* Paper prepared for SPLS 302, School of Physical Education, University of Otago.

Atkinson, J. (1994). Structures of television news. In P. Ballard (Ed.), *Power and responsibility* (pp. 43–74). Wellington: Broadcasting Standards Authority.

Bernstein, A. (2002). Is it time for a victory lap? *International Review for the Sociology of Sport, 37*(3–4), 415–428.

Bruce, T. (2009). Winning space in sport: The Olympics in the New Zealand sports media. In P. Markula (Ed.), *Olymic women and the media: International perspectives* (pp. 150-167). Hampshire: Palgrave Macmillan.

Bruce, T. (2008). Women, sport and the media: A complex terrain. In C. Obel, T. Bruce, & S. Thompson (Eds.), *Outstanding: Research about women and sport in New Zealand* (pp. 51–71). Hamilton: Wilf Malcolm Institute for Educational Research.

Bruce, T., Falcous, M., & Thorpe, H. (2007). The mass media and sport. In C. Collins & S. Jackson (Eds.), *Sport in Aotearoa/New Zealand society* (2nd ed., pp. 147–169). Auckland: Thomson.

Cameron, J. (2000). The issue of gender in sport: 'No bloody room for sheilas'. In C. Collins (Ed.), *Sport in New Zealand society* (pp. 171–185). Palmerston North: Dunmore.

Cameron, J. (1992). *Gender in New Zealand sport: A survey of sport and its national administration.* Christchurch: University of Canterbury Sociology Department.

Cameron, J., & Kerr, R. (2007). The issue of gender in sport: 'No bloody room for sheilas'. In C. Collins & S. Jackson (Eds.), *Sport in Aotearoa/NewZealand society* (2nd ed., pp. 335–354). Albany, Auckland: Thomson.

Carpinter, A., & Mackay, J. (1994, January). *The representation of young people in New Zealand newspapers.* Wellington: Ministry of Youth Affairs/Te Tari Taiohi.

Chapman, S. (2002a). *A quantitative newspaper report on the Waikato Times in 2002.* Paper prepared for SPLS 305, Leisure, Sport and the Media. Hamilton: University of Waikato.

Chapman, S. (2002b). *Media images of sportswomen in the Waikato Times newspaper and an analysis of the results.* Paper prepared for SPLS Investigations. University of Waikato, Hamilton, New Zealand.

Cooper, R. (1981). Investigation of discrimination in sporting and other leisure activities. In *Papers and reports from the 1981 conference on women and recreation* (pp. 43–69). Wellington, NZ: New Zealand Council for Recreation and Sport.

Dixon, S. (2000). Pay inequality between men and women in New Zealand. *Occasional Paper 2000/1.* Wellington: New Zealand Department of Labour, Labour Market Policy Group. Retrieved March 29, 2007, from http://www.dol.govt.nz/PDFs/op2000-1main.pdf

Ferkins, L. (1992a). New Zealand women in sport: An untapped media resource. *New Zealand Journal of Health, Physical Education and Recreation, 25*(4), 15–18.

Ferkins, L. R. (1992b). *New Zealand women in sport: An untapped media resource.* Unpublished thesis, Victoria University of Wellington, Wellington.

Fountaine, S. (2005). Who's the boss? The girl power frame in New Zealand newspapers. *Occasional paper #11.* Belfast: Queens University Centre for Advancement of Women in Politics.

Fountaine, S., & McGregor, J. (1999). The loneliness of the long distance gender researcher: Are journalists right about the coverage of women's sport? *Australian Journalism Review, 21*(3), 113–126.

McGregor, J. (2000). The mass media and sport. In C. Collins (Ed.), *Sport in New Zealand society* (pp. 187–200). Palmerston North: Dunmore Press.

McGregor, J. (1994). Media sport. In L. Trenberth & C. Collins (Eds.), *Sport management in New Zealand: An introduction* (pp. 243–255). Palmerston North: Dunmore Press.

McGregor, J., & Fountaine, S. (1997). Gender equity in retreat: The declining representation of women's sport in the New Zealand print media. *Metro, 112,* 38–44.

McGregor, J., & Melville, P. (1995). Bitter chocolate: Gender equity and prime time magazine sport on New Zealand television. *Metro, 102,* 30–36.

McGregor, J., & Melville, P. (1992). The invisible face of women's sport in the New Zealand press. *Australian Journal of Leisure and Recreation, 2*(4), 18–27.

McGregor, J., & Melville, P. (1993). The invisible face of women's sport in the New Zealand press. *Metro, 96,* 35–39.

Middleton, L., & Tait, D. (1981). *Are women given a choice? An assessment based on information from the New Zealand Recreation Survey.* Monograph Series No 1. Wellington: Department of Internal Affairs Research Unit.

OECD. (2006). *Women and men in OECD countries.* Paris, France: Organisation for Economic Co-operation and Development Publications. Retrieved March 29, 2007, from http://www.oecd.org/dataoecd/45/37/37964069.pdf

O'Leary, E., & Roberts, N. S. (1985, June 15). Bad track record. *New Zealand Listener,* 14–16.

Scott-Chapman, S. (2007). *Results of 2006 Commonwealth Games and 2007 everyday newspaper coverage.* Unpublished data from PhD in progress, The University of Waikato, Hamilton, New Zealand.

Scratchley, M. (1988). *The media space accorded to women in sport in New Zealand.* Unpublished paper, The University of Waikato, Hamilton, New Zealand.

Shanks, M. (2005). *Content analysis: Gender representation.* Paper prepared for SPLS 304, University of Waikato, Hamilton, New Zealand.

Shaw, S., & Cameron, J. (2008). "The best person for the job": Gender suppression and homologous reproduction in senior sport management. In C. Obel, T. Bruce, & S. Thompson (Eds.), *Outstanding: Research about women and sport in New Zealand* (pp. 211–226). Hamilton: Wilf Malcolm Institute for Educational Research.

Short, C. (2006, December). *The visibility of female journalists at major Australian and New Zealand newspapers: The good news and the bad news.* Paper presented at the joint Journalism Education Association (JEA) and Journalism Educators Association of New Zealand (JEANZ) conference, Auckland: New Zealand.

SPARC Facts (1997–2001). (2007). Wellington: SPARC. Retrieved March 21, 2007, from http://www.sparc.org.nz/filedownload?id=97addb2b-23c1-4c91-928c-304a63decda0

Thompson, S. M. (2003). Women and sport in New Zealand. In I. Hartmann-Tews & G. Pfister (Eds.), *Sport and women: Social issues in international perspective* (pp. 252–265). London: Routledge.

Webber, A. (1992). Women in the media: Wrestling with old values. In M. Comrie & J. McGregor (Eds.), *Whose news?* (pp. 181–188). Palmerston North: Dunmore Press.

Wensing, E. H. (2003). *Print media constructions of New Zealand national identity at the 2002 Commonwealth Games.* Unpublished master's thesis, School of Education, University of Waikato, Hamilton, New Zealand.

Wensing, E. H., & Bruce, T. (2003). Bending the rules: Media representations of gender during an international sporting event. *International Review for the Sociology of Sport, 38*(4), 387–396.

Whitaker, S. (1993). The construction of the gendered body within the discourse of sports reports. In J. Cameron (Ed.), *Just for fun...? Readings in the sociology of sport and leisure* (Vol. 1, pp. 1–18). Christchurch: Department of Sociology, University of Canterbury.

Who do you trust now, New Zealand. (2007, June). *The New Zealand Readers Digest, 170*(1022), 35–44.

Toni Bruce and Susan Scott-Chapman
University of Waikato
Hamilton, New Zealand

JORID HOVDEN, TONI BRUCE AND PIRKKO MARKULA

21. THE BIG PICTURE: DATA COMPARISONS AND IMPLICATIONS

INTRODUCTION

In this concluding chapter we synthesise and compare some of the key trends reported in the previous chapters to make cross cultural comparisons. We then reflect on both the potential and limitations of content analysis as an instrument to support strategies for gender equality. The chapter ends with a short summary and conclusions about further research directions.

TRENDS IN THE GENDERING OF OLYMPIC NEWSPAPER COVERAGE

Looking at the data as a whole, it is remarkable to register the similarity of some of the main trends in all participating nations; independent of geographic, cultural and economic differences. One key trend is that female athletes in non-Olympic newspaper coverage are invisible and marginalised globally (see Table 1). However, we also trace another global trend; that successful female Olympic athletes contribute to closing the gender gap in media coverage. In several of the participating countries, women received Olympic coverage relative to their proportion of the Olympic team and/or relative to the medals they won. Among other factors, the overall results indicate that sport journalism, like sport itself, represents in some ways a global culture.

Within the similarities, however, the national analyses show that media environments differ significantly across countries and we find some substantial variations in how newspapers in different countries covered the 2004 Olympics. For example, the proportion of sports news coverage given to Olympics stories ranged from 99.8% in China to only 30.1% in Turkey. The global importance of the Olympics as an event was demonstrated by the finding that Olympics stories took up more than half the sports news in 11 of the 16 countries for which we have this data.

In addition, the overall results presented in the national analyses reveal that researchers from each of the 18 countries made their own decisions about what data was of most relevance for their purposes. Thus, most chapters do not report on all aspects of the overall project design, which complicates and limits the potential for overall comparisons. Different tables draw on results based on either numbers or space, depending on which data was reported or was most appropriate to the specific comparisons. However, we note that, while there are small percentage differences, there is no statistical difference in results based on measuring space or

T. Bruce, J. Hovden and P. Markula (eds.),
Sportswomen at the Olympics: A Global Content Analysis of Newspaper Coverage, 289–304.
© 2010 Sense Publishers. All rights reserved.

on counting numbers for the Olympic data (see Methodology chapter). Except where otherwise stated, the comparisons focus only on the female and male coverage, and exclude the mixed and neutral categories.

Table 1. Average percentages for the overall project by type of coverage

Type of coverage	Female articles average %	Male articles average %	Female photos average %	Male photos average %
Non-Olympic	5.0	87.6	7.3	84.0
Olympic	25.2	40.2	32.3	49.7
Total	15.0	64.3	23.7	56.4

GLOBAL GENDER DISPARITIES IN TOTAL NEWSPAPER COVERAGE

The 12 countries that measured gender disparities in the total coverage (combined Olympic and non-Olympic sport) during the 2004 Olympics found that women generally receive a distinctly lower level of coverage than their male counterparts both regarding text and pictorial space (see Table 2). It is, however, remarkable to register the similarities in the gendered patterns across countries and continents.

Table 2. Total coverage by gender

Countries (n=12)	Female articles %	Male articles %	Female photos %	Male photos %
Belgium (n)	13.1	72.1	16.8	66.3
Hungary (n)	11.2	54.3	13.3	45.2
Japan (n)	20.3	52.2	30.7	60.6
New Zealand (n)	19.0	59.4	24.6	38.9
Norway (n)	17.0	61.5	20.2	59.5
South Africa (n)	20.8	57.7	21.8	67.9
South Korea (n)	15.6	43.5	25.3	48.7
Spain (n)	11.1	61.0	18.7	72.2
Sweden (n)	21.4	54.3	30.1	51.8
Turkey (n)	10.1	78.0	-	-
USA (space)	14.0	60.0	-	-
United Kingdom (n)	6.3	58.9	35.6	53.2
Average	**15.0**	**64.3**	**23.7**	**56.4**

We find that the range for women's coverage globally is only about 12% and varies from 6.3% (United Kingdom) to 21.4% (Sweden). Men's coverage shows a larger span, but most countries are in the 50–70% range. The biggest margin between the genders is found in Turkey with a difference of almost 70%. Although the pictorial coverage for women reveals a slightly higher level than text coverage, the textual and pictorial coverage show similar patterns.

FEMALES MARGINALISED IN NON-OLYMPIC SPORT

The non-Olympic data shows extremely low coverage of female athletes all over the globe (see Table 3). Our results reproduce the gender inequalities reported in existing research, and the distinct trend is that women are still marginalised when it comes to non-Olympic coverage. As a result, newspapers give the impression that female athletes outside the Olympics hardly exist. Only South Korea and South Africa do not closely follow this trend, although coverage of Korean female domestic sport reached only 4.3% of articles and 13.6% of photographs (cf. the South Korean chapter). Several of the authors have characterised the situation in their countries in correspondence with the term 'symbolic annihilation' (Gerbner, 1978); meaning that female athletes competing outside the Olympics or in domestic female sports competitions were symbolically erased during the period of analysis.

Table 3. Non-Olympic coverage by gender

Countries (n=14)	Female articles %	Male articles %	Female photos %	Male photos %
Belgium (n)	3.9	89.0	-	-
Canada (space)	1.9	96.1	-	-
Denmark (n)	2.0	84.0	-	-
France (n)	5.8	84.2	4.0	86.9
Hungary (n)	8.7	84.1	5.3	84.2
Japan (space)	2.3	85.7	5.3	90.5
New Zealand (space)	4.3	86.5	3.9	92.9
Norway (n)	1.5	75.0	<1.0	83.0
South Africa (n)	11.3	69.5	6.7	90.3
South Korea (n)	13.0	60.5	20.0	62.3
Spain (n)	1.7	94.3	-	-
Sweden (n)	6.8	80.6	12.9	81.9
Turkey (n)	2.6	95.2	-	-
United Kingdom (n)	<1.0	63.9	-	-
USA (n)	4.9	77.7	-	-
Average	**5.0**	**87.6**	**7.3**	**84.0**

We register, for example, that all but two of the countries report women's article coverage under 10%, and 10 countries found results under 5%. Three of the countries who reported photographic coverage results found a slightly higher percentage of images, while five found lower levels.

Despite the enormous increase in sport coverage and the rapid growth in women's sport participation during recent decades, newspaper coverage has not increased correspondingly and non-Olympic sportswomen remain almost invisible in most countries. Rather than progress and increased visibility, our results signal a backlash or, at best, a continuation of the status quo.

Commenting on their results, several of the national authors (e.g., Belgium, Germany, Canada, Sweden, New Zealand) emphasize that men's non-Olympic coverage is dominated by national and international professional men's sports, particularly soccer (football), rugby union, ice-hockey and golf; sports that generally dominate the routine newspaper coverage. The data also signal that for several countries (e.g., Canada, Norway, Denmark, USA) sports events like the Olympics influence the routine coverage of men and women differently; men's sport seems to dominate even more in non-Olympic coverage than in regular periods, with the consequence that female athletes competing outside the Olympic arena may be even further marginalised during major events such as the Games. This may also suggest that major events have little influence on the coverage of the dominant male sports, while women's non-Olympic sports are unable to compete with the Olympic news. From this point of departure, we register that women's major events such as world championships in football are strategically planned; moved to time periods outside the main seasons for men's dominant professional sports to obtain higher media attention and coverage.

CLOSING THE GENDER GAP IN OLYMPIC NEWSPAPER COVERAGE

The most remarkable finding is that women's Olympic coverage in all 18 countries rose to a much higher level than for non-Olympic coverage (see Table 4). However, we can still see that male athletes receive more coverage than their female counterparts in all countries except China and Sweden. Further, over half the countries show a difference in article coverage between the genders that is greater than 10% in favour of men. In pictorial coverage we trace a pattern where the differences between the genders decrease because the increase in female pictorial coverage is, in most cases, higher than for men, even though we also register big variations between countries.

In women's Olympic article coverage, only one country registered below 10% and more than three-quarters exceeded 20%. In photographic coverage, the trend is similar but higher, with only one country registering below 15% and more than half exceeding 30%. The overall trends show similarities with previous research that demonstrates variations between continents and countries. Within Europe, there is a clear regional variation, with Northern and Western European nations all exceeding 23%, while no Eastern or Southern European nation passed 18%. English-speaking countries produced results within a narrow range of between 21.2% and 26.5%. Even though previous studies are not directly comparable, the amount of coverage of female Olympians in Europe has tended to be slightly higher than in North America. This also seems to be the case in this study, with the North American countries reporting women's coverage of around 25% and the European countries averaging 26% (within a range of just below 10% to above 35%). Our results demonstrate that Asian countries performed well overall, with China, Japan and Turkey ranking in the top seven countries for female articles. At the same time, three of the four countries that provided the lowest percentages of female coverage were European; the Czech Republic and Hungary in Eastern Europe, and Spain in Southern Europe. Overall, the results average just under 26%, which is consistent with and only slightly below the 2000 Olympics results for European newspaper coverage (Capranica et al., 2005). Of the three European countries for which we have 2000 and 2004 data, Belgian women received slightly more while Danish and French women received about 10% less coverage during the 2004 Olympics (cf. Capranica et al., 2005).

Table 4. Male and female Olympic coverage as a percentage of all Olympic coverage

Countries (n=18)	Female articles %	Male articles %	Female photos %	Male photos %
Belgium (space)	35.4	39.8		
Canada (space)	25.2	28.6	40.6	50.3
China (space)	34.5	31.9	41.5	44.6
Czech Republic (space)	17.8	30.1	38.9	50.6
Denmark (n)	26.0	55.0	33.0	56.0
France (n)	24.0	45.4	30.0	54.2
Germany (n)[1]	31.5	49.1	44.1	54.2
Hungary (space)	9.6	32.8	13.3	33.1
Japan (space)	32.0	39.9	32.0	58.3
New Zealand (space)	26.5	45.0	32.4	46.8
Norway (space)	29.0	43.0	39.0	46.0
South Africa (space)	21.2	46.8	29.7	51.6
South Korea (n)	15.6	43.5	25.3	45.7
Spain (n)	14.6	48.9	23.3	65.8
Sweden (space)	32.6	31.8	39.8	33.8
Turkey (n)[1]	28.7	37.2	33.0	39.8
United Kingdom (space)	23.9	34.2	20.9	70.5
USA (space)	25.5	41.1	32.8	43.3
Average	**25.2**	**40.2**	**32.3**	**49.7**

[1] Germany and Turkey excluded the neutral category.

When we consider mixed coverage, which includes both females and males, we again see a wide variation between countries. A number of countries with low levels of female-only coverage did, however, have high levels of mixed coverage (see Table 5). These include Hungary, South Korea and Spain, all of whom had mixed coverage in excess of a quarter of Olympics coverage.

Three Asian and two Western European countries featured female athletes in more than 50% of coverage when mixed coverage was included. Thus, when taking into account all the coverage that features females, we can see that the Olympics provide much higher visibility for women than non-Olympic coverage. In this respect, these results indicate that the 2004 summer Olympics can be seen as a "path-breaking event" for women in newspaper coverage (Capranica et al., 2005, p. 214).

Table 5. An overview of Olympic coverage by female and mixed category

Countries (n=18)	Female articles %	Mixed articles %	Female + Mixed[1] %
Belgium (n)	30.4	25.2	55.6
Canada (n)	22.7	9.6	32.3
China (space)	34.5	16.6	51.0
Czech Republic (n)	23.0	17.5	40.5
Denmark (n)	26.0	9.0	35.0
France (n)	24.0	16.1	40.1
Germany (n)[2]	31.5	19.4	50.9
Hungary (n)	12.7	34.3	47.0
Japan (n)	30.6	21.2	51.8
New Zealand (n)	27.6	10.4	38.0
Norway (n)	33.0	3.0	36.0
South Africa (n)	27.6	11.7	39.3
South Korea (n)	16.9	25.7	42.6
Spain (n)	14.6	24.5	39.1
Sweden (n)	31.5	16.7	48.2
Turkey (n)[2]	28.7	34.0	62.8
United Kingdom (n)	21.0	25.8	46.8
USA (n)	26.6	21.2	47.8
Average	**25.7**	**19.0**	**44.7**

[1] The female+mixed percentage is based on the original data and may vary slightly from the total of the previous two columns because of rounding.
[2] Germany and Turkey excluded the neutral category.

VARIATIONS IN OLYMPIC COVERAGE RELATIVE TO GAMES PARTICIPATION

The proportion between women's coverage and women's national participation rate was a central analytic issue in the project and most of the national analyses discuss this issue. Previous studies have shown that although variations in gender disparities across continents and countries derive from many factors, one of the most decisive is the proportion of women and men on national Olympic teams. Historically men's participation has been higher than women's, and it is still so in most countries in this study (see Table 6). Women's participation has, however, shown a gradual increase over time. This trend is a result, besides other factors, of conscious gender equality policies within participating countries as well as initiatives taken by the IOC to increase women's participation and women's events in the Games (Capranica et al., 2005).

Overall, women appeared in almost 45% of Olympic newspaper coverage (see Table 5), which is higher than the 40.7% proportion of women participating in the Games. A more detailed comparison of participation and coverage by individual country shows some support for the overall trend identified in recent Olympic studies that women tend to obtain newspaper coverage relative to or slightly higher than their participation on their national Olympic teams (e.g., Pemberton et al., 2004; Urquhart & Crossman, 1999). Note that in order to more directly compare proportions of coverage, participation and medals, we calculated the male and female coverage based only on the raw data for men and women (excluding mixed and neutral coverage) in Tables 6 and 7. The proportion of coverage for men and women thus equals 100%.

Table 6. Male and female Olympic coverage relative to proportion on Olympic teams

Countries (n=18)	Male coverage %	Male team %	Female coverage %	Female team %
Belgium	57	60.8	43	39.2
Canada	55	49.6	45	50.4
China	48	34.5	52	66.1
Czech Republic	61	56.3	39	43.7
Denmark	68	52.0	32	48.0
France	65	64.0	35	36.0
Germany	61	56.0	39	44.0
Hungary	74	58.9	26	41.1
Japan	55	45.2	45	54.8
New Zealand	62	55.0	38	45.0
Norway	59	67.3	41	32.7
South Africa	64	62.0	36	38.0
South Korea	68	52.1	32	47.9
Spain	77	56.7	23	43.3
Sweden	53	54.0	32	46.0
Turkey	56	69.7	44	30.3
United Kingdom	68	61.2	32	38.2
USA	57	52.0	43	48.0
Average	**61.6**	**56.0**	**37.6**	**44.0**

Overall, the percentages were similar for both genders, although males received 5.6% more coverage and females 6.4% less coverage than their proportions on the team would predict (see Table 6). However, even though a majority of the participating countries in this study concluded that women receive an equitable amount of coverage or even relatively more coverage than their male counterparts compared to their ratio on the Olympic team, the results in Table 6 show large variations both between countries and continents, and do not present a clear overall pattern. For instance, based on our analysis of the raw data, in only three countries did females receive more coverage than their proportion on the Olympic team while in two countries the percentages were very similar; in each case the female percentage of these Olympic teams was less than 40%. In six other countries the percentage difference was within 10%. This leaves several countries where females received a noticeably lower proportion of coverage in relation to their proportions on the team, including Denmark, Hungary, Japan, Spain and Sweden. China is an interesting case because it had the highest proportion of female athletes (66.1%) and was the only country where female coverage exceeded 50% (see Table 6). However, Chinese men received 13.5% more coverage than their proportion on the team.

VARIATIONS IN OLYMPIC COVERAGE IN RELATION TO OLYMPIC SUCCESS

Another central question related to the 'medal hypothesis' which suggests that female athletes who win or are expected to win medals will receive more newspaper coverage, and as much as their successful male counterparts. Only about half of the participating countries have argued for this connection by using descriptive statistics, although others have discussed it.

Table 7. Male and female coverage compared to Olympic medals won

Countries (n=12)	Male coverage %	Male medals %	Femalecoverage %	Female medals %
Belgium	57	33	43	67
Canada	55	50	45	50
China	48	37	52	63
France	65	52	35	49
Germany	61	43	39	57
Hungary	74	59	26	41
Japan	55	54	45	46
New Zealand	62	60	38	40
Norway	59	67	41	33
Spain	77	68	23	26
Turkey	56	90	44	10
USA	57	57	43	40
Average	**60.5**	**55.8**[1]	**39.5**	**43.5**

[1] Medal % does not always equal 100%; mixed medals are not included.

A large majority of the participating countries report that female Olympic success means that female Olympians receive more coverage; a finding that seems to support the argument that Olympic media coverage may be 'performance biased' (Urquhart & Crossman, 1999, p. 198). In the most obvious example, Turkish female athletes received 44% of the male/female coverage but won only 10% of the medals.

However, the combined results reveal tendencies in both directions. The overall findings provide support for the medal hypothesis although, on average, men received a slightly higher proportion of coverage compared to the medals they won and females received 4% less. According to our analysis, Turkey, Norway and the USA were the only countries where females received a higher percentage of coverage than medals won.

Overall, the findings indicate that gender still matters. For example, the nation showing the highest success for female Olympians in the 2004 Olympics, China, maintained that female medal winners were extensively under-represented in Chinese newspaper coverage, receiving only 52% of male and female coverage (and receiving only 1.08 stories to every male story), despite winning almost 63% of the medals (see Table 7). Countries such as Germany, Hungary and South Korea also reported little correspondence between women's coverage and women's Olympic success.

Most of the national analyses discussing the medal hypothesis point to another interesting finding; that women's coverage is mostly concentrated around a few top female Olympians, while the coverage of male athletes and male sports in general gives attention to a much broader range of male Olympic athletes and sports events. For example, the Norwegian analysis shows that the two female gold medallists received over 60% of the total female coverage, and Sweden's highest profile athlete, Carolina Kluft, received twice the coverage of the two male gold medal winners. A similar pattern is found in several other countries such as Canada, Denmark, Belgium, United Kingdom, New Zealand, Turkey and South Africa. A recently published European study[1] that also analyses the 2004 Olympics (Olafsson, 2006) documents a similar pattern.

GENDER SIMILARITIES IN PICTORIAL COVERAGE

The overall results show clear similarities with previous Olympic research which finds that both men and women are most commonly represented in sport action or sport-related settings. Overall, the most common images are sport action, at close to half of all images, followed by sport-related at around one-third of all images (see Table 8). Non-sport images make up a very low percentage of the overall Olympic photographs.

The trend is robust and the averages across the data set show remarkable similarities by gender. In 9 of the 10 countries for which we have data, female sport action images are the most common, and they constitute more than half the images in 5 countries. In all countries, women receive distinctly more pictorial coverage in sports action/sport-related settings than in non sport settings; a trend that is similar for male athletes except in South Korea.

Table 8. Types of Olympic photographs by gender[1]

Countries (n=10)	Sport action (%)		Sport-related (%)		Non sport (%)	
	F	M	F	M	F	M
Canada	49.8	46.1	32.2	31.9	6.8	8.3
Germany	53.1	50.5	28.3	36.9	18.6	12.6
Hungary[3]	46.2	31.9	46.2	36.2	0.0	6.4
New Zealand	52.6	51.7	26.3	32.2	11.4	11.1
South Africa[3]	31.7	31.1	66.7	55.5	0.8	11.7
South Korea	36.5	55.3	35.6	60.0	28.0	44.4
Spain	42.9	48.3	35.2	32.9	14.3	7.6
Sweden	61.0	50.0	21.0	27.0	15.0	22.0
United Kingdom[2]	60.0	62.0	21.0	18.0	14.0	10.0
USA	66.4	65.4	32.9	25.6	0.4	5.9
Average	**47.3**	**46.3**	**32.6**	**34.3**	**13.1**	**15.4**

[1]   Percentages may not total 100% because other categories of images, such as 'medals' or 'other', are not included in this table.

[2]   These are estimates drawn from the Figures presented by the authors.

[3]   These percentages are from the total newspaper coverage.

FEMALE PORTRAYAL AND THE 'FEMININITY HYPOTHESES'

One central concern in the study was to examine which sports and which female athletes were given most attention in the Olympic newspaper coverage and to consider if there were preferences for 'feminine appropriate' sports (Matteo, 1986) such as gymnastics, diving, cycling, swimming, beach volleyball and field hockey, or a special focus on physical attractiveness and 'emphasized' femininity. This tendency, which has been noted in previous Olympic research especially in the USA, often leads to a corresponding marginalisation of female athletes participating

in sports requiring strength, muscularity, power or physical contact, which are perceived as masculine traits.

In this study, very few countries reported coverage that was biased towards 'feminine appropriate' sports, showed a tendency to use female athletes for their appearance, glamour and sex appeal, or mirrored the 'femininity hypothesis'. Most of the authors emphasized that women's coverage mirrored the sports and athletes who won or were expected to win medals. Only the Japanese, South Korean and Turkish analyses indicated partial support for the 'femininity hypothesis' and they revealed very interesting findings in this respect. All three reported that gender-biased coverage based on feminine appropriateness of sports or emphasized femininity was not apparent in coverage of athletes from their own country (i.e., Japan, Korea or Turkey) but that eroticisation of female athletes was evident in coverage of women from Western countries.

The overall results regarding the 'femininity hypothesis' may indicate a shift towards greater cultural acceptance of women's participation in a wider range of sports as well as in traditional male sports (see also Reimer & Visio, 2003; Vincent et al., 2002). On the other hand, many of the national authors commented that it was difficult to decide by quantitative content analyses how and why certain female athletes were portrayed more than others. We ask whether the lack of support for the 'femininity hypothesis' and the limited use of sexualisation of female athletes in the 2004 Olympic coverage can be explained by nationalistic agendas through which female Olympic medal winners are regarded and celebrated as national icons.

NATIONALISTIC AGENDAS OVERRIDE MEANINGS OF GENDER

When discussing the medal hypothesis, several other factors besides meanings of gender seem to determine the priority and content of the Olympic coverage. For example, reasons like high national medal expectancies, achievements and prioritising sports linked to national identity play an essential role in which athletes and sports are seen as newsworthy. Previous research suggests that the Games are used as a tool of nation building: The focus on national representatives as winners becomes a means to show success as a nation and, as a result, nationalist discourses override the usual meanings of gender (e.g., Wensing & Bruce, 2003).

Several of the national analyses maintain that success for the nation results in increased coverage, and several examples describe how female gold medal winners are celebrated as national heroines, covered on an equal footing with men and valued for the glory and pride they reflect to the nation (e.g. Sweden, Norway, Denmark, Belgium and Turkey). As some of the national authors have actualised, a crucial question regarding this issue is whether women's sporting performances are primarily of interest only when they contribute to nationalism. Is it the case, then, that the increasing media coverage of female athletes in large international events like the Olympic Games is linked more to ideologies of nationalism than to ideologies of gender equality? The answers to such questions are of course complex and cannot be stated as either/or answers. Perhaps more importantly, they cannot be sufficiently examined by quantitative content analyses alone. Despite these limitations, however, most of the national analyses conclude that winning for the nation is acknowledged and valued for female athletes, while their excellent performances in everyday or domestic sporting events are correspondingly ignored.

FEMINIST CONTENT ANALYSIS AS TOOL FOR GENDER POLITICAL CHANGE: LIMITATIONS AND POSSIBILITIES

Feminist Agendas and New Liberal Media Enterprises

During recent decades a global neo-liberal political climate has influenced the dominant gender structures of powerful societal institutions like the media (e.g.,

Creedon, 1998; Hovden, 2005). The dominance of neo-liberal ideology has, among other factors, led to increased privatisation of media institutions and, thus, to a decline in public control and increase in corporate control. We are witness to an extensive use of profit and market logic to justify what is newsworthy and, thus, a strengthening of an ideology shaped by consumerism and competition (Coakley, 2007; Knoppers & Elling, 2004; Lowes, 1999).

This political transformation has resulted in more entertainment-type newspaper articles. For female athletes, this means a focus on what sells the most; what is assumed to attract the male sports consumer. Creedon (1998) notes that in the USA this means an emphasis on "...little girls and 'sweethearts', heroines and 'lipstick lesbians" (p. 98). Other researchers demonstrate how women athletes are used as décor and profiled by stereotypes (e.g., Bach, 2002; Duncan & Messner, 1998; Lippe, 2005; Olafsson, 2006). Several of the national analyses in this study have identified some of these characteristics with the extensive focus given to a few popular and heterosexually attractive female Olympians. When the core of media enterprises is money, socio-ethical values like democracy, gender equality and social justice are downplayed and, when profiled, are used as instruments for branding, image-building and profit (Creedon, 1998; Hovden, 2005).

Liberal feminist ideals aiming at equal gender distribution of media coverage disturb this new liberal logic and challenge the profit interests of the media owners as well as sponsors. As economic institutions, media enterprises are competing in a marketplace for audiences and advertisers and they know that sport coverage sells newspapers. Political arguments about gender equality, or that women deserve as much coverage as men, are not taken into consideration. Rather, it is more likely that women's sport and female athletes will remain almost invisible, ignored and denigrated as long as they cannot prove to be profitable and attract new audiences or market segments. The increasing sexualisation of elite female athletes in routine sports coverage found during recent decades can be seen as one structural expression of this status (Hovden, 2000; Lippe, 2005).

Most of the newspapers analysed in this study represent money-driven media corporations, in which gender equality issues are considered less relevant as long as the gender-biased coverage does not hurt their reputation and market position. However, this does not mean that critical content analyses such as those produced in this project have lost their change potential in all respects.

Women's Role as Audience and Media Consumers

Several recent media studies suggest a significant power base connected to women's roles as audience and media consumers (e.g., Caldera & Danielson, 2006; Coakley, 2007; Creedon, 1998; Monday Morning, 2002). Because women consist of half the world's population, most media institutions are concerned about how to include women in their market segment. They attempt to do this by listening to women's 'consumer voice'; their needs and desires. From this perspective, women athletes and supporters are already exercising 'power' by choosing not to read the sports pages, not to buy male-dominated sports magazines and in general by paying little or no attention to the sports media. It is argued that women and girls are mostly interested in seeing other women in many realms of social life, including sport (e.g., Bruce & Saunders, 2005; Caldera & Danielson, 2006; Capranica & Aversa, 2002). Scandinavian and US studies suggest that there is some evidence that women athletes and sports fans are frustrated and disillusioned with the current media sport's failure to cover women's sport and celebrate female athleticism in the same way that it does for men (e.g., Bruce, 1998; Caldera & Danielson, 2006; Monday Morning, 2002). Surveys clearly demonstrate that the 'audience' for media sport is predominantly male, as is the content they consume. However, the rise in the female audience during Olympics coverage, and evidence that there was no audience preference for men's sport (see Capranica & Aversa, 2002), suggests that the "market-driven argument that men's sport is the only interest of the audience" is "a merely ideological justification for what is in fact *a socially constructed 'audience preference'* for men's sport" (Capranica & Aversa, 2002, p. 347, emphasis added).

Surveys of the Scandinavian sports press have also identified an ongoing trend towards a decline in readership of printed sports media and a dwindling of the public interest in elite and competitive sports (Monday Morning, 2002). An interesting question is whether a decreasing interest in male professional sport may open up new possibilities for women's sport. However, sports journalists appear, so far, to have given little attention to addressing this crisis and fading interest, or to have started rethinking their priorities in relation to women and other target groups (Monday Morning, 2002). On the other hand, the fact that newspaper enterprises survive by selling papers suggests that the fading public interest in male professional sports may gradually force sport journalists and editors to widen their scope. In this process, the printed sports media enterprises will need critical analyses as well as increased knowledge about women as sport consumers; about their values, desires and dedication to sport. Content analyses, such as those conducted in this study, may become of renewed interest and relevance.

Content Analysis as an Instrument in the Global Strategy of 'Gender Mainstreaming'

While the privately owned media mainly examined in this project are predominantly interested in profit margins, at the same time national governments and policy-makers evaluate the media based on how they disseminate information to strengthen democracy, civic interests and public enlightenment. Similarly, while the results of feminist analyses are persistently ignored by the sport media (Claringbould & Knoppers, 2004; Fountaine & McGregor, 1999), public institutions and policy makers in sport organisations are often more responsive to such research.

The European Commission and European Union member states as well as the United Nations (Council of Europe, 1998; UN, 2007) have made a commitment to using gender mainstreaming[2] as a new strategy to promote gender equality globally. In this process, critical feminist knowledge is seen as a necessary knowledge tool (Rees, 2003). It is, for example, underlined that gender mainstreaming policies seek to identify if and in which ways "the existing systems and structures are 'institutionally sexist' – however unintentionally and however sub-consciously – and to neutralise the gender bias" (Rees 2003, p. 3). For this purpose, the first means mentioned is gender-disaggregated statistics. Gender-disaggregated statistics, such as we have produced in this project, are considered as a central management tool to review the effectiveness of equalisation policies and to establish patterns in the allocation of resources. The EU Council report, edited by the "Group of Specialists on Mainstreaming" (Council of Europe, 1998, p. 28), emphasizes that having data on the current situation of women and men is absolutely necessary for the implementation of gender mainstreaming policies. Research in gender studies has to be carried out and made available (e.g., analyses of current imbalances between the sexes in all policy fields including the media field). From this perspective, feminist content analyses mapping gender inequalities in media coverage are assessed as valuable and relevant gender political instruments, both nationally and globally.

CONCLUDING REMARKS

The sports media is a powerful medium for telling us who and what 'counts' as important. Media coverage is essential for the sponsorship and corporate support that funds the international travel, training, coaching, marketing and public relations necessary for elite level success in sport today. Lack of coverage is thus part of a vicious circle that not only affects women's sporting conditions but also hampers the development and visibility of much amateur or semi-professional men's sport. While there is an argument to be made for celebrating the increased visibility of female athletes during the Olympics, the consistency across our studies, particularly the almost complete absence of female athletes outside of the Games, raises the question of whether it is worth continuing to fight for such coverage or whether women athletes and their supporters should just walk away and find other fields on which to 'play'. However, the symbiotic relationship between sport and the media and the immense symbolic power the media exercises over public understandings of women's sport means that feminists as well as sport politicians cannot turn a blind eye to the content of sport media coverage.

Studies examining policy processes of gender equalisation (e.g Bacchi, 1999; Borchhorst & Dahlerup, 2003) maintain that progress towards increased gender equality can only be achieved and maintained by hard, continuous and knowledge-based political work. Even though content analysis is just one of many contributions in this process, it represents an important tool in providing hard data that is trusted by governments, funding agencies and the public and, thus, in contributing to promoting public awareness and debate.

The benefits and limitations of content analyses, as well as several other implications linked to the design, analyses and results of this project, indicate a further need for both quantitative and qualitative studies with a multi-faceted and broad theoretical and analytical scope. Firstly we see an increasing relevance for longitudinal studies of Olympic media coverage across countries and continents.

Such analyses can precisely map how gender disparities in coverage change over time and produce data that are directly comparable. Secondly, we need content analyses anchored in more radically-oriented feminist perspectives with potential to highlight new forms of gender dynamics, gender inequalities and mechanisms of gendered power structures operating in both 'old' and 'new' media coverage. For example, it will be valuable to further examine whether and how entrenched notions of gender remain a significant obstacle to offering coverage that jointly respects men and women athletes and provides for equal opportunities. Thirdly, looking at the previous research body, we acknowledge relatively few studies about the way media users 'read' media representations of gender. We find, for example, very few analyses of how the trivialisation of women's sporting achievements affects different groups of readers. Finally, a valuable research direction that is still not much highlighted in Olympic studies, and has only been sporadically actualised in this study, is how power and inequalities of gender are woven into the perception of whiteness, nationality and heterosexuality, for example. Meanings of gender are thus not operating separately but are always activated and transformed in the encounter with other categories of social power. Our study and others indicate that disparities in coverage not only are found between the genders but also, for example, between different groups of female athletes. From this point of departure, it will be very interesting, important and theoretically ambitious to conduct future Olympic analyses from intersectional perspectives; analytic perspectives in which intertwined meanings of gender, race, nationality and sexuality can be grasped and special forms of oppression examined. Such studies can bring us closer to an understanding of why some categories of athletes become attractive and newsworthy while others remain invisible and symbolically annihilated.

NOTES

[1] In this study media coverage from 5 European countries, including 2004 Olympic articles, was analysed. The European countries that participated in the study were Lithuania, Norway, Italy, Iceland and Austria.

[2] However, there is considerable confusion as to what gender mainstreaming means and what it implies in terms of new policy approaches. According to Rees (2003), gender mainstreaming is "the systematic integration of gender equality into all systems and structures; policies, programmes, processes and projects; into cultures and their organizations, into ways of seeing and doing" (p. 2).

REFERENCES

Bach, A. R. (2002). *Kvinder på banen – sport, køn og medier*. København: Rosinante.

Bacci, C. (1999). *Women, policy and politics*. London: Sage Publications.

Borchorst, A., & Dahlerup, D. (2003). *Likestillingspolitik som diskurs og praksis*. Fredriksberg: Samfunnslitteratur.

Bruce, T. (1998). Audience resistance: Women fans confront televised women's basketball. *Journal of Sport and Social Issues, 22*(4), 373–397.

Bruce, T., & Saunders, R. (2005). Young people, media sport and the physical education curriculum. *Physical Education New Zealand Journal, 38*(1), 51–66.

Caldera, E. A., & Danielsson, M. (2006). *Om aktiva herrar, for aktiva herrar: Mediesporten och dess publik*. Retrieved July 1, 2007, from http://www.idrottsforum.org/articles/abalo_danielsson/abalo_danielsson060118abstract.html

Capranica, L., & Aversa, F. (2002). Italian television sport coverage during the 2000 Sydney Olympic Games. *International Review for the Sociology of Sport*, *37*, 337–349.

Capranica, L., Minganti, C., Billat, V., Hanghoj, S., Piacentini, M. F., Cumps, E., et al. (2005). Newspaper coverage of women's sports during the 2000 Sydney Olympic Games: Belgium, Denmark, France, and Italy. *Research Quarterly for Exercise and Sport*, *76*, 212–223.

Claringbould, I., & Knoppers, A. (2004). Exclusionary practices in sport journalism. *Sex Roles*, *51*, 709–718.

Coakley, J. (2007). *Sport in society: Issues and controversies*. Colorado Springs, CO: McGraw-Hill.

Council of Europe. (1998). *Gender mainstreaming. Conceptual framework, methodology and presentation of good practice*. Final report of activities of the croup of specialists on mainstreaming (EG-S-MS). Strasbourg: Council of Europe Publishing.

Creedon, P. (1998). Women, sport, and media institutions: Issues in sports, journalism and marketing. In L. Wenner (Ed.), *MediaSport* (pp. 88–99). London: Routledge.

Duncan, M., & Messner, M. (1998). The media image of sport and gender. In L. Wenner (Ed.), *MediaSport* (pp. 170–185). London: Routledge.

Fountaine, S., & McGregor, J. (1999). The loneliness of the long distance gender researcher: Are journalists right about the coverage of women's sport? *Australian Journalism Review*, *21*(3), 113–126.

Gerbner, G. (1978). The dynamics of cultural resistance. In G. Tuchman, A. K. Daniels, & J. Benet (Eds.), *Hearth and home: Images of women in mass media* (pp. 186–215). New York: Oxford University Press.

Hovden, J. (2000). The value of gender in the globalized sport system. *Kunnskap om idrett*, *4*, 13–20.

Hovden, J. (2005). Fra likestilling - til nytte og nytelse? Kjønnskonstruksjoner og markedsstyring i idretten. *Sociologisk Forskning*, *1*, 19–27.

Knoppers, A. L., & Elling, A. (2004). 'We do not engage in promotional journalism': Discursive strategies used by sport journalists to describe the selection process. *International Review for the Sociology of Sport*, *39*(1), 57–73.

Lippe, G. v. d. (2005). Sporten som dominerende maskulin eksponeringsindustri. *Norsk Medietidsskrift*, *12*, 237–255.

Lowes, D. L. (1999). *Inside the sports pages: Work routines, professional ideologies, and the manufacture of sports news*. Toronto, ON: University of Toronto Press.

Matteo, S. (1986). The effect of sex and gender-schematic processing on sport participation. *Sex Roles*, *15*, 417–432.

Monday Morning. (2002). *Industry or independence? Survey of the Scandinavian sports press*. Paper presented at "Play the Game", 3rd international conference for media and professionals in a globalised sports world, Copenhagen.

Olafsson, K. (Ed.). (2006). *Sports, media and stereotypes. Women and men in sports and media*. Acureyri: Center for Gender Equality. Retrieved from http//:www.mujerydeporte.org/documentos/docssms_summary_report.pdf

Pemberton, C., Shields, S., Gilbert, L., Shen, X., & Said, H. (2004). A look at print media coverage across four Olympiads. *Women in Sport and Physical Activity Journal*, *13*, 87–99.

Rees, T. (2003). *A new strategy: Gender mainstreaming*. Paper presented at the "Gemeinsam an die Spitze" conference, Dusseldorf.

Riemer, B. A., & Visio, M. E. (2003). Gender typing of sports: An investigation of Metheny's classification. *Research Quarterly for Exercise and Sport*, *74*, 193–204.

United Nations. (2007). *Women 2000 and beyond women, gender equality and sport*. New York: Division for the Advancement of Women of the United Nations Secretariat.

Urquhart, J., & Crossman, J. (1999). The globe and mail coverage of the winter Olympic games. *Journal of Sport & Social Issues*, *23*, 193–202.

Wensing, E. H., & Bruce, T. (2003). Bending the rules: Media representations of gender during an international sporting event. *International Review for the Sociology of Sport*, *38*, 387–396.

BIOGRAPHIES OF AUTHORS

Bengu Arslan holds two BA degrees, from the Department of Sports Sciences (2007) and the Department of Radio, Cinema and Television (2008) with Honours at Baskent University, Turkey. Her research interests include female athletes' representation in media and gender discrimination in sport organisations. She received the Best Oral Presentation Award in the 1st Mediterranean Sports Sciences Student Congress in 2006 and the Best Poster Presentation Award in the 2nd Mediterranean Sports Sciences Student Congress in 2007. She has publications in the *Annals of Leisure Research* and the *Hacettepe Journal of Sports Sciences*.

Toni Bruce is associate professor in Sport and Leisure Studies at the University of Waikato, New Zealand. Her research interests focus on gender, national identity, race and ethnicity, particularly as these are expressed in the sports media and thought about by sports journalists. A former news and sports reporter, her PhD research (1995, University of Illinois, USA) investigated women sports writers' experiences reporting on male sport. She has co-edited the *Waikato Journal of Education* for six years and is on the editorial board for the *International Review for the Sociology of Sport*. She has published in a wide range of sport and communication journals and is co-editor of *Outstanding: Research about New Zealand Women in Sport* (2008), with Camilla Obel and Shona Thompson.

Susan Chapman is a PhD student at the University of Waikato, New Zealand. Her thesis, entitled "What you see is what you get (influenced by): The representation of New Zealand athletes in print media", examines the intersection of media, sports and gender in relation to sports photographs, including their production and reception by elite female athletes. As an amateur photographer and sports enthusiast, her interests focus on the power of visual communication and the impact of gendered images, particularly in a society where sports and the sports media have always been considered masculine environments. The thesis is written under the direction of Toni Bruce and Carolyn Michelle. She has presented her work at international conferences in South Africa and Australia.

Andrea Gál is a senior lecturer at the Semmelweis University, Faculty of Physical Education and Sport Sciences, Budapest, Hungary. Her master's degree is in Physical Education and Sociology. In 2007 she received her PhD. In her doctoral thesis she dealt with the media representation of female and male athletes in the Hungarian printed media. She is the general secretary of the Sport Sociological Section of the Hungarian Sociological Association and the Hungarian Association of Sport Sciences. She was the co-editor of *Sport és társadalom*, a collection of PhD student papers published in 2003, and *New Social Conditions in Sport*, which also contains selected papers by PhD students.

Ilse Hartmann-Tews is professor of Sport Sociology and Gender Studies at the German Sport University, Cologne, Germany. She has an MA in Social Sciences at the University of Cologne (Germany) and University of Essex (Great Britain), a PhD in Sociology (1989, University of Cologne) and an Habilitation in Sociology of Sport (1995, German Sport University in Cologne). Ilse was Vice-president of the International Sociology of Sport Association (2004–2007) and a member of the ISSA Extended Board from 1999–2003. Her main research areas are the social construction of gender in sport and sport media, and comparative studies on sports development and the structure of sport. She has published widely, including co-editing three recent books: *Handbuch Sport und Geschlecht* (2007, Hofmann) with Bettina Rulofs, *Social Issues in Women and Sport: International and Comparative Perspectives* (2003, Routledge) with Gertrud Pfister, and *Soziale Konstruktion von Geschlecht im Sport* (2003, leske + budrich).

Aina Hindenes is a master's student at the Norwegian School of Sport Sciences, Oslo, Norway. She has been a football (soccer) player and holds several elected posts in the Norwegian Football Association (at the district level).

Jorid Hovden is professor in sociology in the Department for Sociology and Political Science at the Norwegian University of Science and Technology, Trondheim, Norway. Her research interests include gender relations in sports organisations and sports politics, gender, sports and identity, and the gendering of sports media. She has held several elected posts in Norwegian sport organisations. She has served as referee and guest editor for scientific journals. From 2002–2004 she was elected president of the Norwegian Association for Women and Gender Studies. From 2007 she is a member of the extended board of the International Sociology of Sport Association (ISSA). She was guest co-editor of Volume 14(1) of *NORA (Nordic Women's Studies Journal)* in 2006, and published two articles in English in this special issue, entitled "Gender, Power and Sports" (with Gertrud Pfister), and "The Gender Order as a Policy Issue in Sport. A Study of Norwegian Sport Organizations".

Takako Iida is a professor of Sport Sociology in the Faculty of Human Science at Tezukayama Gakuin University, Japan. She established the Japan Society for Sport and Gender Studies with several women researchers in 2002, and became the first president of this academic society (http://www.jssgs.org). She has also been an advisory board member of Women Sport International (WIS). She published *An Introduction to Sport and Gender Studies* (with Itani Keiko, Akashi-syoten) in 2004, and has also written extensively on the topic of women in sport. Her research interest is especially women and sport media. Recently she has been interested in GLBTIQ and sport.

Canan Koca is an assistant professor at the School of Sports Sciences and Technology at the Hacettepe University, Turkey. She worked as a research assistant in the University of Edinburgh between 2007 and 2008. She holds a PhD in Sport Pedagogy from the Hacettepe University (2006). Canan received a Young Scholar Award from the International Association of Physical Education in Higher Education (AIESEP) in 2006. She is an executive board member of the International Association of Physical Education and Sport for Girls and Women (IAPESGW) since 2005. Her key interest is in socio-cultural aspects of physical education and sport such as gender, class, religion and media. Currently she is writing a chapter on Muslim women and physical activity in Turkey for the forthcoming book: *Muslim Women and Sport* (edited by Tansin Benn, Gertrud Pfister & Haifaa Jawad). Her main publications are in *Sex Roles, Women in Sport and Physical Activity* and *Sport, Education and Society*.

Eunha Koh is currently working as a senior researcher at Department of Policy Research & Development, Korea Institute of Sport Science, Korea. She received her master and doctorate degrees at Seoul National University, Korea. Her major research areas include nationalism and globalisation in Korean sport, women's sport and national/international sport policies/politics. She has published in *Sport in Society, International Journal of Applied Sport Sciences, Korean Journal of Sociology of Sport* and has extensively written books on Korean sport. She is an extended board member of the International Sociology of Sport Association and serves on government advisory boards in South Korea including the Gender Equality Board (Ministry of Culture, Sport & Tourism) and the Advisory Board for Human Rights in Sport (National Human Rights Commission).

Árpád Kovács is working for the National Institute for Sport Talent Care, Budapest, Hungary. As a researcher in the Informatics and Research Department, he is working on the overall informatics system of this institute. His master's degree is in Sociology and History and he has expertise in the Statistical Package for the Social Sciences (SPSS) analysis system. He is interested in working up the Informatics System of the Hungarian Talent Care Programs. He is taking part in a longitudinal study dealing with changing the social status of the youth in the Sport Central School and the talent programs.

Stefanie Laenen graduated in Physical Education (2006) from the K.U. Leuven, Belgium. In her master's thesis she focused on gender and media representation in sports. For the moment she is working for the local government of the city of Lier in Belgium.

Chia-Ying "Judy" Liao is currently a PhD student in the socio-cultural studies of sport and physical activity at the University of Alberta, Canada. Her research interests include poststructuralist analysis of women's sport, specifically women's basketball, cultural analysis of media, and psychoanalytical theories.

Katrin Linters holds a master's degree in Physical Education (2006) from the K.U. Leuven, Belgium. The research focus of her master's thesis was on gender and media representation in sports. She also graduated in Dietetics and Nutrition (2008).

Gregory Quin is a PhD student at the University of Lausanne (Switzerland) and Paris-Descartes (France). He is also an assistant at the University of Lausanne at the Institute for Sport Sciences (ISSEP). He is writing a thesis on medical power in the history of French physical education from the middle of the eighteenth century to the end of the nineteenth century, including especially what doctors have said about feminine bodies. Although not only focused on gender, the thesis is still thought through a gendered point of view. The thesis is written under the direction of Bancel Nicolas (Lausanne) and Rogers Rebecca (Paris-Descartes). Gregory is also working on the history of football in Switzerland and has published an article entitled "Football et 'imaginaire national' helvétique (1920–1942). Les matchs Suisse-Allemagne au cours de l'entre-deux-guerres, vus par la presse suisse romande" in *Revue Historique Vaudoise*, *116*, 149-160.

Margaret MacNeill is an associate professor in the Faculty of Physical Education and Health at the University of Toronto, Canada, and is cross-appointed to the Faculty of Medicine. She is the former Director of the Centre for Girls' and Women's Health and Physical Activity Research and is currently affiliated with the Canadian Centre for Sport Policy Studies. Key areas of research include youth and physical activity, gender and health mediacy, health risk communication, communication for social change, and sport media studies. Her work has been published in journals such as the *Journal of International Communication, International Journal of Sport History, Olympika, Journal of Urban Health, International Review for the Sociology of Sport, Studies in Physical Culture and Tourism, Sociology of Sport Journal, Brazilian Journal of Sport Sciences*, and *Media and Culture Reviews*.

Pirkko Markula is professor of socio-cultural studies of sport and physical activity at the University of Alberta, Canada. Her research interests include poststructuralist analysis of women's sport, fitness and dance, cultural analysis of media, ethnography, autoethnography, and performance ethnography. She is an author, with Richard Pringle, of *Foucault, Sport and Exercise: Power, Knowledge and Transformation* (Routledge). She is an editor of *Feminist Sport Studies: Sharing Joy, Sharing Pain* (New York State University Press) and *Olympic Women and the Media: International Perspectives (Palgrave)*, co-editor with Jim Denison of *Moving Writing: Crafting Sport Research* (Peter Lang) and co-editor with Sarah Riley, Maree Burns, Hannah Frith and Sally Wiggins of *Critical Bodies: Representations, Practices and Identities of Weight and Body Management* (Palgrave).

Montserrat Martin is a lecturer in sociology of sport in the Faculty of Education of University of Vic, Catalonia, Spain. Her main area of research is gender and sport, with a particular focus on team contact sports like basketball or rugby and the narrative experience of the players at all levels. She is also interested how sport print media builds Catalan nationalism in Olympic sport and how this notion of nationalism relates with issues of gender in sport. Her PhD drew upon an

Irigarayan sexual difference perspective to explore her own and other women's rugby experiences, presented through narratives of the self. She has published in *Revista Internacional de Sociologia.*

Bert Meulders is a doctoral student at the Department of Human Kinesiology at the K.U. Leuven, Belgium. He holds a master's degree in Physical Education (2002) from the K.U. Leuven and a master's degree in Sport Management (2004) from the University of Windsor (Canada). He was one of the editors of the book, *Sport and Development,* published in preparation for the international conference Unlocking the Potential of Sport for Youth Wellness and Development (2006, South Africa), and guest editor of the *ICSSPE Bulletin* (No. 53, May 2008) focusing on Mega Sport Events in Developing Countries.

Fabien Ohl has been professeur at the University of Lausanne in the Faculty of Social and Political Sciences since 2006. He is the head of ISSEP, the Institute of Sport Science. He has published books on sociology of sport and marketing of sport, including *L'épreuve du dopage* (2008) with C. Brissonneau and O. Aubel; *Sociologie du sport: Perspectives internationales et mondialisation* (2006); *Les marchés du sport* (2004) with G. Tribou; and *Marketing du sport* (1999) with G. Tribou and M. Desbordes. Fabien is the Associate Editor of the *International Review for the Sociology of Sport* and is Executive Board member of the International Sociology of Sport Association (ISSA) in charge of relations with the International Sociology Association (ISA). He is currently working on the question of doping and on sport careers and on media.

Gertrud Pfister is professor in the Department of Exercise and Sport Sciences, University of Copenhagen, Denmark. She was professor at the Freie Universität in Berlin, Germany, from 1980–2000 and was awarded an Honorary Doctorate at the Semmelweis University, Hungary (2007). She has a PhD in history (1976, University of Regensburg) and sociology (1980, Ruhr-Universität Bochum). Gertrud's sport and leisure research interests include gender, organisations and structures, health, and the experiences of immigrants. She has authored or edited more than 20 books and published more than 200 articles in books and peer reviewed journals. Gertrud served as President of the International Society for the History of Physical Education and Sport (1983–2001) and was elected President of the International Sociology of Sport Association in 2004. She has been a keynote speaker at more than 20 international congresses, and is on the editorial boards of 12 scientific journals.

Kelly Redman is a graduate from the School of Sport and Health at the University of Exeter, UK. She continued her studies in the School of Education, completing her postgraduate certificate in education (physical education) in 2006.

Bettina Rulofs is an assistant professor in the Department of Gender Studies/ Institute of Sport Sociology at the German Sport University, Cologne, Germany. She was a visiting professor at the University of Vienna in 2007. Bettina is a member of the Extended Board of the International Sociology of Sport Association (ISSA). Her areas of specialisation include the social construction of gender in sport, representation of women and men in the sports media, sport and diversity, sport and violence, and sport and social work. She has published widely, including co-editing *Handbuch Sport und Geschlecht* (2007, Hofmann) with Ilse Hartmann-Tews, and publishing her PhD thesis, *Konstruktion von Geschlechterdifferenzen in der Sportpresse?* (2003, AFRA Verlag).

Jeroen Scheerder is professor in the Department of Human Kinesiology at the K.U. Leuven, Belgium. His research focuses on socio-economic aspects of sport and physical activity. He lectures in the field of sport policy and sport management. He has published in international journals, including the *International Review for the Sociology of Sport*, the *European Sport Management Quarterly*, *Sport, Education & Society*, the *European Journal for Sport & Society* and the *European Physical Education Review* and has written books on European sports policy, participation in sports, and sports segmentation.

Irena Slepičková is an assistant professor in the Faculty of Physical Education and Sport at Charles University in Prague, Czech Republic. She is involved in sport sociology, leisure sports, sport governance and public sport policy. She has written several scientific articles and chapters in monographs. She is the author of several books, in the areas of sport and leisure, sport and leisure of adolescents, sport, state and society, and sociology of sport organisations. Her research interests focus on sociological aspects of sport and societal conditions of lifestyle. Irena works with doctoral students, mostly on topics of public sport policy, stressing the municipal level. She has also participated in European projects and co-operates with several European universities.

Nancy E. Spencer is an associate professor in the School of Human Movement, Sport and Leisure Studies at Bowling Green State University, Ohio, USA. She received her doctorate in Kinesiology from the University of Illinois in Urbana-Champaign in 1996. Her research focuses on issues of race, gender, ethnicity, and the making of celebrity in professional women's tennis. She has published research articles in the *Journal of Sport & Social Issues*, *Sociology of Sport Journal*, *Journal of Sport Management*, and *Sport Marketing Quarterly*. She published a chapter on Venus Williams in *Sport Stars: The Cultural Politics of Sporting Celebrity*. Nancy is Past-President of the North American Society for the Sociology of Sport (NASSS), and served on the Editorial Board for the *Sociology of Sport Journal*.

Helena Tolvhed earned her PhD in history in 2009 and is a teacher in History and in the Sports Sciences programme at Malmö University, Sweden. Her dissertation (in Swedish) has the English title *Sporting the Nation: "Swedishness" and the Body in the Representation of Olympic Games in Swedish Popular Press 1948 – 1972*. She has published articles on gender and nation in Swedish sports media during the Cold War period.

Bart Vanreusel is professor and head of the Department of Human Kinesiology at the K.U. Leuven in Belgium. He is doing research in the sociology of sport and human movement. He has published in the *International Review for the Sociology of Sport* and recently published an essay on the sociology of endurance sports. He is chair of the Flemish sport council, the advisory board for sport policy issues in Flanders, Belgium.

Attila Velenczei is working for the National Institute for Sport Talent Care, Budapest, Hungary, as leader of the Informatics and Research Department. In that capacity he is responsible for working up the informatic systems of the Hungarian talent care programs and the National Sport Informatics System (as the member of the committee of public procurement). His Master's degree is in Physical Education and Adapted Physical Education. Currently he is a PhD student at the Semmelweis University, Budapest, and his research work is concerned with social inequality in the ways of becoming a top athlete. Between 2002 and 2004 he was an expert of Sport Affairs and he did research on the background of soccer in Hungary and the opinions of the participants about school sports, among other topics.

Emma Wensing completed a Masters in Sport and Leisure Studies at the University of Waikato (New Zealand, 2003) and a Bachelor of Sports Administration (University of Canberra, Australia, 2000). She studied at the University of Toronto, Canada, from 2003–2007 and is currently working in the sports industry in Australia. Her research has focused on intersections of national identity, race and gender in the sports media, particularly during major sporting events like the Olympics. She has published in the *International Review for the Sociology of Sport*, the *Waikato Journal of Education* and the *International Review of Women and Leadership*.

Elodie Wipf is a PhD student at the University of Lausanne (Switzerland) and Marc Bloch (France). She is also Outdoor Sports Policy Officer at the Local Authorities in the area of Strasbourg (France). She is writing a thesis on policy-making in the field of outdoor sports, analysing especially the frames of discursive and deliberative practises in policy making. The thesis is written under the direction of Fabien Ohl (Lausanne) and Gary Tribou (Marc Bloch).

Lucy Webb is currently a PhD student in the Qualitative Research Institute, the School of Sport and Health Sciences at the University of Exeter, UK.

Ping Wu is a senior lecturer in sports journalism and media at the University of Bedfordshire, UK. She was a professional sports journalist in China between 1997 and 2003. In July 2007, Ping was awarded a PhD degree for her research on the complex relationship between the news media and sports administrative organisations in contemporary China. Ping's research interest is the sociology of mediated sports production. She has published in a range of books and journals on topics such as the interdependence between sport and the media, media treatment of women's sport and female athletes, the media build-up of the Beijing Olympic Games, and the Chinese elite sports system.